Gracián, Wit, and the Baroque Age

Renaissance and Baroque
Studies and Texts

Eckhard Bernstein
General Editor

Vol. 17

PETER LANG
New York • Washington, D.C./Baltimore • San Francisco
Bern • Frankfurt am Main • Berlin • Vienna • Paris

Arturo Zárate Ruiz

Gracián, Wit, and the Baroque Age

PETER LANG
New York • Washington, D.C./Baltimore • San Francisco
Bern • Frankfurt am Main • Berlin • Vienna • Paris

Library of Congress Cataloging-in-Publication Data

Zárate Ruiz, Arturo.
Gracián, wit, and the Baroque Age/ Arturo Zárate Ruiz.
p. cm. — (Renaissance and Baroque studies and texts; vol. 17)
Includes bibliographical references.
1. Gracián y Morales, Baltasar, 1601-1658—Knowledge—Literature.
2. Wit and humor—Philosophy. 3. Rhetoric. I. Title. II. Series.
PQ6398.G4Z37   868'.309—dc20   94-42889
ISBN 0-8204-2688-1
ISSN 0897-7836

Die Deutsche Bibliothek-CIP-Einheitsaufnahme

Zárate Ruiz, Arturo:
Gracián, wit, and the baroque age/ Arturo Zárate Ruiz. - New York;
Washington, D.C./Baltimore; San Francisco; Bern; Frankfurt am Main; Berlin;
Vienna; Paris: Lang.
(Renaissance and baroque; Vol. 17)
ISBN 0-8204-2688-1
NE: GT

Cover art by Manuel Robledo Treviño.

Cover design by James F. Brisson.

The paper in this book meets the guidelines for permanence and durability
of the Committee on Production Guidelines for Book Longevity
of the Council of Library Resources.

Printed in the United States of America.

Para mis papás

Copyright Acknowledgments

Illustrations:

Texts:

Sales, St Francis de. *The Sermons of St. Francis de Sales for Lent given in the year 1622.* Edited by Father Lewis S. Fiorelli, O.S.F.S. Trans., by Nuns of the Visitation. Rockford, IL: Tan Books and Publishers, Inc. © 1987 by the Visitation Monastery of Frederick, MD, Inc. Reprinted by permission of the publishers. All rights reserved.

Smith, Hilary Dansey. *Preaching in the Spanish Golden Age.* © 1978 by Oxford University Press. Reprinted by permission of Oxford University Press. All rights reserved.

Contents

Preface

I WROTE THIS BOOK ORIGINALLY IN ENGLISH IN BEHALF OF THE AMERICAN professors who evaluated it as a dissertation, and in behalf of the public to whom this edition is devoted. Even so, I still wonder whether Spanish would have been a better choice for explaining Baltasar Gracián's doctrines. After all, Spanish is my first language. Moreover, it is *his,* too.

Somehow, I fancy about deserving Brunetto Latini's fate. He was plunged into Hell by his otherwise devotee, Dante. Why? Latini "subverted" his own "nature", in a sort of spiritual sodomy, by not originally writting his *Livres dou tresor* in Tuscan, his mother tongue.[1] Fortunately, I do not have to worry about it, since I have neither produced any masterpiece nor enjoy the devotion of disciples, yet, as to be cursed by them for writing in a foreign language.

However, I disillusioned some of my professors. Brian Dutton, of happy memory, strongly regretted my approaching of Gracián's ideas through English. The reason was that each language has its peculiar strengths, and that dealing particularly with Gracián's rich but sharp—universal and yet "Spanish"— doctrines would have been better accomplished with the use of Spanish itself.

Some opinions I have developed about these languages seem to support this point. Spanish excels because of its ample concepts, prompting a wholesome understanding of life in its subtlest shades and in its deepest aspects. Gracián accomplished this to an extreme perfection. His concepts do not arise only from Castilian's unique and *señoril* words, less "pregnant" of meaning than of meaningfulness. His concepts also arise from this language's very complex syntax, hinting at ideas through the greatest net of relationships. Ordinary English is rather a relatively explicit, practical, and thus uncomplicated tongue, whose power resides in its concrete terms, the most abundant of any natural language. It seems animated by Locke's empiricism which aims at coining one

---

[1] See Francisco Montes de Oca "Note 3" to his edition of *Divina Commedia* Inf., XV., (México: Editorial Porrúa, S. A., 1973). Montes de Oca's note refers to André Puzard's essay *Dante sous la pluie de feu,* published in 1946.

term for each sensible thing.[2] This English is the ideal media to convey already established understanding. Nevertheless, my purpose here is not to convey established understanding, but to produce understanding—*an understanding of understanding itself*, as Gracián aimed at it in his *Agudeza*, strongly relying on the special virtues he mastered, of Spanish language, for that purpose.

Although English as a choice for this book is questionable, the choice was made. At the end, this tongue has not only been my means of communication, but also my means to reach the final understanding of the subject.

This experiment has rendered some interesting results. Thinking in English of Spanish "words" has not been only a practice of languages. It principally was experiencing two scholarly and cultural traditions, and in an enhanced way thanks to the keen understanding gained through the comparison and contrast of these traditions. Somehow, this venture does justice to Gracián, who believed that any original effort of understanding consists in the "matching of extremes."[3]

My use of English includes translations from most texts cited from other languages. By means of footnotes, I also quote the text in its original tongue, if its source is Baltasar Gracián, its discourse is poetic, or its language is different from English or Spanish. These footnotes would serve as correctives to imperfect translations.

I thank professors Lloyd Bitzer, Brian Dutton, and Hanns Hohmann for their suggestions concerning the contents and language of this text, originally revised by them in the form of a dissertation. Their recommendations have helped me improve my work; their support has encouraged me to persevere in my research; and their example has been my model of scholarship. The inadequacies which still blemish this work are my complete responsibility. I also thank professors Lloyd Bitzer, Michael Leff, and Don Abbott for endorsing my book, and Manuel Robledo Treviño for the illustration of this edition's front cover.

I should thank many others for their help, and my loved ones for their support. Their care has made me succeed in this enterprise.

---

[2] See *Essay Concerning Human Understanding* III.

[3] See *Agudeza* Discourse 2.

Introduction

IN THIS BOOK, I EXPLAIN THE MORAL AND LOGICAL THEORIES contained in Baltasar Gracián's complete works in order to establish their relevance for and relationship with rhetoric. Gracián's theories on wit deserve special attention because his major theoretical contribution is *Agudeza y Arte de Ingenio*, a treatise devoted to elucidate and give method to the mind's wit. But I also pay attention to Gracián's other works, since the structure of his complete theoretical system can be appreciated only by including these works in my study.

I propose that Gracián's theories on wit respond to the need to give method to the mind's first logical operation, the apprehension of ideas. Gracián, belonging to the most traditional schools of logic, did not confuse the apprehension of ideas with judgment or with inference. Nor did he confuse the apprehension of ideas with the imagining of ideas. According to Gracián, ideas are discovered and apprehended from contact with reality; and ideas, even when created, or produced, are abstract representations, not sensible images.

For Gracián, the method of wit produces discernment. Concerning discernment, he believed that, in the beginning, our perception of things is vague, without distinctions, as when children confuse all men with their fathers. The advancement of learning thus consists in going from unclear generalities to well defined particulars; it consists in specifying the details. Its result is the sharp understanding of a case through precise abstract concepts. Gracián by no means believed that this result could arise from the vagueness of sensible images. He only recognized these images as material foundations of abstract concepts or as a sensible element of persuasion.

Gracián identified wit as the method of discernment because wit performs the most basic operations for the precise perception of details. Comparisons between extreme cases lead reason to detect subtle similarities or distinctions between cases. It is in these subtle distinctions apprehended through wit that discernment gains precision, and the mind makes clear sense of its objects of understanding. Only when the ideas are thus clarified can the mind go on to test them through judgment, and if needed, draw inferences.

Gracián's theories on wit are both richly detailed in artistic rules and comprehensive in their few and systematic general principles. These theories are relevant to rhetoric since their generality applies to every rational process which involves discovery of ideas, and since these theories also pay special attention to the discernment of specific and contingent cases, rather than simply to theoretical issues. Moreover, these theories relate to a seventeenth-century renewal of rhetorical studies concerned with giving method to invention. Gracián's theories also explain the emphasis on witty discernment which orators exercised during the seventeenth century.

Not only the specific theories on wit, but also Gracián's larger system of theories is relevant to rhetoric. Gracián's theories on wit belong to a more general theoretical system: his comprehensive doctrine of mastery. This doctrine subsumes all his works and embodies his most profound philosophy. Though not centered on wit, the doctrine of mastery captures the character of the wit, the heedful person, the prudent politician, the discreet and disabused orator—in summary, he who is master. This doctrine not only sheds light on the notion of character in a rhetorical theory, but on the nature and purpose of rhetoric itself.

The most central theses that I will establish in this book are the following: According to Gracián,

1. His theories on wit explain and give method to every apprehension of ideas.

2. Wit is essentially the mind's faculty that abstracts and discerns sharp and clear ideas within originally vague or unclear materials.

3. Wit's most basic and comprehensive method for the apprehension of ideas is the comparison of odd things in order to discover their similarities or differences.

4. The ideas discovered by wit are abstract and the foundation of every rational thinking.

5. Ideas, although abstract and thus universal, can capture the uniqueness of the most contingent case if assisted by artistic wit.

6. The moral character, moral activities, and potential happiness of persons rest on the mastery of good habits of reason (which include wit).

By relating Gracián's theories with rhetoric, this book also intends to establish that:

7. Gracián's theoretical system is relevant for the theory of rhetoric and the history of rhetorical theory and eloquence.

Some Problems in the Establishing of these Theses

Several problems make difficult the corroboration and explanation of these theses. For example, the theses differ from very common scholarly beliefs concerning what wit is and what Gracián's theories on wit are meant to propose on the subject. Also, Gracián's writings avoid declarative statements which clearly define his positions on a subject; his writings are rather suggestive, like riddles, and rely on the reader to reflect on and achieve understanding of what is suggested.

Concerning the most common scholarship on wit and on Gracián's theories on wit, authors often fail to see the rational function of wit and the rational component that Gracián identified in wit. As I will discuss later, Aristotle usually treated wit as a stylistic device for crafting pointed sayings; Cicero and Quintilian associated wit with the use of laughter as an emotional proof in rhetoric; for some renaissance authors, wit was the creative power of fancy; to some degree, Pellegrini linked wit to the abuse of extended metaphors; Tesauro thought wit to be the symbolic power of the mind; and Vico recognized in wit the mind's power of grasping truths through imaginative universals—that is, an imaginative vision of the world. Rationalists snubbed wit, though they used it, I believe, in their best works, as did Pascal in his *Pensées*. And among other scholars, although the empiricists produced heavy volumes on the subject, they reduced wit to a derailed imagination.

Contemporary scholars often interpret Gracián's theories on wit by imposing over them these common views on the subject and some other external criteria.

Thus these scholars fail to see the rational component defining Gracián's theories. Under the Aristotelian lens, Gracián's theories should appear as concerned with a literary device. If this literary device is then associated with usual views on wit such as Pellegrini's and the empiricists', then Gracián's *Agudeza* should appear as devoted to the abuse of extended metaphors and to a derailed imagination. Not surprisingly, many literary critics have identified *Agudeza y Arte de Ingenio* as the aesthetic code of bad taste.[1] And if numerous literary and rhetorical critics prudently refrain from endorsing this belief, they still relate these theories to pure style and to what they call farfetched metaphors and unnecessarily complicated language attributed to Spain during the seventeenth century.[2]

Some rhetoricians recognize in Gracián a method for invention. They see in Gracián an alternative to prevalent managerial rhetorics which only give method to inference from already established facts and which are silent about the methods for discovery. However, probably imposing views such as Tesauro's or Vico's on *Agudeza*, these rhetoricians reduce Gracián's understanding of wit to the creation of meaning through symbols or to an imaginative vision of the world.[3] When listening to these interpretations, old guardians of logic often

---

[1]Cf. Marcelino Menéndez Pelayo, *Historia de las Ideas Estéticas en España*, (México: Ed. Porrúa, S. A., 1985) 584. See, for example, Adolphe Coster, *Baltasar Gracián*, trans. by Ricardo del Arco, (Zaragoza: Institución Fernando el Católico, 1947); Benedetto Croce, "Los tratadistas italianos del conceptismo y Baltasar Gracián," *La Lectura. Revista de Ciencias y Letras*. 2nd. ser. 12 (1912).

[2]A sample of intepretations of *Agudeza* as concerned with a complicated literary style would be the following: Edward Sarmiento, "Gracián's *Agudeza y Arte de Ingenio*." *The Modern Language Review* XXVII (Cambridge: 1932) 280–292, 420–429; E. R. Curtius, *European Literature in the Latin Middle Ages*,(New York: 1953); and Michael Mooney, *Vico in the Tradition of Rhetoric*, (New Jersey: Princeton University Press, 1985), who relates this "elaborate" and "exaggerated" style to rhetoric.

[3]See, for example, Don Paul Abbot, "Baltasar Gracián's *Agudeza*: The Integration of Inventio and Elocutio." *The Western Journal of Speech Communication* 50 (Spring 1986): 133–143; Emilio Hidalgo Serna, "The Philoshopy of *Ingenium*: Concept and Ingenious Method in Baltasar Gracián." *Philosophy and Rhetoric* 13.4 Fall: 1980; T. A. May, "An

react by summarily blaming Gracián for sophistry (vivid symbols or imagination do not make a good argument). Only a few dissociate Gracián from imagination and style, and associate him with the most traditional systems of abstract logic and rhetorical invention. For example, Parker saw in *Agudeza* a theory explaining the apprehension of ideas,[4] and, more specifically, Wood saw a theory of topical invention.[5] Nevertheless, I have not found, as yet, a scholar noticing and elucidating Gracián's most general claim, that his method embraces *every apprehension of ideas.*[6] No doubt this fact helps explain why no scholarship to date reflects an accurate understanding of the structure and specifics of Gracián's methods of wit.

Even so, scholars should not be fully blamed for failing to see in Gracián a theory concerning the apprehension of ideas. He did not transparently expound his theories, but he purposely searched for obscurity to challenge the reader to think and prompt the reader to produce an intepretation. This interpretation cannot come from simply pointing out what Gracián declared in the specific place in question—which usually is purposely obscure—but by also establishing textual and contextual associations.

Another major problem for establishing the book's theses—particularly the thesis that Gracián's theories on wit are relevant to rhetoric—is that Gracián had a very different view of rhetoric than the view I think his theories enrich. Gracián believed rhetoric was an art of tropes—of pure stylistic ornament.[7]

Interpretation of Gracián's *Agudeza y Arte de Ingenio*," *Hispanic Review* XVI (1948): 257–300, and "Gracián's Idea of the concepto," *Hispanic Review* XVIII (1950): 15–41; Ernesto Grassi, *Rhetoric as Philosophy. The Humanist Traditon,* (The Pennsylvania State University Press, 1980).

[4]See Alexander A. Parker, "'Concept' and 'Conceit': and Aspect of Comparative Literary History," *MLR* 77 (4) (1982 Oct.): xxi–xxxv.

[5]See M. J. Woods, "Gracián, Peregrini, and the Theory of Topics," *MLR* 63 (1968), and "Sixteenth-Century Topical Theory: Some Spanish and Italian Views," *MLR* 63 (1968): 66–73.

[6]See *Agudeza* Discourse 5.

[7]See *Agudeza* "Al Letor."

However, I think his theories contribute to a broader view—to rhetoric conceived as an art enabling reason to persuade on public or moral matters.

Method and Structure of the Book

I intend to uncover Gracián's theories and their relevance to rhetoric by placing them in their cultural and theoretical context, by closely studying Gracián's texts and their interconnections, and by establishing the relationships, distinctions, and implications of Gracián's theories concerning rhetoric.

I principally address the contextual topics in Part One of this book. Although centered in "The Age of Wit", Part One comprehends, among other issues, reviews of classical rhetoric in so far as relevant to understand the development of baroque theories on ingenuity.

Part Two, "A Rhetoric for Wits", is the core of this study; it explains the structure, concepts, and methods of Gracián's theories; it is the place where the major theses here proposed are demonstrated with more detail; particularly, it establishes the most numerous and important implications concerning the relationship between the theories of wit and rhetoric. Although I still rely on the context to shed light on the body of theories, I ordinarily support my explanations with a direct analysis of Gracián's texts.

Part Three, "The Eloquence of Wits", finds additional relationships between Gracián's system and rhetoric by paying attention not as much to their theories as to their practice in oratory, the analysis of texts, and, generally, the task of discovery and invention in many other fields of life. Part Three has a special emphasis in its discussion: it aims at conclusively correcting the failure to see in wit and its concrete applications something already on the rational level, and pertaining to the general operations of human understanding.

Part One

The Age of Wit

1 Spain, the Baroque, and the Jesuits

BALTASAR GRACIÁN LIVED FROM 1601 TO 1658 IN SPAIN. This period was one of striking contrasts in his country. Although this nation then suffered a political and socio-economic decline, nevertheless it enjoyed an artistic and literary prosperity for which this period is called the Spanish Golden Age.

Socially and politically, Spain entered into an age of decline which did not echo her accomplishments of the previous century. During the seventeenth century, there were a strong financial and economic impoverishment aggravated by a substantial decrease of population, either because the remaining Moors were then expelled from her territory, or because many Spaniards left their land to go to America, or just because of disease, the lack of good conditions to live in Spain, or the many foreign wars suffered. There was indeed a long series of military defeats and diplomatic failures which meant the gradual loss of her territories in Continental Europe, the independence of Portugal, and continuous rebellions of other kingdoms within the Iberian peninsula, such as happened with Catalonia. There was mismanagement and corruption in the handling of public business. There was an abusive centralization of power which took away much of the typical autonomy previously enjoyed by the Spanish provinces. There was a pompous, greedy, and incompetent court, led by irresponsible kings who left their duties in the hands of favourites. Some would also say that there was a decrease in Spaniards' patriotic feelings and religious commitment.

Even so, the intellectual, literary, and artistic life strongly contrasts with the dim socio-political picture. From the famous scholars of the sixteenth century, the greatest of all the metaphysicians was still writing in the seventeenth century—the Jesuit Francisco Suárez, who died in 1617—, and then rivaled by other outstanding theologians and philosophers such as Juan Cardinal de Lugo, Pedro de Hurtado de Mendoza, Rodrigo de Arriaga, Francisco de Oviedo, and the controversial Juan de Mariana who boldly denied the divine right to monarchies. Moreover, this period was particularly outstanding because of its literary and artistic accomplishments—for example, Miguel de Cervantes published his major works, *Don Quixote*, in 1605 and 1615, and the *Novelas* in 1613. A new generation of vigorous authors arose: Lope de Vega and the dramatic writers of his school performed for the first time their best *comedias*, setting the parameters of Spanish national drama, which strongly influenced European authors to depart from the strict classical rules and to search for new ones for the modern theatre. Pedro Calderón de la Barca and his followers came with an even newer conception of drama which covered almost the whole of the century, since Calderón died in 1681. Luis de Góngora's *Polifemo* (1612), and *Soledades* (1613) were widely read. Francisco de Quevedo published his poetry, his *Buscón*, and his *Dreams*. Góngora and Quevedo were both very influential and set the models for baroque poetry in Spain and her dominions. Quevedo and Baltasar Gracián himself became the greatest exemplars of baroque prose writing. All these writers produced the most distinct works of the Spanish Golden Age, an age which spanned two centuries: the sixteenth and the seventeenth. For some people, the final, or baroque, stage of this age is the one which better defines Spanish national literature, and the one which constitutes the richest point of Spanish literary history.

Not only literature, but other arts flourished in this age. Hernando de Cabezón and Tomás Luis de Victoria were famous composers of that time. Also, some of the greatest Spanish artists then gave shape to the national school of painting: El Greco (1541–1614), Ribera (1588–1656), Zurbarán (1598–1662), Velázquez (1599–1660), Murillo (1617–1682), etc. This prosperity in literature and arts was not restricted to Spain but was shared by the Spanish dominions overseas, where such writers as Balbuena, Ruiz de Alarcón, Sigüenza y Góngora, and Sister Juana arose. Thus, this age is called golden in both the old and the new Hispanic worlds. To all these achievements, I can add that Spanish was then the international language of European courts.

Very revealing is the fact that Mazarin, the great enemy of the Spanish monarchy, kept his notebooks in a mixture of Italian and Spanish; as they were intimate jottings they prompt the conclusion that Mazarin *thought* in Spanish. This perhaps was a legacy of his Italian upbringing, since in Italy the prestige of Castilian was even greater than it was in France.[1]

The Baroque Age

In spite of the great variety of achievements and authors, there still was, to some degree, a common style of doing art and literature among the *learned* writers of this period. This style is called *baroque*. To explain it, critics usually contrast it with the style tendencies of the previous century. Thus, by baroque it is commonly understood the "artificial and complicated" style of the seventeenth century, as opposed to the "natural and spontaneous" which identifies Spanish renaissance literature. Baroque is the newer style which "formally becomes more complicated, and also is overloaded with strange words and a twisted syntax."[2] Some elementary surveys of Spanish literature contain simple illustrations in order to provide a quick and general idea of the changes which took place from one century to the other. For example, José Manuel Blecua compares Garcilaso de la Vega's and Luis de Góngoras's descriptions of the flow of a river. Garcilaso wrote:

> Danubio, río divino,
> que por fieras naciones
> vas con tus claras ondas discurriendo,[3]

---

[1]Domínguez Ortiz, *The Golden Age of Spain 1516–1659*, trans. James Casey (London: Weidenfeld and Nicolson, 1971) 247.

[2]José Manuel Blecua, *Historia y textos de la Literatura Española* (Zaragoza: Librería General, 1963) 1:289–290.

[3]As quoted by Blecua 1:289:
> You, Danube, divine river,
> that flow with clear waves
> through fierce nations.

Góngora otherwise wrote using this complicated baroque style:

> En roscas de cristal serpiente breve,
> por la arena desnuda el Luco yerra,
> el Luco, que con lengua al fin vibrante,
> si no niega el tributo, intima guerra
> al mar, que el hombre con razón le bebe
> y las faldas besar le hace de Atlante.[4]

I should note that, as an illustration of what baroque literature is, this poem may only be helpful to exemplify one of three main trends in fashion in this age: *culteranism*, also called *Gongorism* in remembrance of Góngora, its main model. The other two trends were *conceptism*, and an exaggerated *naturalism*.

As a term, culteranism means the use of refined or *cultivated* modes and motifs of expression, as contrasting to other modes and motifs which were reputed as ordinary. Its practitioners introduced a large amount of foreign words into Spanish, especially from Latin and Greek. They also borrowed from classical languages their syntaxes, and, in spite of the structural violence, they applied them to Castilian. They used abundant and very complex imagery and metaphors sharply appealing to the senses. They strongly relied on classical literary motifs, such as mythology.

As a term, conceptism comes from the interest some baroque writers had in producing *concepts*.[5] These writers emphasized the ingenious discovery or

---

[4]Blecua 1:289:
> Through crystal rings, a brief serpent—
> through naked sand, the Luco wanders,
> the Luco, which with a tongue at the end vibrating,
> if it does not deny the tribute, it wages an intimate war
> to the sea, that the man for that reason drinks of it
> and, kissing its skirts make him like Atlas.

[5]Concerning baroque theories of wit, "concept" is a key concept whose multiple meanings will be weigh in this book. Some scholars have equaled concepts to conceits, or exaggerated metaphors. For instance, see Edward Sarmiento, "Gracián's '*Agudeza y Arte de Ingenio*'" *Modern Language Review* 27 (1932): 280–292. Other critics have said that concepts should

creation of ideas, words, and new uses for ordinary terms, abundantly used elaborate wordplays, witticisms, antithesis, hyperbole, and symbols, and expressed keen forms of judgment, maxims, and humor. One kind of conceptism searched for the most extreme concision when phrasing thoughts. Another kind of conceptism was emblematic and used complex symbols.

Conceptism was a correlative to culteranism. Their difference was that conceptism strove to create abstract thought, whereas culteranism strove to produce a new universe of striking sensations. Conceptism was mainly used in prose writing. Culteranism appeared mainly in poetry.

Picaresque and satiric literature of this age may be properly characterized as a third trend of the baroque. This trend emphasized an exaggerated *naturalism* focused on uncovering disagreeable aspects of reality. Their practitioners strove for the grotesque, caricatures, the ugly, the dark, and—some novel readers may not be aware of it— enlightenment. Yes, after all, they strove for light. Their works usually took the form of narratives.

In spite of these distinctions among the trends, baroque writers hardly practiced a single kind in an univocal way. They rather mixed them in different degrees. Moreover, these tendencies shared some general characteristics. In spirit, they reacted against renaissance idealistic views of organic beauty and harmony of life.

Concerning modes of expression, it is often said that although there was not a strict rupture with renaissance practices, there was a intensification of these practices; that the result was the development of a taste for affectation, complication, and extreme modes and motives of expression which sharply contrasted with classical criteria; and that the taste would strongly respond to a search for novelties: authors were more than imitators who reproduced nature

---

keep their logical meaning: a mental apprehension or idea. For example, see Alexander A. Parker, "'Concept' and 'Conceit': An Aspect of Comparative Literary History," *MLR* 77 (1982): xxi–xxxv. Other group of critics would describe concepts as both, an intellectual act and its expression in a literary structure. For example, see T. E. May, "An Interpretation of Gracián's 'Agudeza y Arte de Ingenio,'" *Hispanic Review* 16 (1948): 257–300, and T. E. May, "Gracián's Idea of the Concepto" *Hispanic Review* 18 (1950): 15–41.

or copied classical models; they rather strove to be ingenious; they strove to create *new forms*, and produce *new art*.

Several negative qualities have often been associated with the complex style of the baroque era, for example, extravagance, irrationality, bombastic forms and ideas, and the excessive use of purposeless ornament, amplification, and artifice.

Once this style started to become widespread, it began to have its enemies. The classicist Pedro de Valencia censored Luis de Góngora's innovations, in 1613, telling him that "the more [his] style is inflated and estranged with bombastic words, the more swollen and difficult is such a cold form of expression."[6] Also, in 1618, Juan de Jáuregui denounced these innovations as "some soulless poetry...only a body of shapeless thoughts and void judgments, without a fixed purpose, coherence, and relation among its parts." He found some of the poetry containing "only ornament and only the dress of words...only a fantastic exterior." Thus, Jáuregui saw the writers of this poetry as "slaves of mere words" who were drawn by their expressions instead of having control over them.   Their excesses, said Jáuregui, even made these authors "*metaphorize* metaphors themselves."[7]

Not only Spain's, but also much of European literature of this age has been characterized in similar negative terms. Spanish *Gongorism* and *conceptism*, which are the main Hispanic versions of the baroque, are put together with other literary movements of Europe, such as *Marinism* and *conceptism* in Italy, *mannerism* and the style of *preciosity* in France, and *Euphuism* and, in a higher degree, *metaphysical* poetry in England.

Champions of Reason in the eighteenth century, such as the Encyclopedists, would abhor these baroque movements, and would characterize them as chaotic, barbarous, particularly permeated with fanaticism, and lacking any scientific rigor. A label for this style is coined by borrowing from logic the term *baroco*,

---

[6]*Censura de* LAS SOLEDADES, POLIFEMO *y obras de don Luis de Góngora, hecha a su instancia por Pedro de Valencia, cronista de su Majestad.* (Madrid, 1613), as quoted by Marcelino Menéndez Pelayo, *Historia de las Ideas Estéticas en España* (México: Ed. Porrúa, S. A., 1985) 565.

[7]*Rimas de D. Juan de Jáuregui,*(Sevilla, 1618), as quoted by Menéndez Pelayo 567–572.

applied to a strange form of "ridiculous" syllogism—nonetheless valid. Since 1755, thanks to Winckelmann, baroque would be strongly associated to the idea of bad taste in art. Moreover, in the nineteenth century, Jacob Burckhardt would generalize the concept of baroque, and would apply it to what he regarded a decadent style of late renaissance architecture in Catholic countries. Thus, baroque architecture and literature would be described—following Wölfflin—by noticing the picturesque, and the importance of depth, multiplicity, openness, and obscurity in their forms, as opposed to both renaissance architecture and literature which are described by noticing linearity, and the importance of surfaces, unity, closeness, and clarity in their forms.[8]

The baroque, as an anomalous form of style, has been attributed not only to literature but also to oratory of the seventeenth century. Michael Mooney says:

> Stolen, then jilted by logic, rhetoric's "logical" arts of invention and arrangement had a modest career in the seventeenth century. Their companion arts of *verba*, meanwhile, namely *elocutio* and *pronuntiatio*... rather enjoyed their freedom.
>
> ....
>
> In part this occurred through the development of an elaborate, exaggerated form of oratory to which scholars have applied a term from art history—*baroque*...[9]

Mooney then explains:

> The style could be elaborate and intrincate, or it could be sharp, concise, and witty, but always it aimed to be subtle and tense, affected and artificial, to take the plain and simple statement and turn it into language (or gestures) that strained syntax and imagery.[10]

---

[8]The association of baroque art with architecture is strongly held, today. In fact, some contemporary critics borrow categories used for analyzing baroque buildings, and apply them in the study of baroque literature. Cf. Heinrich Wölfflin, *Kunstgeschichtliche Grundbegriffe* (Munich, 1915).

[9]Michael Mooney, *Vico in the Tradition of Rhetoric* (Princeton University Press, 1985) 60–62.

[10]Michael Mooney 65.

On this belief Mooney applies to the seventeenth century the label of "the age of splendor and wit."[11]   Thomas M. Conley describes seventeenth century rhetoric in similar terms, as highly dissociated from reason, and as showing an "increasing focus on affect, or emotion."[12]

Either as literature or as oratory, and regardless of the different positive and negative views held on it, baroque style is seen as finding its richest and most elaborate expression in the Hispanic world. It is often stated: 1) that it was in Spain and her dominions overseas where baroque was practiced in its most intense and extensive way; 2) that it was in these places where baroque style produced the most influential, representative, and diverse works, thus making this movement have a Hispanic twist in the whole of Europe; and 3) that it was in Spain that this style qualified to be included in a literary Golden Age. Baroque writing had indeed a strong imprint in Hispanic countries, where it continued in fashion among many authors until the late eighteenth century. It is even said that this style has infused the ordinary way Spaniards and Hispanic Americans would express themselves for ever.[13]

Baroque, as a style, was so peculiar to Gracián's times that it has been used to label and define the whole period, in spite of this period's very diverse cultural developments. The baroque also has served as a lens through which are seen and understood quite different events of the seventeenth century:

> This is the century of the Baroque—says Domínguez Ortiz—, a term that being
> made to mean so much means almost nothing. The attempt to stretch it to cover the

---

[11]Michael Mooney 60–67.

[12]Thomas M. Conley, *Rhetoric in the European Tradition* (New York: Longman, 1990) 152.

[13]Cf., for example, Ángel del Río, *Historia de la Literatura Española* (New York: Holt, Rinehart and Winston, 1966) 391–392, who quotes Hatzfeld, "El predominio del espíritu español en la literatura del siglo XVII" *Revista de Filología Hispánica* 3 (1941) 9–23: "We believe that the baroque indeed existed as a European movement, and that it was a result of the Spanish spirit and style influencing everywhere, and replacing the Italian and classical character of all European literature during the sixteenth century."

many-sided activities of a whole century has caused it to lose all precise meaning. To some critics it is the expression of courtly life; to others it is first and foremost a popular phenomenon. There are those who see it in terms of post-Tridentine religious feeling, others who maintain that it marks a secularization of life and society. At one moment we are told that it is connected with the economic depression of the period, at another that it is a culture based on ostentation and wealth.[14]

In this view, a fair understanding of the baroque period in Spain seems as elusive as the subject of wit, and thus unreliable to appreciate Gracián in terms of his specific time and place.

The 1640's and the Jesuit Theories on Wit

There is something which strongly pertains to Gracián's specific cultural environment. It is the rise of many treatises theoretically inquiring on the subject of wit.[15] Several authors, mostly Jesuits, like Gracián, although Italians, were interested on this subject during the 1640's. For example, Matteo Pellegrini published *Delle acutezze*, a treatise explaining the genres of witticisms, in 1639, and *I fonti dell' ingegno*, in 1650, a treatise which analyzes the role and methods of mind's ingenuity in the invention of all kinds of discourse, and particularly sciences. Pietro Cardinal Sforza Pallavicino published *Trattato dello stile e del dialogo*, in 1646,[16] a book on the style to be used in writing sciences—a book

---

[14]Domínguez Ortiz 254.

[15]Cf. Parker xxxv. From the main group of theorists of wit who I study, Pellegrini seems to be the single one not described as a Jesuit. Croce's brief biography of Pellegrini seems to indicate that this seventeenth century scholar was just a priest. In any case, he was not by any means unrelated to the Jesuits: for example, his important promotion as custodian of the Vatican Library's archives was effected through the influence of Cardinal Sforza-Pallavicino, *S. J.*, who is another of the theorists of wit analyzed here. Cf. Croce 253–254.

[16]My edition of this treatise is the one published in Rome, 1662.

which, among other things, gives rules to the the use of wit in this endeavor. Emanuele Tesauro wrote *Il cannocchiale aristotelico* in 1654,[17] a book which extensively and very systematically theorizes on all forms of wit, but particularly emphasizes the use of wit in some baroque literary fashions.

The rise of these treatises is very meaningful for contemporary critics. Since the last century, many scholars have seen in these authors' and Gracián's treatises of wit a direct theorizing on baroque literary writings.[18] These scholars have discovered in the baroque theories on wit an instrument to study from specific pieces of poetry to the links and common features of different baroque trends in all of Europe. Their scholarship has revaluated both literature and oratory[19] of this age by finding that, instead of being irrational or just emotional, the baroque is often highly intellectual because of the recourse to wit.

Wit is accordingly identified as the backbone of baroque intellectualism, and

---

[17]My edition of this treatise is the one published in Turin, 1670.

[18]There are many examples of scholars of this kind. Among others, I have already mentioned Menéndez Pelayo, Croce, E. Sarmiento, A. Parker, and T. E. May. My list can be enlarged by mentioning Ernest Robert Curtius, *European Literature in the Latin Middle Ages* (New York, Pantheon Books: 1953); J. M. Aguirre, "Agudeza o arte de ingenio y el Barroco" *Gracián y su época* (Zaragoza: Institución Fernándo el Católico, 1985) 181–190; Ricardo del Arco, "Baltasar Gracián y los escritores conceptistas del siglo XVII" *Historia General de las Literaturas Hispánicas*, ed. by Díaz-Plaja (Barcelona: Ed. Vergara, 1953) 693–726; Ignacio Arellano Ayuso, "El ingenioso estilo de don Francisco de Quevedo. Otros aspectos," *Poesía satírico burlesca de Quevedo* (Pamplona: Ediciones Universidad de Navarra, S. A., 1984) 288–311; S. L. Bethell, "Gracián, Tesauro, and the Nature of Metaphysical Wit" *Northern Miscellany of Literary Criticism* 1 (1953); John Williams Van Hook, "'Concuspiscence of Wit': Baroque Poetics and the English Metaphysical Style" diss., U of Washington, 1983; and Joseph Anthony Mazzeo, "Metaphysical Poetry and the Poetics of Correspondence" *JHI* 14 (1953), "A Seventeenth-Century Theory of Metaphysical Poetry" *RR* 42 (1951), and "A Critique of Some Modern Theories of Metaphysical Poetry" *MP* 50 (1952). This list, however, is very far from being exhaustive.

[19]Examples of studies of oratory illuminated by baroque treatises of wit are Hilary Dansey Smith, *Preaching in the Spanish Golden Age* (Oxford University Press, 1978), and Manuel Herrero García, "La literatura religiosa" *Historia General de las Literaturas Hispánicas* ed. by Guillermo Díaz Plaja (Barcelona: Ed. Vergara, 1953) 1–78.

writers of this age are described as exercising their mind's wit to uncover unexpected similarities, relationships, analogies, or correspondences between ideas, images, or unusual dimensions of reality. They also are described as authors depending on their power of ingenuity in order to create new forms and expressions in their artistic endeavors. If immoderation is now found in baroque writings, it is not as much identified with the picturesque, the passionate, or the sentimental as with conceptual abstractions, the witty, and the novel.

It can be strongly disputed that intellectualism and wit are the features of discourse which serve to define baroque writing and speech. On the one hand, these features are insufficient to explain the many facets of the baroque. On the other hand, these features are also found in many other literary and rhetorical ages. The mentioned treatises of wit show it through their most diverse illustrations comprehending authors of all centuries. Several scholars have adventured it as a successful hypothesis when, by using theories of wit, they have elucidated poetry of different eras. For example, Walter J. Ong did it when revaluating medieval Latin hymnody.[20] Also, Keith Whinnom used Gracián's *Agudeza* to uncover the intellectualism of love songs written during the times of the Catholic Monarchs in Spain.[21] Nevertheless, it is unique to the baroque era the rise of the many treatises on wit, especially among the Jesuits.

From these treatises, Benedetto Croce[22] regards Gracián's *Agudeza y arte de ingenio*[23] and Emanuele Tesauro's *Il cannocchiale aristotelico* the theories

---

[20]Walter J. Ong, S. J., "Wit and Mystery: a Revaluation in Mediaeval Latin Hymonody" *Speculum* 12 (1947).

[21]Keith Whinnom, *La poesía amatoria de la época de los Reyes Católicos* (University of Durham: 1981).

[22]Benedetto Croce, "Los tratadistas italianos del conceptismo y Baltasar Gracián" *La Lectura, Revista de Ciencias y Letras* 2nd ser. 12 (1912) 247.

[23]The title of this work could be translated into English as *Wit and the Art of Ingenuity, The Mind's Wit and the Art of Ingenuity,* or, as Leland Hugh Chambers did, *The Mind's Wit and Art.* Cf. Leland Hugh Chambers, "Baltasar Gracián's 'The Mind's Wit and Art'" diss., U of Michigan, 1962. However, throughout this study, I will keep the Spanish brief form of the title: *Agudeza.* I think this choice is better because *agudeza* is a word which comprehends

which better explain the baroque literary fashions in the whole of Europe. However, Marcelino Menéndez Pelayo does not believe that Gracián's treatise applies to all of the different baroque trends. He rather restricts its range to a "conceptist rhetoric."[24] Even so, instead of limiting the *Agudeza*, Ernest Robert Curtius expands its theoretical power to all forms of mannerism. By mannerism, Curtius understands "all literary tendencies which are opposed to the Classicism of all periods. Understood in this sense, Mannerism is a constant in European literature. It is the complementary phenomenon of the Classicism of all periods."[25] Appraising the *Agudeza*, Curtius says:

> ...the book is unique in its kind. It was a fruitful and timely idea to submit the widely ramified tradition of Mannerism to systematic consideration, to obtain an intellectual apprehension of its central source, to sort its forms, while guarding the dignity of their spirit. Gracián's book is an intellectual achievement of high rank.[26]

For Curtius, classical rhetoric is insufficient to explain the forms of mannerist discourse, in so far as it does not fully address the nature and forms of wit, which is the source of this kind of discourse.

> ...Gracián's originality consists precisely in the fact that he, first and alone, declares the system of antique rhetoric to be insufficient and supplements it by a new discipline, for which he claims systematic validity.
> ....
> Gracián produced a "Summa" of *agudeza*. It was a national achievement. The Spanish tradition from Martial to Góngora was brought into a universal context.[27]

---

both wit as a power of the mind, and wit as a product of discourse. Moreover, this choice is still the most commonly used by English scholars interested on the treatise. Finally, it is necessary to keep the Spanish version of the title in order not to confuse it with Matteo Pellegrini's *Acutezze*, a title which is also translated into English as "Wit."

[24]See Menéndez Pelayo 582.

[25]Curtius 273.

[26]Curtius 301.

[27]Curtius 297, 301.

2   Cultural Practices

THE RISE OF BAROQUE THEORIES OF WIT can be associated with several cultural practices of the age.

Baroque Passion for Originality

Baroque authors did not conceive of originality as an easy achievement in so far as they felt that the writers of antiquity took the lead in most arts and disciplines. For example, Baltasar Gracián observed:

> Some would have been phoenix in their employments, if some others had not taken the lead before.
>
> ....
>
> Those who follow stand as imitators of their predecessors; and, regardless of their effort, they can not purge it of the presumption of imitation.[1]

Concerning this difficult achievement of originality, Gracián could thus say:

> Today more is required of one sage than in ancient times of seven.[2]

Even so, the public of the seventeenth century set strong demands of originality because they were weary of renaissance works. Baroque authors had to answer the challenge and surpass their splendid but already dated predecessors in some fashion:

---

[1]*El Héroe* Primor 7: "Hubieran sido algunos fénix en los empleos, a no irles otros delante." "Son tenidos por imitadores de los pasados los que les siguen; y, por más que suden, no pueden purgar la presunción de imitación."

[2]*Oráculo* Aphorism 1. "Más se requiere hoy para un sabio que antiguamente para siete..." As a piece of judicious wit, this aphorism may serve to ponder many other issues besides of an author's originality.

Taste always moves forward, and never turns back; it is not sated with things already out of date, and always itches for novelty.[3]

Fortunately, originality was possible. Gracián pondered that a first place in time did not necessarily warrant a first place in fame. The best achievements always were the best in excellence, regardless of the centuries when they were accomplished. Moreover, when authors could not surpass their forerunners in the best category of accomplishments, they at least should strive for a first place in minor categories of accomplishments. To do so, authors should apply their *ingenuity* and find new ideas and techniques to set themselves free from things which had become old, repeated, or ordinary.[4]

Gracián was so serious in requiring originality from authors, that he illustrated his point with a famous Spanish painter[5] who did not follow the refined manners of Titian and rather used rough brushstrokes. This painter was first in roughness, said Gracián, rather than second in refinement.[6]

This illustration should be extended to every employment, and every unusual man should understand clearly the trick. He should find in outstanding novelties an extravagant course towards greatness.[7]

If an author could not go beyond the most repeated ideas, said Gracián, this author at least should renew these ideas by renovating the manner in which they

---

[3]*El Discreto* Realce 22: "Siempre va el gusto adelante, nunca vuelve atrás; no se ceba en lo que ya pasó, siempre pica en la novedad..."

[4]See, for example, *El Héroe* primores 6, 7, and 8.

[5]Gracián probably had in mind the great Diego de Velázquez. Cf. Adolphe Coster, *Baltasar Gracián* (Zaragoza, Institución "Fernando El Católico:" 1943) 90. However, in his edition of Baltasar Gracián's works, Arturo del Hoyo rather believes that Gracián was just repeating a common place of the renaissance about the artistic search for novelties.

[6]Cf. *El Héroe* Primor 7, and *Oráculo* Aphorism 63.

[7]*El Héroe* Primor 7. "Extiéndase el ejemplo a todo empleo, y todo varón raro entienda bien la treta, que en la eminente novedad sabrá hallar extravagante rumbo para la grandeza."

are stated.

> Even if things were very well known, if the orator's manner of saying them, and the historian's way of writing them were new, they would be more appealing.[8]

In the context of bad baroque literature, these recommendations from Gracián would certainly be a code of bad taste. They could be associated with the worst kind of writing of this age, and could be seen as reflecting writers whose only merit would be:

> ...exerting their ingenuity to come out from banality. Some writers search for novelties in subtleties of thought (...) Others, poorer in mental gifts, would hide their indigence of thought under the richness of expression. (...) Finally, some others...would adopt the showcase of pedantic erudition as an instrument of success.[9]

Italian writers also suffered a passion for the novel. Contrasting with Gracián, Matteo Pellegrini approached the issue of novelty with an unfavorable attitude. For Pellegrini, most of the contemporary writing vices rested on the abuse of witful sayings which stressed the novel without observing appropriateness.[10]

Yet, Gracián's views may reflect indistinctly the search for originality which authors of his period undertook, regardless of how successful these authors were in their search. Not only bad poets, but also great writers strove for novelty.

Thus far it is important to note that their source of creation—the springs of originality—departed from the renaissance methods of Platonic poetic furor or Aristotelian imitation of models. The source at this point was the author's own *ingenuity*. Hence the greatest writers of this century are described as *wits*. Lope

---

[8]*El Discreto* Realce 22. "...aunque las cosas sean muy sabidas, si el modo del decirlas en el retórico y del escribirlas en el historiador fuere nuevo, las hace apetecibles."

[9]Coster 194.

[10]See *Acutezze*, for example, Chapter 12, 196, and Chapter 13, 249.

de Vega was *the Phoenix of Wits*. Góngora was *the Swan of Wits*. Cervantes was *the Prince of Wits*. His creation, Don Quixote, who is the most important literary character of this age, was *the Ingenious Gentleman of La Mancha*. The last of the great baroque authors in the Hispanic world, Sister Juana Inés de la Cruz, was not a writer inspired by the Muses, but she was the *Tenth Muse* herself because of her outstanding ingenuity.

Therefore, it is not only the passion for originality which should be associated with the rise of treatises of wit—any truly new cultural period contains a touch of originality. What differentiates the baroque era is that the highly sought after originality rested mainly in an author's conscious exertion of his own ingenuity. Baroque treatises of wit can thus be seen as attempts to explain this fashion.

Continuity of the Courtly Tradition of Witty Poetry

Unsympathetic to the baroque search for novelty, Menéndez Pelayo explains it as the exhaustion of the courtly tradition of witty poetry. In his view, this search was not a renewal which ripened classical renaissance modes and motives of expression, but a ruinous effort to keep alive two moribund literary traditions which polluted the renaissance era.

> ...isolated from popular art...inside the palaces of kings and magnates...an intellectual aristocracy...introduced...within all European literature, a plague worse than the locust—the plague of eclogues, madrigals, sonnets, metaphysical songs of a Tuscan fashion, pastoral novels, allegorical farces—a species of poetic nightmare which was not classical, but which preserved all the bad habits of the courts of love and of the medieval troubadour schools...which with the exception of the elegant form, it united the worse vices of two literary decadences: the Alexandrine decadence, and the Toulousean decadence—the false Antiquity, and the false Middle Ages.[11]

---

[11]Menéndez Pelayo 563–564.

Regarding the Alexandrine tradition, Curtius associates, as already noted, Gracián's treatise of wit with all mannerist periods—that is, the sophistic, the Alexandrine, the second sophistic, and other similar periods. Curtius supports his position by making an inventory of Gracián's illustrations of witticisms, as found in the *Agudeza*.

> ...Gracián circles around an ideal canon of the masters of the *concepto*. He gives different versions of it. The one in his Forword (Ambrose, Martial, Seneca, Tacitus, Pliny, Ausonius, Florus, Tasso, Góngora, Camoes) we must regard as a carefully considered selection. Another compromises Augustine, Ambrose, Martial, and Horace...There is a corresponding résumé at the end of the book: Tacitus, Velleius Paterculus, Florus, Valerius Maximus, Pliny, Apuleius, Martial...But if we ask ourselves what literary "experiences" and preferences formed the basis for Gracián's canon, the answer is plain: Martial and Góngora.

> We have already seen that Ambrose and Augustine belong to the conceptist canon. Peter Chrysologus appears with them. But Greek Fathers, such as Clement of Alexandria, Basil, Gregory of Nazianzus, are also taken in.

> Yet he is able to find examples of the use of *agudeza* in epic and the romance (Homer, Virgil, Heliodorus, Mateo Alemán...) and in the complications of dramatic intrigue (Lope de Vega, Calderón...)[12]

Regarding the Toulousean tradition, it is true that many European courts continued practicing troubadour fashions for several centuries. It was a sign of nobility to be involved in love affairs,[13] and to express this love through poetry and songs. This poetry has been described as "stiff, cold, and artificial,"[14]

---

[12]Curtius 299–301.

[13]The masses were regarded as too vulgar to experience the refinements of love. Cf., the classical treatise of courtly love: Andreas Capellanus, *The Art of Courtly Love*, Trans. John Jay Parry (New York: Frederick Ungar Publishing, Co., 1959). In this book, beyond the code of chivalry, Capellanus offered to us an excellent rhetoric of love—an understanding of the rationality behind wooing and being wooed.

[14]"Gaya Ciencia," *Enciclopedia Universal Ilustrada Europeo-Americana* (Barcelona: Ed. ESPASA, 1924) 4:1116.

possibly because critics neglect its very high intellectual component.[15] During the reign of the Catholic Monarchs (1479–1516) many courtly songs were written and collected in what today are known as *cancioneros*. Rather than being a display of sentimentality, these songs were exchanges of playful jests and riddles between the lover and the beloved. If on the surface they expressed commitment to the idealistic and standarized code of love which ruled between courtly sweethearts, they also gave place to an intentional ambiguity which allowed readings of the most carnal erotism, and which nevertheless kept the text itself strictly free from what the mind's wit would be prone to deviate into extremes of obscenity.

Among the theorists of wit, Gracián relied highly on courtly poetry of this tradition to conceive his art of ingenuity. Correa Calderón says:

> From Spaniards of the fifteenth century, who he called *old fashioned authors*, he quotes many examples. He would frequently work with the *Cancionero General*, of Hernando del Castillo, and he was extremely pleased, without doubt, by the conceptual twining of the poets there found.[16]

In his edition of Gracián's works, Arturo del Hoyo registers twelve pages of the *Agudeza* fully illustrated with quotes taken from this *cancionero*.[17]

Regarding other Spanish renaissance and the baroque illustrations for Gracián's treatise, Coster finds that Gracián preferred the kind of conceptist, witty, and playful poetry which would be specifically similar to the one of the

---

[15]Referring specifically to poetry of the Catholic Monarchs' court, Keith Whinnom defines it as "an intellectual poetry, or, if wanted, a metaphysical one" which it is wrong to judge "by criteria unapplicable to the case" as it is wrong to expect from this poetry that it be "romantic, picturesque, and passionate." He then explains that "the merits which is legitimate to expect from this kind of poetry are: lapidary concision, original, witty, and sometimes pungent concepts, and opportune rhetorical, metrical, and wordly inventions." See Whinnom 17.

[16]E. Correa Calderón, "Sobre Gracián y su 'Agudeza y Arte de Ingenio'" *Revista de Ideas Estéticas* (1944) 81.

[17]See Baltasar Gracián y Morales, *Obras Completas*, "Estudio preliminar, edición, bibliografia y notas" by Arturo del Hoyo (Madrid, Ed. Aguilar: 1960) 1298.

cancioneros,[18]   and more generally associated with the Toulousean and Alexandrine traditions as referred by Menéndez Pelayo. Gracián would rather ignore to a high degree, says Coster, the properly culteranist illustrations of baroque literature.

> Gracián will take [Góngora] as an inimitable model for his *Agudeza.* He quotes him seventy four times...Nevertheless... Gracián did not choose the most "Gongorist" samples from this poet. With relish, he quotes his *comedia* entitled *Isabela* from 1613, and several times. However, *Polifemo* and *Soledades,* which are the most definite models of the cult style, he only quotes them twice...[19]

As a professor of grammar in Jesuit colleges, whose *Agudeza* is said to be the result of his lectures,[20] Gracián showed the preferences he had about current literary practices. Thus it was not only the stress on ingenuity as a source of originality and a foundation for creativity during the baroque which influenced Gracián. It was eminently the baroque stress on ingenuity as a practice of intellectual and witty discourse which captured Gracián's attention.

The Italian theorists of ingenuity could not be untouched by the fashion of witty poetry. This trend was also common in Italy during the seventeenth century. A century later, Giambattista Vico would reflect on this development:

> We Italians...are endowed with a language which constantly evokes images. We stand above other nations by our achievements in the fields of painting, sculpture, architecture, and music. Our language, thanks to its perpetual dynamism, forces the attention of the listeners by means of metaphorical expressions, and prompts it to move back and forth between ideas which are far apart. In the keeness of their

---

[18]Gracián would be personally interested in the *cancioneros* because of his regionalism. He was an Aragonese writer who profoundly admired the last king of his country, Ferdinand the Catholic, spouse of Isabella I of Castile, and, with her, Founding Parent of Spain. Any cultural development of Ferdinand's age, such as the *cancioneros,* would have been of strong interest of Gracián.

[19]Coster 221.

[20]Miguel Batllori S. I., *Gracián y el Barroco* (Rome, Edizioni di storia e letteratura: 1958) 35.

perception, the Italians are second only to the Spaniards.[21]

For Gracián and Emanuele Tesauro, Italians would be the first in practicing the courtly tradition of emblems and mottos, and Andrea Alciati would particularly be the first author cultivating these genres of witticisms.[22] Tesauro was distinctly responsive to these courtly practices, and included in his *Cannocchiale* a theory of emblems, mottos, and lapidary and coin inscriptions. And although faultfinding, Matteo Pellegrini also wrote his *Acutezze* as a concrete explanation to these literary endeavors of his time.

Prudence, Moral Subtleties, and Casuistry

Several of Gracián's works cannot be dissociated from another courtly development of the renaissance and the baroque—the fashion of reviewing ancient works, or of writing new books, on the rules which govern and enhance the life of princes and the nobility, as distinct from the ordinary ethics and manners guiding the common people. Gracián's *El Héroe, El Político, El Discreto,* and *Oráculo manual y arte de prudencia*[23] clearly belong to this tradition. To a less obvious degree, his other works also share this connection with literature which sets aristocratic standards. Either assenting or dissenting, Gracián's books relate to works such as Plutarch's *Parallel lives,* Tacitus's *Annals,* and Pliny the Younger's *Panegyric to Trajan,* from antiquity. Gracián's works also relate to Alciati's *Emblemata,* Castiglione's *The Courtier,* Machiavelli's *The Prince,* Giovanni Botero's *Della ragione di Stato* and *Detti*

---

[21]Giambattista Vico, *De studiorum ratione, Opere* 1.95, as quoted by Mooney 104–105.

[22]See *Agudeza* Discourse 6; *Cannochiale,* Chapter 15, 626.

[23]Viginia Ramos Foster renders these titles into English respectively as *The Hero, The Politician, The Discreet Man,* and *Oracle. A Manual of the Art of Prudence.* See her book *Baltasar Gracián* (Boston, Twayne Publishers:1975) 118–138. I keep the titles of Gracián's books in Spanish in so far as there is not yet a standarized version for them in English.

memorabili di personaggi, Juan Rufo's *Las seiscientas apotegmas*, Giovanni della Casa, *Galateo, ovvero de' costumi* (which was adapted into Spanish by Lucas Gracián Dantisco's *El Galateo español*), and Nicolás Faret's *L'Honneste Homme*, among others from the renaissance and the baroque, which address as diverse courtly problems as, for example, palace etiquette, the prince's reputation, the reason of State, the lesser evil as a choice, and the conquering of new principalities.[24] Through Gracián, this courtly tradition continued in other works such as Madame de Sablé's *Maximes*, La Rochefoucauld's *Maximes*, and La Bruyère's *Caractères*.[25]

These works reveal more than ideas. They reveal a culture and a way of life which took place in European aristocracies at the dawn of modern age. Rafael Solana explains this development by saying that "the term honor lost its contents and was replaced by something lacking any relationship with it: honors." He adds:

> That which prescribed a king not to lie, to deceive, or to betray his word started to meet exceptions...the most honorable army was the most numerous one, and nothing was more honorable than succeeding in the battle regardless of the means used. The Homeric hero was not Hector...but Ulysses, the deceitful one...[26]

And as I found stated in another place: what in the Middle Ages was courage,

---

[24]Besides Gracián's, other major and Spanish works on aristocratic rules of morality were Francisco de Quevedo's *Política de Dios y gobierno de Cristo* (1617–1626), and Diego Saavedra y Fajardo's *Idea de un príncipe político cristiano representada en cien empresas* (1640) and *República literaria* (1655).

[25]It should be noted that Jorge M. Ayala detects in Blaise Pascal some direct influences received from Gracián's sententiae, and generally from this tradition of condensing moral problems in aphorisms. See Jorge M. Ayala, *Gracián: vida, estilo y reflexión*, (Madrid: Editorial Cincel, 1987) 23–34.

[26]Rafael Solana, "Tratemos de conservar lo único que no se ha perdido: el humor" *Siempre!* (Agosto 8 de 1990) 9–10. Regarding the *Odyssey*, Gracián held this epic was one lively painting "our pilgrimage through life" (*Agudeza* Discourse 56), and "a book to read from the beginning to the end...Know that the dangerous sea is the Court with its Scyllas of deceit and its Charybdis of lies." (*El Criticón* I, Crisi 12).

honor, and wisdom, became prudence in the renaissance, and plain shrewdness and ingenuity in the baroque age. Gunpowder introduced massive warfare into human affairs, and made senseless the chilvaric code of nobility. Very famous works—such as *Don Quixote*—came to express this renaissance common place. Gracián himself believed that courage as a norm of behavior became either senseless or reckless in military affairs after gunpowder appeared.[27] And the seemly quiet courts were not a peaceful heaven for Gracián: etiquette and good manners themselves were trifling preoccupations compared to the task of survival within the moral jungle of palaces.[28]

The works of aristocratic rules of conduct were contemporary to some great Catholic treatises of moral theology. Certainly, some issues which demanded urgent attention led moral theologians to propose bold answers. Francisco de Vitoria addressed the issue of the conquest of America. He did not only condemn this conquest and the enslaving of Americans; he also contributed to the foundation of International Law, and led popes and Spanish kings to outlaw slavery in the New World—although with less success than a warm expression of good intentions. However, many other issues could not get answers as bold as Vitoria's. For example, without denying either freedom or grace, famous Spanish scholars of the sixteenth and seventeenth century discussed the extent to which these gifts operated on the human will. The Dominicans, led by Domingo Bañez, emphasized grace. The Jesuits, led by Luis Molina, emphasized freedom. Within the Jesuits, Francisco Suárez tried to draw a subtle line between the two admissible extremes. The Holy See continuously tried to remind theologians about admitting their differences as probable opinions within the frame of the Faith, and, more important, as a charity duty of not quarreling amongst themselves.[29]

---

[27]*El Criticón* II, Crisi 8.

[28]See *El Criticón* I, Crisi 9, where Baltasar Gracián mocked Lucas Gracián Dantisco's *El Galateo Cortesano*—a manual of courtly etiquette.

[29]In this age, there were many other serious and subtle theological issues besides defining the balance between freedom and grace. For example, concerning casuistry, theologians

If moral theology met with admissible theoretical probabilities, moral life then faced an obscure realm where the line between right and wrong was not clearly drawn. During the seventeenth century, therefore, casuistry strongly developed efforts to determine the moral obligation and the nuances between better or worse which were comprehended in complex moral cases. Some specific actions appeared as morally possible under certain principles, whereas they were unacceptable under other principles. There was the question of either always following the safest opinions, or sometimes giving place to other probable opinions supported by two or more doctors. Theologians took sides on this controversy. The Jesuits usually supported the second position, thus gaining a reputation of being lax in morality.[30]

Casuistry as such consisted in theological speculations carried over syllogistically from moral principles to particular cases. However, priests very often took it to real life in order to give concrete counsel to their parishioners. There they found new challenges. It was not enough to know moral principles and rules of inference:

> The laws...do not consider the particulars but what is common and general: that is, not what particularly applies to persons, but what generally applies to what is common in everybody...[31]

---

debated the moral validity of just safe opinions in view of safer ones, and, concerning the history of salvation, other discussed whether the Immaculate, in so far as preserved from sin, suffered or not death—a consequence of sin—before her Assumption. Neither councils nor popes have settled these questions yet, but they rather have warned theologians to tolerate each other's admissible opinions on the name of charity, and have encouraged theological inquiry from the fountains of Faith to illuminate these issues. Regarding the question of casuistry, in the eighteenth century St Alphonsus Liguori provided some guidelines which allow the choice of safe opinions without neglect of safer ones. Regarding the debate of the balance between grace and freedom, I have already mentioned that Suárez supplied some answers. Regarding the lot of Our Lady, Pope Pius XII defined the dogma of her Assumption without detailing the circumstances of it.

[30]In his *Provincial Letters*, Blaise Pascal attacked the Jesuits for their lax criteria in using casuistry.

[31]Fr Luis de Granada, *Guía de Pecadores* "Prólogo Galeato."

Priests also needed a keen mind and training to identify the kind of case at issue, in order then to judge it from a given principle. Thus, perspicacity took precedence over argumentation.[32]

Miguel Batllori finds that Gracián's theories of ingenuity were not merely applied to witty language, but that they were also concerned with giving rules to the perspicacious mind of a casuist, in his discerning of specific cases.[33] Gracián was not just a professor of moral theology in the Jesuit college of Gandía. As a priest, one of his main duties was to be a confessor and counselor of souls. He dealt with very complex cases, and some of his solutions brought him criticism because he was too "lax" even for the Jesuits themselves. Gracián preferred to follow his keen spirit than to remain in the narrow boundaries of "rigorism".[34] As I said before, the theorists of wit usually were Jesuits, and, like Gracián, they were confessors and they would deal with acute moral problems and counseling.

Seventeenth century aristocratic prudence, theological probabilities, casuistic inquiries—all these endeavors confronted moral nuances which challanged the mind's wit. Theorists of wit often worked in the midst of these problems. Therefore, I believe that the rise of treatises on ingenuity in this century should not be analyzed in the absence of these moral contexts.[35]

---

[32]A very important and controversial work of casuistry in the seventeenth century was a handbook which helped priests to minister the sacrament of penance, by giving guidelines to identify sins: *De paenitentia*. This treatise was written by the Jesuit Juan de Lugo, a Spanish Cardinal during the times of Pope Urban VIII.

[33]Cf. Batllori *Gracián y el Barroco* 113.

[34]A notable example was Gracián's sacramental absolution given to a priest who repented of womanizing. Gracián "laxly" applied a pontifical bull to the case, instead of turning this case over to higher authorities. Cf. Arturo del Hoyo xxxiv. Nevertheless, Gracián strongly recommended "rigorism" if the case in question is not clear enough. That means that if the judge knows little about the case on which he must *immediately* pronounce a veredict, then the judge should follow not just the safe opinion, but the safest opinion. See *Oráculo* Aphorism 271.

[35]Tesauro, Pallavicino, and Pellegrini's involvement in issues of morality and prudence are expressed in several of their works. Pellegrini published a *Politica massima*. Pallavicino for

Intensification of Religious Life

The developments of moral theology and casuistry examined above can be placed within a broader religious context: the reform which the Church underwent around and after the Council of Trent.

In Spain, this reform can be traced back to the reign of the Catholic Monarchs, who found that the current life of the clergy was too lax to reinforce the place Catholic religion had in Spain as a component of national identity, and as a motive finally to expel the Moors from the peninsula. They appointed Fr. Francisco Jiménez de Cisneros as Primate of Spain, and made him the leader of the reform. Universities were invigorated and founded, promoting a revival of Scriptural studies and scholasticism within their cloisters, and of preaching throughout the whole country. Religious orders were disciplined by reforming their rules, by intensifying their spiritual practices, and by keeping a check on them through the Inquisition. New militant orders—such as the Society of Jesus—were created to defend the Faith. By the time the Protestant movement appeared, the Spanish Church was among the most vigorous in Europe, and was ready to be a leader in the sessions of the Council of Trent.

> In composition the Council had a marked Mediterranean character, with the Italians enjoying a large numerical superiority. The Spaniards came the second, though in respect of the eminence of their representatives perhaps they should be given first place; for they had outstanding names, like the Jesuits Laínez and Salmeron, pontifical theologians, the Dominicans Domingo de Soto and Melchor Cano, and the Franciscans Alfonso de Castro and Andrés de Vega.[36]

Started in Spain, the reform then became part of the religious revival in all of the Catholic countries. And religious education and discipline were not only

---

example published *Massime ed espressioni civile ed ecclesiastica prudenza*, and *Del bene libri quattro*. Tesauro published *La filosofia morale derivata dall' alta fonte del grande Aristotile*.

[36]Domínguez Ortiz 202.

promoted within the clergy but also within the laity.[37]

In spite of having a wide span of interests different from religion, Gracián, Pellegrini, Pallavicino, and Tesauro were outstanding members of the post-Tridentine clergy and could not be dissociated from the intense Catholic life of the seventeenth century. For example, there are very obvious religious concerns in Gracián's *El Comulgatorio*, which he published when he was professor of Holy Scriptures in Zaragoza. This book is a collection of meditations on the Holy Eucharist. Of strong Jesuitical affiliation, this book develops like *The Spiritual Exercises* of St Ignatius, and as a whole expresses the Jesuitical voluntarist stand of practicing frequent communion.[38] Gracián's other books' association with religious goals is not as clear as it is seen in *El Comulgatorio*. However, this association strongly exists, particularly in his *Agudeza*.

Here, I should point out the links between the seventeenth century Catholic revival and the development of theories of wit. As an intellectual ability to perceive relationships between disparate things, wit is associated with many religious practices. Scriptural studies to a high degree consist in establishing concordances between different places of the Writ. Important forms of prayer and meditation imply the consideration of connections between the contents of the Faith and the personal life of the faithful. Preachers very often explain the Gospels by finding correspondences of the texts' contents with the moral behavior of the parishioners. Thus, Alexander A. Parker believes:

---

[37]Along with the popes, St Charles Borromeo and St Robert Bellarmino were leaders of the reform in Italy. In France and Switzerland, St Francis de Sales became one of the greatest promoters of spiritual devotion as part of lay vocations. A sign of the laity's religious education and involvement—says Domínguez Ortiz 206—was that, in Spain, they were "capable of understanding the *autos sacramentales*, plays based on theological symbols which take for granted an unusual degree of religious instruction on the part of the audience." The creation of numerous Jesuit colleges made available Catholic training to most members of the European nobility, and to the raising bourgeoisie.

[38]The Jesuits' voluntarism and strong stand for frequent communion responded to Protestant denials of the free will and of the Real Presence in the Eucharist. It would later respond to Jansenist emphasis on predestination and on infrequent communion.

The connexion of preaching with Wit goes back to the Fathers of the Church. Sermons form, with Martial and Góngora, the three principal sources of Gracián's examples. Sermons and the literature connected with them are the sources from which Gracián's terminology springs; nearly all his characteristic terms, in addition to *concepto* and *agudeza*, derive from there, such as *ponderation, careo,* and *reparo.* His method of analysis through pondering on the new ideas arising from the examination of the initial concept in its relation to each of its 'circumstances' and 'adjunts', thus following 'the lines of ponderation' which the mind discovers in its 'discourse', was the technique of meditation and contemplative prayer. Manuals of meditation called the first stage the 'consideration', which was the first review of the subject; the second stage was frequently called the 'ponderation', or the amplification of the first stage in new or more complex directions.[39]

But preaching, prayer, meditation, spiritual exercises, Scriptural studies were more than a theoretical influence for Gracián and the theorists of wit considered here. Immersed in an intense religious environment, these scholars made these "witty" religious practices a part of their daily life. They could not abstain from being continuous practicioners of wit.

Moreover, among the religious developments of the late sixteenth century and the whole of the seventeenth, I should emphasize the extensive practice of mystical prayer because of its relevance to theories of the mind.[40] Transcending the guidance of external models of prayer, the mystic retreated into his soul and, by means of self-abandonment, he spiritually united to the Eternal Spouse. Now, an outstanding feature of post-Tridentine mystics was the careful recording of their experiences. Works such as St Teresa's *Interior Castle* and St Francis of Sales's *Treatise on the Love of God* reveal a strong analytical and descriptive effort to distinguish the structure of the mind, and the stages which the soul

---

[39]Parker xxxiv.

[40]Famous mystics in Spain and her dominions were St Teresa the Great, St John of the Cross, St Rosa of Lima, and Sister María de Agreda. Famous Italian mystics were St Mary Magdalen dei Pazzi, St Catherine dei Ricci, St Charles Borromeo, St Philip Neri, and St Robert Bellarmino. Famous French mystics were St Francis of Sales, St John Eudes, St Margaret Mary Alacoque, Bl Claude La Colombière, and François de Fénelon.

undergoes in her raptures. They turn mysticism into a psychological inquiry, and this inquiry into psychological empiricism. Miguel Herrero García thus says that St Teresa's works are "the most enlightened experimental documentation of Christian mysticism" which raised this spiritual endeavor to the level of experimental sciences.[41]

Of this religious development, I should stress its strong parallelism with the most important of the seventeenth-century schools of thought. Mystical inquiries implied putting aside external objects—such as models of prayer—and turning the mind into itself to have a direct experience of its properties, contents, and structure while they were in contact with God. In a similar way, Cartesians in France, empiricists in Great Britain, and, to some degree, the theorists of ingenuity in Spain and Italy, very often put aside external objects—such as the learning models of Antiquity—and turned their inquiries into the mind itself, as the departing point in the construction of their theoretical systems.

Preaching

As mentioned some pages above, oratory, and particularly preaching, adopted much of the literary fashions of the age, becoming strongly interested in novelty, complex style, subtle ideas, ingenious interpretations of the Writ, and the display of both sacred and human erudition. Figures such as Fr. Hortensio Paravicino (1580–1633) rose as *Góngoras* of the pulpit. Although they did not neglect their duty to edify their audiences, they also strove to surprise, entertain, and make their learned parishioners marvel with their preaching artistry. This role of pulpit entertainers displeased Church authorities very much, and particularly the Jesuits, who strongly and officially opposed this practice, although not with much success.

Besides these mentioned practices, there was an increasing recourse to

---

[41]Miguel Herrero García, "La literatura religiosa," *Historia General de las Literaturas Hispánicas*, ed. by Guillermo Díaz-Plaja (Barcelona: Ed. Vergara, 1953) 3: 67.

collections of sermons and to other kinds of preaching topics, as materials ready for use when novel preachers had to speak from the pulpit. The collections were readily available in the form of *sermonarios, florilegios, sylvae,* and *thesauri.* The preaching materials ranged from complete sermons to compilations of examples, phrases, scriptural quotations, and other religious topics appropriate for different subjects, occasions, and publics.

With these materials at hand, the preacher only had to build up his sermon by knowing some tecniques of amplification. Among the most common techniques of the age was the use of comparison and contrast, which implied a review of all the *circumstances* relating or separating two things or religious topics borrowed from a collection. To make the job of a novel preacher even easier, tables of comparisons, similes, and concepts[42] suitable for sermons were published. Examples of these works are Juan Pérez de Moya's *Comparaciones o símiles para los vicios y virtudes* (1584), Alonso de Ledesma's *Conceptos espirituales* (1600), Rafael Sarmiento's *Promptuarium conceptum* (1604), Melchor Fuster's *Conceptos predicables* and *Misceláneas predicables* (1611-1612), González de Critana's *Silva Comparationum* (1611), Francisco Labata's *Apparatus concionatorum* (1614), Fr Tomás Ramón's *Conceptos extravagantes y peregrinos* (1619), and Francisco de Hontiveros's *Conceptos predicables políticos y morales a diferentes asuntos* (1663).

This technique of amplification—of comparisons and contrasts—is a very direct precedent of some theories of wit. Gracián implicitly addressed it when explainig some of his *concepts* as consisting of comparisons reviewing the shared or differentiating circumstances of the things matched.[43] Tesauro openly addressed the *concetti predicabili* inserting a whole section on this issue in his *Cannocchiale.*[44]

---

[42]Here, *concept* means an extravagant and fully developed simile or methapor.

[43]See, for example, *Agudeza*, Discourse 4.

[44]*Cannocchiale* Chapter 9: 501–540. For Tesauro, the *concetti predicabili* were a kind of metaphorically fallacious enthymemes useful for preaching.

Theoretical Problems

SOME THEORETICAL PROBLEMS IN THE FIELDS of poetics, rhetoric, and Jesuit education can be related to the rise of baroque theories of wit.

Poetics

A very brief and simplified summary of the changes observed in Spanish and Italian theories of poetics from the sixteenth to the seventeenth century could be the following:

a) Sixteenth-century poetics focused on the *external* sources and processes which inspire and lead the poet to create his works. These poetics rested either on Plato's theories of poetic furor—the recall of *Eternal Ideas*—or on Aristotle's theories of imitation—*the forms* contained in models.

b) Seventeenth-century baroque poetics focused on the *internal* power of ingenuity and its processes which allow the poet to think about and even *produce* his sources, and, moreover, to create and also understand poetry.

These changes separating seventeenth-century from sixteenth-century poetics are related to several theoretical problems faced by critics in the period preceding the rise of theories of ingenuity. These problems were about the role of the mind in creating and understanding poetry.

For example, there was a new awareness of the mind's power to imitate not necessarily Eternal Ideas, not necessarily the forms contained in models, but rather its own internal products as created through its fantasy. John Williams Van Hooks explains some poetic problems faced by the Italian Jacopo Mazzoni when writing *Della difesa della* Comedia *di Dante* in 1587:

> ...to Mazzoni, imitative poetry did not have to be accurate to any objective world beyond itself. Indeed, he preferred that the poet imitate things which he "has conceived in his phantasy." He could call such images "imitative" only by redefining the term... Although Mazzoni does not exclude the direct copying of Nature, his

poet would aim to communicate... images whose "usefulness consists solely in representing well" an idea "conceived in the phantasy" óf the poet.[1]

Explaining Mazzoni's poetics, Van Hook also says:

> Mazzoni... gave the phantasy a more active and positive role to play in the process of thinking... phantasy was a positive "faculty of the mind, ...or power," capable of making "forms" on its own.[2]

The Spaniard Juan Huarte's *Examen de ingenios,* published in 1575, is another example of a transitional work which signals the change from theories of imitation of forms or ideas to theories of ingenuity producing its own poetic forms. In a proper sense, *Examen de ingenios* is not a book on poetic theory. It is rather a book written by a physician who was inquiring about the structure of the mind, its different classes, and the different mental aptitudes which would be appropriate for succeeding in different professions. His views on the structure of the mind did not differ much from traditional studies: the mind is a compound of memory, understanding, and imagination. Even so, Huarte's method of studying the mind was quite innovative: it was experimental.[3] His findings were relevant to poetics because he strongly related the psychological power of imagination with the creation of poetry. In a renaissance context of neo-Platonic poetics, *Examen de ingenios* stole the poet's inspiration from the

---

[1]John Williams Van Hook "'Concupiscence of Wit': Baroque Poetics and the English Metaphysical Style" diss., U of Washington, 1983, 3–4, who quotes Jacobo Mazzoni, *Della difesa della* Comedia *di Dante* (1587; rpt. Casena, Italy: 1688) 1: 560, 559.

[2]Van Hook 5.

[3]Huarte's experimental methods included the recording of correlations and variations as observed in particular cases. Huarte's views on the mind's faculties, his use of the experimental approach, and his classification of sciences according to the human faculties are said to have influenced Francis Bacon's development of his theories on the nature of human mind. Cf. Juan Luis Alborg, *Historia de la Literatura Española,*(Madrid: Ed. Gredos, 1987) 1: 1016; Menéndez Pelayo 431.

ethereal region of ideas, and plunged it into the physical realm of mind's humors and temperament.[4]

Other poetic problems which preceded the rise of theories of wit consisted in defining the role of erudition in the creation and understanding of poetry. An example of this concern can be found in the Spaniard Luis Carrillo y Sotomayor's *Libro de la Erudición Poética*, published in 1611, and regarded as a *culteranist manifesto*. Carrillo y Sotomayor still endorsed the theory of imitation of ancient models. However, his strong emphasis on being completely familiar with ancient modes and motifs of poetry turned imitation into a display of erudition. A plain experience of poetic objects became insufficient for the mastery of poetry. Both the creation and the understanding of poetry relied heavily on vast erudition. Moreover, this learning was not merely the result of acquiring knowledge of antiquity; it was also a result of a skillful—ingenious—use of the instrument of learning: the mind. Thus the critic had to face up to the fact that the poetry promoted by Carrillo y Sotomayor was not only a challenge to erudition, but it also strongly challenged the mind regarding its power to handle such an erudition packed in a difficult, obscure, and hermetic form. This poetry was elitist not only because of its devotion to the learned, but also because of its devotion to the *smart*.

The theoretical turn to the internal powers of the mind was also reflected on several debates concerning whether the plastic arts should be included among the liberal arts. The reasons for this debate were rather vulgar: Philip IV's heavy taxation over those who were not noble practicioners of the liberal arts.

---

[4]It seems that Gracián and some of his scholarly friends were acquainted with Huarte's book. In his granting of approval to Gracián's *El Discreto*, Juan Francisco Andrés de Uztarroz defended the choosing of vocations by youth according to their own inclination, talents, and genius—a doctrine popularized by Huarte. Gracián's own contact with Huarte's theories could be inferred from some fragments of *El Discreto* Realce I, and particularly from *El Héroe* Primor III. There we can see that Gracián disagreed with the idea of having several kinds of "ingenuities"—several kinds of faculties of understanding—according to different types of people. For Gracián there was only one kind of human understanding. What made people differ in their professional talents, believed Gracián, was their specific kind of wills, inclinations, and *genius*.

However, these debates accomplished an interesting analysis of the complex mind's processes necessary to create a work of art. Philip IV himself settled the question by bestowing the Order of Santiago on the great painter Diego de Velázquez.[5]

These examples of Mazzoni, Huarte, Carrillo y Sotomayor, and the plastic arts reveal seventeenth-century critics' need to address the active role of the mind in poetry or any other art—a role fully addressed later by the theorists of wit, when inquiring the faculty of ingenuity.

Rhetoric and Jesuit Education

Rhetoric in Spain and Italy before the rise of theories of wit could be briefly summarized by describing it as a Jesuit Ciceronianism. The spread of Jesuit education made rhetoric in principle a mixture of Ciceronian and Aristotelian theories fully covering all the parts of this art—from invention to delivery. But their rhetoric emphasized a managerial role in invention, the use of emotions in persuasion, the recourse to ornament in style, and dramatic effects in delivery. Also, a peculiar development among some authors was the belief that invention and style were not strictly separate parts of rhetoric, but that they could replace each other in their functions.[6]

The institutionalization of Ciceronianism by the Jesuits was the result of a long controversy among the humanists about restoring classical rhetoric and eloquence in European universities.

In sixteenth-century Spain, some rhetoricians strove to correct and purify scholastic Latin and to return to the usage of the Roman Golden Age, personified

---

[5]See Menéndez Pelayo 615.

[6]My account of sixteenth-century and seventeenth-century rhetorics emphasizes Spanish treatises, and may not fully apply to Italy and to other Catholic countries. However, after reading Pellegrini's depiction of rhetoric in his country in *I Fonti Dell' Ingegno*, I strongly believe that Jesuit Ciceronianism was as prevalent in Italy as it was in Spain at the dawn of theories of wit.

principally in Cicero. They made classical rhetoric—Cicero's, Quintilian's, and also Aristotle's—the theory supporting the use of classical Latin in schools. Grammarians such as Antonio de Nebrija, and Jesuits such as Cipriano Suárez published summaries of classical rhetoric to simplify this restoration of Latin in the universities.[7]

For many humanists, a strong Latin was seen as the language which would keep European scholarship united, within a continent fragmented since the rise of vernacular languages and the increasing national spirit in many countries. For the Church, a strong Latin would help keep Europe spiritually unified. And in Italy, nationalistic figures, such as Lorenzo Valla, saw that a strong Latin would be a means of reconstructing the Roman Empire—at least spiritually—and a means of restoring the ancient Italian glory.

An enthusiastic and strict Ciceronianism was not welcomed by all humanists. Other groups of rhetoricians believed that the use of Ciceronian models for the study of Latin would threaten the Christian mold of schools and encourage the increasing "paganization" of many Church activities and life. They did not mean to reject classical eloquence. They meant that this eloquence could also be found in the Scriptures, the Holy Fathers, and many other great orators of Christianity. Thus, to help Latin recover its eloquence of antiquity, it was not necessary for students to follow pagan models. They could very well follow Christian exemplars of eloquence and thought. In Spain, figures such as Fr. Luis de Granada explained Ciceronian theories of rhetoric within a Christian frame of thought and with Christian models of eloquence.[8] Works like his were late fruits of the Christian humanism promoted by Erasmus and Luis Vives in the North of Europe, and Marsilio Ficino and Giovanni Pico della Mirandola in

---

[7]See Antonio de Nebrija, *Artis Rhetoricae compendiosa coaptatio ex Aristotele, Cicerone et Quintiliano* (1515); Cypriano Soarez, *De Arte Rhetorica libri tres, ex Aristotele, Cicerone et Quintiliano praecipue deprompti* (1569).

[8]Ludovicos Granatensis, *Ecclesiasticae Rhetoricae, sive de ratione concionandi libri sex, nunc primum in lucem editi* (Olyssipone, 1575). My edition of this treatise is Fr. Luis de Granada, *Los seis libros de la rhetórica eclesiástica*, trans. by Josef Bishop of Barcelona (Barcelona, 1770).

Italy.

The Christianizing of rhetoric led some authors to insert this art inside the wide frame of scholastic learning needed for the training of priests, and particularly preachers.[9] Some late sixteenth century rhetoricians wrote treatises which included summaries of this learning, or even treatises which themselves consisted in such kind of summaries. Thus, in spite of its Ciceronian structure, the art of rhetoric itself was explained as a method of approaching and managing the contents of these summaries, and the scholastic subjects to be studied in other books. Moreover, both scholasticism and the emphasis on rhetorical managment made these authors attend carefully on the nature and structure of the human mind in order to teach how to improve its powers and explain the psychological handling of ideas.[10]

---

[9]How wide the scholastic learning then was can be appreciated in Melchor Cano's *De locis theologicis*. Just regarding theology, this Tridentine Father defined ten topics which should be substantive sources and grounds of inquiry and argument: 1) The Holy Scriptures, 2) Tradition, 3) the authority of the Catholic Church, 4) the Councils, 5) the authority of the Roman Church, 6) the Holy Fathers, 7) the Scholastic Theologians themselves, 8) natural reason, 9) philosophers and jurisconsults, and 10) human history. See Melchioris Cani, *Opera* (Bassani, 1746.)

[10]An example of this kind of Christian rhetoric is Diego Valadés, *Rhetorica Christiana* (Perugia, 1579). Valadés included in his treatise several summaries of the Writ, and of the most diverse areas of scholastic learning. He simplified these summaries by means of diagrams. Although not very systematic, his scholastic discussion of the structure of the mind and particularly his rhetorical study of memory give a psychological explanation and a method of handling the summaries of his treatise. The peculiar character of this work is emphasized by its abundant reference to rhetorical practices and illustrations from Mexican Indians. Comentators like Antonio Martí [*La preceptiva retórica española de los siglos XVI y XVII* (Madrid: Consejo Superior de Investigaciones Científicas, 1973) 225–227] ignore that Diego Valadés, General Procurator of the Franciscan Order during the times of Pope Gregory XIII, indeed was an Indian from Tlaxcala—the freest republic of ancient Mexico, and archienemy of the bloody Aztec Empire. [A trivia fact: Valadés illustrated deliberative speeches with an oration proposing the change of the Viceroyalty capital from Mexico City to any other place, since the old Tenochtitlan was doomed because of pollution, disease, and overpopulation.] Among the theorists of wit, Emanuele Tesauro would strongly resemble Valadés's trend: to a high degree, his *Cannocchiale* is a large summary of scholasticism to be approached through the art of ingenuity.

If a reinvigorated Latin—either Ciceronian or from the Holy Fathers—was seen as an instrument to keep Europe spiritually unified, a fortified vernacular language was seen by its respective country as an instrument of national integration and imperialism. Even so, Ciceronianism found defenders among promoters of national languages, in so far as its theories and models would reshape the modern language into the classical standards of eloquence. With this spirit, Antonio de Nebrija published his *Arte de la Lengua Castellana* (1492), the first grammar of a vernacular language. Also, Miguel Salinas published the first rhetoric in a Romance language in Alcalá, 1541: *Rhetorica en lengua castellana*. His work demonstrated that classical rhetoric and models could be assimilated into the practice of Spanish. However, it was not until 1604 that a Spanish rhetoric was fully illustrated with Spanish models of eloquence, when Bartolomé Jiménez Patón published his *Elocuencia Española en Arte*, and showed that Spanish could be as powerful and as complicated as classical languages.

A final group of rhetoricians did not believe that restoring classical rhetoric and eloquence would be critical for the enhancement of scholarly life in Europe. What was needed, they thought, was a thorough reform of the system of education. In France, Peter Ramus dismembered rhetoric in order to have simpler and more neatly defined theoretical areas. He reduced the study of language to grammar, and the study of invention to dialectics or logic; the study of rhetoric only comprehended ornamentation and delivery. The unified art of eloquence became a series of unrelated pieces of knowledge. In Spain, authors such as Fradrique Furió Ceriol and Francisco Sánchez de las Brozas attempted reforms of the same kind in order to simplify the theoretical treatment of subjects in the universities.[11]

The dispute among different groups of Ciceronians and anti-Ciceronians cooled off with the spread of Jesuit colleges, and the Jesuit choice of Ciceronian rhetoric and models of eloquence to be imparted in their classrooms. However,

---

[11]Cf. Walter J. Ong, S. J., *Ramus. Method and the Decay of Dialogue* (Harvard University Press: 1983). The works of Furió Ceriol and Sánchez de las Brozas were respectively *Institutiones Rhetoricae*, 1554, and *Organum Dialecticum et Rhetoricum*, 1579.

this dispute left its marks in the kind of Ciceronianism practiced by the Jesuits.

The Jesuits' choice for classical rhetoric and models could be explained in terms of their endorsement of classical Latin as an instrument to keep Europe spiritually united. The inclusion of Aristotle with Roman rhetoricians such as Cicero and Quintilian could be explained in terms of the esteem that Aristotle enjoyed as the *Philosopher* in the scholastic environment of Jesuit colleges. The use of his rhetoric could encourage this scholastic spirit in the classrooms. I should also say that the Jesuits might have chosen Aristotle's, Cicero's, and Quintilian's rhetorics simply because of the strong tradition behind these works, and because the Jesuits saw in these theories some of the best ever written on this subject.

Rhetoric as such was not, however, a primary concern of the Jesuits in their universities, but a means of teaching the Latin language. To a high degree, rhetoric was part of the *literary* training which their students received. A sign of this was that, of Aristotle's *Rhetoric*, the third book was the one emphasized, particularly its prescriptions on metaphor and ornament. Moreover, the study of his *Rhetoric* was interchangeable with the study of his *Poetics*. Furthermore, as old treatises, such as Suárez's, were replaced by new treatises, the summaries of rhetoric which Jesuits published as elementary introductions to the art increasingly stressed figurative language.[12] Also, Cicero's central place in this training was due to his being chosen as the model for the classical style of

---

[12]The expansion of Cipriano Suárez's outline of rhetoric (a 200-page treatise) fulfilled several Jesuit pedagogical concerns. For example, in Spain, Bartolomé Bravo's additions in his *De Arte oratoria* (1596) consisted in providing a series of rhetorical exercises of imitation and progymnastics. Francisco de Castro wrote his *De Arte Rhetorica* (1611) using the pattern of questions and answers proper for a catechism. José de Olzina offered an *Oratorias Instituciones* (1656) in a bilingual presentation (Latin and Castilian). Nevertheless, one of the most ambitious Jesuit rhetorics was published in France: Nicolas Caussin's *De eloquentia sacra et humana* (1619); with its more than one thousand pages, this treatise was less a rhetorical summary for students than a rhetorical *summa* to keep professors extensively informed of their art, including littler details, such as minor authors and theories on the history of rhetoric, and emphasizing areas which were important in the oratory of the era, such as style and emotions.

imitation exercises. Finally, topics and other resources of invention sometimes served more to teach composition—for example, the creation of emblems—than for the teaching of argumentation.

I am not ready to describe Jesuit rhetoric as one reduced to the mere cultivation of pure style. The fact is that, contrary to the Ramists, there were some Spanish and Italian rhetoricians who could not see invention and style as separate arts. They regarded the rules of style and invention as interchangeable methods for the finding of materials, the explaining of these materials through argumentation, and the expressing of them through appropriate language. Their belief might not rest on a profound speculative basis, yet it had a strong pragmatical support in so far as the practitioners of rhetoric found that tropes could prompt their minds to find materials as did topics, figures of thought could help them polish the structure of an argumentation, and tropes could be analyzed through and subsumed into topics, making a tropological expression meet with its material foundations.[13]

Examples of this position could be detected in Miguel de Cervantes and Diego García Rengifo's belief that oratory, logic, and poetry could meet in their ultimate and common source of materials, which is human experience.[14] From that belief, rhetoricians could indistinctly apply topics to invent either arguments, stylistic expressions, or even poetry—as Luis de Granada suggested. Moreover tropes expressed and could replace topics, in so far as tropes were transferred words referring to a thing through its "genre...species, definition, properties, accidents...and other [topics] of the same kind."[15] Furthermore, a trope could contain an argument in so far as the signifier could implicitly express its relationship with the thing signified in the form of a proposition, and thus

---

[13]See, for example, Luis de Granada's *Rhetorica eclesiástica* (II, ix, 1, and V, vi, 28–29.) Cf., also, Diego Valadés 278–283, who discusses ratiocination, accumulation, induction, enumeration, subjection, dilemma, contrast, retort, and conclusion under the headings of figures and schemata, even so recognizing their argumentative function.

[14]See Diego García Rengifo's *Arte poética*, and Miguel de Cervantes's *Coloquio de los Perros.*

[15]Luis de Granada *Rhetórica eclesiástica* V, vi, 28.

participate in the making of an argumentation.[16] Among the Jesuits, this fusion of invention and style would be learned through their reading the third book of Aristotle's *Rhetoric*, specially his theory of metaphor.[17] A full expression of this fusion would be contained in the theories of wit, and the clearest case would be Tesauro's *Cannocchiale Aristotelico.*

If strong theorizing about style did not indicate that rhetoric was purely concerned with problems of style, the strong emphasis which rhetorics placed on emotion would not indicate either that they prescribed making a case rest on pure emotions. Conley defines Jesuit rhetorics as motivistic.[18] He would be right if he understood motivation as stirring the will of unmotivated souls by exposing them to a desireable good defined through reason and expressed through powerful style and techniques of amplification.[19] However, Conley thinks motivistic rhetorics are those which manipulate audiences' emotional responses.[20] I think he misses the rational component of the Jesuit theory of the emotions. The desireable good that a speaker should use to motivate the audience was a reasonable one, which could be carefully analyzed—thus amplified—through the inventional topics, and consequently argumentatively proven.[21] If a listener was moved through this amplification, it was not because

---

[16]Cf., for example, Granada *Rhetórica eclesiástica* V, vi, 29.

[17]Cf., Aristotle, *Rhetoric* Book III, for example, Chapter 10, 1410b, 5-35.

[18]Conley 152–155.

[19]Spanish rhetorics of the period gave an important role to emotions in the persuasion of audiences. For example, the Jesuit Cypriano Soarez's *De Arte Rhetorica* divides its first book, on invention, in two parts. The first deals with invention as the finding of arguments and their use in argumentation. The second part is devoted completely to amplification as the technique to conciliate audience's emotions with the expounded arguments. The Dominican Granada's *Rhetorica eclesiástica* would even devote a whole book to the art of amplification. This stress on emotions were also taken by the Jesuits to France. Nicolas Caussin's *De Eloquentia Sacra et Humana*—an advanced rhetorical treatise—would devote almost one hundred pages to the emotions as tools of persuasion.

[20]See Conley 23.

[21]Cf. Soarez's and Granada's sections on amplification.

there were reasonless stimuli in the speech, but because his reason perceived in detail and more clearly the desired good, and thus willed it. According to Fr Luis de Granada, the will is a blind faculty which is not moved to any emotion if, beforehand, the understanding has not presented to the will the motives and causes to be thus moved.[22] Even the ill-regulated passions are moved by a perceived good. Their wrong character does not spring from lack of understanding but from ill understanding. Thus, the correctives of inordinate passions are the same as the correctives of wrong understanding: a detailed, true, and precise perception of the object.[23] It should not be forgotten that many of these rhetoricians worked in a scholastic environment which had not yet split the psyche into two completely separate units—understanding and will—as modern theorists of the faculties would later do. There was a single human reason which understood the truth and willed the good. The role of reason in persuading the will would be part of the problems addressed by theorists of wit, particularly Gracián.

The unity that these rhetoricians perceived concerning reason did not make them unaware of reason's different ends. For centuries, preaching had often been classified into two great genres: teaching Christian doctrine, and moving the people toward virtue and away from vice. In the Middle Ages, for example, these ends were respectively theorized by the *artes praedicandi* and the *artes concionandi*. In the seventeenth century, probably influenced by the prevalent Ciceronianism, these preaching genres were somehow fused with the classical genres of oratory. The awesome *contemplation* of the Christian mysteries and of virtue as embodied in the Saints belonged to the epideictic genre. The *moving* of the souls toward virtue and away from vice pertained to "moral oratory," which subsumed the judicial and deliberative genres in as much as both were concerned with persuading about particular human actions.[24] Concerning the

---

[22]See Fr Luis de Granada, *Guía de Pecadores* "Prólogo Galeato."

[23]See Fr Luis de Granada, *Rhetórica eclesiástica*, Book 3.

[24]Cf., for example, Francisco Terrones del Caño, *Instrucción de Predicadores* Prólogo y notas del P. Félix G. Olmedo, S. I. (Madrid: ESPASA-CALPE, S. A., 1946, from 1617

contemplation of Christian doctrine, the preacher should concentrate on a type of discourse which fosters understanding (that is, the apprehension of new ideas), as Baltasar Gracián would come to propose when preparing his theories of wit.[25] But concerning the moving of the souls to concrete actions, the preacher should expand his resources to rhetorical argument (that is, judgment).[26]

If it is mistaken to dissociate the Jesuit emphasis on style and emotion from a theory of reason, it is also mistaken not to see how this stress on style, and, in general, the Jesuits' literary training promoted some developments in the fields of pure style and pure delivery.

Officially, the leaders of the Jesuits were outraged by the elaborate style in fashion among many preachers of the seventeenth century.[27] However, the same training offered in their colleges contained the seeds of stylistic excesses. The study of Latin had its effects not only in promoting this language, but also in setting linguistic models for vernacular languages. The exemplars of elegance were found in Latin, and they were to be imitated—with all their complication—in the national tongue, or even surpassed through ingenuity. Vernacular languages could not avoid the violence of superimposing Latin on

---

edition) Tratado Segundo, Capítulo I; *Sermões do Padre António Vieira* ed. by Margarida Vieira Mendes (Lisboa: Editorial Comunicação, 1987) Sermão da Sexagésima (1655) VI; José Francisco de Isla, *Fray Gerundio de Campazas*, ed. Russell P. Sebold (Madrid: ESPASA-CALPE, S. A., 1960, first edited in 1758) 3:176.

[25]See *Agudeza* Discourse 4, where Gracián directly related his methods of wit to epideictic oratory, apparently because the power of wit consists in bringing forth more than understanding, namely the contemplation of the celebrated subject-matter.

[26]See, for example, Isla 3:176. Epideictic oratory was not deprived of the power of moral persuasion; however, epideictic oratory's force rested more on the saintly model offered than on rhetorical arguments proposing concrete actions.

[27]Cf. Correa Calderón, *Baltasar Gracián. Su vida y su obra.* (Madrid: Gredos, 1961) 51–52; Arturo del Hoyo, "Estudio preliminar, edición, bibliografía y notas," Baltasar Gracián y Morales, *Obras Completas*, (Madrid: Ed. Aguilar, 1960) cxiii-cxiv. They refer to Father Vitelleschi, Superior General of the Jesuits, who tried to stop the stylistic excesses in preaching at least from 1623 to 1631, but unsuccessfully.

their structures.[28]

Latin as a linguistic standard also made writers of national rhetorics focus their theorizing on style in order to demonstrate that the vernacular language could accomplish or even exceed the complexities of its classical model. That was Jiménez Patón's goal when he wrote his *Elocuencia Española en Arte*. In describing this rhetoric, Antonio Vilanova says:

> The main purpose seems to be the attempt to exalt the Spanish language and to enshrine its literature, as rising from the tradition of classical humanities, and as worthy of being put on the same level as Greek and Latin antiquity.[29]

Jiménez Patón is notorious for having offered us one of the narrowest definitions of rhetoric:

> Rhetoric is an art which teaches how to *embellish* a speech—what is said and what is pronounced. Its parts are style and delivery.[30]

Rhetoric was not even style, but just pure ornament.[31] Thus, the theory expounded in Jiménez's *Elocuencia* did not go beyond an enumeration of tropes and figures. His only merit was illustrating them, for the first time, with Spanish examples.

Regarding the presentation of discourses, some of the speech exercises

---

[28]This violence which Castilian suffered in the baroque era made it more similar to its mother tongue. Many seventeenth-century syntactic and word innovations could be described as already assimilated into today's practices.

[29]Antonio Vilanova, "Preceptistas españoles de los Siglos XVI y XVII," *Historia General de las Literaturas Hispánicas*, ed. by D. Guillermo Díaz-Plaja (Barcelona: Ed. Vergara, 1953) 3:662.

[30]Bartolomé Jiménez Patón, *Eloquencia Española en Arte* (Toledo, 1604.), as quoted by José Rico Verdú, *La retórica española de los siglos XVI y XVII*, (Madrid: Consejo Superior de Investigaciones Científicas, 1973) 150.

[31]Jiménez Patón's popularity among literary critics may be the reason for the very widespread notion—in Spain and the Hispanic countries—of rhetoric as pure ornament.

which Jesuits taught were declamation, drama, and public contests of oratory. These practices could promote a strong concern on pure questions of delivery, and could encourage the delivery of dramatistic effects common among preachers of this era.

A result of this Jesuit stress on display was that, by the time the theorists of wit wrote their works, rhetoric had lost its hold on the field of invention, to such a degree, that Gracián, Pellegrini, Pallavicino, and Tesauro had to find a substitute.

For Gracián, neither logic—an art of syllogizing—nor rhetoric—principally an art of tropes—could fulfill the duty of discovering subject-matter.[32] Moreover, their common tool of topics had only a very partial and secondary role in this task: mainly defining and amplifying the relationship between materials already discovered.[33] Matteo Pellegrini also believed contemporary logic had more to do with scholastic subtleties and exercises, rhetoric with emotions, and topics with the management of ideas, than they had to do with finding data from experience.[34] Pallavicino and Tesauro were also unhappy with current logic and rhetoric. They showed their discontent when, in writing their treatises, they departed from the standard explanations for the discovery of subject-matter given by logic and rhetoric in their times and places.

It was Matteo Pellegrini who expressed his dissatisfaction with logic and rhetoric in a most explicit way. As rational arts, he believed, logic and rhetoric should assist mind's wit in its three functions: 1) to get information from reality, 2) to make judgments, and 3) to express and generate emotions.[35] He also believed that logic and rhetoric claimed to cover the first two functions, although pursuing different ends—logic pursued truth, and rhetoric the efficacious and the

---

[32]See *Agudeza*, "Al Letor", and Discourse I.

[33]See *Agudeza* Discourse IV.

[34]*I Fonti Dell'Ingegno* "A'Lettori", and Chapter III and IV.

[35]See *I Fonti dell'Ingegno* Chapter IV, 49: "Gli vfficii dell'Ingegno humano si riducono a trè capi generali. Il primo hà per oggetto la *Notitia*, il secondo l'*Opinione*, il terzo l'*Affetto*."

beautiful. As well, he thought, rhetoric really covered the third function in so far as it was its most legitimate field.

From the three functions of ingenuity, Pellegrini remarked, the first was the most important since it was the foundation of the other two. He felt, too, that the topics were the closest tool which logic and rhetoric provided to assist ingenuity in finding the subject-matter of discourses. However, for Pellegrini, topics either were too confusing to use, or only helped in the tasks of recalling, managing, and judging ideas, but not in the task of finding them. Regarding judgment, he explains:

> It does not seem...that the great Masters... would consider *topoi* except for any other use than supplying enthymemes and syllogisms, that is to say, with the goal of providing Ingenuity only in its second function, which dims to give foundations to, and fix judgments; either promoting or deterring belief.[36]

Topics could assist the recall of ideas and judgments already made. However, topics could not give real assistance in finding new ideas:

> Topics are only very weak stimuli, and display very confused lines of thought...[Their power] only consists in reminding somebody of the things he needs, or the things which would be opportune for him; but this is not to offer these things to him, or to put him on the track to find them quickly.[37]

To compensate for this lack of tools for invention, Pellegrini prepared one of his theories of wit, the one contained in his *Fonti dell'Ingegno*. In similar ways, the other theorists of wit would try to supply answers to this problem

---

[36]*I Fonti dell'Ingegno* Chapter IV, 54: "Ne pare altresì, che gl'istessi gran Maestri ponessero insieme i luoghi Topici, per altr'uso, che per somministrare entimemi, e sillogismi: Cioè a dire mirando a proveder il bisogno dell'Ingegno nel solo secondo Capo, che travaglia per fondare, e fermare opinione; e piantar fede, e spiantarla."

[37]*I Fonti dell' Ingegno* Chapter IV, 57-58: "...i luoghi della Topica sono eccitanti deboli assai e segnano traccia troppo confusa...questo è solamente ricordargli di che cosa egli ha bisogno, e che cosa gli sarebbe opportuna: e non già un offerirgliele, vn porlo sù la strada, che lo conduca a speditamente trouarla."

when writing their treatises.

More about Jesuit Education

Besides rhetoric, some other aspects of Jesuit education were relevant to the rise of theories of wit, for example, the solid scholastic training, and the extensive literary learning aimed at in Jesuit colleges. A very specific problem of Jesuit education is also a direct antecedent of the theories of ingenuity: the lack of a detailed theory of grammar, rhetoric, or poetics which could offer explanations for some works contained in the canon of Latin readings, particularly, Martial's *Epigrams*.

Regarding scholasticism, Jesuits relied on the Aristotelian-Thomist heritage, studying the numerous works of these authors, and their commentators, generally to learn philosophy, and, particularly, logic, physics, metaphysics, psychology, and theology. Compared with other religious orders of the time, the Jesuit approach to scholasticism was innovative, promoting not only the study of Aristotelian and Thomist doctrines, but also their discussion, correction, and amplification through philosophical research and the occasional introduction of rudiments of the new sciences. Jesuits would be the greatest innovators of sixteenth and seventeenth-century neo-scholasticism.[38]

Scholastic logic, psychology, and metaphysics would provide important theoretical background for the treatises on ingenuity here discussed. An example of this is given by Alexander A. Parker, who finds links between some seventeenth-century theories of logical conceptualization, and Gracián's and Tesauro's theories of concepts.

> ...contemporary philosophy divided the term *conceptus* into twenty-five types. Of these I need mention only three basic to Gracián's *concepto* and to Tesauro's

---

[38]The scholasticism of the theorists of wit is reflected in Tesauro's *Cannocchiale*, and *Filosofia morale*, and in Pallavicino's *De physico auditu*, *De generatione*, *De Anima*, and *Breviarium Logicae aristotelicae*, which are commentaries on Aristotle.

concetto: conceptus simplex, which is the act of immediate apprehension of an idea or image (called the first operation of the intellect); *conceptus compositus seu complexus*, which relates one idea to another (called the second operation of the intellect). Both Gracián and Tesauro use this latter phrase when referring to the association, comparison, or contrast of ideas. The philosophers grouped the third type, *conceptus analogiae seu comparationis*, with *conceptus compositus seu complexus*. The disctinction between simple and compound concepts corresponds to Gracián's basic distinction between simple and compound or complex *agudeza*.[39]

Gracián's foundation of prudential judgment on ingenuity and experience, as St Thomas had taught it, is another example of scholastic background behind the theories of wit.[40]

Beyond scholasticism, the Jesuit literary studies would be reflected in the wide learning that baroque treatises on wit exhibited and recommended to practitioners of wit. The literary studies would preserve not only the humanist tradition, but, by promoting erudition, they would also preserve the most diverse European traditions of thought. The preservation of this learning and traditions would play a role in the every day life of an educated man of the renaissance and baroque ages. For example, M. J. Woods finds that topics were more than theories; they were part of the thinking apparatus that many learned people of those ages used in numerous ordinary situations.[41] Yet, the topics which usually assisted thinking were more than void rhetorical commonplaces. They were substantial places containing the common culture of Europe: Judeo-Gentile, Christian-Greek and Roman, Middle Ages-Renaissance, Gothic-Islamic. They contained the common experience of this continent: from the history of their kings to the that of the Church, from classical mythology to the esoteric science

---

[39]Parker xxxi. Parker's comparison of Gracián and Tesauro is with Ludovicus Castanaeus, *Celebriorum Distinctionum Philosophicarum* (Leyden, 1614).

[40]See, por ejemplo, *El Discreto* realces 1 and 5; cf., Arturo del Hoyo clvii–clx.

[41]M. J. Woods, "Sixteenth-Century Topical Theory: Some Spanish and Italian Views" *MLR* (1968) 63: 66–73. Woods quotes the playwriter Lope de Vega, confessing in 1604 that he could not create any of his dramas without the assistance of commonplaces.

of numbers, from the epics of Homer and Virgil to the hymns and martyrology of the Church. It expanded to bestiaries, herbals, lapidaries, heraldries, and other fields of ideas, whose value was strongly symbolic, if not a form of knowledge. This cultural heritage was still a strong element of language among the learned in Italy and Spain during the age of wit, but would later be nostalgically missed by the last of the humanists, such as Giambattista Vico, when the renegades of the modern era pretended to sweep it away, in order to start their inquiries from a blank slate.

If Jesuit scholasticism and literary erudition permeated the thinking of the theorists of ingenuity, a very specific problem led them to theorize on wit: Jesuits lacked a detailed theoretical explanation for the *Epigrams* of Martial, which were part of the canon of Latin readings in their colleges.

> The Jesuits were, among so many other things, the school-teachers of Catholic Europe. They had devised a curriculum, or Ratio Studiorum, in which the study of rhetoric through Latin authors played a very important part. The problem with Martial, who now had to be added to the select list, lay in the fact that what differentiated him from the other Latin authors was this now popular but undefined Wit.[42]

According to Alexander A. Parker,

> Some treatises on Wit therefore arose as commentaries on Martial.[43]

The first Jesuit answer to this problem, says Parker, was from the Polish professor Casimir Sarbiewski, who gave a lecture on Martial at the Jesuit Academy in Polotsk in 1626–27, and whose notes were contained in a manuscript, *De acuto et arguto*, which was not published until 1958. Sarbiewski, explains Parker,

---

[42]Parker xxxii.

[43]Parker xxxii.

...might have given this course earlier in Rome. Sarbiewski said that when there he searched for a work on Wit and could find none. He discussed the subject with rhetoricians in Rome and wrote to fellow-Jesuits in Germany and France, among them the two dramatists, Biedermann and Rader, asking for their definitions and explanations. He summarized this correspondence in his treatise.[44]

Sarbiewski's concern of theorizing on wit would be answered in 1639 by Pellegrini, in 1642 by Gracián, in 1646 by Pallavicino, and, among others, in 1654 by Tesauro. Parker summarizes:

> The close association of the Jesuits with this century-long speculation on literary Wit is a remarkable fact. The most likely explanation is their special pedagogical interest in rhetoric and their philosophical training with its neo-Aristotelian direction; also the fact that they were an international society whose members travelled freely from country to country and were in touch with other members of the Order who shared their special interests.[45]

---

[44]Parker xxxii.

[45]Parker xxxiii.

4   Classical Rhetoric and Wit

IN SEPARATE WAYS, PELLEGRINI AND GRACIÁN CLAIMED being the first who elucidated the puzzling subject wit.[1] Both considered their treatises as setting the foundations of a new art which was ignored or poorly addressed by former rhetoricians. Pellegrini started his *Acutezze* and *I Fonti Dell'Ingegno* with a review of the literature. In these works, he denied there existed a satisfactory treatment of wit by such classical rhetoricians as Cicero, Quintilian, and Aristotle. Pellegrini would then propose his systems as a solution to this deficiency.[2] Gracián, more confident of his innovations, started his *Agudeza* without making the least review of literature. Gracián just asserted his originality, declaring that, before his *Agudeza*, the exercise of the mind's wit only rested on talent and completely lacked any artistic guidelines.[3]

Pallavicino and Tesauro, who wrote their treatises several years later, also

---

[1]In spite of Gracián's and Pellegrini's mutual accusations of plagiarism, and the controversy around the possibility of Gracián borrowing materials from the earlier treatise of Pellegrini (Cf., for example, Coster 233–242; Arturo del Hoyo clxi–clxii; Croce 254–256; Correa Calderón *Baltasar Gracián* 273–274), Gracián and Pellegrini seemed to have worked very independently from each other when preparing their treatises of *Acutezze* and *Agudeza*. Gracián was an enthusiast of wit, whereas Pellegrini was very cautious on this topic. More important, their theories are very different. Pellegrini principally proposed some criteria to produce and judge witticisms, whereas Gracián offered artistic rules and plenty of models for the practice, not only of witticisms, but of ingenuity in general as well. Finally, Gracián had reached his peculiar understanding of ingenuity before Pellegrini had published *Acutezze*. As early as 1637, Gracián had already discussed some of the essential attributes characterizing the faculty of ingenuity. See, for example, *El Héroe* Primor 3, which was then published.

[2]See *Acutezze* Chapter 1, 7–20, whose review of literature applies to theories of witticisms, and also see *I Fonti Dell' Ingegno*, principally Chapter 2, whose revision of literature applies to theories of invention (ingenuity).

[3]For Gracián, his *Agudeza* provides art to the practice of the mind's wit—a practice previously "orphan" of any theory, and left to "the swagger of ingenuity" ("...la valentía del ingenio.") See *Agudeza* "Al Letor" and Discourse I.

made claims to originality. Although Pallavicino acknowledged the *Acutezze*'s precedence, he assured that he had prepared his own theory of "concepts"[4] before having read Pellegrini's treatise.[5] Tesauro's claims of originality are the most peculiar: he denied true originality, but he asserted his merit of finally making, for the first time, a thorough review and interpretation of Aristotle's separate works, thus to construct the theory of ingenuity which wits missed for centuries.[6] Pellegrini's, Gracián's, and Tesauro's spirit of innovation is also expressed, to some degree, in their treatises' complete dedication to the issue of wit, something seemingly without precedent in the history of rhetoric.[7]

Many critics agree in identifying true theoretical progress in these authors.[8] However, some critics rather emphasize the strong classical and rhetorical foundations of their systems, and explain them in terms of this background. For example, Sarmiento explains the theories of wit in terms of classical tropes,[9] Woods does it in terms of classical topics,[10] and Abbott does it in terms of both

---

[4]A "concept" is an important artistic term shared by the baroque theories here studied.

[5]See *Trattato Dello Stile* Chapter 10, 115–118. Pallavicino's claim of originality is a legitimate one. Even if he had conceived the same theories systematized before by Pellegrini, Pallavicino still could do it again by himself. Originality does not necessarily rest on being the first one, but on thinking something by oneself, even if, as we say in Mexico, we come to "discover" the Mediterranean Sea, the black thread, or the wheel.

[6]See, for example, *Il Cannocchiale Aristotelico* Chapter 1, 1–3.

[7]A good example of the extraordinary baroque interest in this subject is Tesauro's *Cannocchiale*, which devotes its almost 800-small-type pages completely to the art of wit.

[8]Besides Parker's study, there are other articles and works noticing the innovative character of theories of wit, for example, Curtius's, Correa Calderón's "Sobre Gracián...", and Hugh H. Grady, "Rhetoric, Wit, and Art in Gracián's 'Agudeza.'" *MLQ* 41:21–37.

[9]See Sarmiento, "Gracián's 'Agudeza'..."

[10]M. J. Woods, "Gracián, Peregrini, and the Theory of Topics," *Modern Language Review* 63 (1968). Woods does not just find links of Gracián with common classical theories of topics, but even with more specialized versions of them, such as Boethius's theories of maximal propositions.

classical tropes and classical topics.[11] There are also critics who deny any originality in seventeenth-century treatises on wit. For example, Benedetto Croce regards these works as blown up commentaries on classical theories of metaphor, and as reductions of all rhetoric to metaphor, without any real contribution to clarify the problem of wit.[12] In a similar way, Coster describes Pellegrini's and Gracián's systems: they are wrong interpretations of Aristotle's theories of metaphor.[13]

In fact, Pellegrini, Pallavicino, and Tesauro were well read on the works of Cicero, Quintilian, and Aristotle, and, in their treatises, these Italian authors often quoted critical passages of the classical rhetoricians to elucidate important issues of wit. Gracián apparently was an exception. He certainly snubbed any previous theory of wit; he blatantly dismissed direct and specific references to them in his *Agudeza*.[14] He probably wanted to emphasize his own theoretical originality. Or he might have wished to stress *Agudeza*'s critical function over its theoretical character.[15] Some of his omissions could rest on avoiding explicit references to commonplaces of his times.[16] Nevertheless, Gracián's claims of innovation still are expressed in terms of solving a deficiency suffered by ancient rhetoricians:

---

[11]Don Paul Abbott, "Baltasar Gracián's 'Agudeza': the Integration of Inventio and Elocutio," *The Western Journal of Speech Communication*, 50 (Spring 1986), 133–143.

[12]See Croce 246–247.

[13]See Coster 233–242.

[14]Gracián knew well the classical rhetoricians. His elephant-like erudition betrays him. Aristotle, Cicero, and Quintilian are often quoted in *Agudeza*. However, Gracián used them just for the sake of illustrating his own theories of witty sayings!

[15]In its appearance, *Agudeza* is more a critical collection of witticisms than a theory of ingenuity. Gracián's emphasis may respond to the pedagogical need of explaining Martial.

[16]For example, in *El Comulgatorio* "Al Letor", Gracián said: "I do not cite the quotations taken from the Holy Scripture because it is superfluous for the learned, and long-winded for every one else." ""No cito los lugares de la Sagrada Escritura, porque para los doctos fuera superfluo y para los demás prolijo").

> ...I dedicate this [work] to Ingenuity, to mind's wit in art, a resplendent theory—for even though some of its artifices glimmer in Rhetoric, they nevertheless do not amount to insights...
>
> ....
>
> The ancients found method in syllogisms, and an art in tropes; they sealed wit...[17]

Moreover, in his *Agudeza*, Gracián included many references to methods of classical rhetoric: topics, tropes, lines of argument, maxims, etc. His acquaintance with these methods might not have come directly from studying particular texts, but it still could have been the result of the common understanding of classical rhetoric shared by scholars during his period.

Thus, regardless any true innovation offered by seventeenth-century theories of wit "beyond" classical rhetoric, these theories were still linked to the ancient art. Their authors at least defined their works as responses to what they regarded as an unsatisfactory, insufficient, or misunderstood system, and as older explanations to wit to be supplemented, corrected, or even replaced by newer explanations.

Classical Theories of Witticisms

In their rhetorics, Aristotle, Cicero, and Quintilian included very concrete and narrow discussions on the subject of witticisms. Cicero and Quintilian to some degree acknowledged the relation of witticisms to the broader problem of wit and to the most diverse kinds of subject-matter for speeches. However, their approach to witticisms was narrowed down principally to humorous sayings, as emotional means of persuasion in speeches.[18] Aristotle's treatement of

---

[17]*Agudeza* "Al Letor" and Discourse 1. "...éste dedico al Ingenio, la agudeza en arte, teórica flamante, que aunque se traslucen algunas de sus sutilezas en la Retórica, aun no llegan a vislumbres..." "Hallaron los antiguos métodos al silogismo, arte al tropo; sellaron la agudeza..."

[18]Cicero's discussion of humorous witticisms is found in *De Oratore* II, 217–290;

witticisms was developed under the heading of lively and smart sayings.[19] It was not focused on the issue of the laughable; although Aristotle had something to say about it.[20] The way he narrowed this subject was by studying it under his discussion of style. He explained witticisms in terms of stylistic tecniques, but nonetheless there are some indications that he recognized that this treatment was too narrow.

Aristotle characterized lively sayings as remarks which vividly convey new facts or new ideas. These ideas should be particularly surprising and unexpected for the listeners. And the remark itself should have a personal application and display some merit in its expression, without being far-fetched or a hackneyed. Aristotle identified three main stylistic features in smart sayings: antithesis, metaphor, and actuality or vividness in words. According to Aristotle, these features are the sources of liveliness in sayings. Regarding metaphor as a source of liveliness, Aristotle explained:

> We may now consider...the way to devise lively and taking sayings...We will begin
> by remarking that we all naturally find it agreeable to get hold of new ideas easily:
> words express ideas, and therefore those words are the most agreeable that enable
> us to get hold of new ideas. Now strange words simply puzzle us; ordinary words
> convey only what we know already; it is from metaphor that we can best get hold

---

Quintilian's is placed in *Institutio Oratoria* IV, iii. My editions of these treatises are the following: Cicero, *De Oratore*, in two volumes, trans. E. W. Sutton and H. Rackham (Harvard University Press, 1979); Quintilian, *The Institutio Oratoria*, in four volumes, trans. H. E. Butler, M. A., (Harvard University Press, 1985.)

[19]Aristotle's discussion of witticisms is found in *Rhetoric* III, chapters 10, 11, and, to some degree, 18. My edition of this treatise is the following: Aristotle, "Rhetoric" trans. W. Rhys Roberts, *The Rhetoric and the Poetics of Aristotle*, ed. by Friedrich Solmsen, (New York: The Modern Library, 1954.)

[20]Aristotle's brief discussion of jests introduces the subjects of humor and its propriety, in *Rhetoric*, III, 18. A more detailed treatment of these subjects is found in his *Nicomachean Ethics*, IV, 8: tactful humor is proper for a ready-witted man, and is a virtue of social intercourse. Supposedly, Aristotle's best exposition of the laughable was found in his lost second book of *Poetics*, on comedy.

of something fresh.[21]

Besides metaphor's power of conveying new ideas, Aristotle identified metaphor's power of doing it promptly, and with unexpected twists. Compared to a simile, a metaphor is briefer, and thus quicker to express an idea.[22] Moreover, metaphors provide unexpected turns to a word usage; thus they make the reception of the new idea more surprising and pleasant.

Of the four kinds of metaphors, Aristotle considered that the most taking was the proportional kind. However, he regarded antithesis as the source of balance between the phrases of a saying. Also, in the contrasting power of antithesis, he saw a source of impressiveness and firmness for the ideas conveyed.

According to Aristotle, a third feature of lively sayings is the "actuality" of the expression used.[23] To assure vividness, a metaphor should not be static or unappealing to the senses, but it rather should make hearers see things in activity, as if events were actually taking place before their eyes; that is, metaphors should be graphic.

Among the types of metaphor useful for smart sayings, Aristotle included similes and hyperboles. Kinds of smart sayings he mentioned are epigrammatic remarks, riddles, burlesque words, jokes, proverbs, and jests.[24]

Although Cicero and Quintilian detached witticisms from the tight limits of style, they still studied them through a narrow lens: the laughable. Cicero and Quintilian confined their discussion of the laughable, moreover, to the realm of humorous sayings, in spite of acknowledging wider boundaries which comprehended humorous narratives and long and ironic speeches. Their narrow

---

[21]*Rhetoric*, III, 10. This quotation was very often referred by Pellegrini, Pallavicino, and Tesauro in their books.

[22]This does not mean that Aristotle discarded similes as a means of expressing smart sayings.

[23]Gracián would later identify in wit a power that is not ordinary in *re*presenting ideas, but extraordinary in *presenting* them, in complete actuality, to the mind for the first time.

[24]On Aristotle's treatment of witticisms, see *Rhetoric*, III, chapters 10, 11, and 18.

conception of wit responded to a very concrete and tactical function which they much appreciated in humorous sayings, namely, that such sayings assist emotional persuasion by releasing undesired stress experienced by an audience, or they serve as opportune weapons with which to ridicule an opponent during debate.[25]

In Cicero's and Quintilian's rhetorics, this tactical function implies that opportunity is crucial to the use of humorous sayings. Thus, their discussion emphasizes the importance of propriety in the use of witticisms in speeches. Laughter and ridicule should be used only on few and appropriate occasions. Even so, neither Cicero nor Quintilian felt able to provide specific artistic guidelines to identify these occasions for laughter and what is particularly laughable about a given occasion. Although Quintilian thought that rhetorical topics[26] may be of some help in the analysis of a humorous situation, he and Cicero offered only some general rules of judgment concerning this matter.

Cicero's and Quintilian's rules of judgment generally identify some occasions for laughable sayings: for example, as said above, some turning points of the controversy when audience's emotional stress should be released or an opponent ridiculed. Propriety also rests, they believed, on a right understanding of what kinds of things are proper objects of laughter in speeches. These things belong to the class of slightly ugly objects; thus, rhetors should not try to cause laughter by pointing out what is very ugly. But noticing the slightly unseemly is not enough; its presentation in speeches requires seemly style, too. Moreover, the humorous ideas which are conveyed should be presented in a quick and pointed manner in so far as their placement occurs within a very dynamic debate. Therefore, the brevity of witticisms makes them the best choice to cause laughter during a controversy.

Cicero's and Quintilian's study of humorous sayings divides the sources of

---

[25]Aristotle also believed that jests are of some service in controversy. "Gorgias said that you should kill your opponents' earnestness with jesting and their jesting with earnestness; in which he was right." *Rhetoric*, III, 18.

[26]Rhetorical topics: who, what, whom... etc.

witticism in two kinds: either words or ideas. Thus, Cicero first discussed witticisms of language according to their sources: ambiguity, the unexpected, wordplay, quotation, literal meaning, allegory, metaphor, irony, and antithesis. Then he discussed witticisms of ideas according to their sources: narratives, comparison, caricature, understatement, irony, farcical jests, assumed simplicity, hinted ridicule, unexpected turns, and personal retorts. In spite of accepting this classification, Quintilian did not clearly follow it in his explanation of witticisms. He broadly described the sources of witticisms: wordplay, substitution, etymology, new applications for words or things through resemblance and ambiguity, dissimilar and contraries, definition, topics (particularly consequents) tropes (particularly hyperbole, irony, insinuation, quotations, retorts, the absurd, and the unexpected). In any case, both Quintilian's and Cicero's analyses rest on the distinction between witticims of words and witticisms of ideas. And although they recognized in some quick and opportune gestures some sources of humor, they tended to find witticisms of ideas or of words as the only kind of humor becoming to an orator, discarding from the orator's arsenal such tactics as grimaces, mimicry, mannerisms, affected intonation, and indecency. Quintilian's prim modesty would even make him wonder about the rightness of humor at all. He saw in humorous sayings a mean method of persuasion because—he believed—they essentially consist in distortions of the true and natural meaning of words.[27]

Limits of Classical Theories of Witticisms

There are many merits in the classical theories of witticisms. Although they can be described as narrow in their approach to the problem of wit, their theoretical restraint results in rich specificity. For example, Aristotle was not only rich but also suggestive in his discussion of metaphor as the backbone of lively sayings.

---

[27]Cicero's discussion of humorous witticisms is found in *De Oratore* II, 217–290; Quintilian's is in *Institutio Oratoria* IV, iii.

Cicero's and Quintilian's theory of the laughable illustrates not only how humor had a tactical use in Roman oratory, but also how emotional appeals generally did in controversies. In fact, seventeenth-century authors appreciated these qualities since, in some way or another, they expanded, simplified, or reinterpreted many of the witty forms Aristotle, Cicero, and Quintilian previously conceived.

However, it seems that classical discussions of witticisms were not satisfactory enough for the theorists of ingenuity two thousand years later. For them, the problem was not that classical descriptions of the witty forms were mistaken. The main problem was that these witty forms themselves were not so much rules to find or produce the witty as they were forms to explain or judge witty sayings already found or produced.

Although Quintilian did not venture that humor was altogether independent of art, he still insisted that "it depends mainly on nature and opportunity."[28] A more skeptical Cicero said:

> Jesting too and shafts of wit are agreeable and often highly effective: but these, even if all else can be taught by art, are assuredly the endowment of nature and in no need of art.[29]

And Aristotle confessed his inability actually to teach how to find or produce the lively and smart in sayings: "Their actual invention can only come through natural talent or long practice."[30]

Without denying the importance of natural gifts in the exercise of wit, seventeenth century authors would not give up all to talent, or as Gracián said, leave it to "the swagger of ingenuity."[31] They would rather believe, as Gracián did, that "Every skill begs for guidance, and all the more does the skill consisting

---

[28]*Institutio Oratoria*, VI, iii, 11.

[29]*De Oratore* II, 216.

[30]*Rhetoric* III, 10.

[31]*Agudeza* Discourse I. "...la valentía del ingenio."

in subtleness of ingenuity."[32]

To make the problem more difficult, what that skill or talent is—what its realm is—does not appear very clear in classical rhetorics. For example, Aristotle presented it as a stylistic skill of providing lively worded sayings by means of metaphors, antithesis, and graphic terms. However, in Aristotle's illustrations, that skill also seems to enable rhetors to accomplish highly intellectual operations:

> When the poet calls old age 'a withered stalk', he conveys a new idea, a new fact, to us by means of the general notion of 'lost bloom', which is common to both things.[33]

The metaphor of this example does not seem just to express or state a new idea. In addition, the metaphor seems to be the instrument for discovering the new idea by allowing both the rhetor and the listener to see the common features between the signified and the metaphorical signifier—common features which not only transcend the separate peculiarities of the compared terms but are apprehensions or intellectual abstractions of what is shared by both terms.[34] The intellectual power of metaphors is also suggested in a parallelism between metaphors and philosophical thinking made by Aristotle:

> Metaphors must be drawn...from things that are related to the original thing, and yet not obviously so related—just as in philosophy also an acute mind will perceive resemblances even in things far apart.[35]

---

[32]*Agudeza*, Discourse I. "Mendiga dirección todo artificio, cuanto más el que consiste en sutileza del ingenio."

[33]*Rhetoric* III, 10.

[34]Emanuele Tesauro would point out later that metaphors do not only show what is generic between two terms, but also what differentiates them. Thus, a metaphor is like a definition: it states both the genre and the differentia of the things referred. See *Il Cannocchiale*, 454 and 554.

[35]*Rhetoric* III, 11.

Cicero and Quintilian dealt with a talent of discovering and expressing an emotional appeal: humor. However, this talent does not consist merely in "feeling" or making others "feel" an emotion. It rests rather on the quickness and acuteness of a mind which observes the opportunity and discovers the objective grounds for laughing in a given occasion. Thus, this talent is intellectual. But the grounds or sources of humor are both ideas (or things) and words actually taking place in a controversy. Hence, the talent is also stylistic. According to Quintilian, "It has the same primary division as other departments of oratory, that is to say, it is concerned with things and words."[36] Moreover, Cicero and Quintilian identified this talent with "acumen" or other similar terms.[37] Thus this talent exceeds the realm of humor and involves other rhetorical tasks, such as, for example, the appropriate choice of proofs in an argumentation, which rests less on topics than on an "acute" attention to the case, as explained in *De Oratore*.[38] Also, as a mental power to observe what fits a given occasion,[39] and a mental power which resists the rules of art, acumen may be paired with other similar talents discussed by Quintilian, for example, sagacity.

> It is enough, I think, to say that there is nothing not merely in oratory, but in all the tasks of life that is more important than sagacity and that without it all formal instruction is given in vain, while prudence unsupported by learning will accomplish more than learning unsupported by prudence. It is sagacity again that teaches us to adapt our speech to circumstances of time and place and to the persons with whom

---

[36]*Institutio Oratoria* VI, iii, 22.

[37]See, for example, *De Oratore* II, 236; *Institutio Oratoria* VI, iii, 12.

[38]*De Oratore* II, 162–176.

[39]Aristotle's definition of rhetoric may be too narrow to this elusive talent, in so far as rhetoric refers to a faculty which *observes* the available means of persuasion only. Quintilian's definition of rhetoric may apply better to this talent; in so far as rhetoric is an art of speaking well, it thus better relates to a talent *to observe* whatever fits in a given occasion, not just a persuasive occasion.

we are concerned.[40]

Classical theories of witticism become more problematic if one abandons the elusive talent which produces witty sayings, and studies the theories on witty sayings themselves.

In the case of Cicero and Quintilian, these theories are not properly restricted to humorous sayings, in spite of the authors' intention.[41] These theories also refer to all kinds of *serious* subjects as expressed by means of sayings, for example, sententias and apothegms.[42] Quintilian's discussion is particularly interesting because he recognized many qualitative nuances among sayings. He did not just split sayings into humorous and serious, but he also found them charming, graceful, urbane, pungent, and more.[43] However, he was reluctant to abandon the laughable as the central issue. That led him into problems when he tried to define urbane sayings. Previously Domitius Marsus had defined *urbanity* as anything well said, and that, for Quintilian, included all rhetoric—an art of speaking well.[44] Quintilian's oddity consisted in trying to restrict the concept of urbanity by keeping it tied to the laughable. According to Quintilian, urbane sayings are those

> ...that are of the same general character as humorous sayings, without actually being humorous.[45]

---

[40]*Institutio Oratoria* VI, v, 11. When discussing sagacity, Quintilian also deals with judgment and appropriateness.

[41]Aristotle wisely avoided reducing his theory of lively sayings to humorous expressions. He rather included all kinds of smart sayings, regardless of whether they were serious, graceful, humorous, charming, etc.

[42]See *De Oratore* II, 250; *Institutio Oratoria* VI, iii, 16–21, 36, and 102–112.

[43]Ways used by Quintilian to describe sayings are, for example, *urbanus, venustus, salsus, facetus, ioucus,* and *dicax.* See *Institutio Oratoria* VI, iii, 17–22.

[44]*Institutio Oratoria* VI, iii, 102–110.

[45]*Institutio Oratoria* VI, iii, 110. Statements like this exasperated Matteo Pellegrini, when

If classical theories of witticisms cannot be restricted to humorous remarks, they may not be described either as methods particularly designed to make witty sayings. Classical rhetorics do not explain witticisms through a concrete theory specially conceived for them, but through the most diverse instruments of oratory: topics and tropes, retorts and wordplay, comparison and metaphor, narrative and antithesis, etc. Even though these rhetorical tools are useful to understand some features of witty sayings, and although they throw much light on the issue, they still are general tools and as such do not specify the distinctive features of these remarks: for example, they do not specify the witty component.

Finally, in dealing with the subject of witticisms, classical theories sometimes exceed the boundaries of what a brief saying is, and address long forms of discourse such as narratives and ironic speeches, as happens in Quintilian's and Cicero's rhetorics.[46] Cicero indeed said:

> For, there being two sorts of wit, one running with even flow all through a speech, while the other, though incisive, is intermittent, the ancients called the former 'irony' and the latter 'raillery.'[47]

In summary, in spite of their intended narrow focus either on humorous or on lively sayings, classical theories of wit actually deal with broader and more complex issues. The problem of wit seems to be of a larger scale than just crafting witty remarks. As seventeenth-century scholars saw it, the scope of this problem extends to the whole issue of ingenuity.

Other Classical Theories Related to Wit

Classical rhetorics do not confine their instructions about wit to the narrow

---

reviewing the classical theories of wit. See *Acutezze*, Chapter one, 13–14.

[46] See, for example, *De Oratore* II, 218–220; *Institutio Oratoria* VI, iii, 35–45.

[47] *De Oratore* II, 218.

treatments of witty sayings. To some degree, additional explanations and methods can be identified by looking at other sections whose subjects have some relation to wit. Theorists of ingenuity could pay attention to these sections when conceiving their systems, and these authors could even expand their inquiries to treatises other than the rhetorics.

Wit could be approached as a species of the art of invention in so far as, to be witty, a speaker should find the witty subject-matter of the remark. Thus, wit would be produced by the general tools proposed by classical rhetoric for the purposes of invention: for example, the topics. The scope of classical theories of wit consequently is enlarged to every section which elucidates the topics. Even though baroque theorists of wit often denied to topics a crucial role in the discovery of subject matter, in fact these authors still payed attention to those sections of classical treatises. Moreover, they often integrated the topics into their broader corpus of theories, usually by turning them into a means to define the link which dissociates or associates the ideas compared by ingenuity.[48]

The need to classify or even produce witty subject-matter led some seventeenth-century theorists of ingenuity to look at the general system of classification proposed by Aristotle in his logical treatises.[49] Pellegrini and Tesauro incorporated Aristotelian categories as a part of their methods of ingenuity. For Tesauro, categories had an analytical and classificatory function. For Pellegrini, categories themselves were "sources" or "seats" of subject-matter, and they seemingly replaced the topics (as empty places or headings to scan subject matter) because of the categories' more systematic and clear-cut appearance.[50]

---

[48]See, for example, *Acutezze* Chapter IX; *Agudeza* Discourse IV; *Trattato dello Stile* Chapter IX, 109; *Cannocchiale* Chapter III, 82.

[49]This attention to Aristotelian logic may be a result of baroque scholasticism. Aristotle's dialectics particularly seems to have influenced the fashionable use of disputation in baroque sermons, and the theoretical discussion of these disputations under the lens of wit, as Gracián did in *Agudeza*, for example, discourses 6–8, 36–39.

[50]See *I Fonti Dell' Ingegno* Chapters V, and VIII–XIX; *Cannocchiale*, for example, Chapter III, 107–115, and Chapter VII, 305.

Aristotle enshrined metaphor and her sisters—the tropes—as a means of expressing lively remarks. Baroque theorists of wit extended this devotion to metaphor's cousins. From stylistic similes, they moved forward to logical comparison, analogy, and example, all of which imply some sort of comparison. These authors did not overlook the methods of amplification, which answered the need to detail the comparisons made. And from figurative language, they passed to the whole realm of figures. They could study much of this rhetorical arsenal in classical treatises.

Seventeenth-century authors payed attention to Cicero's and Quintilian's recognition that witty remarks are not necessarily laughable, but could be of the most serious nature; they specifically noticed Quintilian's identification of apothegms and sententias as forms of witty sayings. Baroque authors somehow expanded their attention from Roman sententias to Aristotelian maxims, and from Aristotelian maxims to enthymemes, in so far as Aristotle regarded maxims as parts of enthymemes, and sometimes even as complete enthymemes.[51] Concerning enthymemes and argumentation, Aristotle had also identified, in his logical treatises, quick wit as "the faculty of instantaneously hitting upon the middle term."[52] Although brief and lacking any method, his comment would support the baroque view of wit as a method for discovering and creating arguments.

Aristotle's use of antithesis to craft witty sayings had some theoretical derivations. For example, some seventeenth-century writers would associate antithesis with antithetical periods, and, sometimes, with periods in general. Moreover, they particularly noticed Aristotle's characterization of antithesis as a form of speech having the effect of logical argument;[53] the Philosopher said:

> Such a form of speech is satisfying, because the significance of contrasted ideas is easily felt, especially when they are thus put side by side, and also because it has the

---

[51] See *Rhetoric* II, Chapters 20 and 21.

[52] *Posterior Analytics* I, 34.

[53] See, for example, *Cannocchiale* Chapter VII, 441–460.

effect of a logical argument; it is by putting two opposing conclusions side by side that you prove one of them false.[54]

Thus, theorists of wit would not find it difficult to pass from a theory of antitheses, to a theory of enthymemes.

Finally we should notice another important expansion in the scope of classical texts as read by baroque authors. In his theory of lively sayings, Aristotle described metaphor as having the power of uniting the pleasant, the new, and the useful in a single expression.[55] Widening their horizon, baroque scholars would relate Horace's ideas of the new, the useful, and the pleasant in poetry to the Aristotelian metaphor. They would specially consider these doctrines of the Roman author:

> Poets aim at giving either profit or delight...The man who has managed to blend profit with delight wins everyone's approbation, for he gives his reader pleasure at the same time as he instructs him. This is the book that not only makes money for the booksellers, but is carried to distant lands and ensures a lasting fame for its author.
> ....
> It is hard to be original...A theme that is familiar can be made your own property as long as you do not waste your time on a hackneyed treatment...[56]

Other Theories of Wit Before the Baroque Age

Theories of wit from the Dark, Middle, and Renaissance ages do not seem to be explicit precedents of seventeenth-century treatises on ingenuity, since baroque authors directly defined their theoretical achievements in contrast with classical

---

[54]*Rhetoric* III, Chapter 9.

[55]See *Rhetoric* III, Chapter 10.

[56]Horace, "On the Art of Poetry" *Aristotle/Horace/Longinus—Classical Literary Criticism* trans. T. S. Dorsch. (Penguin Books, 1965) 90–91, 83.

rhetorics. However, that does not mean that the fifteen centuries separating Quintilian and Pellegrini lack any theory related to wit.

This can be appreciated, for example, in William M. Purcell's survey[57] of theories of *transsumptio* and *metalepsis*, as made from the age of Quintilian to our times, but with an emphasis on the rhetorical doctrines of the thirteenth century.[58] Although Purcell does not link his survey to the issue of wit, his discussion addresses theories which baroque scholars found crucial in explaining ingenuity. Purcell's survey is focused on theories which describe the power of a trope—specifically *transsumptio* and *metalepsis*—to comprehend an enthymeme in itself. His survey starts with Quintilian and lists works of Donatus, the Venerable Bede, Alexander of Villedieu, Matthew of Vendôme, Geoffrey of Vinsauf, Eberhard the German, John of Garland, Gervasius of Melkley, Alexander of Hales, St Thomas Aquinas, Peter of Spain, Dante Alighieri, John Buridan, Johannes Dorp, and George Trebizond.[59] According to Purcell, these authors would not regard "the river runs" as a phrase just tropically ornated. The phrase would rather comprehend in itself a logical component—an argument:

---

[57]William M. Purcell, *"Transsumptio:* A Rhetorical Doctrine of the Thirteenth Century," *Rhetorica* Autumn 1987.

[58]There are other possibilities to illustrate the mentioned point, for example, a survey of theories of preaching, which, like Robert of Basevorn's *Forma Praedicandi* (1322), prompt discourse through correspondences, congruences, circuitous developments, and convolutions discovered in the examination of a theme (see *Three Medieval Rhetorical Arts* ed. James J. Murphy (University of California Press, 1971)). It could also be useful to survey Ciceronianism through the centuries, paying attention to the survival of Ciceronian theories of witty remarks and acuities.

[59]In his survey on *transsumptio*, Purcell includes several renaissance authors. However, he finds that these authors tended to reduce tropes to an ornamental function, particularly when Ramist rhetorics developed. After the renaissance, Purcell only considers three other authors who payed attention to the logical component of tropes: Cesar Chesneau, from the eigtheenth century, and Perelman and Olbrechts-Tyteca, from the twentieth century.

To run (A) is to move (B).
A river (C) moves (B).
Therefore, a river (C) runs (A).[60]

Summarizing this tropical doctrine, Purcell says:

> ...*transsumptio* entails the rationale for tropical changes in meaning. Each of the six transsumptive tropes, metaphor, metonymy, synecdoche, antonomasia, allegory, and catachresis, contains its own mini-argument which produces understanding by relating its point to a similar phenomenon in the communication target's field of experience. They are the essence of rhetoric. They engender understanding and through the understanding, persuasion. *Transsumptio* is the master trope, the key to understanding.[61]

---

[60]Purcell 392. This argument is fallacious as it stands in the quotation. However, as Tesauro would notice with his theory of urbanely fallacious enthymemes in *Cannochiale*, the argument helps the reader abstract a new idea. Thus, in this quotation, the idea of movement is abstracted from rivers and running. Afterwards, the syllogism can be recasted into a perfect BARBARA argument: *What moves runs; rivers move; therefore, rivers run.* Its lack of soundness could now be traced only to the false major premise, which nevertheless is poetically possible.

[61]Purcell 397. Purcell's survey illustrates the fact that seventeenth-century theories of wit were not dealing with issues ignored during the fifteenth centuries which separate them from Quintilian. Purcell's survey reveals the recurrent emergence of inquiries about the relationship between style and invention; it particularly reminds that the scholarly interest on *transsumptio* rested on the finding that this tool was something different than purely ornamental similitudes: the latter embellished already known ideas whereas the former served to discover and reveal the ideas. Cf., for example, Boncampagni's *Rhetorica Novissima* IX, ii, as found in *Scripta Anecdota Glossatorum* ed. Augustus Gaudentius (Bologna: Bibliotheca Juridica Medii Aevi, 1892). Purcell's study concretely pays attention to this problem as observed on an instrument which, since Aristotle's times, has been strongly associated with witty remarks: transferred words.

5   The Theorizing Climax

SEVENTEENTH-CENTURY STUDIES ON WIT PEAKED AT THE 1640'S with figures such as Matteo Pellegrini, Baltasar Gracián, Pietro Sforza Pallavicino, and Emanuele Tesauro. Their effort followed a transition from mannerist theories on imagination to conceptist theories on wit.

The Transition and Sarbiewski's Pioneering Work

After Mazzoni's defense of the poet's fantasy as an alternative to poetic imitation in 1587, several Italian poeticians wrote works inquiring into the nature of poetic concepts. Examples of this trend were Giulio Cortese's *Avvertimenti nel poetare* (1591) and Camillo Pellegrino's *Del concetto poetico* (1598). Alexander A. Parker notices that the term *concept* is central in these authors' theories, as it was later in baroque scholarship on wit. Thus, says Parker, Pellegrino and Cortese are often identified as the first expositors of baroque conceptist theories.[1] However, Parker believes that the term does not yet reflect the intellectual twist which seventeenth-century theories of wit would imprint on it. Parker explains that Pellegrino's and Cortese's poetic *concept* remained in the realm of sensuous imagination—rather than in the realm of wit—in a fashion similar to Torquato Tasso's mannerist speculations on poetry in *Discorsi dell' Arte poetica.*

Tasso does not yet represent the seventeenth century because his imagery is bound

---

[1]See Parker xxiv. His example of critical studies identifying Pellegrino and Cortese as the first conceptist theorists is L. P. Thomas, *Le Lyrisme et la préciosité cultistes en Espagne*, Beihefte zur Zeitschrift für Romanische Philologic, 18 (Halle, 1909), p. 32. *Conceptism* is usually a term applied to seventeenth-century theories on wit. Camilo Pellegrino's *Del Concetto poetico* seems to be close to the issues of conceptist theories since this work addresses "concepts" as expressions resting on the use of metaphor and antithesis. Cf. Croce 243-244 (note 7).

to sensuous experience of the real world and not to the experience of language in an elaborate exploration of words.[2]

Also, in the beginning of the seventeenth century, there were some other works that made the term *concept* central in their expositions. Parker cites Rafael Sarmiento's *Promptuarium conceptuum* (1604) and Tomás Ramón's *Conceptos extravagantes* (1619). However, Parker discards them as pioneers of conceptism. Parker explains that these books were not theories of concepts, but collections of *preaching concepts*, that is, collections of themes for sermons.[3]

Literature on witticisms was abundant throughout the renaissance era. It ranges from reprints of Martial's *Epigrams* to works such as Alciato's *Emblemata*, Juan Rufo's *Las seiscientas apotegmas*, Melchor de Santa Cruz's *Floresta española de apotegmas y sentencias*, and Francisco Asensio's *Floresta de Agudezas*.[4] Correa Calderón sees these works as direct sources which Gracián used to theorize on wit.[5] However, those books were not theories of wit, but collections of witty remarks from which Gracián often borrowed illustrations.

According to Matteo Pellegrini, seventeenth-century rhetoricians—such as Nicolas Caussin—addressed the subject of wit in their treatises. However, said Pellegrini, they did not depart from classical accounts of the issue, and they did not provide a theoretical explanation of what makes sayings "witty".[6]

---

[2]Parker xxiv.

[3]See Parker xxxiv.

[4]In England, in the 1580's, the literary use of witticisms reached its most fashionable level with John Lily's *Euphues*, and the correlative *Euphuism* which was then practiced by witty writers. Cf. D. Judson Milburn, *The Age of Wit 1650–1750* (New York: The MacMillan Company, 1966) 36.

[5]See Correa Calderón *Baltasar Gracián* 262–283.

[6]See *Acutezze* Chapter 1, 17.

True theories of wit did not arise until the middle of the seventeenth century, when the concern for theoretically elucidating the nature of poetic concepts was associated with the enigmatic but then popular witty literature.[7] According to Parker, the first work meeting with these criteria was *De acuto et arguto*, a series of notes prepared by the Polish professor of rhetoric, Casimir Sarbiewski, for his lectures on Martial given in 1626–27 at the Jesuit Academy of Polotsk—a course probably taught earlier in Rome.[8]

Although *De acuto et arguto* was not published until 1958, it still came into being as a manuscript reflecting a wide scholarly discussion on wit that Sarbiewski maintained with scholars such as Biedermann and Rader.[9] Sarbiewski's notes particularly found diffusion in Germany where the Jesuit Michael Radau published excerpts of *De acuto et arguto*, in his *Orator extemporaneus*, in 1640.[10]

Explaining Sarbiewski's major doctrines, Parker says:

> *Acutum* for him denotes true Wit; *argutum* he applies to any statement that is clever and ingenious but lacks what he considers the essence of Wit. This is defined as a statement that is both impossible and possible at the same time. He gives the example from Martial of a hare playing in front of the open jaws of a hungry lion which yet does not devour it. Impossible, says the reader. No, answers the poet, because the lion belongs to Caesar, who is a merciful and magnanimous man. Wit causes surprised wonder, and this gives pleasure.[11]

Parker notices Sarbiewski's disagreement with Biedermann and Rader, who, following Aristotle, still put the foundations of wit in metaphors, or at least in

---

[7]Cf. Parker xxv.

[8]See Parker, xxxii.

[9]Parker xxxii.

[10]See Parker xxxiii. Parker mentions other German Jesuits, who, as theorists of wit, followed Sarbiewski's work: Daniel Morhof (1639-91), with his *De disciplina argutiarum* and *De arguta dictione*, and Jakob Masen (1606-81), with his *Nova ars argutiarum* (1649).

[11]Parker xxxii.

some sort of comparisons. For Sarbiewski, says Parker, wit did not necessarily rest on metaphor since "the relationship between the lion and Caesar is not metaphorical."[12] Parker also indicates that Sarbiewski recorded that for other rhetoricians of his times wit involved a fallacious reasoning, something which would be fully developed later by Tesauro.[13]

In spite of the pioneering character of Sarbiewski's notes, Croce, Mazzeo, Mooney, and Parker rather agree in selecting Matteo Pellegrini's, Baltasar Gracián's, Pietro Sforza Pallavicino's, and Emanuele Tesauro's treatises on wit as the most representative of the seventeenth century.[14] The special character of these works comes from going beyond pure poetic concerns and from addressing complex rhetorical and logical issues such as the mind's wit—the perspicacious and creative power of understanding, serving the most diverse discursive endeavors.[15]

Matteo Pellegrini

Matteo Pellegrini was the first author to publish a baroque theory on wit. His *Delle acutezze che altrimenti spiriti, vivezze e concetti volgarmente si appellano* was published in Genoa, in 1639, three years before Gracián's first edition of *Agudeza*. A year after *Agudeza*'s second edition, in 1649, Pellegrini

---

[12]Parker xxxii.

[13]See Parker xxxii–xxxiii.

[14]Cf., Croce 247, 252, 261; Mazzeo "Metaphysical Poetry and the Poetics of Correspondence" 222; Mooney 65; Parker xxv. Despite their basic agreement, these authors differ on emphasis and additions of other authors to their respective lists. For example, Mazzeo includes in his list Pierfrancesco Minozzi, who published *Gli Sfogamenti dell'ingegno* in 1641.

[15]Cf., Parker xxv; Emilio Hidalgo Serna, "The Philosophy of *Ingenium*: Concept and Ingenious Method in Baltasar Gracián," *Philosophy and Rhetoric* 13.4 (Fall 1980) 245. Parker and Hidalgo Serna particularly refer to Gracián as the example of author who extends his concerns beyond mere aesthetic aspects.

published another treatise, this one on ingenuity, his *I Fonti Dell' Ingegno Ridotti ad Arte*, in Bologna.

Acutezze and *I Fonti Dell' Ingegno* are two different theories. The first aims to explain the art behind witty remarks, whereas the second addresses the broader issue of ingenuity, understood as mind's discursive inventiveness. In the *Acutezze*'s prologue to the reader, Pellegrini defines the contents of this book as follows:

> If you enjoy witty remarks, you may easily delight in this discourse which considers their nature, species, method, vices and virtues, uses, and abuses.[16]

Contrasting with the restricted focus of the *Acutezze*, Pellegrini's *Fonti dell' Ingegno* seemingly aims to explain an art of invention which would empower the orator to speak richly—in a Gorgian fashion—about any subject without any previous investigation:

> The Duke, moved by a great desire of having a method to display his marvelous and genteel speed of mind's wit, he many times requested of me a brief and easy art, by means of which, said he, without any other study, he could have in each case plenty of materials to exhibit his talent.[17]

Actually, *I Fonti dell' Ingegno* inquires into the ways people apprehend and organize their experience. It is on these grounds that *I Fonti* can later discuss

---

[16]*Acutezze*, "Lettore." "Se ti diletti d' Acutezze, potrai facilmente gradire questi discorse nel quali si considera *la Natura, le specie, la miniere, i vitii, & pregi, l' vso et abuso loro.*" Here, I translate "acutezze" as witty remarks since Pellegrini restricts acuteness specifically to sayings. Cf. *Acutezze* Chapter I, 3: "...acuteness does not consist on a reasoning but on a saying." ("...l' Acutezze non consiste in vn ragionamento, ma in vn detto...") As the title of the treatise itself indicates, *spiriti, vivezze,* and *concetti* are synonyms of *acutezze,* thus of witty remarks as well.

[17]*I Fonti Dell' Ingegno* "L' Autore A' Lettori" 10. "Preso egli duque da gran vaghezza di hauer capo da far la proue della sua maraugiliosa, e gentile velocità de' Ingegno; mi richiese più volte d' alcun' arte breue, e facile, mercè della quale, senza altro studio potesse, diceua egli, hauer in ogni proposito larghezza di panno a suo talento."

methods of inventiveness and development of speeches.

In spite of their differences, both treatises share something very important. To some degree, their methods for producing discourse both rely on systems to link or associate terms or ideas, in order to bring about new ones.

In his *Acutezze*, Pellegrini wondered about the many possible kinds of sayings, in order to identify those which could be regarded as "witty" or "acute". Pellegrini found a first criterion to classify the sayings in the classical purposes assigned to style: to teach, to move, or to please.[18] Since sayings are compounds of materials (words and ideas) and relationships (the way materials are associated),[19] Pellegrini introduced a new criterion to classify sayings: whether the acute element of a saying resides in the materials or in the relationships. An additional and very important criterion was either the plain or figurative expression of the materials and relationships stated by the saying.[20]

Pellegrini thus classified sayings: if plain statements of materials teach or move, they are *serious* sayings; if plain statements of materials please, they are *pleasant* sayings; if figurative statements express serious materials, they are *acute* and *serious* sayings; if statements simply rest on a skillful and pleasant wordplay, they are *acute* and *graceful* sayings; if statements appeal to listeners not because of the materials plainly or figuratively expressed, but because of the figurative linkage which holds the matters of the statement together, the saying is *acute* and *admirable*.[21]

Therefore, something which differentiates *admirable witticisms* from the other kinds in the *Acutezze* is that this kind of sayings is not focused on stating materials (ideas or words), but on setting a relationship between these materials.

---

[18]See *Acutezze* Chapter two, 21.

[19]See *Acutezze* Chapter three, 30.

[20]See *Acutezze* Chapter three, 40–42.

[21]See *Acutezze* Chapter two. Pellegrini's terms for the five categories of plausible sayings are: *plausibili gravi, plausibili dilettevoli, acutezze gravi, acutezze leggiadre,* and *acutezze mirabile.* In defining these categories, I am doing more than translating Pellegrini's words. I am rather interpreting large portions of his doctrines.

Moreover, the link established by admirable witticisms is figurative.

Other kinds of sayings may simply involve plain relationships between different materials, for example, this statement:

Margaret Tatcher's achievements are now to be judged by historians.

These relationships do not cease to be plain regardless that the materials are expressed figuratively, if the figurative element of the expression remains in the terms and does not extend to the link:[22]

The Iron Lady has passed to the shelves of history.

For Pellegrini, the feature which differentiates admirable witticisms from the statements made above is that the figurative element is made extensive to the link. An example of this kind of remark is the following:

The Iron Lady has passed to the armory of history.

Or this other example may be even better:

English ballots provided to the Iron Lady a sheath.

According to Pellegrini, the figurative link established by admirable witticisms has an enthymematic force. From the Iron Lady/armory remark I can infer the survival of Margaret Tatcher's legacy in Great Britain. From the ballots/Iron Lady/sheath remark I can infer that the ballot is mightier than the ruler. However, the witty enthymeme is not a logical but a figurative one, believed Pellegrini, since the correspondence or linkage between the terms rests on figurative not real elements, as in this ancient remark from Suetonius:

---

[22]Pellegrini opposed the figurative or *witty* association of terms to the *logical* association of terms. See *Acutezze* Chapter three, 40–42.

Who denies that Nero's ancestry comes directly from Aeneas? This one lifted up his father; that one lifted up his mother.[23]

Or in this more recent observation from Taft:

If "pro" is the opposite of "con," then "Progress" is the opposite of "Congress."[24]

Moreover, the association between the terms should be new, unusual, extreme, and unexpected.[25] Because of these properties and the figurative enthymematic force, this category of sayings is the only one which truly suspends the listener's understanding in a state of wonderment;[26] thus, this category of sayings is the truly acute or witty.

Pellegrini classified *admirable witticisms* as pure and mixed, depending on their subject matter. The pure ones are either serious or joyous. Serious in their turn deal either with sensible judgments or with emotions. And joyous or pleasant remarks deal with either graceful or ridiculous subjects.[27] But since the link is what makes these sayings witty, Pellegrini's discussion concentrates not on the kinds of witty subject-matter, but on the linkage that makes the remark possible.

---

[23]"Quis neget Aeneae magna de stirpe Neronem? Sustulit hic matrem, sustulit ille patrem," as quoted in the *Acutezze* Chapter 7: 102. Aeneas lifted up his father to escape together from Troy's destruction; Nero lifted up his mother to strangle her.

[24]"Taft' Law" *1,001 Logical Laws, Accurate Axioms, Profound Principles, Trusty Truisms, Homey Homilies, Colorful Corollaries, Quotable Quotes, and Rambunctious Ruminations for All Walks of Life* Compiled by John Peers. (New York: Fawcett Gold Medal, 1988) 17.

[25]On the essence of the acute or witty, see *Acutezze* Chapter 3.

[26]See *Acutezze* Chapter 3, 36. This state is rendered in Italian as "meravìglia." Tesauro would be the author who more fully addressed this wonderment as a result of acute speech.

[27]See *Acutezze* Chapter 4. *Acutezze seriose* are either *sensate* or *forti*, and *acutezze givcose* are either *gratiose*, or *ridicolose*. Again the main classificatory principle is the three kinds of stylistic purposes: either to teach, to move, or to please.

This emphasis can be appreciated in Pellegrini's treatment of the laughable. This is the only kind of subject-matter for witticisms which he addresses in a fuller fashion, probably because of the classical association between the witty and the laughable. However, although Pellegrini tended to agree with classical authors in identifying the laughable with the slightly ugly, he would depart from classical authors in strongly emphasizing that the witty in laughable remarks rests not so much on the subject as on the artistic linkage uniting the terms of the remark. He thus believed that a witty link could even make the most ugly, evil, and painful subjects laughable for a sharp mind.[28]

Given the figurative nature of the witty, Pellegrini held that several stylistic devices are the tools that provide the figurative component to the saying. Tropes, insinuation, amphibology, and evident fiction (or allegory) supply and explain the changes of meaning of the terms in the remarks,[29] but, more important, they are also the departing points for the unusual or deviated association of terms in the remark, and therefore they are the principal artistic means generating what Pellegrini called sources of acuteness,[30] for inventing witty sayings: the incredible or unthinkable, the deceitful, harmony, imitation, enthymeme, insinuation, and ridicule.[31]

So far, a witty link is figurative since it associates terms on the basis of the terms' figurative expression. However, the link in itself is not figurative. According to Pellegrini, the invention of a linkage between figurative terms is not artistically supplied or expressed by tropes but through the topics. The latter establish the kind of correspondence which associates figurative terms: a genre

---

[28]See *Acutezze* Chapter 5.

[29]See *Acutezza* Chapter 8. Pellegrini's terms are *traslato, noema, amfibolia,* and *fintion palese*.

[30]Acuteness: the "acute," "sharp," or "pointed" component of witty sayings.

[31]See *Acutezze* chapters 6–8. Pellegrini's terms for the sources of acuteness are: *l' incredibile* or *inopinato, inganneuole, concerto, imitatione, entimemmatico, sottointeso,* and *derisiuo.*

with a species, a cause with its effect, similars, the greater with the lesser, etc.[32] Here I want to point out Pellegrini's innovative understanding of the topics: they are not empty places to find materials; rather, they are places which express relations—the links—between two or more terms. Thus, there cannot be a genre without its species, a cause without its effect, etc. Therefore, Pellegrini's topics do not come alone but in pairs or more.[33]

Pellegrini previewed these findings concerning witty remarks in the beginning of *Acutezze*: 1) the "witty" resides in a saying, not in a true reasoning; 2) thus, its study pertains to the realm of the beautiful, 3) which entails hierarchies, 4) where the "witty" may find a high position, 5) and this position rests not on the subject-matter of the saying, but on the artifices making possible the saying: concretely, the figurative link.[34] Thus, according to Pellegrini, witty remarks are issues belonging to the realm of style, and specifically to ornament. Hence Pellegrini advocated caution and extreme moderation in the use of witticisms, lest their abuse lead to affectation in language or to sophistry in logic.[35]

Pellegrini wrote a second treatise, *I Fonti Dell' Ingegno*, setting out a distinct theory of ingenuity without any explicit association with his former theory of witticisms. By ingenuity, Pellegrini meant something very broad: the

---

[32]See *Acutezze* Chapter 9.

[33]Both Pellegrini and Gracián departed from classical theories of witticisms in making the linkage and sources of acuteness the main principles explaining witticisms. However, Gracián would define the sources of acuteness not so much in terms of their nature (as Pellegrini did: the unthinkable, the deceitful, etc.) as in terms of the method producing acuteness. Moreover, Gracián would diverge from Pellegrini's theories in making enthymematic, tropological, and topical methods not necessary for the generation of sources of acuteness. Gracián would reduce his method to its essential element: the link. And he would expand the link's consequences from the realm of witticisms to the whole field of human understanding. For Gracián, the "witty" and the "ingenious" would become one.

[34]See *Acutezze* Chapter 1: 3–4.

[35]See *Acutezze* Chapters 11–13.

art of human understanding, communication, and inventiveness.[36]

At first, *I Fonti* may appear extremely disappointing. After Pellegrini's denial that topics are a reliable method for discovering subject-matter and his promise of a new and true method of invention,[37] his great innovation is an adaptation of Aristotelian categories as a substitute for topics, in their function of empty places useful to screen, sort, store, and prompt subject matter for speeches.[38] The categories even become the *fonti* or sources of ingenuity, and they preexist either as the supreme forms predicable of any being, or as mental "shelves" where information is naturally stored.[39] Moreover, in an obvious display of "the latest thing," Pellegrini announced that these sources of ingenuity are excited by using six *trascendental questions: is it?; is it possible?; should it be?; is it often?; if it is, what does follow?*, and *why?*[40] Finally, Pellegrini crowned the delineation of his methods of invention by surreptitiously

---

[36]According to Pellegrini, ingenuity's three main functions are to acquire knowledge of the facts, to judge, and to move. Each of these functions in their turn are manifest through the learning of reality, and through its fruitful and inventive communication. See *I Fonti* Chapter four.

[37]See *I Fonti* "A' lettori" and Chapters 2–4.

[38]See *I Fonti* Chapter 5. Lacking the neatness and depth of Aristotelian categories, Pellegrini proposed the following list: 1) relationship between the person knowing and the object known, 2) constituents of the object, 3) quantity, 4) quality, 5) beginnings, 6) ends, 7) action, 8) passion, 9) place, 10) time, 11) substance (subject of properties), and 12) correspondents or relatives. In proposing these *fonti*, Pellegrini answered less speculative concerns than he inquired into for a handy art of discourse. And in including, among others spurious *fonti*, the first one, Pellegrini seemingly conditioned all knowledge to the knower, in a very relativistic fashion: the knower is not just an observer, but a predicate defining the object observed. See *I Fonti* Chapter 8.

[39]See *I Fonti* Chapter 1: 27–30. Although Pellegrini seemed to lean towards mentalism, he actually avoided any endorsement of either realism or mentalism. He just endorsed categories in so far as he found them practical for prompting discourse. Even so, Mooney regards Pellegrini as a formalist since Pellegrini gave much importance to pure arrangement and pure relations as sources of acuity and ingenuity. Mooney grounds his judgment on his study of the *Acutezze*, not *I Fonti*. See Mooney 145.

[40]See *I Fonti* Chapter 6: 69.

reintroducing the topics: discussing lines to develop answers for the trascendental questions, he proposed five kinds of steps or *trapassos* generating speech, consisting in relating the subject in question to its *genre*, or to its *species*, to its *adjuncts*, etc.[41]

However, a closer analysis reveals that *I Fonti* reached some adequate choices in method. The sources of ingenuity and the trascendental questions both refer to the categories.[42] Thus, these methods are not arbitrary, but suitable metaphysically and logically to study a subject. At least, they are the supreme storerooms of a taxonomist. Pellegrini's repetition of the categories in these two stages of his method of ingenuity may be justifiable since the sources help to establish the subject of a discourse, and the questions help to inquire into predicates for such a discourse.

So far, these two stages do not suggest more than a simple, formal, and general frame to research and communicate any subject matter.[43] For Pellegrini, in fact, these stages only accomplish the job of arranging or storing of data. The *fonti* themselves are mental cabinets which merely store concrete information.[44] And the questions only lead to the identification of concrete data's predicates, without adding any new components to the concrete data already stored.[45]

---

[41]See *I Fonti* Chapter 7.

[42]The questions refer to issues of actuality (or existence), possibility, necessity (or obligation), frequency, causality, and finality (or purpose). The questions, like the categories themselves, address the most general ideas that can be predicated from a subject.

[43]Later Tesauro would make the system of categories a taxonomical frame to prepare a written inventory of subject matter, helpful to organize the orator's learning and keep it ready to use for the purpose of discourses. See *Cannocchiale* Chapter three, 107–112. This inventory would be one of Tesauro's elementary methods of exercising ingenuity.

[44]See *I Fonti* Chapter 1: 29–30.

[45]See *I Fonti* Chapter seven, 74–75, and 84, where Pellegrini described the first movement of ingenuity—to bring forth a predicate—as circular, not advancing or making a "step" into new learning. Cf., Pallavicino's *absolute apprehensions* which consist in perceptions of isolated pieces of concrete data without allowing the mind to compare thus far, and to ascend from concrete experience to scientific, conceptual, or abstract knowledge. See *Trattato Dello*

To go beyond pure experience and make the mind reach new grounds of knowledge and true inventiveness, Pellegrini conceived a third stage for his method: the steps of ingenuity.[46] The steps are rules to make the mind artistically zigzag, thus establishing correspondences between the data stored—particularly between the subjects and predicates of different statements.

The steps involved in inventiveness consist in different kinds of shifts from one discursive line to another, in order to explain a subject. The first three steps imply a single shift from one discursive line to another: 1) explaining a specific idea through its *genre*, 2) explaining a general idea through one of its *species*, and 3) explaining an idea through its *colaterals (equals, similars, differents, proportionals, contraries)*.[47] These single shifts do not include changes from sources of ingenuity (categorical subject) or from trascendental question (categorical predicate). The fourth step does include these changes, thus doubling or tripling the possibilities of shifts. Indeed, with Pellegrini's steps of ingenuity, I could omit, single, double, triple, or multiply the shifts from one discursive line to another. Consider the following example:

1) Omission of shifts: I could discuss the subject of *envy* (stored in the category of actions) straightforwardly, without making any shift or step of ingenuity, and thus I would just advance predicates by answering the trascendental questions applied to it in a direct way.

2) Single shift: I answer the question of consequents specifically attached to envy, by rather answering the same question as applied generically to *capital sin* (which still is stored in the same category of actions). The single shift is from species to genre.

Stile Chapter 7: 79–80.

[46]See *I Fonti* Chapter 7.

[47]It is in these steps that I see how Pellegrini reintroduced the topics. He unwillingly seemed to recognize it in one place: "Therefore, these three first kind of steps are of the most important use in eloquence...from them is supplied every matter of tropes, comparisons, and other rhetorical artifices." ("Questi dunque sono trè primi Trapassi, d' vso grandissimo nell' eloquenza...da essi n' è ministrata tutta la materia de' traslati, comparationi, & altra supellettile retoricale.")

3) Double shift: I answer the question of consequents attached to envy, by rather answering the question of cause as applied to capital sin: *fruitless life*. The shift is double because it goes from species to genre, and from one question to another.

4) Triple and multiple shift: I could go beyond the change of discursive lines (from species to genre) and the change from one question to another (from consequents to cause), so that I even reach a change from one source of ingenuity to a different one—let's say, from action to quality. I would then say: the quality of fruitlessness is manifest through the *color green*, and therefore *green is the color of envy*. Moreover, following a series of further shifts, for example, metaphorical ones, the ingenious mind could relate greenness to *immaturity*, and then understand as such the "greeness" of envious people.

In spite of the knottiness of this illustration, it reflects Pellegrini's very sensible concern for technical precision in explaining the mind's methods of associating ideas. Taken into practice, these methods may rather flow smoothly and powerfully, serving the mind in its effort of elucidating difficult subject-matters.

Consider an illustration of Pellegrini's shifts at work, say, Gracián's *El Criticón*. There Gracián explained his theories of a person's ages not directly, but through transferred analytical categories: the yearly seasons, the planetary system, the deadly sins, the acts of a play, the domestic animals, etc. The result was Gracián's most celebrated literary and philosophical work.

Consider my general study on Baltasar Gracián. Instead of explaining Gracián's theory on wit directly by its proper predicates, I am now making a "disgression", a shift of ingenuity: I am explaining Gracián through some transferred predicates which properly pertain to three Italian theorists—Pellegrini, Pallavicino, and Tesauro. My disgression does not aim to complicate or inflate my explanations. It aims at understanding the rather obscure but rich doctrines of Gracián. It does so by helping me to establish subtle differences which separate Gracián from the strikingly related Italian theories. In this sense, Pellegrini's steps of ingenuity help me to discover generic and differentiating traits between data in ways which are usually cognitive and abstractive, rather than inferential. These linkages help me reach *concepts* in the epistemological sense.[48]

The above mentioned steps of ingenuity do not only help a speaker to be ingenious in his discourse by artistically establishing associations between his data. Those steps also artistically explain the complicated extremes which the listener's mind may follow when associating the ideas he receives. However, those are not all the steps of ingenuity. A final step—according to Pellegrini—is a continuous updating of the concrete information stored in the sources of ingenuity, because of the constant innovations and changes in the world, requiring the mind to make a new study of the data. This updating, indeed unending, provides new infinite points of linkage on each piece of data which sneaks into the mind. Complication grows, and with it, the swagger of ingenuity.[49]

There are some additional facts which deserve some attention concerning *I Fonti*.

In accord with the seventeenth-century interest in the mind, Pellegrini rearranged the genres of discourses according to the operations of human understanding: to inform, to judge, and to move.[50] This classification is not repeated in an explicit way by other baroque theorists of wit. This innovation led Pellegrini to think that his art of ingenuity, compared to traditional logic and rhetoric, is the only one which fulfills the duty of obtaining and associating

---

[48]This apprehension of concepts is a result which Pellegrini apparently did not notice. But Tesauro seemed to notice it, and Gracián and Pallavicino did not ignore it.

[49]See *I Fonti* Chapter 7: 80–83. Pellegrini believed that updating was crucial for any field of human action, especially prudence, since human affairs are continuously changing. Philosophy may skip this last step since this lofty discipline is not interested in the changing aspects of reality but with the general, permanent, and trascendent ones.

[50]See *I Fonti* Chapter 4: 49–53. Pellegrini derived species of discourse from these genres. For example, persuasion and dissuasion derive from the genre of speeches to judge. And cross-examination is derived as a method to become informed. Other manifestations of Pellegrini's interest in the mind is his relativistic first *fonte*: the knower. See *I Fonti* Chapter Eight.

information to invent discourse, and that his art of ingenuity is also the most complete since it shares with logic the function of judging, and with rhetoric the functions of judging and moving.[51]

As noticed before, Pellegrini surreptitiously reintroduced the topics in *I Fonti*. Any case, he maintained the innovative understanding delineated in the *Acutezze*. Topics work to establish links between genre/species, similar/similar, contrary/contrary, rather than offering empty sources of materials.[52] As sources, topics are sensibly replaced by categories: the latter more properly refer to supreme predicates pertaining to ideas, whereas the former more properly refer to supreme relationships of ideas.[53] The only difference between *I Fonti* and the *Acutezze* concerning topics may be that the former uses them to link ideas, whereas the latter uses topics to link figurative expressions.

After all, in spite of the *Acutezze* and *I Fonti*'s differences, they do not lack artistic contact. On the contrary, these works meet in the most central of their proposed methods: the link. Either dealing with the witty or dealing with the

---

[51]See *I Fonti* Chapter 4. Contrasting with Pellegrini's, Gracián's comprehensive system of ideas keeps a very scholastic view of the operations of human understanding: conceptualization (which is not the same as gathering information), judgment, and inference. Moreover, the moving of the souls to action is not independent from reason. It consists in the reasonable presentation or demonstration of the goods to be pursued by the will.

[52]Written two centuries before *I Fonti*, Rudolf Agricola's *De inventione dialectica* somewhat resembles Pellegrini's treatise in understanding invention as a task of establishing novel relationships between subjects and predicates. However, Agricola and Pellegrini differ much in their understanding of the topics. Agricola saw the topics as the empty places serving as categories either for subjects or for predicates. See Conley 125–128. But Pellegrini saw the topics as the link between the shifted discursive line which replaces the proper one, and the categories as the general empty cabinets to store materials either for subjects or for predicates.

[53]I would recall here the distinction still kept by contemporary schoolmen between categories and categoremes: the former apply to supreme predicates of referents, whereas the latter apply to supreme modes (how predicates relate to each other): genre, species, difference, proper, and logical accident. See, for example, Raúl Gutiérrez Saenz, *Introducción a la Lógica* (México: Editorial Esfinge, 1977) 101–120; Francisco Montes de Oca, *Lógica* (México: Editorial Porrúa, 1974) 74–77.

ingenious, either associating terms or associating ideas, Pellegrini's link becomes the main artistic method prompting inventiveness in discourse.[54]

Pietro Cardinal Sforza Pallavicino

Pallavicino published his *Trattato Dello Stile e Del Dialogo* in 1646, four years after the first edition of Gracián's *Agudeza*. Some characteristics of Pallavicino's treatise may suggest that *Trattato* is not as important as Pellegrini's, Gracián's, and Tesauro's works, in respect to the theory of wit. First, *Trattato*'s main subject is not a theory of wit, but a theory of the style for teaching scientific matters. Wit, as a subject, is not explicitly addressed except in a few chapters[55] where Pallavicino discussed the *concepts*, as he called the witty remarks. Second, after having prepared his own theory of witticisms, Pallavicino read *Acutezze* and felt himself compelled to confess that his own theories to some degree were inferior than those of Pellegrini.[56]

In spite of this unusual scholarly humility and the secondary place of wit among the *Trattato*'s issues, Pallavicino's treatise is very important because it is the one which reveals the intellectualism of the age in the most explicit terms.[57]

It is still true that the *Trattato*'s main concern is to inquire into the style

---

[54]The artistic association of ideas may be the most distinctive feature of the 1640's theories of ingenuity. Gracián would almost make it the single feature of his method in the *Agudeza*, since he discarded or made very secondary other methods such as the topics, the tropes, or the enthymemes.

[55]See *Trattato Dello Stile* Chapters 10 and 14–19.

[56]See *Trattato Dello Stile* Chapter 10: 115–116: "Matteo Pellegrini...has written an excellent treatise *dell' Acutezze*, which I regret I did not have in my hands before preparing this work of mine." ("Matteo Pellegrini...hà scritto vn egregio Trattato *dell' Acutezze*; il qual mi duole che non mi sia capitato in mano prima che io componessi quest' Opera.")

[57]Pallavicino's intellectualism was the key, for me, to understand the rather obscure but much richer intellectualism of Gracián.

befitting the teaching of science. Pallavicino studied the propriety of eloquence,[58] elegance, and technical terms[59]—as those used by schoolmen— when writing with academic purposes.[60] He also discussed more specific problems of scientific writing: advantages and disadvantages of writing either in Italian or in Latin,[61] the difference between emulating, imitating, borrowing, or plagiarizing,[62] and the use of figurative approaches, such as allegories, fiction, and, particularly, dialogues, when expounding a subject.[63]

Even so, *Trattato* studies style not as pure cosmetics to embellish thoughts but as an instrument which brings forth and embodies ideas. At first, *Trattato* seemingly endorses a dictum which separates useful language from pleasant language: scientific style should be useful for teaching and pleasant for keeping the reader interested.[64] However, Pallavicino somehow reduced the pleasant element of scientific writing to teaching, since acquiring new knowledge is what pleases the reader.[65] Thus, most of his treatise is devoted to the artifices of style that he believed participate in offering new knowledge to the intellect (and therefore, please)—sententiae, comparisons, and concepts[66]—and to the forms

---

[58]By eloquence, Pallavicino seemed to mean a grand, intense, and persuasive style. Cf. *Trattato Dello Stile* Chapter 20, where Pallavicino defines elegance in contrast with eloquence.

[59]See *Trattato Dello Stile* Chapter three, 21. Eloquence, elegance, and technicisms are the three major issues defining the structure of Pallavicino's treatise.

[60]Pallavicino was extremely cautious regarding the use of eloquence's tools in the sciences–he particularly forbade emotions and the amplification of matters (with few very extraordinary exceptions). However, he encouraged the austere splendor of the elegant style, and he endorsed the use of technical terms when needed.

[61]See, for example, *Trattato Dello Stile* Chapter 5 and 27.

[62]See *Trattato Dello Stile* Chapters 11 to 15.

[63]See *Trattato Dello Stile* Chapters 30 to 38.

[64]See *Trattato Dello Stile* Chapter 4: 41.

[65]See *Trattato Dello Stile* Chapter 3: 22.

[66]See *Trattato Dello Stile* Chapter 3: 22. Pallavicino made concepts the same as witty

of discourse which are derivations of these three artifices—allegories, imitative fiction, and dialogue. Moreover, Pallavicino's intellectualism is also shown in the stylistic devices which are not especially designed to teach. These devices do not please so much because of their sensuous qualities as they do because of their appeal to the intellect. For example, rhythmical style, believed Pallavicino, appeals less to the ear than to the mind's subconscious reflection of numerical proportion.[67]

In brief, Pallavicino believed language was not only a vehicle of knowledge, but also, and more importantly, an instrument for knowing, since from the mind's handling of pure experience language allowed the mind to ascend to abstract knowledge.

This belief to some degree responds to Pallavicino's question about how people rise from pure experience to abstract knowledge. Pallavicino regarded the human mind as a blank slate at birth,[68] since even the *first principles*, he believed, are learned from experience:

---

remarks (See *Trattato* Chapter ten, 115), and sometimes he made them also the same as sententiae, whenever the witticism operated as a warrant for reasoning, and the sententia met the definition of a concept: "a brief saying encapsulating a wondrous observation." ("...osseruazione marauigliosa raccolta in un detto breue.") (see *Trattato* Chapter ten, 112–115). Both meanings—witty remark and sententia—tend to assimilate one to the other, but not always.

[67]See *Trattato Dello Stile* Chapter 5: 51–53. See also Chapter 30: 294–295, where Pallavicino corrected previous views he expressed in *Del bene libri quattro* (Roma, 1644). In *Del bene*, Pallavicino hold the belief that poetic imitation pleased only on the level of the fantasy or imagination (sensuous images). In the *Trattato* he held that poetic imitation also takes place and pleases on the level of the intellect (abstract thought)—a higher order of poetry than the imaginative one, and the order convenient for expounding sciences. *Del bene* could be regarded as a theoretical expression of mannerist, Gongorist, Marinist, and preciosity poetry. The *Trattato* is an expression of conceptist, and probably, metaphysical poetry—as would be used in the sciences.

[68]At least Tesauro and Gracián also believed in the human mind as a blank slate at birth. Pellegrini rather seemed to lean towards mentalism, although not clearly.

...the first principles are taught to us by the utterances (so to say) of the many objects which each men of average understanding has experienced, and already fixed in his mind; for example, *the whole is greater than the part...*[69]

If first principles govern reasoning without needing further guarantees, thought Pallavicino, it is because the continuous experience of the first principles in every fact assures for first principles their place in the human mind.[70]

According to Pallavicino, the mind apprehends the reality it experiences in two ways:

> The first is called *absolute apprehension*, which simply contemplates an object, purely as it is in itself, without the mind considering the properties and titles which befit such an object by comparing it with other objects. The second is named *comparative apprehension* since by looking at many objects at the same time, the mind finds which correspondences exist between the objects, either of cause and effect, similarity or dissimilarity, proportion or disproportion, friendship or enimity,[71] and so on.[72]

---

[69]*Trattato Dello Stile* Chapter six, 70. "...i primi principii sono insegnati à noi dalle voci (per così dire) di tanti oggeti, che ogni huomo d' intendimento mediocre gli hà da sè stesso auuertiti, e già stabiliti nell' animo; como per esempio; che *il Tutto è maggior della parte...*"

[70]See *Trattato Dello Stile* Chapter 6: 71. According to Pallavicino, sententiae have a status similar to that of first principles. If the latter work as guarantees for all reasoning in sciences, sententiae do it for reasonings on morality. Both first principles and sententiae are constantly verified by experience; however, sententiae require a more perspicacious mind to be learned. Gracián would stress another important distinction of sententiae: true, they are general statements, but usually plausible and not necessary as the first principles are. See *Agudeza* discourses 29 and 23.

[71]Notice that, in contrast with Pellegrini's understanding of topics, Pallavicino does not see them originally as tools enabling apprehensions, but rather as a result of apprehensions since topics are universals abstracted from experience. Notice, however, that Pallavicino's topics are similar to Pellegrini's in that they come in pairs, and that they express a link or correpondence. On the universal character of topics and common places, see also *Trattato Dello Stile*, Chapter Fifteen, 145.

[72]*Trattato Dello Stile* Chapter seven, 79–80. "...la prima chiamasi *assoluta*, la qual contempla vn oggetto com' è in sè stesso puramente, e senza considerar quali propietà e quali

For Pallavacino, it is the second kind which allows the mind to hold new information beyond pure experience, to apprehend abstract knowledge, and to rise to the level of sciences.

> This second kind of cognition better assuages the intellect's appetite, in so far as it is the cognition which grasps the object in a more exquisite fashion, the one which is good for moving from one truth to another, and therefore the one which is the most efficacious instrument of the sciences.
>
> ....
>
> [These apprehensions] are exactly the first steps by which the intellect, guided by the senses knowing particular objects, then ascends to the acquisition of the Science which beholds the universals.[73]

The idea of laughter may illustrate Pallavicino's theory of knowledge. Assuming the possibility that there is such a thing which can be laughable by itself,[74] absolute apprehensions may allow me to identify this laughable object, and even let me laugh about it. However, for Pallavicino, by means of absolute apprehensions, I can not reach theoretical knowledge of laughter. This kind of

----

titoli couenga a lui paragonato con altri oggetti: la seconda è nominata *comparativa*, perche rimirando con vn solo sguardo molti oggetti insieme, scorge qual corrispondeza habbiano essi frà sè di cagione ò d' effeto, di somiglianza ò dissimiglianza, di proporzione ò di sproporzione, d' amistà ò di nimistà; e così dell' altre."

[73] *Trattato Dello Stile* Chapter seven, 80 and 89. "...questa seconda cognizione appaga meglio l' appetito dell' intelletto, come quella che intende più esquisitamente l' oggetto; e che gioua per passare da vna verità in vn' altra..." "...sono appunto que' primi passi con cui l' intelletto guidato dal senso conoscitore de gli oggetti particulari, s' incamina all' acquisto della Scienza che contempla gli Vniuersali."

[74] This assumption is completely abhorrent to any theory of wit, which finds in laughter the clearest case of ideas brought to mind not by looking at singular objects, but by establishing an apt net of correspondences between the unseemingly or the odd. Nevertheless I like to use this example to portray Pallavicino's theory of absolute apprehensions. The example reminds me that Pallavicino's belief in absolute apprehensions is totally abhorrent to Gracián's theories of wit. According to Gracián, there is not any new idea which can absolutely be learned from a single glance at a single object. Rather, all ideas require an act of abstraction empowered by means of a structure of correspondence. Cf. *Agudeza* Discourse 5.

apprehensions can not let me theoretically explain and understand the causes of laughter, such as some sort of incongruities found in the object, some sort of ugliness and painful imperfection, and yet, some sort of levity, and enlightment gained. In Pallavicino's system, these ideas of laughter can only be apprehended from comparing several clear cases of laughable materials, and from abstracting what is generic to all cases from their differentiae. For Pallavicino, theoretical knowledge can only be learned through comparative apprehensions which allow the mind to abstract the ideas.[75]

Even so, forewarned Pallavicino, not every comparison is suitable for the sciences. Good comparisons are between individuals of the same species, and between species of the same genre. The first kind can furnish arguments by example, and the second kind, arguments by similarities. Both kinds of comparisons are reducible to a syllogistic structure. Moreover, sciences do not admit far-fetched comparisons establishing correspondences between units of different genres. This last kind of comparison could only be reducible to a fallacious syllogistic structure, and it could not serve to argue by example or by similarities.[76] Thus, with scientific propriety in mind, Pallavicino discussed several methods of making comparisons: metaphor, simile, explained comparison, concept (witty remark), and their derivations in allegories, fiction, and dialogue.

---

[75]According to Pallavicino, one of the most important results of abstracting the universals is that they lead to the knowledge of metaphysical and insensible truths. Comparative apprehensions even contribute to very important kinds of practical knowledge, which can not be directly obtained from any sensual perception of facts. For instance, consider the notion of a *problem*. I think that, according to Pallavicino's doctrines, absolute apprehensions never could provide to any person an understanding of the notion of such a problem. Problems are not singular and physical objects just there ready to be apprehended by the senses. The person should recur to a comparative apprehension to learn about this notion by considering, for example, the effects which could follow a cause, the pale present compared to the glorious past, the meager actuality in contrast with the wondrous potentials, etc.

[76]See *Trattato Dello Stile* Chapter 7: 90–91. Gracián did not dwell on the scholastic limits of comparisons. Gracián rather admitted "far-fetched" correspondences between objects if these correspondences maintained the propriety required by prudence.

These stylistic devices not only serve to abstract universals from a set of experiences, suggested Pallavicino, but also serve as proofs in argumentation, since if these devices are recognized as furnishing true universals, the inference necessarily proceeds to particulars. Pallavicino often used Plato's dialogues as examples of discourse in which, by means of allegories, universals are abstracted, and then introduced as guarantees of philosophical reasoning.[77] A recent example of witty remark which brought forth a universal, and thus a guarantee, to an argumentation, is from the British Ex-Prime Minister Margaret Tatcher. She said that there was only one thing she hated more than violence: giving in to violence. She applied this remark to the brief 1991 war against Iraq's occupation of Kuwait.

In human communication, these tools of style enable listeners themselves to abstract the universals from a discourse, and, by testing these universals against their own personal experience, listeners make the pertinent inference by themselves.[78] Moreover, truth and its discovery gains an audience's favor. Attached to the listeners' abstraction of universals, there is the great pleasure of wonderment which audience members experience from their own new discovery.

Any kind of comparison to some degree works to please while teaching, according to Pallavicino, but witty remarks are especially useful for producing the effect of wonderment.[79] The basic source of wonderment is the novelty perceived.[80] *Admissible witty remarks*[81] are the best tools to accomplish this end. For example, to gain theoretical understanding of the sort of incongruities which laughter entails, a person could spare many extended comparisons of

---

[77]See *Trattato Dello Stile* chapters 31–35.

[78]See *Trattato Dello Stile* Chapter 7, for example, 85.

[79]See *Trattato Dello Stile* Chapter 10: 114–115.

[80]Here, Pallavicino disagreed with Pellegrini. Pallavicino did not require beauty in witty remarks, only the novel. For Pallavicino, wonderment is a purely abstract and intellectual pleasure consisting in the mind's experience of grasping something new. See *Trattato Dello Stile* Chapter 10: 116–118.

[81]As opposed to defective witty remarks, that is, false concepts.

cases, and rather quickly learn, on his own, the idea in question through a witty remark: "No mind is thoroughly well organized that is defficient in a sense of humour."[82]

Admissible witty remarks produce wonderment by showing the contrary to what is expected, the different from what is expected, or the astonishing despite its being nonetheless expected.[83] False concepts should be avoided because they say something true but falsely astonishing, say something astonishing but false, or refer a true astonishing matter but through a paralogism.[84] Finally, in the sciences, there should be extreme caution in using hyperbolic witticisms, or acute sayings resting on the playful contrasting of words or ideas.[85]

Pallavicino accomplished a meaningful speculation on how style serves for intellectual purposes. However, he did not go very deeply into questions of method to attain these purposes.[86] Pallavicino was writing a treatise on style, not on ingenuity. He indeed limited most of his pieces of advice to the propriety of different stylistic techniques in expounding the sciences. His guidelines on elegance for the sciences are particularly brilliant.[87]

In any case, ingenuity is one of the subjects explained in the *Trattato*.

---

[82]Heard from Samuel Taylor Coleridge, in a table talk. *The Home Book of Quotations Classical and Modern*, selection of Burton Stevenson, 5th. ed. (1934, New York: Dodd Mead & Company, 1947) 938.

[83]See *Trattato Dello Stile* Chapter 16. These three major types of concepts from Pallavicino are similar to Gracián's basic concepts of pondering the proportion, mystery, difficulty, or contradiction between the terms to be associated in a remark: they rest on the difficulty of the association to be established by the witticisms—or the difficulty to discover the novel. See *Agudeza* discourses 4 to 8.

[84]See *Trattato Dello Stile* Chapter 17. Strongly contrasting with Pellegrini and Tesauro, Pallavicino disliked the metaphorical enthymeme and regarded it as a childish form of witticism. See *Trattato* Chapter 17: 159.

[85]See *Trattato Dello Stile* chapters 18 and 19.

[86]For example, he only discussed three major permissible kinds of witty remarks, without detailing much about their formal aspects.

[87]See *Trattato Dello Stile* chapters 20 to 29.

Pallavicino's understanding of ingenuity stresses perspicacity—the discovery, apprehension, and understanding of universals—rather than creativity—the making up of ideas.[88] And Pallavicino's witty remarks are not out of ingenuity's realm, as they were for Pellegrini. Pallavicino rather considered them the sharpest technique of ingenuity to achieve the novel.

Finally, I should point out that the methodical principle of linking terms or associating ideas reappears in the *Trattato*, now under the discussion of comparative apprehension. Again, with Pallavicino, the link is the artistic technique which ingenuity uses to display perspicacity and inventiveness, in order to achieve the witty.

Emanuele Tesauro

Tesauro's *Il Cannocchiale Aristotelico* was first published in 1654, five years after the second edition of Gracián's *Agudeza*.

A first encounter with *Cannocchiale* may lead the reader to find the treatise very paradoxical. On the one hand, its general subject is a lofty one, ingenuity,[89] and its pages offer the most extensive treatment of the most diverse problems related to this issue: intellectual apprehension, inventiveness, the creation and production of ideas, methods of ingenuity, style, witty remarks, wonderment, and humor. On the other hand, *Cannocchiale* concretely applies its theoretical results to what appears to be the most ineffectual activities: heraldic symbols, mottos, emblems, coin, medal, and tomb inscriptions, and, among other activities, masquerades.[90] Moreover, in dealing with the broad issue of

---

[88]Tesauro would stress creativity.

[89]Ingenuity is such a lofty subject that—according to Tesauro—its sumpreme practitioner is God. See *Cannocchiale* Chapter 3: 59–66. Cf., with *El Criticón* I, crises 1–3. In spite of the newer emphasis on ingenuity in this conception, the idea of God as an Ingenious Author and Communicator has deep roots in the Biblical tradition.

[90]See *Cannocchiale* chapters 13–19.

ingenuity, Tesauro continuously centered his discussion on the power of *argutezza*,[91] which is the keen use of fallacious argumentation, and Tesauro crowned this discussion by praising and recommending the "urbanely" fallacious enthymeme,[92] which he identified as the "Intellect's utmost effort."[93] At the end, the association of these paradoxical elements with the complicated structure of the treatise may lead the occasional reader to regard *Cannocchiale* as the baroque's utmost pomposity.

As pompous as it could seem, Tesauro's book deserves inspection.[94] Among the theories of wit here studied, Tesauro's may have greatest title to be the "Summa of Ingenuity," since it is the one which draws, in a scholastic fashion, the most extensive net of theoretical implications within its pages.[95] It also offers a very systematic theory of ingenuity based on an insightful survey of the

---

[91]*Argutezza* in Italian and *argucia* in Spanish often refer to keen but fallacious argumentation. They differ from Italian *acutezza* and Spanish *agudeza* because the latter often apply to keen perception or conceptualization. Another way of distinguishing them would be that *acutezza* applies to pointed sayings, whereas *argutezza* refers to clever ones. In Tesauro's theory, both *argutezza* and *acutezza* can render witty remarks: the first through a fallacious argumentation, the second through the simpler form of a transferred idea or a statement. See *Cannocchiale* chapters 7 to 9. The theoretical difference between the two concepts appearently attracted the attention of the Italian theorists only, and not the attention of the Spaniards, such as Gracián.

[92]See *Cannochiale* Chapter 9.

[93]*Cannocchiale* Chapter 1: 1. "...vltimo sforzo dell' Intelletto..."

[94]If not because of a legitimate reason, this inspection should still proceed to satisfy the impulse to discover why a man writes an 800 page-book to advocate the use of fallacious reasoning on tombstones.

[95]As noted above, Curtius (p. 301) rather claimed the title of "summa" for Gracián's *Agudeza*. In many aspects I also find Gracián richer in illustrations, in theoretical implications, and in method than Tesauro. However, Tesauro was more than suggestive when drawing the implications and extensions of his theories. He explicitly framed them in a complex scholastic system, and thus I think the *Cannocchiale* better deserves the title of "summa."

theory of metaphor.[96] And Tesauro probably offered the boldest attempt to assimilate style into invention.

The *Cannocchiale*'s theories are interwoven in the most complex way. Briefly, I give an idea of the puzzling structure of the treatise by comparing it with the polyphony in fashion during the seventeenth century.[97] Several themes are played at the same time, and their full meaning can not be attained except in relation to one and other. I believe the most important themes dealt with in *Cannocchiale* are the style, the four causes, and the logical operations involved in ingenuity.[98]

---

[96]Tesauro's survey of the theory of metaphor particularly is focused on Aristotle's works. Tesauro's most closely inspected text may be chapter ten from the *Rhetoric*, book three.

[97]This comparison of polyphony with a text is not mine. Gracián already used the idea of harmony between sounds ["...entre los sonidos, la consonancia..."] to explain the whole business of ingenuity, which establishes correspondences between different discursive lines in order to discover a novelty: the intellectual harmony. See *Agudeza* Discourse 2. Defining music to Her Excellency, the Countess of Galve, Sister Juana Inés de la Cruz also used the definition to explain every effort of abstract conceptualization: "...For one measuring alone, although adapted to different senses, demonstrates Harmony to the ears and Beauty to the eyes. Being limited, the senses judge diverse the measurings perceived from the sensible objects. And thus these senses take for granted these distinctions between what is seen or heard, or what is touched or tasted. But there in abstract, the soul recognizes with evidence that it is but one proportion—different as it may appear—the one which there appeals to taste, or flatter touch, delights the eye, or sounds in the ear." ("...Pues una mensura mesma, aunque a diversos sentidos determinada, demuestra la Armonía a los oídos y a los ojos la Belleza. Limitados los sentidos juzgan mensuras diversas en los objetos sensibles; y así dan la diferencia entre lo que ven o escuchan, lo que gustan o que tientan. Mas el alma, allá en abstracto, conoce con evidencia que es una proporción misma, aunque distinta parezca, aquella que al gusto halaga o que al tacto lisonjea, la que divierte a los ojos o la que al oído suena"). *Enconomiástico poema a los años de la Excma. Señora Condesa de Galve.* Concerning music and ingenuity, cf., also José Miguel Oltra Tomás, "Conformación de un texto de Gracián: El político Don Fernando" *Gracián y su época* (Zaragoza: Institución Fernando El Católico, 1986) 164. Oltra Tomás uses a musical analogy of variations on a theme to explain the structure of Gracián's discourse *El Pólitico*.

[98]The major theme is the four causes of ingenuity, as considered through scholastic analysis: instrumental, efficient, formal, and final. This theme clearly appears throughout the whole book. The theme of style mainly reviews the rhetorical tradition of figures and

Tesauro's theory of antithesis may help to illustrate the intricacies of this systematization. Responding to the theme of style, antithesis should be understood as a harmonic figure[99]—as a species of periodic composition whose appeal is to the ear by means of equal size members, contraposition of terms, and similarity of sounds.[100] Regarding the theme of causes, antithesis is a formal cause of ingenuity, producing thought by contrasting ideas.[101] Finally, considering the logical operations involved, antithesis reaches inference by empowering enthymemes.[102]

Tesauro's theory of wit is similar to Pellegrini's and Pallavicino's in that there is first a step of ingenuity which stores pure data, and then a second step which establishes correspondences between the data[103]—a first kind of apprehension which is absolute, and a second one which is comparative.

---

principally dominates through chapters four to six. The theme of logical operations follows the scholastic analysis: ideas, propositions, and inference. It strongly dominates from chapter seven to nine. The treatment of these two last themes indeed is concentrated under the discussion of the formal cause of ingenuity, but not limited to this place.

[99]Harmonic figures included, in Tesauro, the theory of periodical and rhythmical composition, and also the figures of speech. There were two other classes of figures: pathetic figures, as he called the figures of thought, and ingenious figures, as he called the tropes.

[100]See, for example, *Cannocchiale* Chapter 4: 127.

[101]See, for example, *Cannocchiale* Chapter 7: 445–446, where Tesauro listed eight formal means of contrasting ideas.

[102]See, for example, *Cannocchiale* Chapter 7, where Tesauro supported his description of antitheses as enthymemes with the authority of Aristotle (See *Rhetoric* III, 9), and where Tesauro also analyzed antithesis as a form of definition, and explained its different varieties of propositional forms: affirmative, affirmative-negative, and double negative.

[103]Tesauro's doctrines again describe wit and ingenuity as inventional efforts to link terms or ideas: "As dialectical propositions consist in assenting or denying, similarly those which are witty (*argute*) consist on associating or dissociating." ("Sicome le Propositioni Dialettiche consistono nell' Affermare, ò Negare: così le Argute consistono nel congiugnere o diuidire...") *Cannochiale* Chapter 11: 554. Contrast baroque theories with the classical ones. The latter seem not to have clear the conception of ingenuity and wit as associating or linking ideas.

According to Tesauro, ingenuity includes two natural talents: perspicacity and versatility. Perspicacity observes each object as such, and analyzes it through the categories. By means of perspicacity, the mind gets hold of information. After that, versatility quickly confronts, associates, and replaces the separate notions or circumstances learned from the objects by using other circumstances or notions fitting the case.[104] Ingenuity's versatility accomplishes these shifts or associations metaphorically. In this respect, believed Tesauro, ingenuity differs from prudential judgment, because the latter usually remains at the stage of perspicacity, or apprehension of pure facts,[105] whereas the former rises to the creative connection of ideas.[106]

Tesauro's understanding of ingenuity as pertaining to the metaphorical use of language may lead the reader to regard *Cannocchiale* as a book mainly concerned with poetics or with ornaments of style. However, in this treatise, metaphor is not only a broad term applying to any trope, transferred words, or figurative use of language, but also a term which means the substitution of one set of ideas for another, the association of two or more ideas, or even the construction of new sets of ideas.[107] Moreover, Tesauro once defined metaphor as "to mean something by means of another thing."[108] This definition actually extends to any kind of sign. In this way, *Cannocchiale* becomes a book of semiotics—a theory of the meanings produced by an ingenious mind.[109]

---

[104]See, for example, *Cannocchiale* Chapter 3: 82 and 107, Chapter 7: 266.

[105]See *Cannocchiale* Chapter 3: 82–83.

[106]Tesauro thus made versatility the "Mother of Poetry". *Cannocchiale* Chapter 3: 82.

[107]Some examples of Tesauro are "sirens" and "chimeras" (see *Cannocchiale* Chapter 3: 83), but he also included the creations of an engineer (in Italian: *ingegneri*, that is the ingenious one). See *Cannochiale* Chapter 3: 86.

[108]*Cannocchiale* Chapter 15: 638. "Significare una Cosa per mezzo de un' altra..." Cf. *Cannocchiale* Chapter 7: 302, where he narrows down the definition to transferred words.

[109]I perceive in Tesauro a tendency towards *nominalism*. Meanings, general ideas, the association of experience, stand more often as something produced or created than as something apprehended or learned. The association of data produces metaphors, rather than

Tesauro's metaphors are more than the replacement of one word by another. They refer to the ways that one meaning could stand for another, or for a thing itself. In Tesauro's system, this occurs by means of eight general kinds of metaphor. Two of these kinds are absolute metaphors, in which the association made is—as I interpret it—synecdochical, between the object and its own elements and possibilities: (1) *hyperbole* relates an object with its own possibilities of greatness, and (2) *hypotyposis*, or vivid description, associates an object with some of its many possible images. The six remaining kinds of metaphor are comparative since they associate different things. If based on likeness, the metaphors could be either by *similarities* (metaphor in the strict sense, associating similar objects) or by *pun* (associating similar words or sounds). If grounded on contraries, the metaphors frame either contrasting objects, that is *opposition* (antithesis), or contrary opinions, that is *urbane deception* (irony). If based on the adjuncts, the metaphors are either by *attribution* (metonymy), openly recognizing the adjuncts by making them metaphorically replace an object, or by *laconism*, apparently ignoring the adjuncts, but actually recognizing them by making them be missed and mentally reintroduced by the listener's reflection.[110]

---

abstract knowledge. Facts are perceived by the mind separately, and if collected, they are stored by the handy instrument of categorical inventories, without ceasing to contain plain experience. Facts serve prudential judgment. But meaning—the replacement of one thing by another—does not occur until ingenuity metaphorizes and produces correspondences between the facts. The understanding does it in a creative effort rather than an abstractive one. Universals appear as useful *names*, signs, or symbols which pragmatically stand for facts or concrete truths. But universals do not seem to be general truths about reality. Thus, it is not surprising that Tesauro applied his theory of ingenuity more often to productive than to theoretical or practical arts.

[110]See, for example, *Cannocchiale* Chapter 7: 280–304. Tesauro's terms for his metaphors are: *hiperbole, hipotiposi, metafora di proportione, equivoco, opposito, decettione, metafora di attributione*, and *laconismo*. Tesauro's metaphors are not an arbitrary classification, but a systematic attempt to reduce tropes to their general principles. Tesauro's systematization can fittingly be assimilated to Peter Ramus's four master tropes: synecdoche, metaphor, irony, and metonymy (Tesauro's adjuncts). See Conley 131. These four master tropes are a well established rhetorical lore present in ancient rhetoricians such

Although not discussed by Tesauro, the embodiment of these metaphors implicitly rests on an associative topical system like Pellegrini's; that is, on links which associate terms by means of a topical relationship. Tesauro's absolute or synecdochical metaphors express topical links of the intrinsic kind,[111] for example, genus-species, whole-parts, matter-form, name-definition, the actual-the possible, etc. And Tesauro's comparative metaphors express topical links of the intermediate kind;[112] they are either by similars, contraries, or adjuncts. Hence the foundations of Tesauro's theory of metaphor are material.[113] His theory of style is grounded on a theory of invention.

These material foundations of metaphor permit their strong assimilation into Tesauro's logical system. If metaphors produce a new idea by relating things, then metaphors contribute to the first logical operation: simple apprehension. If metaphors assert the relationship between the terms associated, then metaphors contribute to the second logical operation: judgment or the making of propositions. If metaphors produce a new idea, and relate this idea to the terms which prompted it, when these terms are associated in a proposition (here, the terms have increased from two to three), then metaphors contribute to the third logical operation: inference.[114]

For Tesauro, a single metaphor can encapsulate three operations of the mind.[115] An example of this logical richness contained in a single metaphor can

---

as Quintilian, and still recognized by contemporary rhetoricians such as Kenneth Burke. See Kenneth Burke, *A Grammar of Motives* (University of California Press, 1974) 501–517.

[111]Topics of the intrinsic kind refer to properties of the object itself. Cf. Boethius, *De topicis differentiis*, trans. by Eleonore Stump (Cornell University Press, 1978).

[112]Topics of the intermediate kind refer to properties of an object as discovered through other objects. Cf. Boethius, *De topicis differentiis*.

[113]These material foundations at least apply to the level of semiotic relationships in language.

[114]See *Cannocchiale* chapters 7, 8, and 9, which respectively address metaphorical simple apprehension, propositions, and inference.

[115]One may regard Tesauro's theories as absurd if one has been trained to consider words

be illustrated by one of Tesauro's preferred heraldic symbols: King Louis XII of France's porcupine. The porcupine prompts this inference: Do not mess with King Louis because, like the porcupine, he pierces—wounds—from near and afar.[116] Moreover, a single metaphor can encapsulate a complete discourse. Tesauro, for example, discussed *preaching concepts* (*"concetti predicabili"*)—a sort of religious metaphors, which if carefully analyzed prompt full sermons.[117]

Tesauro's insightfulness goes beyond the utterance of speech to address complex problems of human communication—for example, the chain-reaction of meanings potentially motivated by appearently simple messages inside a listener's ingenious mind.

In any case, Tesauro believed that methapors embraced every operation of the mind and that inferences were their crowning effort. This belief may explain why Tesauro considered *argutezza* the supreme effort of ingenuity. However, said Tesauro, metaphorical inference usually involves *puns*, or the equivocal use of language,[118] and thus involves a fallacy. He offered this example of fallacious induction:

My client should not be obliged to make any payment. This clearly follows from the contract. He promised to pay IN PEACE, but now we are at war since the siege of Vercelli has not ended; WITHOUT LAWSUIT, but a lawsuit has been filed by the creditor; WITHOUT PUBLIC DISCORD, but there is a great uproar in the city after the creditor's complaint; WITHOUT NEEDING TO SUMMON BEFORE A COURT, but now my

---

as terms which univocally symbolize simple apprehensions, but not whole propositions, and even inferences.

[116]King Louis's motto was "Eminus et Comminus." See *Cannocchiale* Chapter 15.

[117]See, for example, *Cannocchiale* Chapter nine, 501–540. Compare Tesauro's logically rich metaphors with Gracián's *pregnant words* ("Preñado ha de ser el verbo..."), which are words not stale, but fecund in meanings. See *Agudeza* Discourse 60. Finally, compare Tesauro's understanding of metaphors with Edwin Black's recent analysis of "the cancer of Communism" metaphor's many rhetorical implications. See Edwin Black, "The Second Persona" *The Quarterly Journal of Speech* (April 1970) 109–119.

[118]See *Cannocchiale* Chapter 7: 460–481.

client contradictorily appears before the judges.[119]

Tesauro's analysis of *argutezza* is in fact concentrated on fallacious enthymemes, the fallacious inferences contained—as he thought—in single metaphors. He called them *urbane enthymemes*.[120] An example he quoted was a warning to a great royal warrior about crossing a (an unsteady) bridge carefully, since under him all (enemies) tremble.[121]

Tesauro was not a fool by being an enthusiast advocate of this kind of fallacious reasoning. Tesauro believed that, although the inference was an error, the metaphorical correspondences established between the terms still were true (a bridge trembling and the enemies trembling under the king.) Concealed under the guise of an apparent reasoning, a true association of ideas suddenly is discovered. The wittiest kind of remarks—the most unexpected, unthinkable, impossible—are thus produced because through a fallacy a truth is apprehended.[122] The greatest kind of wonder—error is truth—gives place to the greatest kind of wonderment.[123]

Although every quibble is a *fallacy*, not every fallacy will be an *urbane quibble*, but

---

[119]*Cannocchiale* Chapter 7: 470. "Che il mio Cliente più non sia tenuto à pagamento niuno; dagli Atti medesimi chiaramente risulta. Egli ha promesso di pagare IN PACE: & hor siamo in guerra; continuando l' assedio sotto Vermicelli. SENZA LITE: & hor la lite è contestata dal Creditore. SENZA STREPITO: & ei ne hà fatto vn rumor grande per la Città. SENZA FORMA DE GIVDICIO: & hor si stà in Contradittorio dauanti a' giudici."

[120]See *Cannocchiale* Chapter 9: 487–500.

[121]See *Cannocchiale* Chapter 9: 489.

[122]Since they rise from error, these wittiest remarks are the supreme kind of true apprehensions, and thus the ones which deserve to be called true concepts. Tesauro, like his Italian fellow theorists, did not use the term concept in its broad logical meaning of simple apprehension. He reserved the term concept to those witty observations fashioned by means of an urbane enthymeme. See *Cannocchiale* Chapter 9: 487–500.

[123]The aesthetic experience of wonderment does not seem to be a central issue in Gracián's doctrine, and that strongly differentiates him from the Italian theorists of wit.

only such a quibble that without malice, and rather playfully imitates the truth, but does not supress it, and imitates what is false, but only apparently, in a fashion that lets truth show as if through a veil.[124]

That explains Tesauro's enthusiasm for fallacious enthymemes: it applies to wit. *Argutezza* is subsumed to *acutezza*, and thus the primacy of conceptualization over inference is restated.[125] Considering again Tesauro's example of urbane enthymeme, although it is wrong hastily to infer trembling bridges from trembling enemies, it is valid to conceptualize from the relationship of trembling enemies and trembling bridges the idea of overwhelming power, and just then, after this conceptualization, it is right to infer the careful use which must be attached to that power, whose abuse would not only tear down bridges, but also enemies, subjects, and a whole kingdom. Therefore, the king should be merciful.

Other examples also may illustrate the full sense of Tesauro's belief in *argutezza* as intellect's utmost effort. For Tesauro, Suetonius's remark on Nero would not be just a fashionable and stylistic relationship of ideas, as it was for Pellegrini. In Suetonius's remark, Tesauro would see Nero's depravation as a sign of the corruption which Roman customs underwent through the centuries. Moreover, in Taft's observation, Tesauro somehow could recognize the *Cong*ress's tendency to delay decisions through lenghty *con*troversies as opposed to *prog*ressing in the decision making and in the reaching of an agreement.

The assimilation of style to invention does not occur only in what Tesauro called the ingenious figures (Tesauro's metaphors). It also applies to the other kind of figures and instruments of style. The example of antithesis—which I

---

[124]*Cannocchiale* Chapter nine, 494. "...sebene ogni Cauillatione sia vna *fallacia*; non perciò qualunque fallacia sarà *Cauillatione Vrbana*: ma quella solamente, che senza dolo malo, scherzeuolmente imita la verità, ma non l' opprime: & imita la falsità in guisa, che il vero vi traspaia come per vn velo..."

[125]Although following a convoluted way, Tesauro came to endorse one of the central theses of conceptist theory: the primacy of conceptualization over inference. This thesis was one of Gracián's basic premises when preparing his theory of wit.

mentioned above—illustrates how Tesauro associated periodic style, rhythmical composition, and figures of speech with logical operations. Figures of thought also are very strongly attached to reason. Tesauro indeed gave to these figures the full meaning of *thought*: the different acts performed by human reason. If acts of understanding, reason expresses herself through figures such as knowledge, doubt, ignorance, assertion, denial, testimony, correction, remembrance, interrogation, response, interpretation, narration, oath, reflection, objection, fiction, imagination, argumentation, etc. If acts of the will[126] as such, reason expresses herself through figures such as perplexity, approbation, deliberation, authority, admonition, dissuasion, etc. If acts of embracing or resisting passions, reason expresses herself through figures such as salutation, adulation, appreciation, abomination, hope, fear, threat, deprecation, etc.[127]

I would present two final comments on Tesauro's theories of wit. First, if the reader is concerned with printing his own money, founding a royal dynasty, or assuring his place and memory in history, he should go to *Cannocchiale*.

---

[126]Strongly attached to scholasticism, theorists of wit did not split will from reason. For them, it was an act of reason to will what was understood as good. They did not reduce the movements of the soul to sensuous passions, as modern thinkers often did later. Consider, for example, the rationalist Blaise Pascal, the great enemy of these witty Jesuits. He transferred the persuasion of the will to an "art of pleasing", as if gaining the will rested on bribing it with sweets. See Blaise Pascal, *On Geometrical Demonstration*, Section II. Consider also Bernard Lamy, the great rationalist rhetorician. For him, "men are not to be acted, but by motion of their passions," and by that he meant that a man "follows that which gives him most pleasure." Moreover, "a man is wholly in our power, when we are able to stir in him such Passions." And that is accomplished—according to Lamy—by the figures, whose sensuous features, by resembling real passions, strongly affect the mind of people. See *The Rhetorics of Thomas Hobbes and Bernard Lamy*, ed. John T. Harwood (Southern Illinois University Press, 1986) 362-363, 241–250. Great empiricist rhetoricians were not far from this view. Consider, for example, George Campbell, who regarded passions as the movers to action, and sensations as the exciters of passions. See George Campbell, *The Philosophy of Rhetoric*, ed. Lloyd F. Bitzer (Southern Illinois University Press, 1988) 77-81. With this view, the empiricists' stress on resemblance and vivacity, as qualities of the language which persuades the will, is not surprising.

[127]Tesauro analyzes figures of thought in *Cannocchiale* Chapter 5.

There he will find sound advice about the design of coins, the rules of drawing and explaining coats of arms, and brilliant guidelines about writing epitaphs.[128] Second and not less important, Tesauro's book offers an extraordinary effort to link verbal and rational persuasion with the broad realm of symbols.[129] His book may be a good point of departure for a great field: the rhetoric of semiology.[130]

---

[128]See *Cannocchiale* chapters 17, 15, and 13.

[129]See, for example, *Cannocchiale* chapters 14 and 18.

[130]Clear cases of rhetorical messages from this broad field are political cartoons, which indeed provide witty arguments on forensic, epideictic, and deliberative issues in newspapers.

6   The Age of Reason

THE WORK OF SCHOLARS NEXT TO Pellegrini, Gracián, Pallavicino, and Tesauro did not echo these Jesuits' theorizing effort. The conceptist spirit declined. To some degree, it did not take root because its theories of wit were received as if posing issues of pure style. In a more definite way, wit could not keep its honorable place within the schools because of the irruption of the Age of Reason.

The Franco-Italian Controversy on Wit

This fate was announced by a curious fact of cultural history, reported by Arturo del Hoyo:[1] because of their up-to-date character, Baltasar Gracián's writings became the model from which Spanish language was taught in Europe by the middle of the seventeenth century, and somehow, considering the prominent place of Spanish culture in Europe during that period, these writings were also a model for writing in many countries under Spanish influence, regardless of the language.

This use of Gracián would annoy many educators and students. Gracián may be exquisite, but he would be a torture if his extremely difficult writings were used as models for the elementary learning of a language. In purely stylistic terms, promoting Gracián's use of witty correspondences in every composition offends simplicity—it insults the usually more sensible choice of informing about a subject by following a single discursive line.[2] Finally, an excessively high regard for wit may degenerate into an unbridled ingenuity. What propriety would occasionally use to get an insight into complex subjects, abuse would turn

---

[1]See Arturo del Hoyo cc–cci.

[2]Being a master of wit, Gracián's writings apparently endorse a profuse use of wit. However, Gracián himself was opposed to the abuse of wit in writing. See, for example, *Agudeza* discourses 60 to 62.

into a pure display of cleverness and reduce to a low kind of ornament piled on indiscriminately and meaninglessly.

The fact is that Gracián's popularity provoked a reaction among the new enthusiasts of Reason, and led them to defend what they regarded as simplicity and good taste.[3] In 1660, two years after Gracián's death—reports Arturo del Hoyo—, Claude Lancelot published in Paris a method of teaching Spanish that censored the use of Gracián and Malvezzi as stylistic models. Later, the Jesuit Dominique Bouhours would follow Lancelot's footsteps. In his *Entretiens d' Artiste et Eugène* (1671), Bouhours extensively rebuked Gracián's witty extravagances. Gracián found defenders in France, for example, Amelot de la Houssaie, who translated Gracián's *Oráculo* in 1684 and endorsed Gracián's style. However, Bouhours persisted to object against this Spaniard, when he published *La manière de bien penser* (1687), and in doing so Bouhours trampled on many Italians who were also practitioners of wit. Italians then reacted, either to restore their national pride, separate themselves from Spanish excesses, or truly defend wit as the mind's most excellent activity. Among the works they published are G. G. Orsi's *Considerationi sopra un famoso libro franzese intitolato La manière de bien penser* (1703), Bernardoni, Muratori, Salvini, Bedoni, Torti, and other Italian authors' *Lettere di diversi autori in proposito delle considerationi di Orsi* (1706), Muratori's *Della perfeta poesia* (1706), G. Fontanini's *Della eloquenza italiana. Ragionamento* (1706) and *Ragionamento in difesa delle Consideracioni sobra il libro delle Manière* (1708), and Gravina's *Della ragion poetica* (1708).[4] A paradox behind this dispute—Arturo

---

[3] To some degree, the controversy around Gracián's style promoted the association of bad taste with Spanish literature by the time the Age of Reason started. How much this association sprang only from the abuses of wit attributed to Gracián and other Spaniards, how far it also responded to national cultural rivalries, and to hatred against anything Spanish in times when, in spite of her decadence, Spain still had strong influence in politics and culture in the world, may yet require more careful elucidation. In this period, even syphilis was a Spanish disease, and many ideas like these have endured and permeated broad clusters of beliefs about Spain, such as the Black Legend.

[4] For the Franco-Italian dispute on wit, see Arturo del Hoyo cc–cci, and Mooney 105, 135–158.

del Hoyo ponders—is that Bouhours admired much of Gracián's work. Bouhours weighed Gracián's merits in a third book: *Pensées ingenieuses des anciens et des moderns*. Bouhours even attempted the impossible and futile task of translating Gracián's *Agudeza* into French, a treatise which resists fair translations and only admits adaptations into other languages.[5]

Among the great Italian defenders of the art of ingenuity during the Age of Reason was Giambattista Vico. In his *Institutiones oratoriae* (1711), he tried to restore ingenuity's high esteem by distinguishing between bad and good wit. *Dicta arguta* should be rejected since they consist in sterile cleverness—a bane of mankind. However, *dicta acuta* are

> ...sharp-witted statements...having enthymematic force, with incisiveness equal to their conciseness, born of imaginative, ingenious minds' intent of discovering the true; through them listeners see novel visions an discover new relationships, sinners are reduced to tears, implausible cases are won in courts, legislation is gotten through intractable assemblies.
>
> ....
>
> *Acuta* derive from truth and succeed when they teach; *arguta* arise from playfulness and succeed when they deceive.[6]

Thus, when Vico wrote his *New Science* (1723–1744), a purified ingenuity sheltered within *acutezza*'s boundaries rose as the great master of civilizations.

> ...ingenuity is the source of all innovation and culture...how laboriously it is gained and how quickly lost by men, being as they are "first stupid and rough, later docile and capable of being disciplined, then perspicacious, after which keen [*acuti*] and able to discover, finally shrewd [*arguti*], astute, and fraudulent..." Philosophy, geometry, philology, jurisprudence—the whole of learning shows us how ludicrous it is to fight ingenuity with truth. The acuities of oratory, to cite only one such example, give the pleasure they do because they show relationships that only the ingenious can see. Witty remarks (*dicta arguta*), on the other hand, arise from a "feeble and narrow imagination"...and out of a spirit of trickery.   Led to expect

---

[5]Cf. Arturo del Hoyo cci, and Coster 275–293.

[6]Mooney 157.

one thing, the hearer is told another, and thus convulses with laughter.[7]

Inspired by this purified notion of ingenuity, Vico undertook the task of conceiving his new science of humanity, explaining the natural unfolding which societies and cultures observe through centuries, depending on the different developmental stages of the ingenuity of the peoples involved. Law, institutions, language, cultures and societies themselves are thus the result of this supreme power of ingenuity.[8]

However, this purified notion of wit did not seem to prosper. Although Spain in many ways was alien to the modern trends in Europe, that did not make her a safe shelter for sound theorizing on wit. Her scholars abandoned the insightful approach of Gracián into human conceptualization, and took ingenuity down to the byways of mere puns and quibbles. At least this is the way Menéndez Pelayo describes Francisco José de Artiga's *Epítome de la elocuencia española* (1726),[9] and seemingly that is also the case of Fernando de Velasco y Pimentel's *Arte de Agudeza*, which advertises itself as an "easy school of acuities" and a "nosegay...of clever flashes of wit."[10]

The Rise of Modern Philosophy and the Fall of Wit

In the rest of Europe, the spirit characterizing seventeenth-century theories of wit could not survive as such, since its two principal foundations of classical rhetoric and scholasticism were strongly questioned by the new philosophies of the modern age. Both rationalism and empiricism claimed to depart from a rejection of any previous dogmatism. Any knowledge transmited by tradition was

---

[7]Mooney 158.

[8]Cf. Peter Burke, *Vico* (Oxford University Press, 1985) 32–88.

[9]See Menéndez Pelayo 582.

[10]See Correa Calderón, *Baltasar Gracián* 286.

banished. A new start from zero was announced. Rationalists would commence with the few and general ideas which are clearly and undoubtedly distinguished by the mind, reaching truth through geometrical demonstration. Empiricists would rather acknowledge sensuous experience only, and truth would have a probable character depending on psychological processes by which images fix themselves in the fancy. There was no place for the scholastic principle giving life to baroque theories of wit: that truths (or at least ideas) are abstract and yet apprehended from experience by a complex effort of the mind. For the rationalist, truths are not apprehended, but already given in those ideas clearly distinguished or geometrically inferred by reason. For the empiricist, the closest to abstract knowledge are compounds of images which the fancy processes. The closest to truth is belief, whose sources are the relatively constant images to which a mind is accustomed through forces of vivacity, steadiness, proximity, or resemblance effected by experience. The Age of Reason would not be an enthusiastic recipient of the fruits of the Age of Wit.

This was not completely the case for empiricists writers. Even though empiricism denied abstract knowledge, and with it, the scholastic problem of conceptualization, empiricism nevertheless relied on experience, and to acquire this experience, empiricism strongly endorsed the notion of the association of ideas. However, what the empiricists understood by association of ideas stripped the seventeenth-century theories of wit of their conceptist foundations.

In fact, many works addressing the issue of wit were published in England during the seventeenth and eighteenth centuries.[11] And these works covered the whole spectrum of meanings attached to the elusive power of wit. According to John Oldmixon,

Wit and Humour, Wit and good Sense, Wit and Wisdom, Wit and Reason, Wit

---

[11]A very comprehensive, complete, and alternative account of the age of wit in England can be found in D. Judson Milburn, *The Age of Wit 1650–1750*, (New York: The MacMillan Company, 1966).

and Craft; nay, Wit and Philosophy, are with us almost the same Things.[12]

However, since Thomas Hobbes wrote his treatises in the middle of the seventeenth century, wit in different degrees was associated either with judgment or with fancy,[13] or with their compound which integrated human understanding.[14]

Wit either as judgment or as sound understanding became a very restrained method of associating ideas. The pointed and unexpected turns of wit were unthinkable as pertaining to judgment. Judgment could not accept whims of the fancy that connected distant facts unrelated by sense data.[15] Judgment rather rested on solid experience, with close relationship among the facts associated. Judgment could only associate either sensed facts of the same kind (argument by example), or sensed facts of a similar kind (argument by analogy).[16] Thus, the association of ideas in judgment consisted in a sort of induction[17] which

---

[12]John Oldmixon, *Essay on Criticism* (1727) 21, as quoted by Edward N. Hooker, "Introduction," *Essays on Wit* 1st. ser. 2 (University of California: The Augustan Reprint Society, 1946) 1.

[13]Cf. Hooker 1–2, who quotes Hobbes's *Human Nature* X, iv, and *Leviathan*, I, viii.

[14]Cf. Hooker 1, quoting Walter Charleton's *Brief Discourse concerning the Different Wits of Men*, (1669) 10, 17–19.

[15]Cf. Lord Henry Home Kames, *Elements of Criticism* (1776) Chapter One, 19.

[16]Cf., for example, George Campbell *The Philosophy of Rhetoric*, Ed. Lloyd F. Bitzer. (Southern Illinois University Press, 1974) 43–58. Campbell also included testimony and caluculation of chances in his forms of evidence.

[17]The validity of this kind of induction may be questioned by formal logicians since it does not rest on the sameness of terms—something which I think could only be known or formally granted through conceptualization, an operation of the mind denied by empiricists through their denial of abstract thought. The validity of this kind of induction rather rests on something as *logically* vague and unwarrantable, I think, as sensuous resemblance, contiguity, and custom. (These were Hume's criteria for associating ideas. Cf. David Hume, *An Enquiry Concerning Human Understanding*). If some validity is granted to this kind of induction, its nature is psychological rather than logical since it refers to processes how the human mind may fix its own beliefs. Then empiricism would not surprisingly be described as a

became reliable depending on the many repetitions of an homogeneous set of experiences and its strength of fixation in the human mind.[18]

If these precautions against non-easily identifiable sensuous associations gave solidity to the methods of natural sciences, they often deterred scholars from accepting fields of more abstract speculation involving bolder flights of understanding.[19] Metaphysics was automatically discarded.[20] For some scholars such as Lord Kames, even genuine invention—the reaching of new and unusual ideas beyond the ordinariness of sensuous facts, including the great ideas of geniuses—was not the result of good sense, but of mistaken operations of the association of ideas, which by chance grasped an extraordinary perception of things.[21] Moral reasoning was chained to sensations. Moving people to action was reduced to stirring up their passions.[22] Moral values were not something which required an extreme effort of understanding to be learned, or a conscious and valiant determination of the will to be followed. Values were rather something already instilled in human nature—self-evident in the form of common sense or moral sentiments. Their discovery sprang from feeling those sentiments,[23] and their embracement sprang from just letting oneself be pulled

---

philosophical psychology.

[18]Hume's sources of belief were vivacity of sensations, whose appeal was to the imagination; steadiness of sensations, whose appeal was to memory; and association of sensations, whose appeal was to experience.

[19]Here, I can identify the seeds of what Wayne C. Booth called scientism—the modern dogma of only accepting as reasonable an argument grounded on known and sensuous facts. See Wayne C. Booth, *Modern Dogma and The Rhetoric of Assent* (The University of Chicago Press, 1974).

[20]Not only the abstraction, but also the comprehensiveness of metaphysics made it unacceptable for empiricists. Metaphysical associations extend to all beings and trascend the realm of sensual resemblances and even actual existence.

[21]See Lord Henry Home Kames, *Elements of Criticism* (1776). This view might be related to pop-culture's recent conception of geniuses and scientists as madmen.

[22]See George Campbell 77–81.

[23]Here I found the seeds of what Wayne Booth called motivism—the modern irrationalist

along by those feelings.[24] Therefore, good judgment—or as many authors put it in that age, good taste[25]—did not depend on an active ingenuity but on a given genius's competence to taste experience: the larger amount of natural talents a person is endowed with, the better that person judges or feels that experience. Thus, good judgment was not an action of the mind, but just a fact of being born with a better nature[26]—the result of being a genius.[27]

---

dogma of endorsing values or justifying actions as result of pure feelings. See Wayne C. Booth, *Modern Dogma and the Rhetoric of Assent.*

[24]Cf. Adam Smith, *The Theory of Moral Sentiments*, (1759); Thomas Reid, *An Inquiry into the Human Mind on the Principles of Common Sense* (1764).

[25]Spaniards apparently were the people who introduced the subject of good taste into criticism. Cf. Menéndez Pelayo 584–585, who quotes Bernardo Trevisano, "Introducción" *Reflexiones de Muratori sobre el buen gusto* (Venice, 1736). Baltasar Gracián indeed included rich discussions on the nature of good taste in his *Héroe*, his *Discreto*, and his *Oráculo*. Yet, I wonder how much the Spanish word *gusto* should necessarily and metaphorically be associated with the discerning powers of the tongue (with this metaphorical association present in English language, judgment—in so far as taste—becomes an issue of sensations). *Gusto* in Spanish does not mean only the sensuous enjoyments of cuisine, but also, and in a more ordinary way, it is a word derived from *gustar*, which means to like. *Gusto* thus is a synonym of predilection, very close to election and choice, and it does not always entail, in Spanish, attachments to sensations.

[26]Cf. David Hume, *Of the Standards of Taste*: "Where the organs are so fine as to allow nothing to escape them, and at the same time so exact as to perceive every ingredient in the composition, this we call delicacy of taste, whether we employ these terms in the literal or metaphorical sense." Cf., also, William Duff, *An Essay on Original Genius* (1767) ed. John Mahoney (Florida: Scholars' Facsimiles & Reprints, 1964); Alexander Gerard, *An Essay on Genius* (1774) ed. Bernhard Fabian (Wilhelm Fink Verlag München, 1966). In Spain, the quality of understanding as necessarily the result of genius or special talent was discussed by Juan Huarte in his *Examen de Ingenios* (1575). As I indicated above, Gracián rejected this opinion because, for him, the artistic rules of understanding are general, trascend special natures, and are useful for all people. Even so, *genius*—understood as a particular kind of talents or inclinations—is an important component of Gracián's theories of deliberation.

[27]In his "Introduction" to Gerard's *Essay on Genius* xlvii–xlviii, Bernard Fabian considers the romantic movement as a direct result of eighteenth century theories of genius. Being a good artist only implied being a genius—being endowed with a powerful imagination. Artistic rules—rhetoric—were just accessory, and thus irrelevant.

The lack of good judgment was implied in the narrower understanding of wit as just fancy. Unexpected, adventurous turns of this type of wit were marks of a person naturally endowed with a powerful imagination. But, also, these turns probably were the marks of a person naturally endowed with poor judgment, incapable of controlling the associations made by his fancy.[28] The admissibility of fancyful wit was even questioned in literature, where major works of art were said to imply the intervention of good taste—that means good judgment.[29] Many discussions of fanciful wit were thus narrowed into studying or criticizing minor literary productions whose main features would be humor, clever wordplays, jests, raillery[30]—to some degree, that kind of wit that Vico described as *arguta* instead of *acuta*.

In empiricist systems, an additional characteristic of fanciful wit was that its aesthetic appeal was reduced to imagination. If present in minor works of art, as the kind of playful literature just mentioned above, fanciful wit's appeal would be to the passion of the laughable. If present in major works of art, the appeal of this fancy would be by means of sensuous beauty. However, abstract

---

[28]Cf. Lord Kames 19.

[29]Cf. Hooker 2–3.

[30]See, for example, Sir Richard Blackmore, *Essay upon Wit* (1716); Joseph Addison, *Freeholder* 45 (1716); *Essay on Wit* (1748); Richard Flecnoe, *Of a bold abusive Wit* (1665); Joseph Warton, *The Adventurer* 127 and 133 (1754); *Of Wit* (*Weekly Register*, 1732); John Gay, *The Present State of Wit* (1711). All these works are reprinted in *Essays on Wit* (The Augustan Reprint Society 1st ser. 1–3, 1946–1947). In addition to these authors, I would call attention to the exceptional character of Corbyn Morris, whose description of wit is close to baroque authors: "It is the Province of Wit to *elucidate* or *enlighten* a Subject, not by reasoning upon that Subject, but by a just and unexpected Introduction of another *similar*, or *opposite* Subject; whereby, upon their *arrangement* together, the *original* Subject may be *set off*, and more clearly enlighten'd, by their obvious Comparison." Corbyn Morris, *An Essay towards Fixing the True Standars of Wit, Humour, Raillery, Satire, and Ridicule* (1744) (The Augustan Reprint Society 1st. ser. 4, 1947) 1. An important feature of Morris's theories is his distinction between similes and metaphor in contrast with wit's comparisons. The former imply many sensuous associations which adorn the speech but introduce many points which do not pertain to the case. Wit's comparisons concentrate only in those points which are relevant to the case. See Morris 3–5.

pleasures—intellectual delights similar to baroque wonderment—would not be part of the aesthetic theories of empiricist authors.[31]

In the twentieth century, some philosophers of argumentation still long for an understanding of knowledge as something which requires some mental effort to be reached. For example, Stephen Toulmin believes that "one of the unexamined axioms of modern philosophy" is "the doctrine that 'All our knowledge is either immediate or inferential.'"[32] Behind this axiom is the rationalist belief that true understanding only comes from clear ideas[33] and deductions, and the empiricist belief that true understanding only comes from clear facts and inductions. Contrasting with these beliefs, baroque theories of wit postulated their doctrines of strenuous conceptualization, in which ideas need to be apprehended, intellectually abstracted from experience, before any process of judgment or inference is to be followed.

---

[31]See, for example, Lord Kames's *Elements of Criticism*, Hume's *Of the Standards of Taste*, and Edmund Burke's *The Sublime and the Beautiful*. I should notice that Edmund Burke did not find empiricism sufficient to explain the pleasures of the beautiful and the sublime. He said: "The truth is, if poetry gives us a noble assemblage of words, corresponding to many noble ideas, which are connected by circumstances of time or place, or related to each other as cause and effect, or associated in any natural way, they may be moulded together in any form, and perfectly answer their end. The picturesque connection is not demanded; because no real picture is formed; nor is the effect of the description at all the less upon this account." Edmund Burke 171. This passage echoes the baroque aesthetics of correspondences, and even a theory of topics as general kinds of relationships between terms.

[32]Stephen Toulmin, *The Uses of Argument* (Cambridge University Press, 1958) 247.

[33]Although still grounding his thought on the modern axioms, Edmund Burke nevertheless expressed his dissatisfaction about them as follows: "A clear idea is therefore another name for a little idea." See Burke 63.

Part Two

A Rhetoric for Wits

7   Gracián's Life, Works, and "Rhetoric"

THE SPANISH KINGDOM OF ARAGÓN IS FAMOUS because of the simple-mindedness attributed to its rustic inhabitants.[1] But, in fact, this kingdom has produced some of the most keen-minded personalities of World history: Aragón was the homeland of the wittiest Latin writer, Martial; it also was the country of Saint Laurentius, the wit among the martyrs, a joyous deacon who, displaying extreme composure, still had time to joke gently with his executioner while being grilled alive on a hot rack during Valerian's persecution; Ferdinand The Catholic was Aragón's son and king—a king who was the exemplar of princely shrewdness for Machiavelli, and of active prudence for Gracián, since Ferdinand founded the great Spanish Empire less by military actions than by sensible political maneuvering.

Father Baltasar Gracián y Morales

Baltasar Gracián was not only an additional character in the long line of witty people from Aragón, he was also very self-conscious of his ingenuity and often explained it through his race. For Gracián, Martial was more than a literary preference. Martial was Gracián's countryman in a very close sense. Martial was born in Bílbilis (today's Calatayud), whereas Gracián was born in Belmonte, a suburban area of this ancient city, a place, according to Gracián, where a fool has never been found.[2] Saint Laurentius was born in Huesca, the Aragonese city where Gracián found the most propitious environment for his

---

[1]Although the people of Aragón were not perceived in the seventeenth century with the humourous features of a *Baturro* yet, they already were a paradigm of pigheadedness. See Miguel Herrero García, *Ideas de los Españoles del Siglo XVII* (Madrid: Editorial Gredos, S. A., 1966) 275–276.

[2]See *El Criticón* III, Crisi 6. "...no hay ningún necio en Calatayud..."

literary activities.[3] For Gracián, Ferdinand was the embodiment of all Aragonese virtues—virtues wanting in the morally and mentally deficient Spanish kings of the decadent seventeenth century.[4]

It was in Aragón that Gracián spent most of his life. However, Gracián was not sedentary. He often traveled through many cities of this kingdom and of some other kingdoms in Spain, in order to fulfill his different duties. He moved back and forth from Calatayud to Toledo, Saragossa, Valencia, Lérida, Gandía, Huesca, Madrid, Navarra, Tarragona, Graus, and Tarazona. He became a student, and then a Jesuit, and went on to teach grammar, moral theology (especially casuistry), and philosophy, preach before audiences of thousands, be a confessor of noblemen, the only surviving military chaplain of the Royal Army during bloody battles, act as temporary vice chancellor of a Jesuit College, participate as an elector in a Jesuit provincial convention, and accomplish other activities fitting to his estate.

In his itinerant life, he did not have the opportunity to introduce himself fully into the best of Spanish society and its intellectual elite. Some authors have seen in this failure Gracián's bitter resentment towards the Spanish Court.[5] However, in his youth in Toledo, he could at least hear about the greatest intellectual events of that time such as the evening parties given by Góngora, Paravicino, and El Greco.[6] And in Gracián's every day life, he could also be the friend of important provincial noblemen, for example, Don Vincencio Juan de Lastanosa, of Huesca, and Francesco Maria Carafa, Duke of Nocera, and Viceroy of Aragón, under whose protection and within whose intellectual circles, Gracián

---

[3]In his works, Gracián several times made reference of Saint Laurentius, noticing his ingenuity as often as his holiness. See, for example, *El Héroe* Primor 4.

[4]Gracián summarized his regard for Ferdinand with his opening sentence of *El Político*: "I *oppose* a king to all kings who have already passed; I *propose* a king to all kings who have still to come." ("Opongo un rey a todos los pasados; propongo un rey a todos los venideros.")

[5]Cf., for example, Alborg 2: 836–838.

[6]See Arturo del Hoyo xiv.

could develop his literary activities.

Describing Gracián as a man errant surpasses its physical meaning and reflects also his alternating spirit, keenly responding to contingencies, and trying to balance in the best possible way his many, usually legitimate, but very conflicting loyalties. As a military chaplain, Gracián risked death backing the Royal Army during the Succour of Lérida. However, he did not let his friendship with Nocera falter, when the Viceroy was found guilty of high treason.[7] For the sake of comradeship, Gracián did not complain when the Canon Manuel de Salinas y Lizana laid his hand on the *Agudeza*'s second edition to introduce into it his questionable translations of Martial's *Epigrams* into Spanish. However, in an ultimate effort of persuasion, Gracián did not hesitate to call Salinas a "jackass",[8] to prevent the canon from publishing some badly written Latin verses. Gracián's candor made the canon put an end to their friendship. Although a prominent priest in his community, Gracián swore in the notorious tradition of blaspheming peculiar to Spaniards.[9] Loyal to the ideals of

---

[7]Gracián dedicated *El Político* to Nocera in times when the latter's clemency was already clashing with King Philip IV's harsh punishment against the rebels of Catalunia. After Nocera's imprisonment, ·Gracián openly defended the Duke's policies of clemency in the *Agudeza*, Discourse 55. Gracián also theorized on the political importance of clemency in *El Discreto*, Realce 4, making it one of the most important marks of lordship. Contrastingly, in *El Discreto*, Realce 16, Gracián reproved the vice of *hazañería*, a sort of ineffectual and vulgar display of power beloved by the masses, and currently and notoriously practiced by the king. Cf. Arturo del Hoyo xlii–xlviii and cliv–clv.

[8]See *Gracián's Letter to Salinas, March, 1652*. Refuting some arguments of Salinas about the correct use of Latin, Gracián responded: "...the word *orium*, plural of *os*, *oris*—Your Worship answered that Pliny made use of it; this, my lord, was a mistake of the purist grammarian and most true "Asino" (*jackass*, by purposeful equivocation) Dispauterio, who for the sake of reading *earum* wrote *orium*..." ("...la dicción *orium*, plural de *os, oris*, responde v. m., que Plinio la usa; éste, señor mío, fué un error del puro gramático y verdadero "Asino" Dispauterio, que por leer *earum* puso *orium*...")

[9]See, for example, in *Gracián's Letter to a Jesuit in Madrid, 29 de julio de 1642*, Gracián's explanation of his request to an onlooker of a royal parade: "For the Devil's sake, shut up..." ("Callá, diablos...") Of course, Gracián is still very far from the basest levels of Spanish blaspheming.

the Society of Jesus, Gracián was a visiting professor in Gandía and other cities outside Aragón, in order to promote the values of international brotherhood within a Spain divided by regional strife. However, in spite of his best intentions, Gracián rather stirred up this kind of quarrel because of his impatience with the Jesuits of Valencia, and his partiality for Aragón.[10] He accepted the most unpleasant duties for the sake of the Society of Jesus. For example, he prevented a rich widow from stripping the Jesuit House of Tarragona of an inheritance conferred on it by her husband.[11] However, for twenty years, Gracián had the utmost disregard for getting the Jesuit imprimatur for his books, and, after their publication, he had the greatest ability to cope with and avoid reprimands from his superiors.[12] Gracián's unbiased judgment often surprises his readers. For example, he earnestly praised the Bishop of Puebla, México, for his outstanding piety and wit, regardless of Juan de Palafox's active enimity against the Jesuits.[13] Nevertheless, Gracián has become notorious

---

[10]Cf., for example, Arturo del Hoyo cx–cxiii, and Batllori 62–70. The Jesuits of Valencia's resentment against Gracián caused this writer many troubles. They continuously denounced any kind of fault in Gracián's life to his superiors, aiming to put Gracián in disgrace. The Jesuits of Valencia finally succeeded when they brought to their superior's attention Gracián's continuous disregard for the publishing policies of the Society, and when these Valencians finally were outraged because of feeling themselves alluded by Gracián's satire against religious hypocrisy (*El Criticón* II, Crisi 7).

[11]See Arturo del Hoyo liii–liv.

[12]Cf., for example, Alborg 2: 826–835. Gracián often was tolerated because he did not publish his books with his own name—although it was well known who he was—, and because he strategically combined his mischiefs with the need for his services by the Society. In any case, he was finally disciplined, less because the superiors wanted to punish him than because they wanted to display equity after having punished some Jesuits of Valencia for mischiefs similar to those of Gracián: publishing satires of Jesuits from other kingdoms—in their particular case, a bold satire against Gracián. Cf., also, Arturo del Hoyo lxxxviii–cxviii. The proportionally kind and delayed punishment of Gracián, compared with the harsher and quicker punishment of the Jesuits of Valencia, could be explained by the moral and artistic quality which separated Gracián's satires from those of his Valencian brothers.

[13]See *Agudeza* Discourse 56; *El Discreto* Realce 18. Blessed Juan de Palafox is an extreme case of incorruptibility: his corpse remains fresh and untouched in its coffin.

because of his probably intentional silence about Miguel de Cervantes.[14] Gracián wrote some of the intellectually sharpest prose in Spanish of all ages. However, he was banned from preaching a sermon on the fictional theme of receiving a letter from Hell—a possibly childish trick to startle and entertain his audience.[15]

Gracián's alternating spirit have made some scholars identify his deep morality and religious principles with the tortuosities of a bad casuist.[16] But even in a trivialized assestment of Gracián, his dilemmas are certainly more facinating and genuine than those of some modern professionals who today negotiate and balance their loyalties to their families, communities, profession, corporation, and whims in the light of what better pays the bill. Gracián might have negotiated all that as well, but he did it in the light of what made him grow better in character and wisdom—to be the Wit, the Keen Critic, the Hero, the Politician, the Discreet Person, the Prudent Gentleman, the Saint he advertised in his treatises.

Gracián's Works

Gracián's works are what give him an outstanding place in history. They are among the best prose ever written in Spanish. They introduced key words into Castilian, to express moral issues in ways not achieved yet in other languages.[17] His narrative *El Criticón* is unique in its allegorical class. His *Agudeza* provided an aesthetic and a rhetorical theory for the Spanish baroque. And summarizing all, his moral doctrines act as the unifying impulse which defines and organizes

---

[14]Cf., for example, Ceferino Peralta, S. I., "La ocultación de Cervantes en Baltasar Gracián", *Gracián y su Época*, (Zaragoza: Institución Fernando el Católico, 1986) 137–156.

[15]See Alborg 2: 831; Arturo del Hoyo liv–lv.

[16]See Arturo del Hoyo xxvi.

[17]See Margarita Morreale, "Castiglione y 'El Héroe': Gracián y 'Despejo,'" *Homenaje a Gracián*, (Institución "Fernando el Católico," 1958) 137.

all his works.

In brief, Gracián's books are a meditation on being a superior person by fully exercising the person's moral powers. His doctrines belong to the field of morality, although not so much because they prescribe moral codes or a philosophy of ethics, but the more because they attempt to provide an art for the exercise of a person's highest faculties within his moral environment.

> Here you will have...a reason of state for your own self, a compass guiding you to excellence, a noble art of being—of being superior, expressed in few rules of discretion.[18]

In 1637, already a mature man, Gracián published *El Héroe*—the key for understanding his system of ideas. This book is the one which systematically presents the main concepts which reappear in his later treatises: the *señorío*[19] (or mastery) of a person over his own moral life, the very comprehensive power of understanding which includes ingenuity, prudence, judgment, predilection and election, and the will as the personal force which leads to fruitful actions; moreover, several social circumstances which, if managed properly, may enhance a person's moral powers, and the great end of virtue, as the actualization of all the moral potentials of a person through his life.

Gracián published *El Político, Don Fernando el Católico* in 1640.[20] This

---

[18]*El Héroe* "Al Lector." "Aquí tendrás...una razón de estado de ti mismo, una brújula de marear a la excelencia, una arte de ser ínclito con pocas reglas de discreción".

[19]It is difficult to translate the term *señorío* into English. To appreciate this difficulty, consider, for example, that *señor, señora,* and *señorita*—whose meanings express moral sovereignty, authority, competence, and others ideas discussed later in Chapter Eight—hardly match with the poorer meanings of *sir, mistress,* and *miss*—terms also poorer in word derivations. Without any other better choice, from now on I will use "mastery" as the English translation for "señorío." "Self-mastery" could better express the emphasis of the term on being lord of oneself, in order to be lord of everything else thereafter. But the term "mastery" is more comprehensive than "self-mastery," since it includes the external areas in which the person also exercises sovereignty as result of his self-mastery.

[20]The earliest edition preserved of this treatise is from 1646.

brief book is less a panegyric to Ferdinand than an academic discourse on the virtues of a monarch—virtues exemplarly illustrated by Ferdinand's case. According to Gracián, *El Político* addresses real rules of policy instead of codes of utopian republics.[21] The welfare of a nation is highly dependent on the capabilities of its rulers, especially the monarch. *El Político*'s scheme of analysis for these capabilities follows the pattern already proposed in *El Héroe*: mastery, ingenuity, prudence, judgment, choice, will force, etc. But *El Héroe*'s doctrines on how fully to be a superior person are narrowed down in *El Político*, and they turn into how fully to be a monarch.[22]

As said before, *Agudeza* was first published in 1642. Although mostly propounding a comprehensive theory of ingenuity, this treatise still fits the even more general scheme of *El Héroe*: *Agudeza* studies one of the *hero*'s and *politician*'s desired capabilities which is *wit*, and *Agudeza* raises this wit to the level of an art.[23]

Gracián published *El Discreto* in 1646. This treatise is not as specialized as *Agudeza*, which deals with only one of the human capabilities; nor is it as broad in scope as *El Héroe*, which deals with all of the moral resources of a person. *El Discreto* is rather focused on those powers of understanding which make a person discreet: keen perception and sound judgment. This treatise in fact helps greatly to clarify Gracián's relationship between ingenuity and judgment. Another feature of *El Discreto* is its lesser attention to monarchical concerns

---

[21]See *El Político*: "I will consider true rules, not political paradoxes." ("Apreciaré reglas ciertas, no paradojas políticas...")

[22]Some scholars have recognized other analytical schemes running parallel with the one of capabilities in *El Político* [See, for example, Arturo del Hoyo cxxxv–xli; Jorge M. Ayala, *Gracián: Vida, Estilo y Reflexión* (Madrid: Editorial Cincel, 1987) 66–79; José Miguel Oltra Tomás, "Conformación de un texto de Gracián: El Político Don Fernando," *Gracián y su Época* (Zaragoza: Institución Fernando el Católico, 1986)]. However, for purposes of this study, it is enough to note now that this very complex discourse propounds the same doctrines of *El Héroe*, as personified in King Ferdinand.

[23]*Agudeza* is probably the work of Gracián which has been most controversial and least appreciated through the centuries, and the one which has most resisted any attempt at translation. Cf. Ayala 77; Arturo del Hoyo cci; Coster 275–293.

than *El Héroe* and *El Político*. *El Discreto* shifts the emphasis from the personal capabilities which a leader should actualize in order to achieve his own happiness and the welfare of his nation, to the moral resources which any person should actualize to enrich his life, his position in the community, and the welfare of this community.[24] *El Discreto* also makes a slight shift from what is primordial to assure a superior personhood (*El Héroe*'s chapters thus are called *"primores"* because they address what is primordial) to what enhances an already superior personhood (*El Discreto*'s chapters thus are called "realces", in English, "enhancing features".) This shift makes *El Discreto* bring genius, gallantry, good conversation, fresh acquaintance of news, and other topics into Gracián's theories. Finally, I would observe that Gracián introduced through each chapter strikingly different stylistic forms in *El Discreto*, for example, allegory, academic argumentation, satire, invective, fable, problem, panegyric, dialogue, etc. These changes of form reveal his interest in providing exemplars of stylistic discretion to be imitated by his readers.

Gracián published the *Oráculo Manual y Arte de Prudencia* in 1647. If *El Héroe* identified the primoridal moral faculties of a superior person, and *El Discreto* analyzes the enhancing elements of moral understanding, the *Oráculo* specifies numerous rules about concrete moral action, that is, prudential maxims grouped under 300 headings. These maxims resist a fixed systematization

---

[24]*El Discreto* still reflects some of Gracián's aristocratical bias, in which rank, birth, sex, race, and others often appear strongly tied to the moral capabilities of a person. However, time fortunately purified Gracián's aristocratic beliefs, and made him ground the superiority of one person over another less on birth than on moral character. Compare, for example, *El Político*'s enthusiastic celebration of monarchy with *El Criticón*'s bitter description of monarchs as persons usually suffering some of the worst forms of slavery: being powerless before their own monarchical power (see *El Criticón* II, Crisi 12). Compare also *El Héroe*'s discussion of the natural grace which shines in the commands of those persons who are born as true leaders (see *El Héroe* Primor 14) with *El Criticón*'s grounds for true fame and immortality on pure moral character (see *El Criticón* III, Crisi 12). Now, Gracián's emphasis on moral character is not only present in his last books, but in all of his treatises. I believe that this emphasis and Gracián's call to all persons to reach superior levels of personhood—to become true aristocrats—are among the most appealing features of his writings for all ages and peoples.

because they are open to very different applications and contingent cases, as if they were rhetorical lines of argument. However, a reader can identify, in the *Oráculo*, maxims which define the psychological resources which morally equip a person, maxims which call one's attention to moral traps of different personal, social, and cultural situations, maxims which specify tactics or strategies of behavior, maxims which set moral and religious standards and guidelines, and maxims from tradition and popular wisdom redeveloped and enhanced by Gracián. The *Oráculo* is probably the treatise which better subsumes in a single unit what are regarded the most distinct features of Gracián's doctrines and style: his cautionary prudence and his very rich but laconic expression. This is also the best book of Gracián's as measured by the number of attempted translations of the work into different languages, and by the popularity of the book among the intellectual élites of Europe through several centuries.[25]

Gracián published *El Comulgatorio* in 1655. Of all his works, this book has attracted the least critical attention, probably because of its eminently religious character, its lack of a theoretical purpose, and its apparent disconnection from Gracián's other works.[26] In brief, this book may be nothing more than a collection of meditations to inspire devotion in the receiver of the Eucharist. However, in its own way, *El Comulgatorio*—like *El Héroe*—is a key work for understanding Gracián's system of ideas. Of a strong Ignatian filiation, *El Comulgatorio*'s meditations follow the principles of the *Spiritual Exercises*: building up the soul by addressing the memory/imagination, enlightening the understanding, and then moving the person to action. If concretely illustrated in *El Comulgatorio*, these principles also theoretically permeate all Gracián's works, and inform his doctrines. Moreover, *El Comulgatorio* mirrors Gracián's voluntarist stand, present in all his books: even when receiving grace, a person is not a passive receptacle, but an active seeker of Communion.

---

[25]There is a recent translation of this treatise into English: *The Art of Wordly Wisdom. A Pocket Oracle,* trans. by Christopher Maurer, (Doubleday Currency, 1992). It has the merit—as a best-seller—of making Gracián accessible to Anglo-Americans.

[26]Cf. Ayala 83.

Gracián published *El Criticón* in three different parts in 1651, 1653, and 1657.[27] This work may be his most celebrated in literary terms. As a narrative pertains to the group of masterpieces of the Spanish Golden Age, say, *Lazarillo de Tormes*, *Don Quixote*, and *Guzmán de Alfarache*. It is also the first among a series of European books such as *Gulliver*, *Robinson Crusoe*, and *Candide*.[28] Very unique aspects of *El Criticón* are its strong allegorical nature, and the very abstract delineation of the narrative's characters and situations, all of which serve to provide a discursive frame for Gracián's doctrines on the developmental stages of the person's moral character. I think that, rather than just a piece of literature, *El Criticón* is more a doctrinal book in the same fashion as Gracián's other treatises. I would finally observe that *El Criticón* has often been described as the most pessimistic of all of Gracián's writings. It presents human life as a journey from false conceptions and expectations about what the world offers, to a painful "disabuse"[29] which frees the person from the falsehoods of this world.

---

[27]Paul Rycaut's 1681 English translation rendered this book's title as *The Critick*. In Ramos-Foster's critical study of Gracián's works, she rendered the title as "The Master Critic," without explaining her choice of translation. Although maybe too literal, I prefer to translate *El Criticón* as "the faultfinde", "the censurer", "the harsh critic", or "the severe critic". A less literal and yet even more appropriate translation would be "the keen critic". However, considering the doctrines contained in the book, the most befitting translation for the title would be "the disabused gentleman."

[28]Cf. Alborg 2: 865. See also E. Correa Calderón, "Introducción, recopilación y notas," Baltasar Gracián, *Obras Completas* (Madrid: M. Aguilar Editor, 1944) cxlviii, who quotes Arthur Schopenhauer: "My preferred writer is this philosopher Gracián. I have read all his books. I believe his *Criticón* is one the best books in the world...it may be the greatest and most beautiful allegory which has ever been written...I know three allegorical works of deep breath: the first is the incomparable *Criticón* of Baltasar Gracián...The other two are more sketchy: they are *Don Quixote* and *Gulliver in Liliput*."

[29]"Desengaño" is the word used by Gracián to express this doctrine, and it is usually translated into English as "disillusionment" or as "enlightenment." However, I prefer the translation of "disabuse" or even "undeception." Regarding disillusionment, the fact is that, for Gracián, the journey of life is not one in which a person loses his illusions, but his misconceptions of the world. Rather than lost, Gracián's "illusions" are reasserted in *El Criticón*. At the end of the narrative, the final stage of moral development consists in

Gracián's pessimism is usually perceived in all his books and doctrines because of his emphasis on the hostile environment within which a person morally develops. Either a wicked society or a person's own weakened nature blocks the person from achieving moral growth. Personal salvation will not come automatically to him. He should gain this salvation by continuously rescuing it from unfriendly contexts. And he may use strategies which range from "just say no,"[30] to the most sophisticated forms of cunning that negotiate the person's own terms with his environment.[31]

However, what is often overlooked from Gracián's doctrines is his great optimism on the potentials of moral development attainable by a person. These attainable potentials are nothing less than the fullness of virtue; nothing less than the perfection of the moral character through will force under the guidance of the person's reason; nothing less than the human accomplishment of sainthood—a sign of the reception of eternal bliss.[32]

Outside of Spain, Gracián has been well received by foreign publics. In spite of the difficulty of rendering Gracián's books into other languages,[33] many

---

accomplishing the standards of virtue as highly defined by Gracián. Enlightenment is also a bad translation of *desengaño*. If disillusionment misses the bright side of *desengaño*, enlightenment does the opposite, by not rendering the dark idea of suffering a painful realization that one was living in error.

[30]Cf., for example, *El Criticón* I, Crisi Ten: "Do you see all these blind knots tied by the will with a yes? The will can untie them again with a no." ("¿Ves todos aquellos ciegos ñudos, que echa la voluntad con un sí? Pues todos los vuelve a deshazer con un no...")

[31]Cf., for example, *Oráculo*, Aphorism 13, about discovering other person's second and even third intentions, Aphorism 158, about knowing how to use one's friends, Aphorism 84, about knowing how to use one's enemies, and Aphorism 73, about knowing how to use one's own weaknesses or *pecadillos*.

[32]*El Héroe, El Político, El Discreto*, the *Oráculo*, and *El Criticón* finish their meditation on fully being a superior person by summarizing in one way or another the fullness of accomplishments in sainthood.

[33]Rendering Gracián into another language goes beyond translating his complex terminology or his poetic turns. It also includes finding correspondent syntactic structures to those which Gracián took from Spanish—structures able to express specific thoughts

different translators have accomplished it with different success in various countries and centuries. Important translations are by Nicolás Gervaise (*El Héroe*, 1645) and Amelot de la Houssaie (*Oráculo*, 1684) which stirred up Gracián's popularity in Europe through French. Arthur Schopenhauer reintroduced Gracián into contemporary discussion, with a translation of *Oráculo* into German in 1861.[34]

Regardless the difusion of Gracián outside of Spain, he certainly has been an author with little appeal for the masses because of the hermetic character of his writings, and the degree of learning required to his readers. He is neither popular among scholars who analyze manhood either by defining its abstract essences or by reaching purely factual generalizations. However, Gracián has appealed to some intellectual élites, troubled by the question of the human condition and the concrete tensions of human existence—to people such as Pascal, Voltaire, Goethe, Schopenhauer, and Nietzsche.[35] Friedrich Nietzsche wrote in some of his letters:

> There is nothing today comparable to Gracián's wisdom and perspicacity in the experience of life.
> ....
> I share your assesment of Baltasar Gracián: Europe has not produced yet anything

---

through the witty relationships established.

[34]Examples of unreliable translations are those of Paul Rycaut (El Criticón, 1681) and Leland Hugh Chambers (*Agudeza*, 1962). Rycaut only offered an abbreviation of *El Criticón*'s first part (*The Critic: written originally in Spanish; by Lorenzo Gracian, One of the Best Writers in Spain, and Translated into English, by Paul Rycaut, Esq.* (London: printed by T. N. for Henry Brome at the Gun in St. Paul's Church-Yard, 1681) Pages 257.) Chambers missed the sense of *Agudeza*'s most important terms, *concepto* and *ingenio*, by translating the first as *conceit*, rather than as *concept*, and the second often as *imagination* rather than as *ingenuity* (see Leland Hugh Chambers, "Baltasar Gracián's 'The Mind's Wit and Art,'" diss., U of Michigan, 1962).

[35]On the difusion of Gracián works in Spain and the rest of Europe, see Ayala 23–34; Arturo del Hoyo cxcvii–ccvi.

more refined and complex on the subject of moral subtleties [than his works].[36]

Gracián's Works as a Rhetoric

A central thesis of this book is that Gracián's works are relevant to the theory and the history of rhetoric. However, it is very easy to overlook or even dismiss the rhetorical character of Gracián's works.

Gracián himself was aware of some misleading elements of his *Agudeza*, which induce a reader to mistake its purpose. He believed that the treatise's illustrations would be its most interesting feature for the public. If the presentation of its theories does not please the reader, he said,

> ...the materials may well satisfy, for so many such daring witticisms, so much so well said, will redeem the cost and justify the time [invested in reading.][37]

The problem with this kind of preference would be that *Agudeza* could be appraised as only a collection of witticisms:

> And you, O Book, although what is new and tasteful guarantees you the good will if not the praise of your readers, nevertheless you still pray for the good fortune of coming across someone who understands you.[38]

Moreover, if described comprehensively and in a unified way, the explicit character of Gracián's works does not reveal itself as a *theory* of rhetoric. The

---

[36]As quoted by E. Corréa Calderón, "Introducción, recopilación y notas," Baltasar Gracián, *Obras Completas* (Madrid, M. Aguilar Editor, 1944) cl.

[37]*Agudeza* "Al Lector". "...los materiales bien pueden satisfacer, que tanto tan valiente concepto, tanto tan bien dicho, desempeñarán el coste, lograrán el tiempo".

[38]*Agudeza* "Al Lector". "Y tú, ¡oh, libro!, aunque lo nuevo y lo exquisito te afianzan el favor, si no el aplauso de los lectores, con todo deprecarás la suerte de encontrar con quien te entienda".

most evident contents of his writings are doctrinal in the realm of morality and politics—what makes, and how a person, or particularly a ruler, become great in character. The most popular quality of his writings is literary. His works have an important place in the canon of Spanish literature. School teenagers learn Gracián as the paradigm of laconic expression. Moreover, his works are profoundly religious. Not only *El Comulgatorio*, but also all of Gracián's books engage the reader into an intense and deep meditation. If these spiritual reflections of Gracián are followed seriously, the reader can not skip the realm of the religious. Furthermore, his works are models of eloquence. Some of his writings are clearly discourses, as *El Político*, which specifically illustrates the structural complexities of "polythematic" baroque speeches (not to mention other of *El Político*'s eloquent features). Several of his letters accomplish important tasks of persuasion. All of his works very directly address the reader, trying to convince him to achieve concrete changes in his moral life. All of his works reveal a conscious and artistic use of the most diverse arsenal of eloquence. Gracián himself is the greatest master of Spanish aphorisms and maxims. In addition, some of his works can be identified as pieces of criticism, for example, *Agudeza*, which is principally regarded as a critical collection of witticisms. Finally, some of Gracián works, such as *Agudeza*, clearly reveal theoretical efforts, but on the subjects of ingenuity and baroque aesthetics. None of Gracián's works explicitly presents itself as a theory of rhetoric.

Furthermore, Gracián himself defined his theories of wit as something very different from rhetoric. He specifically distanced his *Agudeza* from areas traditionally related to rhetoric. He relegated inference to the art of syllogizing, or logic. And he reduced rhetoric itself to style, and particularly to tropes.[39] Gracián rather devoted his *Agudeza* to wit. Although he recognized the use of tropes and rhetorical figures as instruments for the expression of witticisms, and he saw in these stylistic devices ornament and materials to dress witty thoughts,[40] and although he also saw the topics as methods to provide a line of

---

[39]See *Agudeza* "Al Lector" and Discourse 1.

[40]See *Agudeza* "Al Lector." "Válense la agudeza de los tropos y figuras retóricas, como

development towards witty ideas,[41] Gracián nevertheless considered the theoretical realm of wit as something different from tropes and topics. For Gracián, the theoretical realm of wit is found in the methods for discovering or producing[42] correspondences between objects which the mind did not relate previously. For Gracián the art of establishing correspondences is not the same as the art of tropes and the art of topics. Moreover, the art of ingenuity is all self-contained in the art of establishing correspondences:

> This kind of correspondence is generic...and embraces all the art of ingenuity.[43]

In brief, for Gracián, his art of wit is not a rhetoric, at least in two of the most classical methods of rhetoric: tropes and topics.

Even so, Gracián's theories are related—and some of them directly pertain—to rhetoric. By just scratching the surface of his *Agudeza*, one can identify the recurrent themes of topics, tropes, rhetorical figures, sententiae, rhetorical arguments, the style used in speeches, etc.[44] If Gracián did not mean

---

de instrumentos para exprimir cultamente sus conceptos, pero contiénense ellos a la raya de fundamentos materiales de la sutileza, y cuando más, de adornos del pensamiento." ("Wit makes use of rhetorical figures and tropes as devices for elegantly expressing its concepts; but they contain themselves within their own limits of the material foundation of nicety and, at best, the ornaments of thought.")

[41]See *Agudeza* Discourse 4. "... líneas de ponderación...esto es...los adjuntos...como son sus causas, sus efectos, atributos, calidades, contingencias, circunstancias de tiempo, lugar, modo, etc..." ("...lines of ponderation (development)...that is...the adjuncts...such as...the effects, the attributes, the qualities, the contingencies, the circumstances of time, place, mode, etc...")

[42]See *Agudeza* Discourse 2. "Si el percibir agudeza acredita de águila, el producirla empeñará en ángel..." "If perceiving the witty establishes one's credit as an eagle, producing it makes one challenge the angels...")

[43]*Agudeza* Discourse 2. "Esta correspondencia es genérica...y abraza todo el artificio del ingenio."

[44]For example, *Agudeza*'s discourses nine to thirteen are devoted to witticisms through similitude, discourses nineteen to twenty two are devoted to witticisms through hyperbole,

to make these methods a necessary part of the art of ingenuity, he at least meant to make them instruments contributing to the exercise of ingenuity. Moreover, many of *Agudeza*'s precepts directly apply to the use of speech for the practical purposes of addressing political and moral situations.[45]   Furthermore, by scratching the surface of his other treatises, one can discover rich and compact discussions on very classical parts of rhetoric, for example, delivery, emotions (pathos), plausible data (evidence and, to some degree, logos), the character of a politician (ethos), the education of this politician, etc.[46] If Gracián meant to limit these issues to prudential judgment and action, these issues nevertheless do not cease to have some relation to problems of rhetoric, as defined in some classical rhetorics.

Moreover, by looking at Gracián's illustrations of his theories, we can acknowledge that he did not dissociate his precepts from the practices of oratory.   It is true that most of *Agudeza*'s examples come from literature, covering all genres of writing such as epic, drama, and lyrical poetry, and that the examples concentrate on the witty offshoots of these literary genres. Nevertheless, we should not forget that at least one third of its abundant illustrations come from oratory.[47]

A deeper inspection of Gracián's treatises should not overlook that, at least,

---

discourses thirty six to thirty eight are devoted to witticisms which produce rhetorical arguments, etc.

[45]See, for example, *Agudeza*, Discourse 3, last paragraph, which classifies subtleties according to the sources of wit producing ingenious speech (correlation, ponderation, ratiocination, and invention). If studied in the context of the speech practices of Gracián's age, these "sources" were either different steps or different methods to develop a sermon. See also Discourses 45 and 46, which respectively address "witty actions" and "witty speech" responding to sudden moral or political problems requiring a prompt and persuasive response from a wit.

[46]See, for example, *El Héroe*, primores 13 and 14, which strongly define Gracián's ideas of delivery, the *Oráculo*'s Aphorism 155, which addresses the reasonable control of emotions, and *El Discreto* Realce 5, which strongly addresses the need to be acquainted with fresh information if one is going to be engaged in any kind of discussion, and even conversation.

[47]Cf. Parker xxxiv.

Agudeza is a theory of invention. It intends to explain and give artistic power to the mind's inventiveness. It aims to sharpen the mind's perspicacity and creativity. It aspires to prompt discourse.

Baltasar Gracián believed that theories of wit can provide explanations and art concerning the ways the human understanding apprehends or produces concepts. He believed that in discovering or establishing correspondences between apparently not associated things, the mind rises from mere experience to abstract ideas. In fact, one of the most outstanding features of *Agudeza* is that it makes techniques of witticism and techniques of conceptualization to be usually the same in so far as they accomplish the same result of bringing forth new ideas.

As an art of invention, Gracián's theories of ingenuity may be too general to be specified as rhetorical. Indeed, Gracián believed that wit serves all the arts and sciences.[48] Nevertheless, in the same way that general theories of argumentation inform the theory of rhetoric[49], in so far as their general methods to some degree shed light on specific methods of a part of rhetoric, which is rhetorical judgment and inference, thus also Gracián's general art of conceptualization should serve similar purposes: in spite of its generality, this art should help to explain rhetorical conceptualization. Moreover, as a method of invention, Gracián's rules of wit should not be seen as serving only the discovery or creation of ideas. Inventing ideas give place to the invention of arguments and inferences, since ideas are a necessary precedent of arguments and inferences, or as Gracián often put it, a necessary precedent of judgment and action.

> Each watchful faculty of the soul—I mean those that perceive objects—enjoys

---

[48]See *Agudeza*, Discourse 3.

[49]Consider for example Stephen Toulmin's, and Ch. Perelman and L. Olbrechts-Tyteca's theories of argumentation. See Stephen Toulmin, *The Uses of Argument* (Cambridge University Press, 1958); Ch. Perelman and L. Olbrechts-Tyteca, *The New Rhetoric. A Treatise on Argumentation*, Trans. John Wilkinson and Purcell Weaver (University of Notre Dame Press, 1969).

some artifice in them [in the objects]... The understanding, then, as the first and foremost faculty of the soul, snatches the prime of artifices, the consummation of the exquisite, in all its differentiation of objects... [Then] Dialectic takes care of the connections of the terms in order well to assemble an argument, a syllogism, and rhetoric [takes care] of the embellishment of words, in order to compose an eloquent flower, as is a trope or a figure.[50]

Furthermore, Gracián's art of wit often and directly relates to argumentation. Some of the most interesting methods of ingenuity proposed in *Agudeza* involve the witty use of argumentation in discourse; and wit itself generates argumentation by discovering relationships between the terms of a syllogism, or between propositions in an enthymeme.[51]

In fact, if placed in and assimilated to the whole scheme of Gracián's political and moral treatises, *Agudeza*'s theories more clearly reveal their rhetorical dimension. Instead of seemingly applying not to rhetoric but to literature, since Gracián strongly stresses the aesthetic element of his art,[52] his theories turn out to be an explanation of wit as a virtue and a faculty forming the

---

[50]*Agudeza* Discourse 2: "Toda potencia intencional del alma, digo las que perciben objetos, gozan de un artificio en ellos... El entendimiento, pues, como primera y principal potencia, álzase con la prima del artificio, con lo extremado del primor, en todas sus diferencias de objetos... Atiende la dialéctica a la conexión de términos para formar bien un argumento, un silogismo, y la retórica al ornato de las palabras, para componer una flor elocuente, que lo es un tropo, una figura." Cf. Don Vincencio Juan de Lastanosa's Dedication of the Treatise "to the Most Excellent Count of Aranda." In dedicating this treatise, Don Vicencio, protector of Gracián, explains that judgment is the heir of ingenuity.

[51]See *Agudeza* discourses 3, and 36 to 38.

[52]In an important distinction that Gracián made between wit and judgment, he asserted that "Wit is not satisfied with just the truth, as judgment does; [wit] also aspires to the beautiful." ("No se contenta el ingenio con sola la verdad, como el juicio, sino que aspira a la hermosura.") By that he meant that any genuine piece of wit presents a novelty to the mind, and thus always entails the aesthetic experience of wonderment. Even so, that does not mean that Gracián's art of wit remains only in the realm of aesthetic activities.

character of persuasive politicians and gentlemen,[53] a mind's talent and art which allows persons to persuade reasonably[54] and deliberate on moral or public issues,[55] and a method of addressing the contingent aspects of human affairs[56] and reaching solutions for practical matters[57] through discourse.[58]

Gracián's doctrines are akin to classical rhetoric not only because they include discussions on invention, but also because of their attention to disposition, style, memory, and delivery in several places in his works.[59]

Beyond classical rhetoric, Gracián's works address important issues which rhetoricians of the modern era made central to their systems, particularly in Great Britain during the eighteenth century. For example, leading the seventeenth-century innovative interest in the mind, Gracián systematized the rules of the art less by looking on the art itself than by looking into the mind of its artist. Although he gave system to these rules by describing the forms, steps, or structures which the different methods observe in themselves,[60] he more

---

[53]See, for example, *El Héroe* Primor 3, and *El Discreto* Realce 1.

[54]See, for example, *El Discreto* Realce 22.

[55]See, for example, the *Oráculo* aphorisms 80, 136, 222 and 227, *El Discreto* realces 7 and 19, *El Héroe* primores 6 to 11.

[56]See, for example, the *Oráculo* aphorisms 250 and 294.

[57]See, for example, *El Discreto* Realce 19, *Agudeza* discourses 39 to 47.

[58]The moral and political context of Gracián's theories of ingenuity distances his rules of wit from those of Pellegrini—serving either literary wit or scientific discourse—, Pallavicino—serving scientific discourse—, and Tesauro—serving symbolic activities.

[59]On disposition, see, for example, *Oráculo* aphorisms 3, 39, 81, 82, 95, 170, *Agudeza* discourses 4 to 8 and 51 to 57. On style, see, for example, *Agudeza* discourses 60 to 63. Gracián's understanding of erudition to some degree can be associated with the classical notion of memory; see, for example, *Agudeza* Discourse 58. Also, on memory, see, for example, the *Oráculo* aphorisms 179 and 262. On delivery, see, for example, the *Oráculo* Aphorism 42, *El Discreto* Realce 2, and *El Héroe* primores 13 and 14.

[60]For example, the discursive forms observed in a speech when using correlations, hyperboles, similes, maxims, antithesis, ponderations, mysteries, contrarieties, etc., to reach a conceptualization.

strongly explained these rules by approaching them through their foundations in the operations peformed by the human mind, and through the psychological structure of human understanding. As mentioned above, the conceptual frame which more comprehensively gives system to his complete works is one based on the operations of the mind: ingenuity, judgment, and the will.[61] Even in *Agudeza*, where Gracián carefully explained many artistic rules through the features of the methods themselves, he nevertheless roughly ordered them according to the operations of the mind involved in conceptualizing: either just ingenuity, or also judgment, or even action.[62] Moreover, several particular concepts link Gracián with modern rhetoricians—for example, the concepts of taste[63] and the association of ideas.

Hence, let's proceed and examine next all those features of Gracián's doctrines which are relevant to rhetoric.

---

[61]Gracián's first treatise *El Héroe* is the one which more clearly follows this scheme of moral faculties to explain its doctrines. Gracián's other treatises also follow this conceptual frame, but by paying special attention to one of the faculties proposed by the scheme. For example, *Agudeza* is devoted to ingenuity, the *Oráculo* emphasizes judgment, and *El Discreto* pays strong attention to the relationship of ingenuity and judgment. Later, in *I Fonti*, published in 1650, Pellegrini applied this scheme of operations of the mind explicitly to rhetoric, classifying the types of discourses depending on if they just inform, or they also seek judgment, or even intend to move people into specific forms of action. See *I Fonti* Chapter 4: 49–53.

[62]The rules in which just ingenuity seems to be involved in the conceptualization are concentrated at the beginning of *Agudeza*'s first treatise, roughly discourses one to twenty one. The rules in which judgment seems to be stressed are concentrated in the middle part of *Agudeza*'s first treatise, roughly discourses 22 to 29. The rules in which action seems to be stressed are concentrated in the final part of *Agudeza*'s first treatise, for example, discourses thirty, and forty five to forty nine. It should be noticed that *Agudeza* is divided into two treatises, the first dealing with simple kinds of subtleties, and the second dealing with compound kinds of subtleties and style—the first giving method to simple concepts, and the second explaining the connection of concepts in a whole discourse.

[63]On taste, see, for example, *El Héroe* Primor 5.

The Rhetor

GRACIÁN'S AIM WAS NOT TO TEACH FRESHMEN RULES for crafting ingenious or prudent speeches; he rather strove for prompting all to be ingenious, prudent—complete *señores*.[1] Thus, Gracián's doctrines should remind us what being a *master* is, and how we can accomplish this end.

Being a Master

Gracián's profile for a *rhetor* matches those of Aristotle's, Cicero's, and Quintilian's; they respectively considered the rhetor as a person of practical wisdom, "able to deliberate well about what is good an expedient for himself,"[2] a person "with the merits of a commander or the wisdom of a statesman-like

---

[1]Most of Gracián's books start by revealing, in their titles, their focus on the artist rather than on the art. These titles refer to heroes, discreet gentlemen, politicians, and keen critics instead of heroic, discreet, political, or keenly critical practices or actions. In particular, *Agudeza*'s title does not refer to an art of witticisms but to an art of our mind's wit. *Oráculo* and *El Comulgatorio* seem to be the exceptions. Their overt titles do not refer to paradigmatic persons or human faculties but to collections of writings: the first, sage aphorisms (metaphorically: "oracles"); the second, religious meditations. Nevertheless, although indirectly, these two books' titles also partake of Gracián's emphasis on the person. According to Correa Calderón, *Oráculo* subsumes some lost manuscripts of Gracián titled *The Heedful Person* and *The Gallant Gentleman*. See E. Correa Calderón, "Introducción," Baltasar Gracián, *Obras Completas*, LXXV–LXXIX; Cf. Arturo del Hoyo cli–clii and cxc–cxciii. Also, *El Comulgatorio*'s was rather titled *El Comulgador* ("the communicant") in the first page of the book. Indeed, Gracián's artistic rules spring from his views on the potentials of human nature. This is clear from the very beginning of his treatises. *El Héroe* starts with a consideration of the faculties of understanding and will exemplified by lordly, heroic, superior people. *El Discreto* commences with a consideration of what genius and ingenuity mean in a discreet gentleman. *Oráculo* starts with an aphorism which refers to the whole comprehensive idea of fully becoming a person. And in *El Político*, Gracián opened his discussion by proposing King Ferdinand—a paradigmatic person—as the model of politician.

[2]*Nicomachean Ethics* VI, 5.

senator,"[3] and a "man of virtue."[4] Gracián did not expect less from his heroes, politicians, discreet gentlemen, etc.

The Human Condition

However in Gracián's books, the rhetor's profile is tainted with some hindrances: the deceptive appearances of the world, and the malice inherent in the rhetor's own human nature and in the society surrounding him. Thus, Gracián's rhetor is not just a person who has grown in wisdom through his life and education, but is also a person who has had to overcome deception and malice in the process of becoming wise. For Gracián, wisdom is not just the result of eliminating ignorance, but is also the victory over deception and malice. Thus, one of the comprehensive virtues of Gracián's rhetor is to be a *"varón desengañado"*[5] whose life is a *"milicia...contra la malicia."*[6]

For Gracián the world was not delusive in itself, as if it were a false shadow of true Platonic ideas; deception rather was the result of a person entering the world without any knowledge, and yet hastily generalizing his first experiences, thus making of any impression a truth—a rule of nature—and making of any momentary pleasure or whim a moral imperative—a final and lasting good.[7] Thinking by means of universals about particulars, human reason at first lacks keeness of perception and discriminating power; consequently reason makes childish mistakes such as regarding every man a father or every woman a

---

[3]*De Oratore* I, ii, 8.

[4]*Institutio Oratoria* XII, i, 1.

[5]See, for example, *Oráculo* Aphorism 100. As said before, "Varon desengañado" should be translated as "disabused man" rather than "disillusioned man", as it is often rendered into English. *El Criticón* is the book which better takes into consideration the concept of disabused man.

[6]*Milicia...contra la malicia*: "a warfare against malice." See the *Oráculo* Aphorism 13. This Spanish saying may be traced to the Book of Job, VII, 1: *"Militia est vita hominis super terram."* (English translations of this quote fail to render the idea of warfare.)

[7]See, for example, *Oráculo* aphorisms 69 and 227; *El Discreto* Realce 6 and 14; *El Criticón* I, Crisis 1–3, 7 and 10.

mother.[8] It is only through the experience of years that people may gain discernment.[9] Then they may distinguish what is truly universal, timeless, and valuable from what is just circumstancial, timely, and passing. Then, the person may be free from his former mistakes or deception. His wisdom would thus be the product of a process of disabuse—a process of overcoming not just ignorance, but also bad habits of thinking and living.

Even so, bad habits tend to get deeply rooted in people, becoming vices which often are difficult to eradicate.

[A person] is reared from childhood, so childishly, that when he cries, any puerility pacifies him, any toy brings him into contentment. [Nature] seemingly receives him into the kingdom of happines, and it is not but into the captivity of sorrows, that, when he finally opens his spiritual eyes, realizing his deception, he is already bound to it without remedy, and he finds himself submerged in the same mud from which he was formed, and then, what could he do but to step on it, striving to get out of it the best way he can?[10]

Deception turns into a real problem when the person becomes so entangled in old and bad habits that he does not abandon them, in spite of realizing their wrongness. Then, what were childish mistakes lose their innocence and become: 1) self-deception, since the person rationalizes his mistakes to save his face,[11] 2) malice, since the person turns to loving and being addicted to what is wrong,

---

[8]See *El Criticón* I, Crisi 1. Cf. Aristotle, *Physica* I, 1; and St Thomas Aquinas *Summa Theologica* First Part Q.85, Art. 3.

[9]See, for example, *Oráculo* aphorisms 146, and *El Criticón* III, Crisi 5.

[10]*El Criticón* I, Crisi 5. "Críase [el hombre] niño, y tan rapaz, que cuando llora, con cualquier niñería [la naturaleza] le acalla, y con cualquier juguete le contenta. Parece que [la naturaleza] le introduce en un reino de felicidades, y no es sino un cautiverio de desdichas; que, cuando llega a abrir los ojos del alma, dando en la cuenta de su engaño, hállase empeñado sin remedio, véese metido en el lodo de que fué formado, y ya ¿qué puede hacer sino pisarlo, procurando salir dél como mejor pudiere?"

[11]See, for example, *El Criticón* I, Crisi 11, III, Crisi 5.

base, and ugly,[12] and 3) vulgarity, since the person finally takes pride and satisfaction in his own ignorance and wickedness.[13]

It is important to notice that the hindrances of deception and malice affect the personality of the rhetor and the nature of his art.

For the rhetor, it is not enough to be wise, talented in persuasion, and knowledgable in the art of rhetoric. He also requires heroic virtue to triumph over the weaknesses inherent in his human nature. Gracián's rhetor thus must be a moral hero. As a man devoted to his own community, the rhetor should not always expect good reasons and good faith in answer to his arguments, but he should expect deception and malice, too, because of the vicious people who also are part of society. Therefore, the rhetor should be a model of cautious prudence, discretion, and, again, of heroism, if not to redeem such a corrupt society, at least to save his own soul:

> Among lions and tigers there was but one danger: losing the material life...but among men, there are many more and greater dangers: to lose one's honor, peace, wealth, joy, happiness, conscience, and even the soul.[14]

Moreover, as a politician, Gracián's rhetor should add a good dose of heedful circumspection—moreover, prudent calculation—to his statemanship, preventing any possible hidden spite and wicked outcomes even from the best manifestations of good will received.[15]

Thus, the rhetor's art seems to be tainted with its quota of cunning. For example, he should not only fight against his own weaknesses, but he often should conceal these weaknesses as well, so as not to expose himself and

---

[12]See, for example, *El Criticón* II, Crisi 9, III, Crisi 2.

[13]See, for example, *El Criticón* II, Crisi 5.

[14]*El Criticón* I, Crisi 4. "...entre los leones y los tigres no había más de un peligro, que era perder esta vida material...pero entre los hombres hay muchos más y mayores; ya de perder la honra, la paz, la hacienda, el contento, la felicidad, la conciencia, y aun el alma".

[15]See, for example, *Oráculo* Aphorism 13.

surrender his own freedom to his enemies.[16] In fact, Gracián admitted this and other extraordinary and expedient occasions in which rhetoric may calculate truths and manipulate means of communication, bordering, in so doing, on the realm of falsehood and iniquity, paradoxically to win over deception and malice. In Gracián's doctrines, even truths have their measure, their mode, their use, their time, their occasion, their place, lest they—and oneself—are surrendered to the surrounding butchers.[17]

There is an overreaching excellence which comprehends a rhetor's heroism, prudence, cautious statemanship, and heedfulness: it is mastery, being a lord of oneself, after being a victor over malice and deception. Although a lordly rhetor—an aristocrat—may be a diligent leader and a smart politician, he is not a true master until he achieves virtue. Only then he becomes a beloved and true leader, and a wise politician.[18]

There is only one excellence which subsumes and transcends mastery: it is sainthood:

> In a single word, saint; that is saying it all at once.[19]

But this excellence is only reached by few persons who, close to death, overcome the last and most difficult deception: thinking that the things of this world are lasting, instead of just temporary and passing:

> Philosophy itself is nothing else than a meditation on death—and indeed, it should be meditated many times before, in order to succeed in doing it well only once later.[20]

---

[16]See, for example, *Oráculo* aphorisms 145, and 181, and *El Héroe* primores 1–2.

[17]See, for example, *El Discreto* Realce 22, *Agudeza* Discourse 55, *El Criticón* I, Crisi 10.

[18]See, for example, *El Criticón* II, Crisi 12, and III, Crisi 12; *El Discreto* Realce 24.

[19]*Oráculo* Aphorism 300: "En una palabra, santo, que es decirlo todo de una vez."

[20]*El Discreto*'s ending sentence: "La misma Filosofía no es otro que meditación de la muerte; que es menester meditarla muchas veces antes, para acertarla a hacer bien una sola

And nothing else but virtue, which belongs to the realm of immortality, lasts for ever.[21]

Mastery

Gracián's rhetor can still be defined as a "man of virtue," in spite of becoming such a person through disabuse. It is on virtue, on good habits of thinking and living, that the rhetor's practical wisdom and statemanship rest. Moreover, through virtue, the rhetor is invested with his most empowering and comprehensive ethos: mastery, since it is also virtue which fully defines this excellence:

...true sovereingty consists in integrity of habits.[22]

---

después". See also, *El Héroe*, Primor 20, and *El Criticón* II, Crisi 12, and III, Crisi 11. Death and sanctity are rather crucial in specifying Gracián's understanding of mastery. They establish the right dimension of human lordship, by addressing the ultimate questions. An interesting quote Gracián made from a sermon for Ash Wednesday by a famous preacher (*Agudeza* Discourse 39) can express well the ultimate dimension of human self-mastery: "que es tierra, que es polvo y nieto de la nada: *Memento homo, quia pulves es, et in pulverem reverteris.*" ("(a human being) is soil, is dust, and grandson of Nothingness, etc.") Beyond these questions, Gracián implicitly, as a religious man, also paid attention to the ultimate answers referring to Who truly is the Lord. For Gracián, just through these disabusing answers the notion of human mastery can be recovered and purified. See, for example, *El Criticón* III, Crisi 9; and the most beautiful Meditation 15 from *El Comulgatorio*, about the Eucharist and the seraphims' reverence before God's throne.

[21]See, for example, *El Héroe* Primor 20, *El Discreto* realces 24 and 25, and especially *El Criticón* III, Crisi 12. Gracián strongly related human virtue to eternal bliss, seemingly making him a sort of Pelagian; he also strongly attached virtue to secular accomplishments and to perennial wordly fame, thus seemingly making him a sort of seventeenth-century secular humanist. However, Gracián's doctrines on virtue should not be divorced from Gracián's religious beliefs and scholastic training. As a Catholic, Gracián knew that virtue (the famous good works) was the free human assent to grace. And although putting it in very simplistic terms, I think that, as a scholastic theologian and philosopher, Gracián knew that virtue was the actualization of the human potentials needed as a passport to the afterlife.

[22]The *Oráculo* Aphorism 103. "...la verdadera soberanía consiste en la entereza de costumbres".

So much empowered, true mastery is thus so much empowering that it does not persuade, but commands; it even does not need to speak, since its presence alone is obeyed.[23]

From a rhetorical viewpoint, this notion of mastery results shocking. It seemingly denies rhetoric. It admits the possibility of a speechless rhetor. Moreover, if mastery is attached to the aristocratic and monarchic environment from which Gracián learned this notion, then mastery seems to consist in nobility's command or the rule of rank rather than argumentation or the rule of reason. These are strong objections against making mastery a defining quality of a rhetor. Yet, although these objections have a dose of truth, a well understood concept of mastery in fact entails very rich rhetorical dimensions which we should not lose sight of.

Certainly Gracián attached strong monarchic and aristocratic connotations to the concept of mastery. His *Político* prominently is a celebration of the Spanish Monarchy and of King Ferdinand's lordship—one largely resting, Gracián believed, on birth and blood.[24] The case is that Gracián not rarely associated mastery with nature, referring to a grace of command and of winning the wills of others, which few persons possess as a gift of genius.[25]

---

[23]See *El Héroe* primores 12–15. See especially Primor 14.

[24]Consider, for example: "Ferdinand was of the Aragonese kings' heroic race...It seems that the moral qualities, and nature's and fortune's privileges and failings, are inherited as much as the natural endowments." ("Fué Fernando de la heroica prosapia de los reyes de Aragón...Parece que se heredan, así como las propiedades naturales, así las morales, los privilegios o achaques de la naturaleza y fortuna.") See, also, in *El Político*, Gracián's celebration of Ferdinand's selection of a spouse, in terms of birth, and Ferdinand's selection of the House of Austria, as the recipient of his vacant kingdom after not having been blessed with a surviving heir.

[25]See, for example, *El Héroe* Primor XIV. "Some people irradiate an innate mastery, a secret ruling force that makes itself be obeyed without exterior precepts, without an art of persuasion... The lion is realized as such by the remaining beasts, in a presaging of his nature, and, without having tried his courage yet, they bow in advance their heads." ("Brilla en algunos un señorío innato, una secreta fuerza de imperio que se hace obedecer sin exterioridad de preceptos, sin arte de persuasión... Reconocen al león las demás fieras, en

Even so, in discussing the subject of mastery, Gracián did not reduce his considerations to the lordship possessed by a king or noblemen through birth. He extended it to all kinds of human activities—regardless of blood or nature—if in these activities a person possess some authority and autonomy in decision making. For example, kingship is participated in by any minister in charge of an area of administration through delegation.[26] But even more important, each person is king in his own sphere of action, in so far as that sphere is his.[27]

Very meaningful consequences follow, for rhetorical theory, from this expansion of mastery from persons of rank to all persons having some realm of authority. In this very basic sense, mastery is primarily binding, not because it is virtuous, wise, or innately "graceful", but because it is nominally autonomous—because it has legal authority to judge and decide about its given set of activities.

Rather than denying rhetoric, recognizing areas of authority whose decisions have binding power to some degree explains rhetorical interaction. The most obvious case is that we, rhetors, persuade assemblies, judges, jurors, courts, government officials because, regardless we like them or not, these institutions and people have authority to pass judgment on the issue of our concern. Moreover, a community needs rhetoric if it truly recognizes the autonomy which each free person has in his own realms. There is no other way than rhetoric to harmonize different judgments and still keep them autonomous in a society.

---

presagio de naturaleza, y, sin haberle examinado el valor, le previenen zalemas.") For Gracián, *innate* mastery is enjoyed by very few persons—such as Ferdinand. However, these few are not only or necessarily princes. In fact, royal blood is rarely a warrant of inborn lordliness; not few monarchs are rather vulgar, ineffectual, and unlordly. See, for example, *El Criticón* II, Crisi 5.

[26]*El Político*: "This great duty of reigning can not be exercised alone; it should be communicated to the complete staff of ministers." ("Este gran empleo del reinar no puede ejercerse a solas; comunícase a toda la serie de ministros".)

[27]See, for example, the *Oráculo* Aphorism 103. Another extreme expression of the Spanish understanding of each person's sovereignty comes from Cervantes: "Under my cloak, I kill the king." ("...debajo de mi manto, al rey mato.") *Don Quijote* I, Prologue.

Furthermore, and in a deeper sense, a primary qualification defining any speaker's ethos when he persuades is the understanding of *who the lord of the judgments pronounced is*: are the judgments just his?, do the judgments belong to him and to an institution, a group of people,[28] or any other person he represents?, do the judgments belong not to him but to somebody else, in which case, the speaker is not the rhetor but just a messenger?

Nominal authority should be legally enough to make its judgments binding in its autonomous realm. However, this kind of authority fails to meet the standards of rhetoric if it is simply based on authoritative decisions without the support of reason and virtue. In the same measure, nominal authority alone fails to meet Gracián's standards of mastery:

> Regardless of the greatness of a person's position, the person should demonstrate he is greater than such a position.[29]

Thus, in its fullest and initially mentioned sense, mastery requires more than positions and an innate grace, and needs to rest on the greatness—the virtue—of a person as such. In short, true mastery consists in the personal sovereignty rooted on fullness of personhood,[30] which backs a person's own judgments and

---

[28]I believe that an important and often legitimate element of the ethos displayed by a well-defined group of *persons*—e. g., some community of interests—is the group's claims of autonomy. For example, "If you pass this general rule that affects us, we still are free to counteract it in this our realm in this way..." Although it seems a threat, it is rather the assertion of the group's freedom and autonomy, which are not surrendered to the state. In cases like this, autonomy itself is more than a reasonable means of persuasion. The assertion of one's autonomy also is one of the most significant rhetorical acts, since it gives the rationale to strengthen separate autonomies through the formation of groups, and, more important, it sets and explains the foundation of free societies.

[29]*Oráculo* Aphorism 292. "Por grande que sea el puesto, ha de mostrar que es mayor la persona".

[30]For Gracián, any actualized personhood—being a person—derives from fullness of virtue; if people lack virtue, they would only deserve to be identified with subhuman types, for example, the mobs, the wicked—that is beasts, and children and puerile individuals. See, for example, *Oráculo* Aphorism 1, 108, and 296; *El Criticón* I, Crisis 5 and 6, II, Crisi 5, III,

actions.[31] In this sense, mastery refers to the most comprehensive and radical element of a rhetor's ethos.

> A speaker's mastery wins the listener's respect, gains the hypercritical's attention, and captures everybody's approval. It furnishes the speaker with words and judgments...
>
> ....
>
> This enhancing and superior condition is dazzling in any of its favored possessors, and especially in those persons in charge of the greatest duties. In an orator, it is more than something circumstancial. In a pleader, it is essential. In an ambassador, it is his splendor. In a leader, it is his commodity. But in a prince, it is his utmost good.[32]

A Manifest Mastery

Although mastery comes through disabuse, it nevertheless rises and becomes the splendor of virtue. This splendor is manifest through its specific perfections and through some critical areas on which a rhetor exercises and establishes these perfections.

The perfections of mastery. Freedom, authority, competence, *despejo* (ease)[33],

---

Crisis 7 and 8; *El Discreto* realces 6, 9, 11, 14, 16, and 20.

[31]The two most comprehensive areas of mastery discussed by Gracián referred to speech (or judgment), and action. See, for example, *El Discreto* Realce 2, and *Oráculo* Aphorism 122.

[32]*El Discreto* Realce 2. "El señorío en el que dice, concilia luego respecto en el que oye, hácese lugar en la atención del más crítico y apodérase de la aceptación de todos. Ministra palabras y aun sentencias al que dice..." "Brilla este superior realce en todos los sujetos, y más en los mayores. En un orador, es más que circunstancia. En un abogado, de esencia. En un embajador, es lucimiento. En un caudillo, ventaja, pero en un príncipe es extremo".

[33]The complex idea which Gracián meant by "despejo" may be quickly translated into "ease." However, the best of Gracián's translators have simply given up in trying to render it into their own languages, by rather calling it—as Corbeville did—the *je ne sais quoi*, not to mean an irrelevant and obscure concept, but to mean an elusive and important idea. The

and responsibility are the intrinsic perfections of mastery. They are the person's own excellences confirming him as lord of his realm. Gracián usually expressed them through prudential rules, for example:

a) Regarding a person's freedom, circumspect reticence should be the safeguard of it, since by carelessly expressing his words, feelings, or judgments, this person not only puts them under the public's dominion (that is, he surrenders the sovereignty he kept over these areas, making them from then on the property of the public), but, dangerously, he exposes the inner-self (that is, his whole freedom and sovereignty) to manipulation by possible enemies.[34]

b) Regarding authority, the greater it is, the greater its master should measure and limit his words, not to risk discrediting his authority[35] with unauthoritative, unhappy, or loose remarks.[36]

c) Regarding competence:[37]

> One should become first lord of the subject-matter, and later...one can speak with a masterful command and an imposing superiority over the audience...it is easy to become lord of the listeners' souls, if, previously, one has taken care of becoming lord of the issue discussed.[38]

---

je ne sais quoi apparently became a central notion in many literary critics of the modern era. See E. Correa Calderón, "Introducción, Recopilación y Notas," Baltasar Gracián, *Obras Completas* (Madrid: M. Aguilar, 1944) 18a, second footnote.

[34]See, for example, *El Héroe* primores 1 and 2.

[35]See, for example, *Agudeza* Discourse 62, the section on the reserve and careful wording which should distinguish a prince's speech.

[36]Notice that the reticent circumspection which is required to safeguard a person's freedom and authority gives moral grounds to Gracián's choice for laconic language.

[37]Competence may match Aristotle's idea of good sense, as a component of the orator's ethos or credibility. See *Rhetoric* II, 1.

[38]*El Discreto* Realce 2. "Hácese uno primero señor de las materias, y después...puede hablar con magistral potestad y decir como superior a los que atienden, que es fácil señorearse de los ánimos después si de los puntos primero".

d) Regarding *despejo*, Gracián believed that ease in accomplishing the immediate areas of competence should set a person free to take again command on himself and on new activities without losing the least control of the initial tasks and the additional ones.[39] *Despejo*, as the luster of such an ease, is what makes a rhetor's mastery resplendent and irresistibly attractive to an audience.[40]

e) Regarding responsibility,[41] a person should have commitments, but he should limit them to what he can accomplish and take command of;[42] he should be the lord of his commitments rather than a "joker card" which is of use to everybody;[43] he should be the first in his area of responsibilities, or the first in openning new fields;[44] he should prefer reputable undertakings,[45] and yet he should honor his commitments and decency even in solitude because he is primarily responsible to himself, rather than to a society.[46] Etc.

The intrinsic perfections of mastery may be enough for a rhetor to assure himself other excellences such as reputation and leadership.[47] But these other excellences do not always rest only on the person's own sovereignty; they often rest on the public response to the rhetor, too.

---

[39] See, for example, *El Héroe*, Primor 13. "*Despejo* (ease) first turns a general into a lord of himself, and later into a lord of everything." ("El despejo constituye primero a un general señor de sí, y después, de todo").

[40] See *El Héroe*, Primor 13.

[41] Responsibility may match Aristotle's idea of good moral character, as a component of an orator's ethos, or credibility. See *Rethoric* II, 1.

[42] See, for example, *Oráculo* Aphorism 252.

[43] See, for example, *El Discreto* Realce 11. A person who is a "joker card" is not a player in the game, but someone who is used in thousand different ways by other players.

[44] See, for example, *El Héroe* primores 6 and 7.

[45] See, for example, *Oráculo* Aphorism 67.

[46] See, for example, *Oráculo* aphorisms 50 and 280.

[47] Reputation and leadership may match Aristotle's idea of goodwill, as a component of an orator's ethos or credibility. See *Rhetoric* II, 1.

> The excellence of personal perfections is not enough to win the favor, although one assumes the opposite.[48]

When the merits of reason are not enough, then the merits of love should adorn a rhetor's mastery[49] to win the people's favor and affection. This love is grounded on the rhetor's respect and honor for his listeners,[50] on his displaying of benevolence, gallantry, and generosity, and, among other things, on his being attentive to the personal and cultural preferences and sensitivities of a public.[51]

Finally, even though Gracián tended to think that a true mastery could be so dazzling as to be effective in the absence of speech, he also believed that personal perfections do not diminish but rather gain considerably if they are discreetly advertised, announced, or displayed to an audience, so that heedless listeners do not miss these perfections.[52]

The areas of mastery. A master's perfections are manifest through his accomplishing them in several areas. Some of these areas are differentially accessible to people; other areas are equally accessible to people by nature.

The special areas of mastery refer to some factors which by themselves contribute to make a person more competent in a given activity than his

---

[48]*El Héroe* Primor 12. "No basta eminencia de prendas para la gracia de las gentes, aunque se supone."

[49]Here, love is not an emotional proof. Love rather expresses an ethical proof: the rhetor's personal attribute of being a lover of the people, which also brings forth another attribute: the rhetor's blessing of being beloved by his people.

[50]Corollary: to make the listeners recognize one's own mastery, one should recognize each listener's own mastery; honor your neighbor to be honored yourself.

[51]See, for example, *El Héroe* Primor 12; *Oráculo* aphorisms 40, 97, and 112; *El Discreto* realces 4 and 22.

[52]See, for example, *El Discreto* Realce 13.

neighbor, for example, genius,[53] fortune,[54] and economic[55] and social opportunities.[56] By themselves, these factors establish differences between people's possibilities of success in the diverse fields of life. By themselves, these factors open to people more areas and opportunities of exercising their mastery.

Other areas in which mastery is exercised are open equally to all people: the understanding and the will. All people share understanding and will in as much as reason is what defines human beings.[57]

Gracián concentrated his analysis on genius, the understanding, and the will, which are intrinsic and inalienable areas of mastery for every person.[58] This is the strongest evidence that Gracián's doctrines of mastery refer to the sovereignty of the person as such, rather than to an established aristocracy.

For Gracián, genius refers to special talents or "happy and superior inclinations"[59] which contribute to make a person (or even cities and nations) especially competent in one area of life rather than in others. Gracián's prudential rules on genius and on other special areas[60] where mastery is exercised usually emphasize that it is not enough to be lucky about having these talents or gifts. It is also necessary that the person recognizes these blessings

---

[53]See, for example, *El Discreto* realces 1 and 9.

[54]See, for example, *El Héroe* primores 10 and 11; *Oráculo* aphorisms 139 and 196.

[55]See, for example, *El Criticón* II, Crisi 3.

[56]See, for example, *El Criticón* II, Crisi 6, the section discussing social patronage.

[57]Gracián rejected different types of reason according to different kind of "ingenuities." In his view, the rules of the mind are the same for all men. Although the human specific way of understanding distinguishes people from the beasts and from the angels, the differences among people are not on types of understanding but on choices made by the will, on how extensively the understanding is exercised, and on natural inclinations due to talents or geniuses. See, for example, *El Héroe* Primor 3; *El Discreto* Realce 1.

[58]The understanding and the will are the axes around which *El Héroe*'s doctrines evolve. Ingenuity and genius are the axes around which *El Discreto*'s doctrines evolve.

[59]*El Discreto* Realce 1: "...una tan feliz cuanto superior inclinación".

[60]Fortune, social opportunity, etc.

and takes possesion of them, in order to make the best use of them and thus affirm his mastery.[61]

Gracián believed that the correct recognition of a given genius is crucial for anybody's success in life; for example, if one mistakes the identification of one's own and the neighbor's genius, one will probably fail in choosing one's vocation, matching a spouse, enjoying friends, finding employment, and appointing employees.[62]

For Gracián, a genius matching important positions of government is "unique in its kind, but not defective in what is general, keener than those of ordinary men, but not extravagant,"[63] it is outstanding in all attributes of nature and also well balanced and mature, high-minded in judgment and strong in spirit, and with a superior discernment and brave in its choice of glorious enterprises.[64] There are many other types of genius which, although extraordinary in a specific field of activity, would be defective in the very comprehensive area of government if they are not associated with other talents. For example, Gracián strongly warned politicians against an unrestrained gay and joking genius which, if it is the single skill of a person, only serves as a talent for commedians.[65]

Some of Gracián's doctrines seem to imply that the diversity of genius and of special areas of mastery are the occasion for argument and public discourse.[66] If people were not different in genius, talents, preferences, or in other areas such as fortune and economic and social opportunities, but completely equal, as if they were clones, there would be no need for rhetoric. Also, by the way,

---

[61]These rules of taking possession of one's special areas of mastery of course apply to the general areas of mastery, too: the understanding and the will.

[62]See, for example, *El Discreto* realces 1 and 10; *El Héroe* primores 9 and 15; *Oráculo* aphorisms 34, 89, 104, 115, 156, 161, 203, and 273.

[63]*El Discreto* Realce 1. "Sea, pues, el genio singular, pero no anómalo; sazonado, no paradojo..."

[64]See *El Discreto* Realce 1.

[65]See, for example, *El Discreto* Realce 9, *Oráculo* aphorisms 76 and 79.

[66]See, for example, *Oráculo* Aphorism 294.

humanity would probably be too boring.

I also find in those doctrines an important condition of rhetoric: there are common areas of mastery, such as the understanding and the will; if these did not exist, there would be no possibility of rhetoric, since there would be no common grounds to be shared by people.[67]

In Gracián's doctrines, the understanding is a very broad human power. Its most comprehensive functions are ingenuity and judgment.[68]

Ingenuity refers to understanding as such, in its narrower sense of discernment.[69] It also refers to the mind's power of conceptualization, either as an apprehension of ideas from reality, or as the mind's production or invention of new ideas.[70] A prominent ingenuity is characterized by bold vigor, promptness, and keeness.[71]

A summary review of Gracián's works reveals that judgment refers to reason's discriminating assent or dissent to ideas, things, or actions as true, good, or beautiful.[72] Some aspects of judgment to which Gracián devoted much attention were prudence, taste, and choice. Gracián's strongest emphasis was on prudence, which tends to embrace all other aspects of judgment, and which is the major topic of almost all his works. Even so, prudence particularly refers to judgments wary of deception and malice; it entails a person's heedful calculation to identify and secure for himself the valuable, in the middle of

---

[67]See, for example, *El Discreto* Realce 8.

[68]See *El Héroe* Primor 3.

[69]See *El Héroe* Primor 3.

[70]See, for example, *Agudeza* discourses 1 to 3.

[71]See *El Héroe* Primor 3.

[72]For a concrete definition of judgment, see, for example, *Oráculo* Aphorism 96. In *El Criticón* I, Crisi 10, concerning the three main values submitted to judgment, Gracián made a different list than the one I have presented above and I fathomed from his works. He listed the honest, the useful, and the pleasant, and in that order.

hostile and very concrete circumstances.[73] Taste refers to the mind's discriminating capacity to identify, appreciate, and enjoy what is valuable. Taste is good taste if it is not easily satisfied and if it is grounded on extensive and eminent experience.[74] Choice refers to judgments discriminating, determining, and contriving the will's means and ends.[75] Good choice rests on good taste and the right dictates of prudence.[76]

Ingenuity and judgment are the areas of mastery which Gracián more overtly codified, by means of either substantive rules of prudence or formal artistic principles.[77] Seemingly, he did not work so with the will, which is another general area of mastery intrinsic to all human beings. If in explaining most subjects Gracián was ordinarily brief and veiled, concerning the will, he was exceedingly laconic and criptic.

Even so, a comprehensive reading of his writings shows their linkage with the long European tradition which systematically has studied the will, for example, through some of its general virtues (fortitude and temperance) and passions (irascibility and concupiscence).[78] Thus, if understanding means the mind's thinking, then the will means putting this thinking into practice.[79] In a psychological sense, the will refers to will power, that is the vehement passions, the lofty movements of the soul, and the personal and spiritual strength which

---

[73]See, for example, *Oráculo* Aphorism 243; *El Discreto* Realce 23.

[74]See, for example, *El Héroe* Primor 5.

[75]See, for example, *El Héroe* primores 6, 7, and 8; *El Discreto* realces 3 and 10; *Oráculo* Aphorism 283.

[76]See, for example, *Oráculo* Aphorism 51.

[77]The substantive rules of prudence abound in *El Héroe, El Político, El Discreto, Oráculo,* and *El Criticón.* The formal artistic principles are mainly found in *Agudeza.*

[78]By irascibility, men of schools meant the movements of the soul in accomplishing ends. By concupiscence, they referred to the enjoyment of an already accomplished end.

[79]See, for example, *Oráculo* Aphorism 18.

carry on and make effective the dictates of reason.[80] In terms of external behavior, the will refers to human efforts, actions, work, or calculated industry to accomplish the mind's ends.[81] Gracián often addressed the will through prudential rules which may direct it; for example, "give your attention to not failing one commitment rather than to succeeding in one hundred of them."[82] However, I think Gracián believed that will power, like physical strength, rested more on exercise than on specific substantive principles or on formal rules. For him, a strong will does not come through a bland life free from challenges, but through austerity, hardship, competition,[83] and difficult quests.[84]

If on one hand the sanctions of reason are not completely effective or meaningful until they are carried out by the will,[85] on the other hand the will itself springs from and is rooted in the dictates and appreciations of reason.[86] It is reason that sees the valuable, that sets the soul in motion, and that should keep a check on and direct every passion and action.[87]

---

[80]See, for example, *El Héroe* primores 2 and 4; *Oráculo* aphorisms 98 and 128.

[81]See, for example, *Oráculo* aphorisms 53, 66, 204, 231, and 251; *El Criticón* II, Crisi 8.

[82]*Oráculo* Aphorism 169: "Atención a no errar una, más que acertar a ciento". Also see, for example, aphorisms 66, 82, 204, 231, and 251.

[83]For Gracián, competition sharpens a politician's skills and quickens all his abilities: "Ferdinand met in time with princes of genius: sagacious, heedful, political...competing each other in courage, and contesting each other for the greatest fame...Kings reciprocally wake one another up, and also they lull each other asleep..." ("Concurrió Fernando con príncipes de su genio, sagaces, atentos, y políticos... compitiéndose el valor, emulándose la fama... Despiértanse unos a otros los reyes, y adormécense también...") *El Político*. However, if competition is a principle which strengthens the will, it should not be the principle guiding judgment; otherwise, judgment would be a mere reaction to competition rather than a creative and leading discretion. See, for example, *Oráculo* aphorisms 47, 165, 180, and 183.

[84]See, for example, *El Político*; *El Criticón* I, Crisi 5.

[85]See, for example, *Oráculo* Aphorism 18, *El Héroe* Primor 4.

[86]See, for example, *Oráculo* aphorisms 290 and 294.

[87]See, for example, *Oráculo* aphorisms 78, 69, 155, 207, and 287.

...the man...should totally be made of brains: Brains in his ears, not to hear so many lies and listen to so much of flattery...Brains in his hands not to err in their control and rightly to hit on the things they are put over. Even the heart should be made of brains, not to let itself be pulled, moreover, drawn by its passions. Brains, and more brains, and lots of brains for the complete, brainy, and substantial man.[88]

For the purposes of rhetoric, it should be noticed that the reasons of the will are not different from the reasons supplied by taste (appreciative judgment) and established by choice (resolved judgment). Also, the will differs from pure passions in that the later are not necessarily stirred up by discriminating reflections of the understanding, but by pure and singular impressions.[89]

A comprehensive assessment of mastery. The superior place of mastery in Gracián's system of ideas can be appreciated through the lens of rhetorical proofs: mastery, as the rhetor's *ethos*, would be of much greater importance than *logos*—the people deciding an issue than to the pure positions on the issue in question.

This may be an aberration if mastery were not a whole subsuming virtue, comprehending, among many other personal qualities, good sense. The fact is that ethos itself assimilates logos and makes it meaningful and plausible. Moreover, good reasons, good decision-making, good deals are nothing in the

---

[88]*El Criticón* III, Crisi 6. "...todo el hombre habría de ser de sesos: Seso en los oídos, para no oír tantas mentiras ni escuchar tantas lisonjas...Seso en las manos, para no errar el manejo y atinar aquello en que se ponen. Hasta el corazón ha de ser de sesos, para no dejarse tirar y aun arrastrar de sus afectos. Seso y más seso y mucho seso para ser hombre chapado, sesudo y sustancial". These are words of the Brainy Man, a person all made of brains, and one of the good monsters who guided Critilo and Andrenio through life.

[89]The will may lose perception of the pleasures associated with pursuing and attaining a good—the will may even be tested with pain and suffering—, and nonetheless the will would still pursue the good because of the reasons supplied by the understanding; however, pure passions would simply cease to move the soul since the motivating feeling or the momentary pleasure dissappeared, and there is nothing replacing them, such a clear understanding of the good pursued. See, for example, *Oráculo* Aphorism 227; *El Héroe* primores 2, 4 and 5.

absence of virtuous persons[90] who, for Gracián, subsume all of the above and, furthermore, character. This happens because nothing, in the absence of moral character, finally actualizes and makes true what has been resolved:

> **Always deal with dutiful people**. A prudent person can deal with them and be sure that they engage in a true commitment. Their duty is the greatest guarantee for the deal made...There can be no good deal with baseness, in so far as baseness is not committed to honesty; for this reason, there is never true friendship among the wicked...honor is uprightness's throne.[91]

Hence, for Gracián, a practical matter is settled more by moral character than by reasoning. For example he believed that words of wisdom were idle even in the King Alphonsus X The Sage of Castile, because he was very incompetent in carrying out these words in his kingly duties. Gracián preferred the less educated Alphonsus V The Magnanimous of Aragón because he could carry out his humbler words in actions.[92] Although Alfonsus V of Aragón was smaller in one area of mastery, he nevertheless was greater as a complete man.[93]

Ethos is greater than logos also because, for Gracián, every issue in moral argumentation (as would be any deliberative, judicial, or epideictic issue) is subordinated and tied to the ultimate issue of attaining moral character. In one

---

[90]The preeminence of the artist over the art seems to be a long rhetorical tradition. Like Gracián, Cicero seemingly identified the success of rhetoric more in the person of the orator than in the art itself. Cicero's best treatises on oratory are focused on the orator rather than the art itself.

[91]*Oráculo* Aphorism 116. **"Tratar siempre con gente de obligaciones**. Puede empeñarse con ellos y empeñarlos. Su misma obligación es la mayor fianza de su trato...No hay buen trato con la ruindad, porque no se halla obligada a la entereza; por eso entre ruines nunca hay verdadera amistad...es la honra el trono de la entereza".

[92]See *El Político*, where Gracián criticizes Alphonsus X: "What is the importance that...Alphonsus was a great mathematician, if he was not even a mediocre politician? He who attempted to correct the fabric of the universe was on the brink of losing his own kingdom." ("¿Qué importa que sea...Alfonso gran matemático, si aún no es mediano político? Presumió corregir la fábrica del Universo el que estuvo a pique de perder su reino").

[93]Cf., for example, *El Discreto* Realce 24; *Oráculo* Aphorism 166.

sense, Gracián meant that a master does not settle an issue simply because it needs to be settled, but because solving it contributes to his honor.[94] In a deeper sense, Gracián meant that the ultimate question at issue is to attain happiness, in an eudemonistic sense, that is, actualizing all the potentials one has as a person through greatness and integrity of character.[95] In the deepest sense, great moral character is the ultimate issue since on it depends eternal salvation.[96] Thus, for Gracián, no prudential issue can be divorced from the question of character; the expedient and the just are subsumed to the honorable.

In Gracián's doctrines, the ultimate issue of achieving good character becomes a very peculiar check to what really matters in an argument.[97] For example, it may seem *logically* inadmissible that two different conclusions of one argument could be equally plausible; nonetheless, in terms of *ethos*—which is an additional premise, after all—, these conclusions may be equally acceptable, if each conclusion respectively is a result of the special character of the different persons arguing.[98] Moreover, Gracián warned against being too attached to a position on a particular issue, as is "a fool with his theme." One should not indiscriminately aim at victory on a particular position, but at the mastery of one's understanding and one's will—which is what makes a person virtuous. Otherwise a person would be the slave of a position on an issue rather than the lord of it. Attachment to a position contrary to the understanding, to the

---

[94]See, for example, *El Héroe* primores 1, 2, and 6 to 8. Honor is a very rich word in Spanish and, although ticklish, it is not limited to the ideas of reputation or fame. It eminently refers to integrity of character. But it extends to the virtue enjoyed by a group or by a particular person through the virtue practiced by each member of the group or by another person who is related to the first one. Don Quixote's great feats were not just to promote his own honor, but ultimately, to promote Dulcinea de Toboso's honor and fame. Also, every Jesuit undertaking is defined in terms of *ad majorem Dei gloriam.*

[95]See, for example, *El Discreto* Realce 24.

[96]See, for example, *El Héroe* Primor 20.

[97]See, for example, *Oráculo* aphorisms 280 and 66.

[98]See, for example, *Oráculo* aphorisms 294, 280, and 66.

will, or to one's own mastery as a whole, is not just stubborness, but perdition.[99]

So, it is clear that a non-defective mastery is necessary in effetive rhetoric. But mastery trascends rhetoric. It is the seat of honor, the grounds of fame, the source of happiness, the garmets of immortality, and the passport for eternal bliss.[100]

Mastery and Other Related Subjects.

There are blemishes staining Gracián's views of mastery. They deserve attention less because of being a dark side of Gracián's thought than because of the unexpected turns his theories of mastery thus suffer, regardless of their darkness or brightness.

The unmanly manly mastery. Gracián is notorious for some of the most sexist comments ever made in Spanish language. For example:

> ...the greatest understanding of the wisest woman does not exceed the understanding of any sound man at the age of fourteen.[101]

But Gracián was also eminent in genuinely celebrating great *señoras* from his close circle of friends, from many places and times of history, or symbolically through impressive emblematic women who were characters in his *Criticón*. Indeed, he extensively referred to real *señoras* in his books as exemplars of wit, discretion, authority, leadership, will power, and other very highly esteemed areas of mastery.[102]   Also, Gracián's denial of mastery to

---

[99]See, for example, *Oráculo* aphorisms 49, 142, 218, 239, and 261.

[100]See, for example, *El Criticón* III, Crisi 12.

[101]*Agudeza* Discourse 23. "...la mayor capacidad de la más sabia mujer no pasa de la que tiene cualquier hombre cuerdo a los catorce años de edad". If there is something which might redeem Baltasar Gracián from expressing that idea, it would be that he offered it as an example of "rare opinions" and that the opinion was not his but of his father Francisco Gracián.

[102]See, for example, *Agudeza* Discourse 7, *El Discreto* realces 6 and 22, and *El Político*,

women seems to rest on something circumstantial:

They do not want to be women yet! Always to be girls![103]

Moreover, immaturity is not a vice which Gracián foresaw in women only. He also bitterly applied it to Spain, which is the single European nation that Gracián placed as still in "Children's Springtime, and Youths' Summertime."[104] Regarding the Royal Court, only some of its extraordinary women such as the Princess of Rosano and the Marchioness of Valdueza were safe from this vice of immaturity.[105]

However, these women were mature, *señorial* persons, because they possessed all the "manliness" the men in Madrid lacked, which brings us back to Gracián's sexism but in a subtler way: maturity, that is mastery, is a masculine quality.[106]

Now and then, Gracián's views of manly mastery even seem unmanly. I won't deny that Gracián wrote beautiful pages on friendship and family life, and

---

which is abundantly illustrated with cases of great women. Considering the women of Toledo, Gracián believed that: "...here, a woman says more by using a single word than in Athens a philosopher with a whole book." ("...más dice aquí una mujer en una palabra, que en Atenas un filósofo en todo un libro") *El Criticón* I, Crisi 10.

[103]*El Criticón* I, Crisi 6. "¡Aún mujeres no quieren! ¡Siempre niñas!"

[104]See *El Criticón* Part One.

[105]See *El Criticón* I, Crisi 6.

[106]Cf., for example, *El Político*: "In Spain manly females have always taken the places of men." ("En España han pasado siempre plaza de varones las varoniles hembras".) Also, *El Político*: Semíramis' sex was better concealed by her understanding than her masculine clothes. Moreover, *El Héroe* Primor 2: Queen Isabella belied the weaknesses of her sex by ignoring the pains of giving birth. How far was Gracián from some of today's sexist concepts of mastery? It seems that women still need to follow some masculine stereotypes of dressing, thinking, talking, or behaving in order to climb the corporate ladder. They even have to renounce some "weaknesses" of their sex such as getting pregnant, childcaring, and family life. They must follow the steps which the "more mature" men have already walked since industrialization.

even on love.[107] He indeed believed that family and friends could be important sources of inspiration, support, and counsel for a politician.[108] Yet, friends sometimes turn out to be only of use for the personal ends of the politician, and the family usually is more a burden to keep in the closet than a contributor to the politician's goals.[109] Thus, Gracián's views on the politician as subordinating friends and family to his political life seem to contradict his doctrines of mastery as requiring completeness and integrity of personhood. Moreover, this subordination of the man's private life to politics seems to surrender mastery to the state. If fully stretched, these views would lead to a fascist state, or, if applied to the economy, they would match many contemporary fascist corporations where individuals are just disposable assets for the use of a company.[110]

---

[107]Gracián argued against the belief portraying Martial as being too cold and unemotional an author, because of his too intellectual type of epigrams. Gracián contended that in this intellectual strength was found the emotional force of Martial. See *Agudeza* Discourse 49. The same argument could be applied to defend Gracián's own works from Jorge Luis Borges who believed that Baltasar Gracián did not know any love at all. See Ramos-Foster 70. Regarding actual family life, Gracián seemed to be in close relations with all his brothers, his father, and his sister, all of whom are extensively quoted in Baltasar's books as exemplars of wit. I believe Gracián even quoted his mother in this unidentified supplication: "My son, may God give you an understanding of the good kind" ("Hijo, Dios te dé entendimiento del bueno"). *El Héroe* Primor 3.

[108]See, for example, *El Político, El Héroe* Primor 15, *Oráculo* aphorisms 44, 156, and 158.

[109]See, for example, *Oráculo* aphorisms 5, 115, and 158; *El Criticón* II, Crisi 10.

[110]I have often been warned against Gracián's nationalism and aristocratic overtones concerning mastery: they have been used to justify fascist states, such as Spain during the times of Francisco Franco, and even the Nazi regime. This warning results from Gracián being often identified with philosophies which proclaim a separate group of superior people or race whose morals transcend the morals of ordinary humans. Nietzsche himself claimed to be indebted to Gracián's thought (see, for example, E. Correa Calderón, "Introducción, recopilación y notas"). Gracián indeed believed in a superior race or people, but his view referred not to something factual but to a moral imperative, mastery; moreover, its achievement consisted not in transcending—ignoring—, but in fully accomplishing the

The masses. Immaturity, as an attribute of children, seemingly denies them any area of lordship. Yet, children are supreme in exercising the intellectual virtue of wonderment, usually weakened with age. In a positive sense, wonderment is a beautiful response to the new, the source of attentiveness, and what keeps open the soul to the marvels of the universe.[111] Even so, in a negative sense, wonderment underlies previous ignorance, which makes it possible for a person to receive indiscriminately a given fact as new or marvelous. It is in this second sense that wonderment separates itself from mastery and becomes a characteristic not of children but of the masses.[112]

The masses are a very important concept to be contrasted with mastery. As a synonym of the populace, the crowds, and the ordinary, and an antonym of mastery, the concept of the masses reminds us that Gracián's doctrines are not pure of classism and of sympathies with an established aristocracy. Even so, unwillingly and without any pretense of introducing new ideas, or revolutionizing his society, Gracián still acknowledged some mastery to the masses:

Better mad with everyone than sane and all alone...but I would qualify this

---

demands of virtue; finally, the call to mastery was not reserved to the few, but was as universal as the call to sainthood. Even so, Gracián was so concerned with restoring the Spanish Empire to its golden age, that he often seemed to identify and even subordinate moral character to the survival of the state (see, especially, *El Político*). Not until old age did he write a book completely addressing the issue of disabuse, *El Criticón*. There he seemed to reach enlightenment and he warned against the previous equation of the politician as a servant of the state. He discovered that there was not a worse slavery than the one suffered by rulers, who become puppets of their own power—see *El Criticón* II, Crisi 12. His most refined conception of mastery, as applied to public issues, may be grasped here. Not the persons but the state is who serves, and it serves the persons. Since the state did not promote Critilo's and Andrenio's virtue, then they estranged themselves from the state and abandoned the political career. It is not mastery that should be subordinated to solving public issues, but solving public issues that should be subordinated to mastery. It is not rhetoric but the rhetors of a society that matter the most; thus, the preeminence of ethos in Gracián's theories is again clear.

[111]See, for example, *El Criticón* I, Crisi II.

[112]See, for example, *El Criticón* I, crisis 2 and 10.

aphorism by saying: "Better sane with everyone than mad and all alone."[113]

In any case, it is important to notice in Gracián's doctrines that the notion of the masses—as it happens with mastery's—refers less to social classes than to character. In Gracián, the strongest synonym of the masses is the vulgar, which is a sin commited by all social classes and positions.[114] Moreover, the vulgar, as a sin of character, appears to be worse than the foolish, the wicked, and even than hypocrisy.[115] Foolishness and wickedness consist in not thinking or doing what is right because of being too meshed and addicted to what is wrong. The fool and the wicked probably miss—and thus assent to—the true and the good in the depths of their hearts.[116] Hypocrisy implies some degree of assent to what is right, since vice hastens to get dressed with the garmets of virtue.[117] It is only the vulgar that is a complete and abhorrent subversion of reason and virtue. Rooted in blameful ignorance and in malice, the vulgar proclaim the foolish as reasonable and the wicked as praiseworthy. The vulgar regard reason as irrational and make the irrational reason. They assent to the subjective, to

---

[113]*Oráculo* Aphorism 133: **"Antes loco con todos que cuerdo a solas**...mas yo moderaría el aforismo, diciendo: 'Antes cuerdo con los demás, que loco a solas'". Cf., with aphorisms 43 and 77.

[114]See, for example, *El Criticón* II, Crisi 5.

[115]Despite the keen variety of defective kinds of character identified by Gracián and his attention to classify them systematically (as he achieved it in *Agudeza* discourses 26 and 27), he nonetheless ignored the category of the weak. Contrastingly, despite the small variety of types of character identified by Fr Luis de Granada (only three: the good, the bad, and the weak), he nonetheless devoted his greatest pastoral attention to the weak (see, for example, Fr Luis de Granada's *Sermón de las Caidas Públicas*, or, of course, his *Guia de Pecadores*.) It seems as if Gracián's voluntarism did not let him have sympathy for the weak and made him subsume them to the category of the wicked.

[116]On foolishness and wickedness, see, for example, *El Criticón* I, crisis 5, 6, and 11, II, Crisi 9, and III, crisis 2, and 5; *Oráculo* Aphorism 168.

[117]See *El Criticón* II, Crisi 7.

whims, and to singular and wild impressions; they deny objective standards.[118] And not content with all this, for the sake of their own survival, the vulgar hasten in the spreading[119] of their sickening taste[120] through all the realms of society.[121]

Vulgarity is such an extreme denial of character and mastery, that it conceals itself behind the anonimity, amorphousness, and facelessness of the masses.[122]

However, Gracián was not fearful of vulgarity. He believed that since vulgarity is irrational, in the long term it is also impractical, and thus self-defeating.[123]

Gravity as the spirit and countenance of mastery. Gracián often described different nations by means of clichés. For example, the English are handsome but cruel,[124] the French are industrious but greedy and frivolous, the Italians are

---

[118]In denying the possibility of objective—shared—standards and making the irrational usurp reason, vulgarity denies rhetoric. Moreover, from a theological point of view—let's here give some leeway to wit—it is not foolishness, wickedness, or hypocrisy which would be so serious as to become sins against the Holy Spirit, but vulgarity, since it is vulgarity that makes a person fully deny the objective standards of God. By means of vulgarity, a person—like, say, Adam and Eve—usurps the determination of what is objectively good or bad, by ruling it through his own whims rather than by the judgments of God, the Creator of all, and the One who defined the value of each thing from Eternity.

[119]Alas!, here we have the sin of scandal.

[120]Notice that taste is not only an aesthetic concept. It extends itself to all the realms of value judgment.

[121]Regarding the vulgar, see, for example, *El Criticón* I, Crisi 9, and II, Crisi 5.

[122]See *El Criticón* I, crises 9 and 10; II, crisi 5. The masses is a topic which has attracted the attention of many other writers in Spain, cf., for example, José Ortega y Gasset's *La Rebelión de las Masas*.

[123]See, for example, *El Criticón* I, Crisi 10, where the vulgar crowds are humiliated by the Arts.

[124]The degree to which Gracián relied on these clichés can be appreciated by considering the legendary origin of the attributes of the English nation. In *Lives of Saints*, Introducton by Father Thomas Plassman, OFM, Editorial Supervision by Father Joseph Vann, OFM (New York: John J Crawley & Co., Inc., 1954) 149, we read about St Gregory the Great: "One

wise and magnificent, but deceitful and treacherous, and the Spaniards are grave but ineffectual.[125]

These stereotypes might be chauvinist, racist, foolish, or of bad taste.[126] What is important to note is that, for Gracián, the best expression of mastery is given in Spanish gravity, if it truly occurs.[127] Gracián's choice of gravity matches his whole notion of mastery. Gravity—with its austerity and seriousness[128]—irradiates the majestic beauty of a mastery grounded just on the recovery of virtue, after having suffered disabuse.[129]

---

day, the story goes, Gregory was walking through the Roman slave market when he noticed three fair, golden-haired boys. He asked their nationality and was told that they were Angles. 'They are well named,' said Gregory, 'for they have angelic faces.' ['Non Angli sed angeli']. He asked where they came from, and when told 'De Ire' he exclaimed 'De ira [from wrath]—yes, verily, they shall be saved from God's wrath and called to the mercy of Christ. What is the name of the king of that country?' 'Aella.' 'Then must Alleluia be sung in Aella's land.' Some modern historians have viewed the tale skeptically, claiming that the serious-minded Gregory would not have descended to punning. However, it seems unlikely that anyone would have taken trouble to invent this delightful anecdote...when Gregory became pope, the evangelization of Britain became one of his most cherished projects."

[125]See, for example, *Oráculo* Aphorism 242; *El Criticón* I, Crisi 13, II, crisis 3 and 8, and III, crisis 2, 4, and 8.

[126]In most occasions Gracián used these clichés as a technique of amplification by distribution, to explain general ideas through figurative species, for example, the cardinal sins: "in Spain this, in Italy that, in England such that...and so on." See, for example, *El Criticón*. However, I wonder how much innocence can be associated to such a technique in an author such as Gracián. In any case, regarding national styles of mastery, following Gracián clichés, and, worse, applying these clichés anachronically, I myself still tend to see pretty and bucolic elegance in Gainsborough's and Reynolds's English country gentlemen and military officials, pompous frivolity in Hyacinthe Rigaud's Portrait of Louis XIV, magnificent sovereignty in Michaelangelo's sibyls, and solemn gravity in El Greco's Portrait of a nobleman with his hand on his breast.

[127]See, for example, *El Discreto* Realce 2; *El Criticón* I, Crisi 13.

[128]Continuing with clichés, I think that in Mexico Spanish gravity is intensified, if not enhanced, with its assimilation of Indian sadness.

[129]Translating again this idea to artistic examples, compare the majestic gravity of Juan

Becoming a Master

For Aristotle, the man of practical wisdom, who is involved in rhetoric, changes his character through his various stages of life.[130] Cicero's stateman and Quintilian's man of virtue require an extensive education in the experience of public life and in the study of many fields of knowledge to possess the character and the competence of an orator.[131] In a similar way, Baltasar Gracián believed that education was of great importance in building a master's character, and that age was very significant in understanding the growth and evolution of the master's personality. In fact, Gracián's doctrines on education and on psychological development are so rich that they may deserve a separate study.[132] Here, nevertheless, a brief reference to these doctrines may be enough to complete this sketch of Gracián's views of mastery.

Education

Gracián endorsed the traditional means of education embracing imitation, practice, and theory.[133] However, he reshaped them as emulation, virtue, and erudition. Thus, Gracián's conception of education centers on the person rather than on his external actions. For example, Gracián explained emulation not so much as the imitation of artistic models but as the creative and adaptive imitation of exemplary persons.[134] Virtue subsumes the practice of an art, and becomes a very broad goal of practicing good habits of thinking and living which build up

---

Pareja—an ex-slave—and Francisco Lezcano—a dwarf—painted by Velázquez, with the idiotic kings he also portrayed.

[130]See *Rhetoric* II, 12–14.

[131]See *De Oratore* III, xv, xx–xxiii; *Institutio Oratoria* I, Preface.

[132]*El Criticón* itself is a reflection on the psychological development and the education of a person.

[133]On the traditional means of education, see, for example, (Cicero) *Ad C. Herennium De Ratione Dicendi*, Trans. H. Caplan (Cambridge: Harvard University Press, 1981) I, ii, 3.

[134]See, for example, *El Héroe* Primor 18.

and define the character of a person.[135] Erudition may be the part of education most focused on subject-matter rather than on the person: it includes the arts, the sciences, and philosophy, and the most diverse kinds of experience from facts and life. However, even regarding erudition, Gracián preferred the study of subject-matter offering heroic models of people to be emulated—for example, history and the great works of literature.[136]

According to Gracián, since the earliest stages of life, education should instill good habits in children and in youth. It should encourage austerity and diligence and oppose indulgence and laxity so as to strengthen their character.[137] Both liberal and mechanical arts are emphasized in the education of the young, whereas more advanced courses should deal with more substantive matters such as those found in theology, philosophy, the sciences,[138] and some experimental studies.[139] The main purpose of all these studies is to contribute to the moral growth of a person:

> ...Moral Philosophy made [the complete person] prudent; Natural Philosophy, wise; History, clear-sighted; Poetry, ingenious; Rhetoric, eloquent; the Humanities, discreet; Cosmography, informed; Holy Scripture, pious...[140]

The adult person further enriches his education by adding to his studies the actual experience he acquires in public life, travels, friendly relationships, and other kinds of observations he makes of the real world. And the elders culminate this process by enjoying especially times of solitude and recollection,

---

[135]See, for example, *El Discreto* Realce 23; *El Criticón* I, Crisi 5.

[136]See, for example, *El Criticón* I, Crisi 11, II, Crisi 4; *Agudeza* Discourse 61.

[137]See *El Criticón* I, Crisi 5.

[138]Cf., *El Criticón* Part One, on children and youth, with Part Two, on adulthood.

[139]See *El Criticón* II, Crisi 2.

[140]*El Discreto* Realce 25: "...la Filosofía Moral le hizo prudente; la Natural, sabio; la Historia, avisado; la Humanidad, discreto; la Cosmografía, noticioso; la Sagrada Lición, pío..."

which make them philosophize in their prime, reflecting on all the things they learned throughout their lives.[141]

All education combines the pleasant and the useful to win the interest of students, and although in youth there is some freedom to enjoy areas of pure amusement, in adulthood, nevertheless, there is no place for pleasant studies which ignore the useful and the substantive. For example, a mature person can enjoy listening to music and reading great epic works, but it would be very unbecoming for him to play ballads or to savor novels of chivalry.[142]

The education of ingenuity may emphasize literary studies, whereas the education of judgment should pay strong attention to philosophical, political, and scientific studies, and, in short, to real problems and information.[143]

There is a very important principle of education which is more potently garnered from the reading Gracián's works than by any specific discussion he made on the subject.[144] Education is not a process of teaching in which a pedagogue expounds, but a process of learning in which the student acquires knowledge and becomes virtuous. As an educator, Gracián did not write in an expositive style, which simply declares or transmits knowledge. He rather wrote in such a way[145] that the reader must heuristically extract by himself the point made, by reflecting on the words said and giving them meaning through his own experience.[146]

---

[141]See, for example, *Oráculo* Aphorism 229; *El Discreto* Realce 25.

[142]See, for example, *El Criticón* II, Crisi 1; *Agudeza* Discourse 55.

[143]Compare *Agudeza* Discourse 58 with *El Criticón* II, Crisi 4.

[144]Referring to Gracián's style of writing, when extending a publishing license for *El Discreto*, Manuel de Salinas y Lizana said: "The style is laconic...it has even mysteries in its punctuation...there is very little to read, but there is much to reflect on." ("El estilo es lacónico...tiene hasta en la puntuación misterios...ofrece poco a la lectura, pero mucho al discurso"). *El Discreto*, License from Don Manuel de Salinas y Lizana, Doctor and Canon of the Holy Church of Huesca.

[145]Gracián called this form of writing conceptist style.

[146]Making the listeners reach for the point made by themselves is the whole business of

Gracián's satire on manuals of etiquette reveals his opposition to purely dogmatic education.[147] His choice rather was an education providing a rationale for the rules imparted,[148] preferable pragmatic reasons contemplating the ends pursued.

I never look at the beginnings but at the end.[149]

Gracián usually stressed long term goals, in so far as they conform to the different and major stages of life. At the end of his youth, a person should have found his own vocation, not only in the broad terms of choosing his religious or his marital estate, but in terms of identifying and accepting his own unique genius.[150] The peak of adulthood should culminate in self-realization—in having reached that fullness and completeness of virtue which being a master means.[151] Even so, old age usually is the last opportunity to become truly wise, since, in the face of death, people may at last reach disabuse and be able to contemplate the actual and limited dimensions of human mastery. The recognition of one's

---

Gracián's conceptist doctrines, and particularly, his theory of conceptist style. Regarding conceptist style, as opposed to declarative or expositive style, see *Agudeza* Discourse 62.

[147]See, for example, *El Criticón* I, Crisi 11.

[148]Gracián's enthusiasm for prudential maxims may illustrate the peculiar way in which he was concerned for an education giving both substantive rules of moral judgment and the rationale behind them. For Gracián, a true maxim should encapsulate a rule and its rationale, which usually is a fact of life disabusing people—openning their eyes against deception—, for example, "In worldly rewards, it is not new that he who deserves more receives less." ("...que en los premios del mundo no es de ahora,/que el que merece más, alcance menos"), as said Bartolomé Leonardo, quoted by Gracián in *Agudeza* Discourse 43. From this plausible fact of life, the reader can infer the rule by himself if he is involved in practical affairs and is called to settle his own expectations in an enterprise.

[149]*El Criticón* I, Crisi 10. "Nunca pongo la mira en los principios, sino en los fines", answered Critilo, when asked why he did not enter in the Inn of Indulgence.

[150]See, for example, *El Criticón* I, Crisi 13, II, Crisi 1.

[151]See *El Criticón* II, Crisi 13.

own limitations is the most liberating act of life because it is then that the self finally opens to the infinite possibilities which the after-life offers, empowering human mastery to do what it could not do alone by itself.[152]

In summary, Gracián's system of education is focused on self-knowledge and on growth in virtue in order that the person may conquer and achieve mastery.[153]

Stages of Life

For Gracián, education is not the only contributor to the growth and evolution of character. Age also is in itself a very significant influence in personality.[154] For example, a virtuous person increases and insures his authority with age.[155] However, regardless of his virtue, an old person should limit his responsibilities not only because he may be weaker in his faculties, but also because he may have too few of years than are necessary to be personally accountable for very large and time consuming projects.[156]

---

[152]See, for example, *El Discreto* Realce 25. The complete novel of *El Criticón* is about the liberating experience of disabuse. However, see especially Part Three on old age, particularly crises 9, 10, and 11.

[153]See, for example, *El Criticón* I, Crisi 9; *Oráculo* Aphorism 89.

[154]See, for example, *El Criticón* II, Crisi I, when Andrenio wonders about the changes of personality from youth to adulthood: "Either here is a mystery or these men have just gotten married..." Argos answered: "What could be more enchanting...than thirty years on their shoulders?" ("Aquí algún misterio hay, o esos hombres se han casado..." "¿Qué mayor encanto...que treinta años a cuestas?")

[155]Authority is not only increased by the experience of years. It is also ensured by an unquestionable reputation for steadiness in virtue which the old person has earned through his life. It does not matter that this person starts losing the strength of his faculties. For example, doting, grunting, erring, and making the young wait are rather ornaments and prerogatives of virtuous elders. Their lives are proof that they have become sovereigns of themselves—and this sovereignty buttresses their authority, fuels their reputation, dresses them with honor, and inspires admiration and emulation in the young for ever. See *El Criticón* III, crisis 1 and 2.

[156]See, for example, Gracián's reproof of old age's impossible and vain projects that he

When writing about the ages of life, Gracián included many variables such as genius, sex, public responsibilities, and other aspects concerning mastery.[157] A glance on some analytical schemes he used to study the stages of life may offer a rapid view of Gracián's doctrines of age. At the same time these schemes may give an idea of Gracián's controversial emblematic style.[158]

For example, he applied to the ages of man the old scheme of seasons, which does not need an explanation here.[159] He also reflected on the changing colors of hair: the blonde speaks of the immaturity of youths, the dark resembles the maturity of adults, and gray hair is similar to the decay of old age.[160] He believed that the virtues of wonderment,[161] bravery, ingenuity, and judgment respectively peak in children, youth, early adulthood, and mature adulthood.[162] If life were a play, the children and the youth would speak with the dead (that is books) in the first act; the adults would speak with the living (that means public life) in the second act; and the elders would speak with themselves (that means, they philosophize) in the final act.[163] He symbolically applied the ancient planetarium to human decades: 1) Moon (because of the changes and moodiness of childhood), 2) Mercury (because of the learning of the arts), 3) Venus (Oh, Venus!), 4) the Sun (because the person is in the prime of his ingenuity), 5) Mars

---

called "chimeras." *El Criticón* III, Crisi 3.

[157]*El Criticón* takes the reader on a journey through the different ages of people.

[158]Voltaire and Jorge Luis Borges disliked Gracián's emblems, regarding them as cold and overdone. Cf. Coster 289 and Ramos-Foster 70–71. With deep personal involvement, Schopenhauer would rather engage in the painstaking job of translating some of Gracián's most emblematic works into German, finding in them significant moral and intellectual challenge. Cf. E. Correa Calderón, "Introducción," Baltasar Gracián, *Obras Completas* cxlviii-cxlix. I belong to Schopenhauer's party.

[159]See *El Discreto* Realce 25.

[160]See *El Criticón* II, Crisi 13.

[161]See, *El Criticón* I, Crisi 2.

[162]See, for example, *Oráculo* Aphorism 298.

[163]See *Oráculo* Aphorism 229; *El Discreto* Realce 25.

(because it is the thoughest time for work), 6) Jupiter (judgment has reached its maturity), 7) Saturn (old age makes the person an obscure, weak, and remote planet), 8) Moon (if the person is still living, he is childish again). If vices are involved, gluttony is especially suffered by children, lust by the youth, greed by mature people, and arrogance by the elders.[164] Quoting a fable from the picaresque writer Mateo Alemán,[165] Gracián explained that the first thirty years of life are the human ones because of people's blind confidence, carelessness, and pride in themselves. The following twenty years are the jackass ones, because people do not have any option but to work like jackasses. Then come twenty dog years, of gruntling and growling. And the final twenty years are the monkey ones, when people hardly have enough strength to cover their shame and hide from the abuse inflicted by thoughtless youths.[166]

A final comment: Gracián's analysis of the stages of life trascends the person's age and applies also to the historical development of nations,[167] and to positions in public life (there are momentous times to take office or to leave it).[168]

---

[164]See *El Criticón* III, Crisi 10 and Crisi 3.

[165]See Mateo Alemán, *Guzmán de Alfarache* Second Part, Book One, Chapter 3.

[166]See *Agudeza* Discourse 56; *El Discreto* Realce 25.

[167]*El Criticón*'s journey through life is also a journey through European countries. Spain is childish or youthful (Part One). From Aragón to Central Europe, there is adulthood (Part Two). Germany and Italy are already old nations (Part Three). See particularly *El Criticón* III, 10. Gracián here seems an important precedent to Giambattista Vico's doctrine of history and of cultural development.

[168]See, for example, *El Discreto* Realce 12; *El Héroe* primores 10 and 11; *Oráculo* aphorisms 39, 59, 110, and 153.

9   Defining Wit

GRACIÁN SEEMINGLY THOUGHT IMPOSSIBLE TO DEFINE such as elusive thing as wit; hopefully its understanding would come by seeing it directly:

> Its being is a being of the kind more easily known by perceiving its mass, rather than by having its precise definition...[1]

His *Agudeza y Arte de Ingenio* thus abounds in illustrations which would let the reader reach a knowledge of wit through experience.[2]

But counting only on illustrations to explain the essence of wit suggests that Gracián neglected the job of theorizing, leaving such a challenge to the student—a neglect which may hardly be justified even by recalling Gracián's pedagogical beliefs, such as, not declaring doctrines, but presenting them veiled so that students reach learning through their own effort.[3]

---

[1]See *Agudeza* Discourse 2: "Es este ser uno de aquellos que son más conocidos a bulto, y menos a precisión..."

[2]Excellent studies of these illustrations exist, for example, Evaristo Correa Calderón "Índice Onomástico" and "Índice de Primeros Versos" Baltasar Gracián y Morales, *Agudeza y Arte de Ingenio* (Madrid: Editorial Castalia, 1969) 2: 259–275; E. Correa Calderón, *Baltasar Gracián. Su vida y su obra*, (Madrid: Ed. Gredos, 1961) 154–168; and Arturo del Hoyo 1257–1302.

[3]Teaching wit with pure illustrations can be misleading. A stick as an instrument could be thought of differently according to its diverse purposes: to hit, to dig, to pick, to scratch, etc. Likewise, Gracián's methods—if just illustrated—could be interpreted in many different ways depending what they are believed to be used for, for example, an art of poetry (see, for example, Curtius 273–201, who believed that the *Agudeza* was a code of mannerist literature of all poetic ages), an art of extended tropes (see, for example, E. Sarmiento, "Gracián's 'Agudeza y Arte de Ingenio,'" *Modern Language Review* 27 (1932): 280–292), an art of imagination (see, for example, Emilio Hidalgo Serna, "The Philosophy of Ingenium: Concept and Ingenious Method in Baltasar Gracián" *Philosophy and Rhetoric* (Fall 1980) 245–263; Hidalgo Serna does not strip Gracián's theories from their epistemological implications, however, Hidalgo Serna still reduces these methods to the power of just addressing the imagination), etc.

Fortunately, Gracián left something more than clues.   He proposed three important definitions.   The first definition refers to an artistic method:

> Hence, this conceptive artifice consists in an exquisite agreement, a harmonious correlation between two or three knowable extremes, expressed by an act of understanding.[4]

A second definition refers to this same act of understanding:

> Accordingly, concept may be defined thus: it is an act of understanding which extracts[5] the correspondence found among the objects.[6]

A third definition refers to a discursive achievement or result:

> The consonance or harmonious correlation itself, which has been extracted, is the objective subtlety...[7]

An Act of Understanding

Without seemingly being specific, Gracián's definitions present wit as an act of understanding.   Which one is it?, since the schools teach that there are three acts of understanding: conceptualization, judgment, and inference.

Clear answers is found in other places of his books.   For example, Gracián

---

[4]*Agudeza* Discourse 2: "Consiste, pues, este artificio conceptuoso, en una primorosa concordancia, en una armónica correlación entre dos o tres cognoscibles extremos, expresada por un acto del entendimiento".

[5]Gracián used here the word "exprimir" which may also be translated as "to squeeze out."

[6]*Agudeza* Discourse 2: "De suerte que se puede definir el concepto: Es un acto del entendimiento, que exprime la correspondencia que se halla entre los objetos".

[7]*Agudeza* Discourse 2: "La misma consonancia o correlación armoniosa exprimida, es la sutileza objectiva..."

did not intend to study judgment under the heading of ingenuity, since he usually separated the one from the other:

> I have devoted some of my works to judgment, and most recently my *Art of Prudence*, but this one I am dedicating to Ingenuity.[8]

He did not mean to study inference either:

> A syllogism is built on rules; with rules, then, let the concept be forged.[9]

However, from this elimination, it does not easily follow that conceptualization is the topic left to Gracián's theories of ingenuity. A doubt springs from Gracián's concepts not looking like formal logic's—not expressed with simple and sharp terms such as *punishment, penance, offense, repentance, pertinacy,* or, better, *x, y,* and *z,* or any agreed and replaceable symbol such as ☺, which declare the concept and transmit it like water through a channel to the unwitting. Rather Gracián's concepts appear as discursive structures—typically subtleties—which establish a complex set of relationships among different objects of understanding. Moreover, these structures are not easily replaceable,[10] and do not transmit but prompt understanding, hoping that an

---

[8]*Agudeza* Al Letor: "He destinado algunos de mis trabajos al juicio, y poco ha el *Arte de la Prudencia*: éste dedico al Ingenio..."

[9]*Agudeza* Discourse 1: "Armase con reglas un silogismo; fórjese, pues, con ellas un concepto".

[10]The uniqueness of a discursive structure is not simplistically explained by Gracián in terms of style or language, but usually in complex terms: the relationships intellectually discovered or established by a person among cognizable objects: "...each person perceives an order in the stars as he wishes." ("...cada uno proporciona las estrellas como quiere" *El Criticón* I, Crisi 2). Thanks to being concerned with the relationships betwen cognizable objects rather than style, Gracián's type of concepts still offers some hope of being translated from one language to another. If the difficulty of translation remains, it is due less to stylistic factors than to the different power of each language of presenting relationships between objects. Words themselves differ in their connotations from one tongue to another; this variance of connotations makes the possible points of contact between the objects expressed

attentive and active mind is its recipient—one who "squeezes out" the idea from the subtlety. For example, Gracián illustrated his structures with Miguel de Ribellas addressing the Heavenly Prince, St Michael Archangel:[11]

> I will postrate myself at your feet,
> And there, where Lucifer lies stretched,
> We will both do penance:
>   For if I have offended the same Lord,
>   There is no difference 'twixt him and me
>   But he is pertinacious, and I repent.[12]

How could these discursive structures be called concepts by Gracián? Shouldn't they be called judgments since they are not usually presented in separate and individual terms, but by means of propositions? Moreover, shouldn't they be called inference in so far as they often are expressed by means of argumentation?[13] Furthermore, shouldn't they be called discourses since sometimes they may require a whole speech to be said?[14]

Certainly, Gracián's discursive structures are often fashioned as

---

diverse. Moreover, languages differ in syntax. Languages with a powerful syntax would be thus more capable of conveying relationships between objects than languages with a simple syntax.

[11]Catholic iconography often represents St Michael Archangel after defeating Satan. St Michael victoriously holds a sword while, with one of his feet, he immobilizes Satan's head.

[12]*Agudeza* Discourse 14:
> Postraréme a tus pies tendido,
> Y allí do Lucifer está tendido,
> Juntos los dos haremos penitencia:
>   Que si al mismo Señor tengo ofendido,
> No queda entre él y mí más diferencia,
> De estar él pertinaz, yo arrepentido.

[13]See, for example, *Agudeza* discourses 36 to 38, which deal with "conceptual argumentation".

[14]See, for example, *Agudeza* discourses 51 to 57, which deal with compounded wit, that is, concepts which spring from complete and elaborate speeches.

propositions, or argumentations, or even complete discourses. Nevertheless, the primary purpose of these structures for the talent of ingenuity is not to assent or dissent about something, that is, to judge; it is not to derive a conclusion either, that is, to infer, but their main function is to allow the understanding to grasp an idea not conceived or thought of previously. Their purpose is to reach the understanding of something new—the discernment of a point not seen before by the mind.

For example, I finally got an explanation, recently, of why DNA has the power to multiply itself, and is therefore the key to life. A friend of mine[15] spent beyond an hour addressing my almost science-proof brains. She patiently used models made of marbles to illustrate her ideas as a teacher would use oranges to make children understand the meaning of an addition. At the end I got a sort of an idea about it:

> Some complex molecules, when they break apart, do it in two simpler molecules which, although halves of the one broken apart, are correlative puzzle pieces the one of the other. Moreover, these pieces only have a power to recombine with a new set of atoms if these atoms arrange themselves as the former half was arranged. Therefore, when the two halves which broke apart recombine, they do it with two newly arranged replicas of the former halves. Thus, instead of having the original two halves which formed one molecule of DNA, then there are two molecules of DNA with four halves, which on their turn, when breaking apart and recombining, would produce eight halves, and then sixteen, and so on, "Be fruitful and *geometrically* multiply..."

My friend supplied some information that I needed, and her explanation was somehow fashioned argumentatively. However, she was neither informing,[16] arguing, proving a point, drawing implications, nor trying to make me advance a judgment of assent or dissent. She just hoped for some understanding on my

---

[15] Irene de de las Peñas, from Mexico City.

[16] For Gracián, plain information by itself does not necessarily render understanding. It provides only the raw materials which are meant to be understood by reason if empowered by wit with structures of correspondence, that is, "concepts."

part of what is meant by DNA as the key to life.[17]

Another example of a discourse directed to my understanding also came from her. She pointed out that frogs have the largest chains of DNA in the animal kingdom. She then explained that this size serves to codify the additional genetic information needed to transform frogs into princes if kissed. She was not concerned with presenting evidence and she was not arguing with me or trying to gain my belief. She was just sharing with me an enjoyable idea.

Both of my friend's examples appealed to my understanding, although they may differ if I were to test them with my judgment. The case is that, according to Gracián, none of these examples invalidate my friend's ingenuity in as much as they were powerful enough to make me grasp new ideas. For Gracián, a talent of ingenuity could be crazy and, nevertheless, still be the most brilliant, whereas judgment and inference could only be valid if they are right and sound.[18]

The fact is that Gracián's theories of ingenuity refer to an act of understanding which is not judgment or inference, but a new conceptualization. Gracián's discursive structures may look like logical propositions and argumentations, but their purpose is to lead the mind to conceptualize an idea for the first time. Their use is not to criticize an idea (either by judgment or inference), but to introduce it to the understanding, that is, to reach a conceptualization.

Moreover, Gracián primarily understood conceptualization in a way which may seem strange to formal logicians. For him, a conceptualization was the introduction of new ideas to the mind, and not a *formal-logic operation*. A conceptualization was not the neat *re*presentation of a preexistent thought in the

---

[17]The discovery of DNA's function could be described as one of the most outstanding examples of wit in action. In 1953, having been known the presence of DNA in the cell for 80 years, Watson and Crick came to hypothesize by "using a great deal of intuition" that the peculiar mirroring structure of the halves of a DNA molecule—distinguishing it from other molecular chains of proteins—might provide an explanation for the mechanisms of reproduction in living creatures. See Robert Wallace, Jack L. King, Gerald P. Sanders, *Biology the Science of Life*. (Scott, Foresman and Company, 1986) 199, 218–220.

[18]See *Oráculo* Aphorism 283. Cf., also aphorisms 56 and 194.

mind by means of a term, as it is for formal logicians. For Gracián, a conceptualization was an *act of understanding*: a concept consisting of the astounding *presentation* of a thought to the mind for the first time. Thus, Gracián's concepts are not those simply expressed by terms or symbols. Gracián's concepts are those prompted by complex discursive structures which produce understanding, and as such belong more to the art of ingenuity. In fact, Gracián believed that ingenuity and logic were two different arts:

> The progress of enterprises already begun is easy; inventing is arduous...The ancients found methods for syllogisms...they sealed wit.[19]

Logic was an art of syllogizing, and as such, was, for Gracián, insufficient for the acquisition of new learning.[20] Thus, he undertook the task of theorizing on the acts of ingenuity, that is, the acts of understanding bringing forth a new conceptualization.

---

[19]*Agudeza* Discourse 1: "Fácil es adelantar lo comenzado; arduo el inventar...Hallaron los antiguos métodos al silogismo...sellaron la agudeza..."

[20]For Gracián, a formal logic of syllogizing was also insufficient as an instrument of judgment. Judgment also needs some material foundations—experience—to ground its conclusions. For now it is enough to say that, interpreting Gracián, ingenuity refers to the ways the mind learns new ideas; judgment, to the ways the mind grounds its assent to ideas on experience; and logic, to the ways the mind criticizes the formal operations reaching conclusions. This view of conceptualization, judgment, and inference as pertaining to different theoretical fields would make Gracián depart from some scholastic logic which still today sees all acts of understanding as pertaining to general logic, the only difference being that, as acts of understanding, they refer to psychological or epistemological logic, whereas as a critical language they refer to formal logic. To amplify this point, some elementary logics from schoolmen may be sufficient, for example, Raúl Gutiérrez Sáenz, *Introducción a la Lógica* (México: Ed. Esfinge, 1977) 69. In any case, the great inspiration of scholasticism, Aristotle himself, made the operations of understanding—those of learning the first principles, the universals from sensations—and the operations of demostration—those of scientific proof—be distinguished from each other. See *Posterior Analytics* II, v, 19.

What "Squeezing" or "Extracting" Concepts Means

The Spanish *exprimir* denotes the act of squeezing the juice from something, and connotes both the acts of intellectually abstracting and verbally expressing. This connotation features the extent of the effort of aprehending ideas according to Gracián.

"Squeezing" and the Different Methods of Conceptualization

There are many methods which help the mind to make sense of—to find meaningful—the raw data. Reviewing these methods, I may, for example, list definition, description, analysis, synthesis, division, comparison, contrast, tropes, and, considering the method usually associated with Gracián, witticisms. In any case, every kind of method on some occasion or another seems to be included in Gracián's illustrations of wit.

For instance, consider this *definition* of one woman, taken from Luis de Góngora:

> He was found in the country by that woman,
> **the life and the death** of men.[21]

From the same song, Gracián quoted a *description* of a man:

> The body, with **insufficient** blood,
> the eyes, with **excessive** night.[22]

Some of Gracián's illustrations imply a task of *analysis*, in which a single

---

[21]*Agudeza* Discourse 5, which quotes Góngora's song "En una fiesta que se hizo en Sevilla a San Hermenegildo":
> Le halló en el campo aquella
> **Vida y muerte** de los hombres.

[22]*Agudeza* Discourse 5:
> El cuerpo **con poca** sangre,
> los ojos **con mucha** noche.

circumstance is isolated from a set of objects considered. Haughtiness is the circumstance in question in this old example borrowed from the *Romancero General*:

> The Tower of Felisalva,
> I will bet that is the one,
> **since it challenges the stars**
> **to harmonize with its haughty lord.**[23]

There are also illustrations implying the task of *synthesis*. Consider, for example, this one from Juan Rufo, when he explained to Don Juan de Austria what comets announce when they precede the death of kings:

> For the comet sent
> when death strikes the kings
> **is lightening threatening their bodies**
> **and a star guiding their souls.**[24]

For Juan Rufo, a comet synthesizes the idea of a providential announcement of both a threatening and a hopeful death for kings.

Presenting a concept to the mind could involve the method of *division*, too, in which a whole is sorted and separately detailed in its parts, in order to make it clear. This illustration is from the Canon Francisco Antonio Fuser:

---

[23]*Agudeza* Discourse 6:
> La torre de Felisalva
> yo apostaré que es aquella
> **que en fe de su altivo dueño**
> **compite con las estrellas.**

[24]*Agudeza* Discourse 9:
> Porque el cometa que envía
> cuando a morir los emplaza,
> **rayo es que el cuerpo amenaza**
> **y estrella que el alma guía.**

Thrice blind, Longinus pierced his God;
blind of his body, as is evident;
blind of his soul, without seeking remedy
and blind by his anger and its fire...[25]

Gracián's method of conceptualization, one of correspondences, is of course often illustrated with *comparisons* and *contrasts* which make things and ideas reciprocally clarify their meanings. This example from *Romancero General* includes very complex comparisons and contrasts:

The two brothers quarreled,
and in such a fashion they quarreled
**that the one who remained alive would be Cain
if the dead one were not he.**[26]

Among the illustrations, Gracián also included *metaphors* and other *tropes* which help to present ideas to the understanding. Here is again an example borrowed from Góngora:

Many centuries of beauty
in few years of age.[27]

---

[25]*Agudeza* Discourse 51:
Longinos hiere a Dios, tres veces ciego;
ciego del cuerpo, como se ve claro;
ciego del alma, sin buscar reparo,
y ciego de la cólera y su fuego (...)

[26]*Agudeza* Discourse 15
Riñeron los dos hermanos,
y de tal suerte riñeron,
**que fuera Caín el vivo,
a no haberlo sido el muerto.**

[27]*Agudeza* Discourse 5:
Muchos siglos de hermosura,
en pocos años de edad.

However, the methods of conceptualization mentioned above are not the ones specifically attracting Gracián's theoretical concern. If they appear as illustrations of *Agudeza*, they principally do so because of their witty features. The fact is that Gracián was more interested in the conceptualizing power of *witticisms*. Consider this subtlety from Alonso Girón de Rebolledo, penetrating further on the mocking event of a rooster signalizing St Peter's cowardice:

> Shouldn't the rooster crow
> recognizing such a glamorous chick?[28]

Moreover, Gracián did not think that witticisms were just one additional method of conceptualization. He believed that all original effort of human conceptualization (for that purpose: definition, description, analysis, synthesis, division, etc.) departed from the use of discursive structures of correspondences as those embodied in witticisms:

> This kind of correspondence is generic to every concept, and it embraces the entire art of ingenuity.[29]

These correspondences consist in the confrontation of objects to discover and abstract the characteristics they share and the characteristics which make them different, a task which leads the mind to grasp well defined ideas. Yet, before explaining further what this confrontation means, it is important to be aware of what it doesn't.

Comparisons Resembling the "Squeezing" of Correspondences

Several methods resemble the "squeezing" of correspondences because of

---

[28]*Agudeza* Discourse 3:
   ¿No había de cantar el gallo
   viendo tan grande gallina?

[29]*Agudeza* Discourse 2: "Esta correspondencia es génerica a todos los conceptos, y abraza todo el artificio del ingenio..."

resting on comparisons between terms. However, not every comparison intends the apprehension of ideas, as wit does. The fact is that some comparisons primarily aim at judgment or even inference.

Arts whose methods strongly resemble Gracián's "squeezing" of correspondences are Aristotle's dialectics, and in general, scholastic disputation. The *Topica* gives art to the critical clarification of terms on the grounds of their relationship in a proposition.[30] For such a study of terms, the *Topica* proposes the use of definitions, comparison, contrast, etimologies, and other tecniques alike, which are also embodied in Gracián's subtleties.[31] Moreover, placed side by side with scholastic disputations, Gracián's witticisms strongly resemble them in the use of techniques to overturn a contrary opinion.[32] However, dialectic's purpose is to criticize terms and propositions to assure that they correctly lead, by means of argumentation, to probable conclusions,[33] whereas Gracián's subtleties are directed *to perceive, to produce, to grasp* such terms—their judgment and implications rather being a posterior and separate aim.[34]

Behind Gracián's belief, there is the understanding that by the unexpected, and thus witty, confrontation of things, previously unnoticed tokens and

---

[30]The four general kinds of relationships of one term with another could be of genus, definition, property, or accident. See *Topica* I, 4. Aristotle also identified more specific kinds of relationships, for example, antecedents, concomitants, and consequents, which are types of accidents. See *Topica* II, 4. Notice that the character of a term as accident, genus, property, or definition, does not rest on the term itself, but on its relationship with other terms. Differently, the categories giving character to a term—such as substance, quality, quantity, etcetera—do not need to refer to the relationship they keep with other terms, in order to define themselves; they are the form itself of the objects studied. See, for example, *Topica* I, 9.

[31]See, for example, *Topica* I, 13 to 18. Cf., for example, with *Agudeza* discourses 9 to 16.

[32]Consider, for example, Gracián's transpositions and retorts (*Agudeza* discourses 17 and 18), and in general Gracián's methods of ratiocination (see, for example, *Agudeza* discourses 6 to 8).

[33]See *Topica* I, 1.

[34]See, for example, *Agudeza* Discourse 2.

relationships of these things are highlighted and revealed to human perception, as if using a telescope[35] to see the stars, or some catalysts to reveal the chemistry of some reagents:

> Cognizable extremes are more easily observed if united[36] with one kind than with another—also their correlate[37]—, that the enhancement of subtlety for one case is a ballast for the other.[38]

And yet, the comparison made between extremes is not judgmental—it is not a comparison in which assent is given either to similarities or to differences of objects. The comparison is rather heuristic in which relationships and tokens shared by objects are abstracted and finally perceived by the mind.

The non-judgmental character of Gracián's comparisons can be appreciated in metaphors and other forms of figurative language that may wittily compare, such as antitheses do. However, their function for ingenuity essentially is to shed light on an issue so that the mind understands; this function is just accidentally stylistic so as to delight the fancy with imaginative embellishments.

In a similar fashion, some of Gracián's argumentative subtleties may look like inferential forms of comparison, such as argument by example and by

---

[35]Emanuele Tesauro used the metaphor of a telescope to symbolize his complete work: the *Cannocchiale Aristotelico*. Baltasar Gracián also used the metaphor of lenses applied to factors sharpening the understanding. However, Gracián sometimes meant something negative by these lenses. For example, Gracián identified one lens with malice, and the second lens with biased affection, one and the other distorting the right perception of the moral character of people. See *El Criticón* II, Crisi 9.

[36]A rewording of this statement could be: "**A** is more easily known if compared with **B**, and vice versa."

[37]"Also the correlate" could be reworded by saying, "moreover, the tokens **x**, **y**, and **z**, etc., that **A** and **B** share are more easily identifiable by means of this kind of comparison."

[38]*Agudeza* Discourse 2: "Resaltan más con unos que con otros los extremos cognoscibles, si se unen, y el correlato, que el realce de sutileza para uno es lastre para otro". Note that Gracián did not believe that all comparisons were equally efficient in highlighting the specific character of **A**, **B**, and their shared tokens. Some comparisons do a better job than others.

analogy.[39]   But these subtleties' primary function is apprehending ideas, discovering a possible argument, as happens with witty argumentation.[40] Their aim is not securing ideas through an inference yet. Certainly, inferences may follow from establishing relationships between terms. However, for Gracián, no inference can proceed if the terms of the reasoning are not previously discovered and well delimited by a conceptualization.[41] If the terms to be conclusively related in an argument are still not defined, then, it is not yet clear what is being conclusively established or discussed.[42]

So, the witty "squeezing" of correspondences is first, and refers to comparisons which lead to the clear apprehension of ideas—to the discovery of the terms. The inferential comparisons come later, and refer to the connection of already clear terms in order to reach their implications, regardless if the argumentation is a deduction or an induction.

For it should be clear that Gracián did not mean an induction when he talked about wit. Wit is the process which abstracts ideas from raw data. It is the most basic rational process, and *the only one* which rises from sensual experience and imaginative stimuli to abstract thoughts. Inference could only occur when those abstract and well delimited thoughts *already exist*.[43] In the scholastic system

---

[39]Subtleties may resemble analogies, regardless of how an analogy is understood, either just as an inference proceeding from picturesque resemblances (see Campbell 53), or as an inference which, grounded on an accidental feature shared by the objects compared, concludes further and establishes additional and more substantial things as shared in common (see Richard Whately, *Elements of Rhetoric* Ed. by Douglas Ehninger (Southern Illinois University Press, 1963) 90–103).

[40]See *Agudeza* discourses 36–38.

[41]See *Agudeza* Discourse 36.

[42]Without having clear ideas yet, people sometimes believe they are already arguing. Nonetheless they would just be talking about completely different things without noticing their failure to understand themselves and each other. A dispute over an issue should then take some preliminary time to delimit the points discussed, before engaging in any effort to prove argumentatively and to conclusively judge such points.

[43]See *Agudeza*, for example, discourses 1 and 2.

within which Gracián worked, inductions as much as deductions should proceed from abstract thoughts. That is considered as possible because abstract thoughts could refer to singular,[44] particular,[45] or universal cases.[46] A deduction would proceed from a well established universal case to its implications in particular or singular cases. An induction would proceed from singular and indeed well defined cases (not vague, just felt, and undefined images, but rather abstract, accurate, and rational ideas) of the same species, to a general conclusion which would establish that a set of singular cases share something universal to all of them.[47] If inference were meant to be the same as conceptualization, then it would be senseless for schoolmen—and for Gracián—to separate the first act of understanding—simple apprehension—from the third one—inference.

Gracián made clear his belief about the primacy of wit—the art of conceptualization—over other acts of understanding:

> Each faculty has a king among its acts, and also a king among its objects; the concept reigns and wit is victor concerning those of the mind.[48]

---

[44]For example, *this Mexican*, Arturo Zárate Ruiz, is both an abstract and a singular idea. When being rationally apprehended, this idea needs not include all of Arturo's image in the mind, for example, features such as a mole behind his left-nostril, and the lack of his vermiform appendix and of another appendix which normally rests on a person's shoulders. Certainly, the idea could be detailed: he is one of the sons of Alfredo Zárate de los Santos and Carmen Ruiz Oronoz, brother of Alfredo, and twin of Roberto, but even this idea is abstract and does not need imaginative thinking. In fact, the specification of the idea does not need to be very complex in order to be singular. Arturo can be properly conceptualized as *this man, this journalist, this patient with a diatal hernia, this hypochondriac*, etc. Moreover, these concepts can be differently used depending the circumstance relevant to the case or to the inference being made with singular instances of the same kind, for example, a generalization from studying particular cases of hypochondriacs.

[45]For example, *some Mexicans*, those living in the Northeast.

[46]For example, *all Mexicans*.

[47]Today, in any systematic experimental research, one should first define well the set of singular objects to be studied, if later one wishes to proceed and reach generalizations.

[48]*Agudeza* Discourse 1: "Tiene cada potencia un rey entre sus actos, y un otro entre sus

He added:

> Understanding without wit and concepts is a sun without light, without rays...[49]

However, Gracián did not regard wit as something bringing understanding to completion. The proving and judgment of ideas should still be reached. If judgment is lacking, if wit is just enjoyed in its purity of subtle relationships, then Gracián did not hesitate to call it the opposite of sound understanding (that is, the opposite of the union of wit and judgment).[50]

In summary, comparison of terms is a method shared by wit, dialectics, metaphor and other figurative expressions, analogy, induction, and deduction. However, wit uses the method of relating terms in order to bring forth new concepts, without securing by itself the judgment or the proving of the idea conceived.

"To Squeeze" is to Grasp and Express Abstract Ideas

Although the material foundation of wit's "squeezed" ideas often gives them an imaginative appearance and expression, for Gracián, these ideas are nonetheless abstract and with an appeal to rational understanding.

Nevertheless, it is easy to regard these concepts as rather addressed to the imagination—to pure fancy. For example, Gracián believed that if a conversation is empowered with conceptist style,[51] it should stimulate the

---

objectos; entre los de la mente reina el concepto, triunfa la agudeza".

[49]*Agudeza* Discourse 1: "Entendimiento sin agudeza ni conceptos, es sol sin luz, sin rayos..."

[50]Gracián's definition of wit as something contrary to understanding (see *Agudeza* Discourse 1) should be interpreted in the whole context of his theories, particularly *Agudeza* discourses 1 to 4, and *El Héroe* Primor 3.

[51]Conceptist style refers to the use of structures of correspondence in a text to suggest new ideas, rather than the use of previously understood terms to declare ordinary ideas. It also refers to the fashion of witty discourse which developed in Spain in the seventeenth century, whose main figures were Baltasar Gracián and Francisco de Quevedo.

audience's imagination, because things are not just said by the speaker, but perceived by the listener through his own experience as evoked by the speaker's words.[52] Gracián also identified metaphor and, in general, figurative language, with the "ordinary office" of discourse,[53] because figures supply the images the mind uses to reflect upon, when "squeezing" concepts.[54]

Even so, it should not be forgotten that Gracián theorized about the art of ingenuity in order to trascend the limitations that he believed belonged to rhetoric. For Gracián, rhetoric was an art of pure tropes and figures of language. He clearly distinguished the art of ingenuity from "rhetoric"—from the pure recourse to imaginative ornaments of speech:

> Wit makes recourse of rhetorical tropes and figures as if instruments cultivatedly to squeeze its concepts; but they [rhetorical tropes and figures] contain themselves within the boundaries of the material foundations of the subtlety, and, at best, they may be ornaments of thoughts.[55]

Gracián seldom used the word imagination in his works, and when he did it, he described it as a "tyrant" to be restrained by the person, lest imagination takes over this person and subdues him with emotional representations of the most diverse kinds.[56] Ingenuity rather illuminates the mind, not with mere material

---

[52]See *El Criticón* I, Crisi 1.

[53]Note that figurative language is *ordinary* for Gracián, and *not deviated.*

[54]See *Agudeza* Discourse 53; see also discourses 9 and 20.

[55]*Agudeza* Al Lector: "Válese la agudeza de los tropos y figuras retóricas, como de instrumentos para exprimir cultamente sus concetos; pero contiénense ellos a la raya de fundamentos materiales de la sutileza, y cuando más, de adornos del pensamiento". Here, I should notice that the closest translation I found of *cultamente* was *cultivatedly*, and that this word has a very technical meaning: it refers to the modes of writing of *culteranist* authors as opposed to those of the *conceptist* school, in the seventeenth century. A *culteranist* author would be characterized by his imaginative, affected, and flowery style, that is, "purely rhetorical," and a *conceptist* author would rather choose a language additionally embodying abstract thoughts and primarily appealing to ingenuity.

[56]See *Oráculo* Aphorism 25.

light as the one perceived from the celestial bodies, but with immaterial rays which enlighten the understanding.[57] In fact, when conceptualizing, ingenuity surpasses what is merely apprehended by the senses, and penetrates into the depths of things by means of reflection.[58]

Therefore, for Gracián, wit reaches abstract thought. Wit conceives ideas which enjoy the properties of abstract concepts. Indeed, Gracián's subtleties present to the mind what is generic or common between two dissimilar things, by means of "proportions."[59] To appreciate this point, consider this epigram from Martial quoted by Gracián in *Agudeza*:

> Not long ago, Diaulus was a physician, now he is a mortician:
> What he practices as a mortician, he had already practiced as a physician.[60]

Gracián's subtleties also highlight the differentia or specifying features separating two things alike, by means of "improportions."[61] For example, this observation Gracián quoted from Ausonius Gallus:

> Unhappy Dido, never well married with either of your husbands!
> This one died and you run away; that one ran away and you die.[62]

---

[57]See *Agudeza* Discourse 1: "...cuantos [rayos] brillan en las celestes lumbreras son materiales con los del ingenio".

[58]See *Oráculo* Aphorism 35.

[59]See *Agudeza* Discourse 4.

[60]*Agudeza* Discourse 4:
> Nuper erat Medicus, nunc est vespillo Diaulus:
> Quod vespillo facit, fecerat et Medicus.

[61]See *Agudeza* Discourse 5.

[62]*Agudeza* Discourse 5:
> Infelix Dido nulli bene nupta marito;
> Hoc pereunte fugis; hoc fugiente peris.

The concepts thus rising reveal themselves as possesing some extension and comprehension. For example, the idea of Dido's husbands extends to Sichaeus and Aeneas, and comprehends the common feature of having offered an unhappy relationship to Dido.

But, by comparing and contrasting two things, I think Gracián's simplest subtleties may enable the abstraction not only of one, but of three or more concepts. First, the common feature is isolated and conceptually delimited, with the possibility of being thought separately from the things from which it has originally been abstracted. Moreover, the two correlated things are conceptually distinguished—defined—by means of the confrontation which highlights both their generic feature and their differentiae. If one goes further in this "squeezing" task, one should also identify the whole idea of the relationship which puts together all the elements.[63] Not only **C** which is the common element, but also the compared objects **A** and **B** are better understood, and even **D** which is the relationship kept by all these elements.[64] The focus on one concept or another may depend on the case in question:[65]

---

[63]As discussed later, the relationship discovered does not reduce itself to establishing links of equality between the circumstances compared. The relationship could also inform about links of cause-effect, genre-species, whole-part, or any other topic. See *Agudeza* discourses 16 and 4.

[64]Hidalgo Serna seemingly considers that Gracián's theories are all about **D**, that is, the concept which comprehends the relationship established between **A** and **B**, "the conceptual expression of correspondences." See Emilio Hidalgo Serna, "The Philosophy of *Ingenium*: Concept and Ingenious Method in Baltasar Gracián," *Philosophy of Rhetoric* 13.4 (Fall: 1980) 251. However, grounded on my understanding of Gracián's notion of "squeezing," his many illustrations of witticisms, and Pallavicino's clear doctrines of abstraction by means of comparative apprehension (see *Trattato* Chapter 7), I believe that Gracián's theories of wit also apply to the abstraction of **C**, that is, the common feature shared by **A** and **B**.

[65]If one is more discriminating, one would identify and isolate two other concepts: the respective differentiae of **A** and **B**. Moreover, one may even identify as many concepts as the mind establishes by paying attention to the many possible relationships of the objects and elements compared, either in isolation or combined, for example: $[(A) \cdot (D)]$, $[(C) \cdot (B)]$, $[(C \cdot D) \cdot (A)]$, $[(D) \cdot (B \cdot C)]$, etc.

[When scrutinizing circumstances and correlative terms, wit] identifies a correspondence or convenience explaining either the main subject, or one subject in relation with others. Then, it squeezes it [the correspondence], reflects on it, and in doing so, the subtlety is given.[66]

The abstraction made sometimes may be an elaboration or creation of the mind.[67] However, it often refers to an already existing reality, to a way of being which is intellectually detected in objects:

The objective subtleties are already present in the objects themselves.[68]

This belief defines Gracián as a realist.

The Objects from Which Concepts are Squeezed

According to Gracián, ingenuity very comprehensively serves all the arts and sciences.[69] Therefore, the objects of ingenuity are those belonging to all fields of knowledge and action. Here, however, it is enough to consider one of the elementary distinctions which Gracián made among subtleties. Subtleties could be abstracted from—or expressed by—ideas, words, or actual events.[70]

Ingenuity can directly pay attention to actions, things, facts, or events, and make them its objects either in the discovery or the expression of concepts.

---

[66]*Agudeza* Discourse 4: "...y en descubriendo alguna conformidad o conveniencia, que digan, ya con el principal sujeto, ya unos con otros, exprímela, pondérala, y en esto está la sutileza".

[67]There are two kinds of concepts: those discovered as already existing in a given reality, and those produced or created by the mind. See *Agudeza* Discourse 2.

[68]*Agudeza* Discourse 63: "Están ya en los objetos mismos las agudezas objetivas".

[69]*Agudeza* Discourse 3.

[70]See *Agudeza* Discourse 3.

Ideas are thus conceived by the observation of unexpected relationships between things. For instance, Gracián mentioned an emblem in which Andrea Alciati first expressed his wonderment about the extraordinary finding of a helmet with a beehive in its inside rather than blood; and then he reflected about the sweet fruits of peace.[71] Another instance: recently, the *Chicago Tribune* published an article recounting how an explanation to the Mayan glyphs started to be advanced in 1960. Tatiana Proskourakoff, a professor from Harvard, finally made sense of some unique inscriptions which only were used in specific places and times for limited periods ranging an average of 75, 35, or 15 years; she then asked:

> What kind of things would last 75 years? A lifespan! What would last anywhere from 15 to 35 years? A reign![72]

Regarding wit of facts, seemingly another and yet forgotten archeologist said:

> One stone is a natural fact. Two stones is a human fact. Three stones is a civilization.

Among the examples of actions rendering themselves concepts quoted by Gracián, there is the one from Alexander the Great, when he ingeniously solved the Gordian knot by cutting it with his sword.[73]

Concepts may also be abstracted from an unexpected confrontation of words, and by exploiting either their meanings or their sound properties. Consider this epigram contrasting the piety of a marchioness with the furtive and

---

[71]See *Agudeza* Discourse 20.

[72]Peter Gorner, "Blood from a stone," *Chicago Tribune* Tempo (November 15, 1990) 6. Inspired by professor Prokouriakoff's idea, scholars began to relate the Mayan glyphs to the recording of events occurring during the reign of specific rulers in a city and in a given period. The idea seems to have been successful so far.

[73]See *Agudeza* Discourse 34.

forbidden pleasures of her husband (or who knows if viceversa, or whatever) from Alvaro Cubillo de Aragón, quoted in *Agudeza*:

> The marquis and his wife
> dismissed each other in happiness;
> she left to visit her God,
> while he enjoyed his God's visit.[74]

A more recent example of a wordplay bringing forth a concept is this one taken from Billings' Notes:

> Infants don't have as much fun in infancy as adults do in adultery.[75]

Ideas which are already abstract could relate in untried ways and be squeezed even more. See this illustration from *Agudeza*:

> A remarkable wit once said of St Francis Xavier that he might have been Apostle of the Indies *de jure divino*, on the grounds that all the Apostles were sent in pairs to the spiritual conquest of the world...Only St Thomas, Apostle of the East, does not find a mate, save in this Jesuit Apostle.[76]

Another instance is from President Benito Juárez, who subsumed the laws protecting individuals and the laws securing peace to nations, into a whole comprehensive principle of equity, by means of this political maxim:

---

[74]*Agudeza* Discourse 33:
> El marqués y su mujer,
> Contentos quedan los dos;
> Ella se fue a ver a Dios,
> y a él le vino Dios a ver.

[75]*1,001 Logical Laws* 85.

[76]*Agudeza* Discourse 23. "De San Francisco Javier, dio un gran ingenio que parece que había sido Apóstol de las Indias *de jure divino*, fundándose en que todos los apóstoles salieron a la conquista espiritual del mundo pareados...Sólo a Santo Tomás, apóstol de Oriente, no se halla otro compañero, sino este apóstol jesuita".

Among individuals as among nations, respect for the rights of others means peace.[77]

The Mind Squeezes Correspondences

Ideas, words, or things may be different kinds of objects from which the mind obtains concepts. However, in any case, the objects, by being discovered together through structures of correspondences, bring forth more than what they offer in isolation. As said, the objects **A** and **B** inform the mind about themselves with more precise terms when correlated, since they also inform about **D**, which is the relationship they thus enjoy, and about **C** which is the correlate that, by being shared, grounds the relationship.[78] A series of four (or more) concepts consequently may rise.

This series of concepts are not grasped through subjective or preexistent mental filters like Pellegrini's *fonti* and Tesauro's categories. Gracián's system can reach conceptualization without the aid of these preconceptions. As in Pallavicino's posterior method, the only thing required is the mind itself, which—although a tabula rasa[79]—still is active, and screens the objects through the objective structures of correspondences which arise from the things themselves when the mind intently perceives them connected:

> Each watchful faculty of the soul—I mean those that perceive objects—enjoys some artifice in them [in the objects]. If a proportion between visible parts, it is beauty; if among sounds, it is harmony; and even the vulgar sense of taste detects

---

[77]Benito Juárez, "Triumph of the Republic Speech," delivered in Mexico City, July 15, 1867: "Entre los individuos como entre las naciones, el respeto al derecho ajeno es la paz".

[78]The job of wit is to perceive these relationships and correlates which are presented to the mind, notwithstanding if they are real or spurious. In any case, judgment later takes care of criticizing the things seen by wit.

[79]"Men are born as naked of knowledge in their souls, as of feathers on their bodies." ("Nace el hombre tan desnudo de noticias en el alma, como en el cuerpo de plumas"). *Agudeza* Discourse 1.

the combinations between the spicy and the delicate, the sweet and the sour. The understanding, then, as the first and foremost faculty of the soul, snatches the prime of artifices, the consummation of the exquisite, in all its differentiation of objects.[80]

Gracián preferred that the correspondences established by the mind were between "extremes," that is, very dissimilar objects. However, his method is not essentially against correspondences established between similar objects, or objects of the same species, if these correspondences bring forth new insights into the things studied. Consider, for example, Andrenio's reaction to his encounter with Critilo, the first man Andrenio ever saw in his life:

Critilo, you ask me who I am, and I wish to know it from you. You are the first man who I have ever seen until now, and in you I see myself mirrored more lively than in any of my mute reflections in a spring...[81]

Moreover, the comparison made needs not even to be made with another object of the same species, but could be established between the same object as placed in different times or circumstances:

Comparisons could be made with the same subject, considering its different affections and times, in such a fashion that the subject is compared with itself, contrasting its effects either by proportion, discordance, or excess.[82]

---

[80]*Agudeza* Discourse 2: "Toda potencia intencional del alma, digo las que perciben objectos, gozan de algún artificio en ellos; la proporción entre las partes del visible, es la hermosura; entre los sonidos, la consonancia, que hasta el vulgar gusto halla combinación entre lo picante y suave, entre lo dulce y lo agrio. El entendimiento, pues, como primera y principal potencia, álzase con la prima del artificio, con lo extremado del primor, en todas sus diferencias de objetos".

[81]*El Criticón* I, Crisi 1: "Tú, Critilo, me preguntas quién soy yo y yo deseo saberlo de ti. Tú eres el primer hombre que hasta hoy he visto y en ti me hallo retratado más al vivo que en los mudos cristales de una fuente..."

[82]*Agudeza* Discourse 15: "Puédese hacer el careo con el mismo sujeto propio, según diferentes afectos y tiempos, de suerte que se carea él mismo con sí mismo, contraponiendo sus efectos, ya por conformidad, ya por discordancia o por exceso".

This rather isolated passage of *Agudeza* nevertheless suggests an explanation to the scholastic belief that from a singular object the mind may get a clear and simple apprehension of what is necessary and what is accidental, what is permanent and what is transitory, in this object. Moreover, through this simple apprehension of one individual object the mind could reach an understanding of the essence of the object's species. Gracián noticed:

> Having seen a lion means having seen all lions, and having seen a lamb, all...[83]

For the understanding, the changes observed during the small period that separates two compared instants are enough to release some meaningful information about what is merely circumstantial and what is substantial in the singular object, and by extension, the species.

Even so, Gracián warned:

> ...but having seen one man means no more than having seen only one, and even such a man is not well known.[84]

Although correspondences may be philosophically or critically useful to abstract from an exemplar object the general essence of a species,[85] Gracián rather was concerned with prudential questions—those addressing the non-repeatable combination of circumstances of singular cases, for instance, the uniqueness of one person, of an action, or of a given situation.

Therefore, the conceptualization of a case through correspondences of the same object is not brought by merely grasping the essential features of the object in question, but by also paying attention to the circumstancial. If the comparison

---

[83]*El Criticón* I, Crisi 11: "Visto un león, están vistos todos, y vista una oveja, todas..."

[84]*El Criticón* I, Crisi 11: "...pero visto un hombre, no está visto sino uno, y aun ésse no bien conocido".

[85]For example, Pallavicino's *Trattato* strove to supply the mind with a method to reach scientific and philosophical principles; it used comparisons which abstracted the essence of things.

made is between different objects, it can not be from completely applying one example to another, because it would only work concerning the common or general features:

> ...one should not act by example, because it usually lacks some of the circumstances.[86]

How then could a singular case be grasped covering all its meaningful circumstances, by means of comparisons? Hasn't the case been defined as unique, and without an equivalent? Although the case is unique, its characteristics can be compared to other characteristics of itself or to those separately found in other objects. The object's characteristics could be initially identified by perceiving, at different times, what is circumstancial and permanent in the same object. Moreover, the perception of the circumstances could be enhanced by means of additional comparisons with other objects which, if not equal in every property to the case in question, they nevertheless share circumstances which could highlight the ones possessed by the object under consideration. The more objects are introduced into the comparison, the more sources that shed light on the circumstances of the case in question, and the more detail in its characterization.

> Uniformity restricts; variety expands; and the more the latter multiplies perfections, the more it is sublime.[87]

The conceptualization of a case is then enriched by means of many and diverse correspondences, in which one subtlety hightlights one circumstance,

---

[86]*Agudeza* Discourse 23: "...no se ha de obrar por ejemplo, por faltar casi siempre alguna de las circunstancias". Even though this quote does not come as part of the body of theories in *Agudeza*, but as an illustration of an extravagant opinion, the passage nevertheless strongly reveals what is often involved in Gracián's method of conceptualizing—the uniqueness of a given case.

[87]*Agudeza* Discourse 3: "La uniformidad limita, la variedad dilata; y tanto es más sublime, cuanto más nobles perfecciones multiplica".

and another makes it easier to perceive additional components of the case in question.

> The subject of reflection and pondering...is like a center from which a discourse develops lines of thought and subtlety to the surrounding entities, that is, the adjuncts which crown it, such as the causes, the effects, attributes, qualities, contingencies, circumstances of time, place, mode, etc., and any other correlative term...[88]

Hence, conceptualizing a case, for Gracián, may need more than the simple movements of one comparison or one contrast. Rather, it may consist in a complex and systematic series of correspondences which present all the pertinent details of the case. The result could be a simple concept by "conglobate" matching, in which "there are many terms in the correspondence."[89] It could even be a compound concept in which many ideas are interrelated into a whole speech.[90] In brief, the wit artistically should introduce, emphasize, belittle, exclude, transpose, and so on, circumstances into a concept by means of correspondences, and thus reach the appropriate understanding of the case he addresses.

Matching Extremes

Gracián's concepts arising from a very complex net of correspondences may be characterized as a rich discourse which, in its expansion, recalls the open hand

---

[88]*Agudeza* Discourse 4: "Es el sujeto sobre quien se discurre y pondera...uno como centro, de quien reparte el discurso, líneas de ponderación y sutileza a las entidades que lo rodean; esto es, a los adjuntos que lo coronan, como son sus causas, sus efectos, atributos, calidades, contingencias, circunstancias de tiempo, lugar, modo, etc., y cualquiera otro término correspondiente..."

[89]*Agudeza* Discourse 15: "En las paridades conglobadas...son muchos los términos de la correspondencia."

[90]See *Agudeza* discourses 51–57.

that the ancients used to symbolize rhetoric. Even so, the basic method of correspondences which gives place to the more complex one still may be better represented as a closed fist, not to symbolize dialectics, but the subtle and brief flashes of wit which build up the discourse, and define it in its most crucial points.

The case is that, for Gracián, a basic witty correspondence between two simple objects should be established between *extremes*; that is, *two very dissimilar things* (for example, Diaulus as a physician and as a mortician) if one wants to discover a common feature (for example, Diaulus's professional abilities), or *two very similar things* (for example, Dido's husbands) if one wants to abstract the differentia (for example, the contrasting fate of Siquaeus and Aeneas).[91] As quoted already,

> Cognizable extremes are more easily observed if united with one kind than with another—also their correlate...[92]

Observing things through extremely subtle comparisons adds precision to the abstraction, although the things may not always be as quickly identified as happens with rough contrasts—for example, a black thread placed over a white piece of cloth. In fact, the extremes may be so different when compared, or so similar when contrasted, that wit may have a difficult time discovering and abstracting the identifying or differentiating correlate:

> When this correspondence is recondite, that the mind needs to reflect in order to observe this correspondence, then, the confrontation is more subtle since it demands more from the mind...[93]

---

[91]See *Agudeza* discourses 4 and 5, which deal with the most basic types of correspondences, either proportions or disproportions.

[92]*Agudeza* Discourse 2: "Resaltan más con unos que con otros los extremos cognoscibles, si se unen, y el correlato..."

[93]*Agudeza* Discourse 4: "Cuando esta correspondencia está recóndita, y que es menester discurrir para observarla, es más sutil, cuanto más cuesta..."

The residue identifying or differentiating things thus obtained from extreme comparisons and contrasts, is so thin that perception is challenged. And yet, the correlates abstracted are the subtlest and, therefore, the ones which take discernment to its limits and keenest precision. Consider this dialogue which Baltasar Gracián's brother, Pedro, conceived as taking place between St Francis Borgia and the Empress' corpse:

> Not long ago, clear eyes,
> you rivalled the sun;
> now, eclipsed, you shed
> on me a brighter light and splendor.[94]

Moreover, thin residues, by opportunely highlighting and identifying subtle circumstances, often supply the most crucial materials to redefine the whole conceptualization of a case in a discourse. For instance, look at this exordium for an Ash Wednesday sermon, quoted in *Agudeza*, wondering about the definition of man:

> The Greek will say he is a *Microcosmos*, a little world. Plato, that he is the measure of all things. Aristotle, the harmony of the universe. Pliny, the hallmark of everything created. Cicero, the bonding of the world. Seneca, the center of knowledge. Cato, a participant of the divine mind. Socrates, a god to another man. Pythagoras, a tree with its roots in the Heavens. Plutarch, the king of the Earth. Diogenes, a sun with a soul. The saintly Moses, the image of God Himself. David, crowned with glory. Saint Basil, a politic animal. Nazianzus, the governor of all creatures. Saint Ambrose, the judge of all. Saint Bernard, a citizen of Paradise. Saint Gregory the Great, the contemplator of God. Saint Augustine, the end and the hope of all the other creatures. But I, with the authority of God Himself, will say that he is soil, he is dust, and the grandson of Nothingness: *Memento homo, quia*

---

[94]*Agudeza* Discourse 5:

> Ojos claros, que en un tiempo
> competíais con el sol,
> cuando eclipsados, me dais
> mayor luz y resplandor.

pulvis es, et in pulverem reverteris.[95]

Thus, Gracián's understanding of wit would differ from Pallavicino's,[96] and from the even later empiricists',[97] who regarded pointed or extreme comparisons unthinkable since they would lack grounding in verifiable sensuous data.

Nevertheless, Aristotle suggested a long time before that bold and distant comparisons were very fitting for philosophy, in the discovery of the principles governing every being:

...in philosophy...an acute mind will perceive resemblances even in things far apart.[98]

And yet, considering the whole of Gracián's writings, what he searched for through the abstraction of thin residues from extreme correspondences were not so much the flights and subtleties of a metaphysician as the dives and keen penetration of a casuist,[99] who must prudently discern the specifying and critical

---

[95]*Agudeza* Discourse 39: "El griego dirá que es un *Microcosmos*, un mundo pequeño. Platón, que es medida de todas las cosas. Aristóteles, la armonía del universo. Plinio, cifra de todo lo criado. Cicerón, vínculo del mundo. Séneca, centro del saber. Catón, participante de la mente divina. Sócrates, dios para otro hombre. Pitágoras, árbol plantado hacia el cielo. Plutarco, rey de la tierra. Diógenes, sol con alma. El santo Moisés, imagen del mismo Dios. David, coronado de gloria. San Basilio, animal político. Nacianceno, gobernador de las criaturas. San Ambrosio, juez de todo. San Bernardo, ciudadano del Paraíso. San Gregorio el Magno, contemplador de Dios. San Agustín, fin y blanco de las demás criaturas. Mas yo, con la autoridad del mismo Dios, diré que es tierra, que es polvo, y nieto de la nada: *Memento homo, quia pulvis es, et in pulverem reverteris.*"

[96]See *Trattato* Chapter 7.

[97]See, for example, Lord Kames *Elements of Criticism* Chapter One, 19 and Campbell 43–58.

[98]*Rhetoric* III, 11.

[99]Even so, Gracián devoted some of his discursive structures not to discern specific cases, but to apprehend general principles of moral conduct, such as maxims. See, for example, *Agudeza* Discourse 43.

features of the most recondite case.

> **One who understands well.** Ratiocination was the art of arts; it is not enough any more: one must find out, and especially concerning disabuses... There are seers of hearts and lynxes of intentions. The most important truths always come half said; the heedful person should receive them with full understanding; if favorable, the reins of belief should be tight; if hateful; they should be loosened.[100]

If done through speech, this task of *discerning cases* becomes perfect:

> Some people have the capacity of those vessels which collect much but communicate very little...Explanation is to the understanding what resolution is to the will...[101]

If so, I think this task may be called rhetoric.[102]

Presenting What is New to the Mind

Concerning subjective properties of ideas, logicians often classify them as clear, exact, and distinct.[103] However, these subjective properties of concepts were not the ones emphasized in *Agudeza*. Gracián's interest was in the novelty perceived

---

[100]*Oráculo* Aphorism 25: **"Buen entendedor**. Arte era de artes saber discurrir; ya no basta: menester es adevinar, y más en desengaños...Hay zahoríes del corazón y linces de las intenciones. Las verdades que más nos importan vienen siempre a medio decir; recíbanse del atento a todo entender; en lo favorable, tirante la rienda a la credulidad; en lo odioso, picarla".

[101]*Oráculo* Aphorism 216: "Tienen algunos la capacidad de aquellas vasijas que perciben mucho y comunican poco...Lo que es la resolución en la voluntad es la explicación en el entendimiento..."

[102]It is not out of place here to recall Aristotle's definition of rhetoric: "...the faculty of observing in any given case the available means of persuasion." *Rhetoric* I, 2.

[103]By subjective properties it is meant that ideas are clear, exact, or distinct not so much in themselves as in the way that a specific mind perceives them.

by the mind in subtleties.[104]

Gracián believed that "invention belongs to ingenious people;"[105] and that invention itself meant "artistically squeezing novelties".[106] Moreover, the reaching of novelties by a person could mean either perceiving ideas or producing them for the first time.[107] Furthermore, when a subtlety does not provide new information but just luminously recalls previous experience, even then its job is not reduced to remembrance but it rises to the level of finally recognizing something for the first time:

> **Helping to understand is greater than helping to remember.** Moreover, sometimes it is enough to remind and other times one should go further and help people to recognize the facts.[108]

Thus, by no means Gracián's concepts should be perceived as pure managment of experience. Even when no new information is provided, the mere rearrangement of previous experience through structures of correspondences leads to the intellectual abstraction of concepts, and that is new since it was not previously beheld and understood.

Like other conceptist authors,[109] Gracián attached a strong aesthetic component to the act of finally understanding something. He believed that

---

[104]I discuss more specific subjective properties of concepts later.

[105]*Oráculo* Aphorism 283: "La inventiva es de ingeniosos..."

[106]*Agudeza* Discourse 47: "...exprime novedad artificiosa..." Although this quote particularly applies to "concepts by ingenious actions", it fittingly refers to all the task of ingenuity, that is, "the strenuous effort of invention" ("arduo es el inventar", *Agudeza* Discourse 1).

[107]See *Agudeza* Discourse 2.

[108]*Oráculo* Aphorism 68: **"Dar entendimiento es de más primor que el dar memoria.** Cuanto es más, unas veces se ha de acordar y otras advertir".

[109]Cf., for example, Pallavicino's *Trattato* Chapter Three, 22.

"novelties are pleasant"[110] to the mind. In this sense, subtleties should necessarily please, since their very essence is to render the novel:

> Ingenuity is not satisfied only with the truth, like judgment, but it aims beauty.[111]

Finally, although Gracián did not elaborate much about it, the aesthetic pleasure which ingenuity reaches is wonderment, that is, the intellectual "emotion"—indeed—of grasping new understanding.[112]

Defining Ingenuity, Concept, and Wit

As seen in the beginning of this chapter, Gracián left us three definitions clarifying the essence of artistic wit: one definition refers to a method, another to an act of understanding, and a third one to a discursive achievement of the understanding.

He also left, in *Agudeza*, three key terms about all this: ingenuity, concept, and wit. Although interchangeable, each one enjoys its emphasis. "Ingenuity" is the mind's talent in charge of the act, the method, and the achievements of understanding defined above. Ingenuity is the mind's power to discern, abstract, conceptualize, create, or produce new ideas. "Concept" stresses the ideas themselves, or their method: their discovery, perception, production, and embodyment in witty correspondences. "Wit" may refer to ingenuity as a talent. However, it usually emphasizes the exquisite achievements of ingenuity. In this sense, a better translation of "agudeza" into English would be "subtlety" or "witticism."

---

[110]*Oráculo* Aphorism 283: "Es lisonjera la novedad..."

[111]*Agudeza* Discourse 2: "No se contenta el ingenio con sola la verdad, como el juicio, sino que apira a la hermosura".

[112]See *El Criticón* I, crisis 1–3. Here Gracián identified the capacity of wonderment in children, since they are the people who more easily enjoy the novel.

Thus, *Agudeza* is a treatise which explains "all the methods and differences of concepts"[113] that, according to Gracián, ingenuity uses to achieve wit.[114]

---

[113]This is a subtitle of the *Agudeza*: "...todos los modos y diferencias de conceptos..."

[114]It does so by identifying the four causes of wit: 1) the efficient: the mind's talent of ingenuity; 2) the material: the things or objects themselves whose nature and circumnstances ingenuity should apprehend; 3) the formal or exemplary cause: the models of wit to be imitated; 4) the final and "modern" cause of wit: the art of ingenuity, which makes the acts of understanding achieve perfection in so far as they do not abandon the understanding to chance, but rather give direction and light to this mind power. Of these causes, *Agudeza* explains the final one, concerning the rules of art, and it also illustrates these rules with exemplary causes, that is, abundant models of witticisms. The efficient and the material causes, concerning the mind's talent of ingenuity, and the objects to be learned, are left to the reader to grasp for himself (see *Agudeza* Discourse 63). If compared, *Agudeza* with Tesauro's *Cannocchiale*, Tesauro theorized not only about man's ingenuity, but also about all kinds of spiritual beings' ingenuity as efficient causes producing wit; moreover, for Tesauro, besides ingenuity, man also resorts to poetic furor and to exercise as efficient causes of wit (Chapter 3). Tesauro regarded both models and things as materials which the mind's ingenuity *uses* to produce ideas. Thus, for him, models and things were instrumental causes of ingenuity (see Chapter 2). For Tesauro, art only existed in formalistic principles; so, art is only the formal cause of wit (see chapters 4–9). And the final cause is just the speech produced by the mind or the orator (Chapter 10). For Tesauro, the efficient cause produces utterances, art only exists in formal principles, models and things remain only as instruments for utterances, and the final product is mere speech. Differently, Gracián saw ingenuity as an efficient cause of learning or abstraction, the objects of reality as a material cause already possessing the principles of art ("Están ya en los objetos mismos las agudezas objetivas...", that is "the objects themselves already contain the objective subtlety" *Agudeza* Discourse 63), the models to imitate as sources embodying the principles of art to be imitated and learned, and the rules of art as the final cause in so far as the final result of a discursive enterprise—a discourse enjoying artistic wit—is perfect if it embodies the principles of art. Tesauro was a nominalist, whereas Gracián was a realist.

10   Artistic Wit

IN THE BEGINNING OF *AGUDEZA*, GRACIÁN WEIGHED FIVE possible approaches for artistically studying the methods of wit:

1) Wit may be explained as a result of pure talent or of talent assisted by art, that is, either as perspicacious wit or as artistic wit.

2) Artistic wit could in its turn be intently studied by its materials: actual events, things, or *acts*, that is, the beings—the primal stuff of understanding—, moreover, *concepts*, that is, the beings' intellection—the ideas or thoughts—, and furthermore, the ideas' embodiment, that is, *words*.

3) Wit may be analyzed according to the direction of the relation between the extremes matched: either a correspondence or agreement, or a contrariety or disagreement.

4) Wit may be considered according to the number of correspondences contained in a simple concept or thought: either pure wit or mixed wit.

5) Finally, wit may be explained according to the kind of connections existing among different simple concepts within a complete speech: either loose or *minor art wit*, or compound or *major art wit*.

However, Gracián discarded these five approaches as the principal ones to make an inquiry into wit. He deplored some of them, like the one on the materials used by ingenuity, as merely accidental to artistic wit, and even vulgar. He saw in every of these approaches few theoretical potentials to gaining detail if used alone, especially in the approach of just two possible directions in a relationship between extremes.[1] Nevertheless, Gracián found a sixth approach which could be fruitful to theorizing. This one refers to the four "genres," "modes," or "sources" of squeezing concepts used to achieve incomplex wit: *correlation, ponderation, ratiocination*, and *invention*:

> The first is that of correlation and agreement of one term with another, and here enter proportions, disproportions, similitudes, comparisons, allusions, etc. The

---

[1] See *Agudeza* Discourse 3.

second is that of judicious and subtle ponderations, and this subsumes *crises* [witty judgments], paradoxes, exaggerations, sententiae, ripostes, etc. The third is that of ratiocination, which embraces mysteries, objections, illations, proofs, etc. The fourth is that of invention, and it comprehends works of fiction, stratagems, inventions in action or speech, etc.[2]

Correlations

Correlations are the first great genre of concepts and the most basic instrument of wit. Gracián included here "proportions, disproportions, similitudes, comparisons, allusions, etc."[3]

Correlations consist in the elementary "squeezing" of correspondences by the matching of extremes, as explained above. As the foundation of every original conceptualization, this method of correlation extends to the three other more elaborate modes of making concepts. According to Gracián, every artistic

---

[2]*Agudeza* Discourse 3: "La primera es de correlación y conveniencia de un término a otro, y aquí entran las proporciones, improporciones, semejanzas, paridades, alusiones, etc. La segunda es de ponderación juiciosa sutil, y a ésta se reducen crisis, paradojas, exageraciones, sentencias, desempeños, etc. La tercera es de raciocinación, y a ésta pertenecen los misterios, reparos, ilaciones, pruebas, etc. La cuarta es de invención, y comprehende las ficciones, estratagemas, invenciones en acción y dicho, etc." It may be disappointing that Gracián did not overtly follow this theoretical approach to wit either; he would thus disconcert many scholars who do not find any true system in his exposition. For example, Benedetto Croce (Croce 249) bewailed that "Besides these rough explanations in Gracián's work...there are...many arbitrary and confused distinctions and classifications." In fact, *Agudeza* is not meant to be the clearest work for theoreticians; it rather aims at sensibly explaining wit to its practicioners, going from the easiest to the most difficult artistic rules. Its expositive order usually allows the reader to be first familiarized with the purest forms of wit, and later with the mixed and the complex varieties. Thus far, in spite of this expositive order, Gracián still fulfilled his analysis of wit according to the four modes of "squeezing" concepts. Here, I skip Gracián's pedagogical interests and focus my study upon his four sources of concepts.

[3]*Agudeza* Discourse 3: "...las proporciones, improporciones, semejanzas, paridades, alusiones, etc."

concept can be reduced to correlations, since it either starts or ends in some sort of harmony between the terms.

Strangely, this general character of correlations makes them a special class: they are the only method of wit which applies to every conceptualization. Particularly, in a unique way, correlations include the apprehension of new ideas in the absence of any previous idea,[4] whereas ponderations can only reach the new in view of the old, ratiocinations can only supply missing premises in view of an existing premise and an existing conclusion, and inventions can not discover existing facts in the abscence of previous ideas, but only create new possible facts in the presence of established facts.

Correlations can be studied according to several different principles:

The Direction of the Relationship

Correlations are *correspondences* or *proportions* when they associate previously unrelated things.[5] For example, Mexicans compare the attention one receives from bad friends with the attention farmers pay to cacti in the desert: in either case a visit responds to selfish interest—to times when the sweet fruits are at hand. For instance, it is said that my brothers chose very different professions: Alfredo is a dentist and Roberto is a proctologist. However, both share a peculiar fascination with a specific end of the digestive canal. A rather keen correspondence is this one quoted in *Agudeza* and borrowed from St Ambrose, who matched the birth and the death of St John the Baptist saying:

> I do not know what to wonder at more, whether his marvelous birth or his marvelous death; truly he died for truth who was born by prophecy.[6]

---

[4]Correlations can take place in minds as empty of ideas as a blank slate. In doing so, correlations discover the purest forms of novelty, and by imprinting the blank slate for the first time, they cause the purest forms of wonderment. Of course, correlations are not produced in the complete absence of anything. The absence of ideas does not mean the absence of objects of understanding from which ideas should be learned.

[5]See *Agudeza* Discourse 4.

[6]*Agudeza* Discourse 4: "No sé de qué me admire más, si de su prodigioso nacimiento o

Correlations are *disproportions* or *dissonances* when they dissociate previously related things.[7] For example, lemons and limes are words used by Americans and by Mexicans; however, Americans differently apply these names to one fruit depending its ripeness whereas Mexicans apply them to two very different fruits regardless their color. For instance, Mexican Border cities are often thought as being quite similar;[8] however, a more discriminating observer would differentiate many things as important as their industrial development and their labor force: Matamoros's workers are very reliable but expensive and organized in the toughest labor unions whereas Tijuana's workers are cheaper and unorganized, though not as reliable. Gracián quoted this subtle disproportion from Juan Rufo:

> Jorge and Beatriz gazed at each other,
> with a burning affection;
> **although it entered them through their eyes,**
> **they never saw such a danger.**[9]

In brief, proportions help to highlight common features between things, and disproportions, the differentiae.

---

si de su prodigiosa muerte; con razón murió por la verdad el que nació por profecía". The *truth* of St John's birth was prophesied by an angel. St John was beheaded for continuing the task of proclaiming the *truth*.

[7]See *Agudeza* Discourse 5.

[8]They are often thought as culturally the same because both border the United States, as if San Diego and Brownsville were equal because both border Mexico, or Boston and Miami were homologous because both face the Atlantic.

[9]*Agudeza* Discourse 5:
> Jorge y Beatriz se miraron
> Con un afecto encendido
> **Que entrándoles por los ojos**
> **Nunca vieron el peligro.**

The disproportion rests on the fact that the more they see each other, the more they go blind of love.

The Matter of the Relationship

As explained before, for Gracián the most general kinds of objects or materials from which correspondences are squeezed are ideas, words, and actual events. Some details about correlations of words now deserve additional attention. They show that Gracián's theories go beyond pure questions of style. Also, some refer to very special materials helpful for "squeezing" concepts: quotations from authorities.

By wit of words Gracián understood ingenious hieroglyphs, acrostics, etymologies, word-formation, word plays, paronomasia, puns, quibbles, and any form of concept founded on the circumstances of the words used as terms: their letters, their sounds, their structure, their various meanings depending the situation, etc.[10]

Gracián to some degree disliked words as the matter of subtleties. He thought them to be a too easy, ordinary, and not a very serious resource to produce wit. He also believed that they suffer a major inconvenience: this kind of concepts may not be translatable into other languages.[11] However, Gracián recognized that all the modes of concepts at one time or another take recourse to words as their matter, because words are very helpful in supplying and specifying meanings in subtleties. By noticing the components and the many circumstances which surround words, a wit may be able to discover, ground, and multiply the words' meanings, and thus, he may be able to conceive new ideas. Rather than promoting an ambiguous use of language, he specifies and enriches the meaning of words by lingering over their contingencies, and by signalizing these contingencies through the structure of correspondences.[12] For example, St Teresa the Great was quite clear when—before one of her mystical raptures—she said:

---

[10]See *Agudeza* discourses 31–33.

[11]See *Agudeza* discourses 32 and 33.

[12]See *Agudeza* Discourse 31.

...I die because I do not die...[13]

And courtly gentlemen were not ambiguous either when they snatched this expression from its religious realm and turned it into a request of profane love.[14] For instance, Lope de Sosa confessed:

> Although life stirs the passions,
> I do not want to lose it,
> not to lose the occasions
> of enjoying having lost it.[15]

The multiplication of meanings by the witty use of words could take place in a single expression, or even a word, if it is strategically placed in a discourse.[16] Consider this Mexican antitrust slogan:

> *Sin* competencia *hay in*competencia.[17]

And look at this phrase which is very typical of Gracián's own writings:

> *Dieron conmigo en un calaboço, cargándome de* hierros, *que éste fue el fruto de los míos.*[18]

---

[13]"...que muero porque no muero..." Cf. *John* 12:24.

[14]Cf. Whinnom.

[15]*Agudeza* Discourse 24:
> La vida, aunque dé pasión,
> No querría yo perdella,
> Por no perder la ocasión
> Que tengo de estar sin ella.

[16]See *Agudeza* Discourse 31–32.

[17]"Without *competencia* (that is both competition and competence) there is incompetence."

[18]*El Criticón* I, Crisi 8: "They took me to the dungeon, charging me with *hierros* (that is

Gracián was extremely open-minded regarding the use of words in crafting witty concepts. He accepted the creation of new words by the most adventurous playing with morphemes, syllables, or letters. He would even applaud the ingenious mixing of elements from different languages.[19] Consider this bizarre and, yet, keen description of President Carlos Salinas de Gortari's administration:

Es una Salinastroika *sin* príisnost.[20]

This witticism, popularized by the Mexican press, mixes Mexican political jargon with Soviet President Gorbachov's political philosophy: *Perestroika* and *Glasnost.*

Just after discussing the verbal wit, Gracián explained the concepts squeezed from quotations of ancient, authoritative, or any other useful text.[21] These explanations are not only a key to understand his whole theory of witty correspondences, but also very enlightening concerning the witty use of quotes in speeches, especially religious ones. In *Agudeza*, quotes are not primarily a type of evidence fashioned as testimonies, in which **A, B,** and **C** sources report witnessing the same event **D**, and therefore, inductively prove **D**. As indicated before, Gracián made conceptualization precede judgment and inference, and this rule even applies to quotations. So, in *Agudeza* quotations **A, B,** or **C** are brought not primarily to judge or prove the idea, issue, or the situation **D**. As in

---

both iron chains and wrongdoings); that it was the fruit of *those of mine."*

[19]See, for example, *Agudeza* Discourse 31.

[20]"It is a *Salinastroika* without *príisnost.*" The clever expression refers to President Salinas's economic reforms, bolder than those of Gorbachov's *Perestroika* (another concept: substitute the "last name" *Pérez* for the one of the Mexican President, and then there is a *Salinas*troika). However, Salinas's administration has been reputed to lack political reforms, such as Gorbachov's *Glasnost.* Therefore, Salinas's lack of *príisnost,* refers to the *PRI,* which is the Mexican leading political party, and also the main organization now needing political reforms.

[21]See *Agudeza* Discourse 34.

any witty correspondence, **A, B, C,** and **D** previously appear to the mind as the most unrelated things. If they are put together, it is because they could shed light on each other, and if sharing any circumstance, they can lead to the presentation of a new idea to the understanding. Consider this illustration from one of Gracián's brothers:

> Father Felipe Gracián reflected, in a sermon, over the great beauty of charity, and how pretty and delightful it appears to God and men. First, because charity has a lovely face: **Love your enemies**, it even pleases the enemies offering them its beautiful countenance...[22]

Gracián celebrated bold applications of quotations to specific situations. For example, he refers to this episode in the life of St Francis Borgia:

> Saint Francis Borgia, then, Duke of Gandía, promised Doctor Villalobos...a silver plate...if, on the next day, he was free of fever as the phsycian assured. In due time, the doctor came and took Francis Borgia's pulse and found him with very little fever, but there was some. And so the Duke said: "Villalobos, what do you say now?" The physician replied: "My Lord, **Amicus Plato, sed magis amica veritas.**" The saintly Duke savored the clever saying and the good news, and ordered the silver plate sent to the physician's home immediately.[23]

According to Gracián, the better the listeners know a quoted text, the easier and quicker a wit could make them notice new and surprising applications of the

---

[22]*Agudeza* Discourse 54: "Ponderó el Padre Felipe Gracián, en un sermón, la hermosura grande de la caridad, y cuán linda y agradable parece a Dios y a los hombres. Primero, porque tiene bellísimo rostro: **Diligite inimicos vestros**; aun a los enemigos lisonjea, haciéndoles buena cara..." Father Felipe Gracián was quoting *Matthew* 6:44.

[23]*Agudeza* Discourse 34: "Prometió San Francisco de Borja, duque entonces de Gandía, al doctor Villalobos...una fuente de plata, si al otro día le hallaba sin calentura, como él lo aseguraba. Vino al plazo señalado, y, pulsándole, hallóle con muy poca, pero alguna; y, pues, dijo el duque, '¿qué decís, Villalobos?'. 'Señor, que *Amicus Plato, sed magis amica veritas*'. Gustó mucho el santo duque del buen dicho y de la buena nueva, y mandó al punto se le llevasen a su casa".

text to unexpected situations.[24]

Gracián was unblushing in recommending equivocally the quoting of texts: one could annex or suppress words from the reference, intermix words of different languages, and use the most bizarre wordplays or adaptations in the quotation, if all this served to prompt the suitable and graceful rendering of new ideas. A good example from *Agudeza* is the following—and almost sacrilegious—diatribe against ambition:

> ...the learned and astute saintly Archbishop of Ravenna applies to ambition that famous text by St Paul on charity, and he says: **Ambition is patient, ambition is kind; it bears all things, it believes everything, it hopes all things, it endures all things**, etc.[25]

Some authors miss the heuristic function of witty quotations and blame Gracián of "Jesuitically misquoting scripture."[26] Even so, many and eminent

---

[24]See, *Agudeza* Discourse 34.

[25]*Agudeza* Discourse 34: "...el culto y agudo santo arzobispo de Rávena, aplica a la ambición aquel célebre lugar de San Pablo a la caridad, y dice: **Ambitio patiens est, benigna est; omnia suffert omnia credit, omnia sperat, omnia sustinet**, etc." The text adapted is from I *Cor* 13:4–7.

[26]Edward Sarmiento, "Gracián's 'Agudeza y Arte de Ingenio'" *Modern Language Review* 27 (1932) 2: 426. Cf., also José Francisco de Isla, *Fray Gerundio de Campazas*, Introduction, edition, and notes by Russell P. Sebold (Madrid: Espasa-Calpe, S. A., 1963) 3: II, iv, 9. In his famous eighteenth century satire against baroque eloquence, Father Isla presented Fr Blas defending what Isla believed mistaken, extravagant, and presumptuous modes of Biblical quotations. Although Isla succeeded in portraying the vanity and the risks of misquoting the Writ by baroque preachers, Isla unconsciously presented Fr Blas with good reasons defending the baroque or "old" method against the "modern" one of quotations: for Fr Blas, modern sermons "resemble the finish of modern buildings in Rome—which is called *coating*—, and make them look like as built with porphyry, marble, jasper, or alabaster, but they really are only covered with a very superficial sheet, which if it deceives the eyes, it also could be removed with a fingernail...and there is as much difference in the method of quoting of the old preachers compared to the modern ones, as there is between new and old buildings. These required a whole mountain to make a jasper urn...those are built up into palaces with the jasper formerly used for the urn." (Isla 3:180). In other words, moderns only saw quotes

saints in the history of the Church have enjoyed this grace of ingeniously bringing out from the "storeroom new treasures as well as old."[27] Look closely to this passage praising the Lord's Incarnation, by St Bernard of Clairvaux:

> It seems to me that..."If the Lord God of hosts had not left us a seed, we should have been like Sodom and reduced like Gomorrha."[28] This seed flowered[29] first in the wonderful doings[30] which were shown forth in symbols[31] and in riddles[32] as Israel came out of Egypt,[33] all along the way[34] through the desert[35] to the Land of Promise[36]...Not without reason do we understand Christ to be the fruit of the flowers sprung from this seed, for David says, "The Lord will look with kindness upon the earth and it shall bear fruit".[37] And again, "I will place the fruit of your womb upon your throne".[38] It was at Nazareth[39] therefore that Christ's birth was first announced

---

as supporting materials or proofs for the ideas whereas conceptist authors saw quotes as the stuff which constitutes the ideas themselves. Fr Blas's defense of conceptism transcends quotations and also applies to other areas of rhetoric, for example, figurative language. Moderns would see it as just an ornament or an attachment to plain language. Conceptist would rather see figures as the stuff which renders the ideas themselves.

[27]*Matthew* 13:52.

[28]*Rom* 9:29.

[29]*Is* 17:11.

[30]*Ps* 78:32

[31]1 *Cor* 10:62.

[32]1 *Cor* 13:12.

[33]*Ps* 114:1

[34]*Ps* 68:4

[35]*Neh* 9:19.

[36]*Heb* 11:9

[37]*Ps* 85:12

[38]*Ps* 132:11.

[39]*Mt* 2:24

...Christ then is the good Fruit[40] which endures for ever.[41]

As Chrysogonus Wadell notices, behind the Mellifluous Doctor's "flights of rhetoric," there is "a use (or apparent abuse) of biblical citations."[42] St Bernard would be certainly and scandalously misquoting the Writ, if every tiny bit of Holy Scripture were reduced to a record of clear historical "facts" and univocal pieces of Revelation from which the theologian, without further reflection, could build inferences and judgments.[43] But like many other religious authors, St Bernard is working with the Bible as a text to be first clarified and interpreted.[44] He indeed is highly esteemed by the Church because of his insightful study of the Scriptures. His adventurous discovery of concordances among very different and unexpected texts opened new avenues of Scriptural inquiry[45] and earned him

---

[40]*Mt* 7:17.

[41]Bernard of Clairvaux, "In Praise of the Virgin Mother, Homily One," *Magnificat, Homilies in Praise of the Blessed Virgin Mary by Bernard of Clairvaux and Amadeus of Lausanne*, trans. Marie-Bernard Saïd and Grace Perigo, introduction by Chrysogonus Waddell, OCSO (Cistercian Publications, Inc, 1979) 7–8. The specification of Scriptural quotations in St Bernard's passage is already given in Saïd and Perigo's translation.

[42]Chrysogonus Wadell, "Introduction," *Magnificat* xi.

[43]Some Protestant theologians—for instance, the Fundamentalists—would reduce the Writ to a clear record of historical facts authenticating a clear and univocal Revelation. Cf.,for example, the controversialist Thomas Sherlock's *Trial of the Witnesess*, typical of the English Enlightment.

[44]Let's remember that Church Tradition has always been aware of the many meanings of the Writ, instructing through Saint Paul, the Church Fathers, and others about the spiritual sense of the Scripture. For example, with the authority of St Paul, St Augustine had already explained that "we in this life enjoy Him 'through a glass' or 'in a dark manner.'" (*On Christian Doctrine* I, xxx, which refers 1 *Cor* 13:12.) And St Jerome searched not only for historical, but also for tropological, and spiritual meanings (allegorical and anagogical) in the Bible. (See, for example, Didaco Valades *Rhetorica Christiana* III, xiii., which reflects on this Tradition within the Spanish Golden Age.)

[45]Just to exemplify these rich avenues of "witty" Scriptural inquiry, consider the most diverse sermons grounded on *Revelation* 12:1, which refers to a great sign: "a woman clothed

a place as the last among the Church Fathers.

An interesting observation to repeat now is that, in Gracián's system, the adventurous discovery of new meanings is not reduced to the study of quotations.[46] It extends to any kind of materials confronted—either words, things, or ideas—in order to squeeze new concepts. Thus, the swagger of ingenuity—daring to see what no other person was able to see before—applies to all arts and fields of knowledge.[47] In a somewhat different context, the Nobel Prize-winning biochemist Albert Szent Gyorgi said:

> Discovery consists in seeing what everyone else has seen and thinking what no

---

with the sun..." Concordances of this passage with others referring either to Christ, or to the Church, or to Our Lady, or to the end of times, etc., have given occasion to preachers to prepare the most different, and yet, not incongruent sermons. This witty discovery of Scriptural meanings is common not only in preachers and sermons, but also in ordinary people and other religious practices such as prayer, meditation, Ignatian spiritual exercises, and, of course, Scriptural theology.

[46]Even so, I can not emphasize enough the great importance which quotations enjoyed in seventeenth century oratory. At least since the sixteenth century, preachers had the prescription of grounding their sermons on ten theological places, as said: 1) the Holy Scriptures, 2) Tradition, 3) the authority of the Catholic Church, 4) the Councils, 5) the authority of the Roman Church, 6) the Holy Fathers, 7) the theologians, 8) natural reason, 9) philosophers and jurisconsults, 10) human history. (See the Tridentine Father Melchor Cano, *Opera* (Bassani, 1746)). From these places, only natural reason did not consist in quotations. Moreover, in the eighteenth century, even Father Isla himself—one of the greatest enemies of baroque eloquence—had to recognize "ten sources of invention" for all kinds of oratory: 1) history, 2) fables and parables, 3) adages and popular sayings, 4) hieroglyphs, 5) emblems, 6) testimonies from antiquity, 7) sententiae, 8) the laws, 9) the Holy Writ, and 10) speech itself and the discreet use of common places. From them, nine of these places involved citing texts, and only the last one referred to the classical sources of invention. Even though Isla expressed this doctrine through the ridiculous and baroque Fray Gerundio, Isla nevertheless offered his qualified approval to it through the young, modern, and "clearminded" scholar of rhetoric, Don Casimiro. (See Isla 4: 31–84.) Notice that if quotes were just "proofs" with an univocal meaning, they would not have any inventional, only managerial value. Quotes nevertheless were regarded as sources of *invention* because of the most diverse and new applications the wit could make of them, depending the case in question.

[47]See *Agudeza* Discourse 3.

one else has thought.[48]

My point here is to insist that Gracián believed his theory of ingenuity in fact was a system of invention not reduced to the finding of new meanings in words or quotations, but extended to all kinds of discoveries, including the realm of actual things and ideas.[49] For example, I finally discovered that brown rice and lentils share their cooking time and water quantity for steaming; this discovery suggested to me the possibility of cooking them together, and this I successfully did. Moreover, the objects of conceptualization do not need to be "logical" ideas or things. They can also be emotions, that is "pathos,"[50] or nobility of character, that is "ethos."[51] Concerning character, Gracián quoted an anecdote from Alexander the Great:

...Alexander used to cover one of his ears when listening to the prosecution. Inquired about it, Alexander answered: "I reserve this one for the defendant."[52]

Agudeza also refers to this admonition from Emperor Augustus:

Listen, young men, listen to this old man who was listened by the elders in youth.[53]

Concerning emotions, Gracián quoted this complaint from Jorge de Montemayor:

---

[48]Dennis J. Sardella, "A Scientist Talks about Prayer," *Catholic Digest* (April 1991) 45.

[49]See *Agudeza* Discourse 1–3.

[50]See *Agudeza* Discourse 42.

[51]See *Agudeza* Discourse 30.

[52]See *Agudeza* Discourse 30: "...Alejandro se tapaba una oreja oyendo alguna acusación, y preguntando por qué hacía aquello, respondió: 'Guardo ésta para el reo'".

[53]See *Agudeza* Discourse 5: "Oíd, mozos, oíd a un viejo, que cuando era mozo los viejos le escuchaban."

> Why do you flee from me
> if you very clearly know
> that when I am before you
> you are even further from me?[54]

From the same author, Gracián cited this expression of profane bliss:

> Is it possible a more joyful life
> than dying from this lovesickness?[55]

The Precision of the Relationship

Together with proportions and disproportions, Gracián grouped similitudes and comparisons among the four general types of correlations. If the first two types explain the direction of a relationship in a correlation, the second ones explain the precision reached in establishing the relationship.

In *Agudeza*, similitudes[56] refer to similes and metaphors, but they may comprehend all kinds of tropes.[57] Similitudes are characterized by not sharply

---

[54]See *Agudeza* Discourse 42:
¿Por qué te escondes de mí,
pues conoces claramente,
que estoy, cuando estoy presente,
muy más ausente de ti?

[55]See *Agudeza* Discourse 42:
¿Qué más vida puede haber,
que morir del mal que muero?
Again, dying means the culmination of profane love.

[56]*Similitudes*: The word used by Gracián is *semejanzas*.

[57]See *Agudeza* discourses 9 to 13, and 20. For Gracián, similitudes are a principle of correlation which comprehends conceptual similarities, dissimilarities, metaphors, allegories, metamorphoses, fiction (see discourse 35, 55, and 56), nicknames (see discourse 48), and many other forms of vivid wit (for all these see *Agudeza* Discourse 9). In fact, all witty tropes—Gracián particularly explained hyperboles—consist in grounding a relationship between terms on an appropriate and specific circumstance, and at the same time giving

segregating the proper grounds of association between two or more terms, from other contingencies surrounding these terms. For example, Gracián's similitudes do not relate a swordfish and a big nose by accurately isolating the size and the pointed features which the nose and the fish's sword share. Gracián's similitudes rather make one term be completely assimilated by the other, incorporating into the relationship all the colorful contingencies which appear with the circumstance properly relating these terms.[58] Consider these hyperboles used by Francisco de Quevedo to describe a man with a big nose (or rather the opposite, a big nose with a man):

> There was once a man glued to a nose;
> it was a superlative nose;
> it was a hangman and scribe like nose;
> it was a very bearded swordfish...[59]

Although the additional contingencies presented may not properly pertain to the point being squeezed by the witticism, they nevertheless colorfully render this point to the imagination, in so far as the terms are assimilated into each other in their full images.[60] The wit is working in the realm of conceptual tropes, and ornately presenting his concepts.[61] Consider this other example, as quoted in *Agudeza*, in which Martial tastefully made clear who were the guests of his

---

occasion to the assimilation of all the surrounding contingencies into the associated terms. (See, for example, *Agudeza* Discourse 20; also see Discourse 53).

[58]See *Agudeza* Discourse 9.

[59]Don Francisco de Quevedo y Villegas, "A una nariz," *Obras Completas*, Estudio preliminar, edición y notas de Felicidad Buendía (Madrid: Aguilar, 1988) 2: 380:
  Érase un hombre a una nariz pegado,
  érase una nariz superlativa,
  érase una nariz sayón y escriba,
  érase un peje espada muy barbado.

[60]See *Agudeza* Discourse 9.

[61]See *Agudeza* "Al Lector".

books:

> The reader and the listener, Aulus, approve my little books;
> but a poet finds them not quite finished.
> Well, I don't care, for, concerning the dishes on my table
> I rather prefer to please the guests than the cooks.[62]

The proper grounds of the similitude may be implicit. In such a case, the similitude, although pure, already contains wit's perfections. The reason is that the foundation of the relationship, although just evoked, is already present in the witticism.[63] Look at this lamentation, by Don Antonio Hurtado de Mendoza, as quoted in *Agudeza*:

> O excessive misfortune!
> To be a Phoenix in love and a Swan in death![64]

Sometimes the grounds of the similitude are explained to make them clearer to the listener. Then, according to Gracián, the similitude properly is called conceptual,[65] since the correlate of the relationship is abstracted. For instance,

> ...Rufo said of a prince who lost a thumb when the barrel of the pistol he was
> shooting blew up, that he who was a lion in arms and valor also had to be a lion in

---

[62]See, *Agudeza* Discourse 9:
  Lector et auditor nostros probat, Aule, libellos;
  sed quidam exactos esse poeta negat.
  Non nimium curo. Nam coenae fercula nostrae
  malim convivis, quam placuisse coquis.

[63]See *Agudeza* Discourse 9.

[64]See *Agudeza* Discourse 9:
  ¡Oh, mal terrible!
  ¡Ser Fénix en amar, y en morir cisne!
Mendoza refers to the misfortune of loving for ever, like the phoenix, and yet, dying, that is, making love, like a singing swan, only once.

[65]See *Agudeza* Discourse 10.

having a claw less: for the lion is unique in this among fierce beasts.[66]

Either implicit or explicit, similitudes should be grounded on a special or unusual circumstance which relates the terms. Without it, the similitude is a cliché. Without the pungency of the proper foundation, it is a dead, cold, and ordinary similitude, like having called the brave prince "lion," and not having indicated the additional and peculiar explanation which makes this trope witty when referring to the prince.[67]

A rich similitude may give occasion to the whole development of a speech, if the speaker argues, explains, or clarifies the different and unexpected circumstances which ground the relationship between the terms.[68] An instance from *Agudeza* identifies St Ignatius Loyola with the first light created by God, and from which the other celestial bodies were derived. The similitude is then developed into a discourse about the history of the Society of Jesus by matching each of these twinkling bodies with different dazzling and saintly Jesuits, such as St Francis Xavier, St Francis Borgia, St Aloysius Gonzaga, St Stanislas Kostka, etc.[69]

For Gracián, a correlation gains precision if, instead of remaining as a rough similitude, it segregates the irrelevant contingencies of the terms' images, and establishes the association by making it rest directly on the proper circumstance linking the terms. Then, the correlation is called comparison, and it is witty if a special and unusual circumstance grounds the concept.[70] An example in

---

[66]See *Agudeza* Discourse 11: "...Rufo, dijo un príncipe que disparando una pistola se le reventó el cañón y le derribó el pulgar, que quien era un león en el valor y en las armas, lo había de ser también en tener una uña menos como el león, singular en esto de las demás fieras".

[67]See *Agudeza* Discourse 11.

[68]See *Agudeza* discourses 11, 12, and 53.

[69]See *Agudeza* Discourse 9.

[70]See *Agudeza* discourses 14 to 16.

Agudeza is taken from St Leo the Great, who compares the effects of two deacons' martyrdom on their respective cities:

> From the glimmering beam of the deacons' glory, Jerusalem was as distinguished by Stephen as Rome would become illustrious by Laurentius.[71]

Contrasting with similitudes, comparisons do not make the terms assimilate themselves into each other in so far as the association only rests on a specified circumstance which gives occasion for a parallelism. For instance, consider this epigram from Martial as quoted by *Agudeza*:

> While the eagle was carrying the boy[72] through the air of heavens,
> the burden was attached unhurt to the dreadful claws.
>   Now, the prey prevails upon Caesar's lions,
> and, safe, a hare plays inside their huge jaws.
>   Which miracle do you think the greater? At each side a supreme
> sovereign: these creatures are Caesar's, that one is Jove's.[73]

Although similitudes could be established by assimilating Caesar to Jove,

---

[71]See *Agudeza* Discourse 14: "Leviticorum luminum coruscante fulgore quam clarificata est Hierosolyma Stephano, tam illustris fieret Roma Laurentio." There is a deeper sense in this apparently cold, ordinary, and unimportant comparison. Pope Leo is asserting the special place Rome enjoys as the spiritual see of Christianity. The saintly Pope was distinguished by being the greatest champion of the papacy during the fifth century.

[72]This boy was the beautiful Ganymedes.

[73]See *Agudeza* Discourse 14:
    Aethereas aquila puerum portante per auras
    illaesum timidis unguibus haesit onus:
    Nunc sua Caesareos exorat praeda leones,
    tutus, et ingenti ludit in ore lepus.
    Quae majora putas miracula? summus utrisque
    auctor adest: haec sunt Caesaris, illa Jovis.
This epigram may be the most critical one in the development of baroque theories of wit. It led Sarbiewski to separate wit from the theory of metaphor or tropes, and to see in wit abstract thought. See Chapter Five; cf. Parker xxxii.

Jove to Caesar, Caesar to the lion, and Jove to the eagle, the epigram is rather focused in one circumstance that Jove and Caesar share: bestowing their magnanimity even through their beasts. The terms compared otherwise remain separate and untouched—they are just paralleled.[74]

For Gracián, comparisons do not limit themselves to parallelisms between circumstances equally shared by two or more different objects. Rather, the parallelism could also discover any link of the topical kind, that is, not only *equals*, but also other topics such as *cause, effects, adjuncts*, and others.[75] When two or more terms compared share many circumstances topically related, a discourse may be developed by explaining each type of correspondence.[76] An example quoted in *Agudeza* is from St Leo the Great, who contrasted Romulus and Remus with St Peter and St Paul. The saintly Pope distinguished between the pagan and the holy Rome founded by them, the error and the truth taught, the political and the spiritual sees established, the fratricidal and the martyrized blood spilled, etc.[77]

Summarizing my interpretation of Gracián's conceptual similitudes and comparisons, I think the former "squeeze out" concepts whose precision only reaches the imaginative level of the tropes, whereas the latter "squeeze out" concepts whose precision reaches the truly abstract level of the topics.[78]

---

[74]See *Agudeza* Discourse 14.

[75]See *Agudeza* discourse 16 and 4. Gracián here shared the seventeenth century theory that the topics are not empty cases to draw materials into the speech. Topics rather are links expressing the relationship existing between the materials. Moreover, Gracián shared Pallavicino's belief that the topics are not pre-existent to the ingenious discovery of ideas (as Pellegrini and Tesauro seemed to believe). Gracián and Pallavicino saw the topics as part of the discovery made: the topics come to the mind as the relationship found between the ideas being thought.

[76]See *Agudeza* discourses 15 and 16.

[77]See *Agudeza* Discourse 16.

[78]I have mentioned before that the topics tend to subsume the tropes in baroque theories of rhetoric. Without denying this trend in Gracián, I nevertheless see him differentiating tropes by attributing to them the power to assimilate the terms compared into a single

The Explicitness of the Relationship

As illustrated above, some concepts clearly specify the circumstance grounding them, and other only imply such a circumstance: the reader himself should abstract it by squeezing the two or more terms matched. Even so, allusions exceed the cryptic character of ordinary implicit wit. They not only omit the foundation of the relationship, but, moreover, they do not specify the terms related, but just imply them. The listener should derive them from the many factors surrounding the situation in which the speech takes place, and from the speech itself. Only then can the listener put the terms together and squeeze the concept.[79]

> The method of this and other similar [concepts] consists in hinting at the point without explaining it completely, for it is enough to cause in him who does not understand hesitation and curiosity, and in he who understands, pleasure.[80]

According to Gracián, "Ordinarily an allusion finds its proportion with the past."[81] Look at this allusion, quoted in *Agudeza*, grounded on the common knowledge of history between the interlocutors:

> When Henry the Great of France, a little while before his unhappy death, told the Spanish ambassador that with the numerous army he had gathered he was thinking of going to Italy, to breakfast in Milan, hear mass in Rome, and get to Naples in time for dinner, the Spaniard replied: "Sire, if Your Majesty must advance with such a haste, at that rate you might very well arrive in Sicily for Vespers."[82]

---

imaginative idea.

[79]See *Agudeza* Discourse 49.

[80]*Agudeza* Discourse 49: "...consiste el artificio desta y otras semejantes, en un apuntar sin explicarse del todo, que basta a ocasionar el reparo y despertar la curiosidad en el que no lo entiende y el gusto en el que lo entiende".

[81]*Agudeza* Discourse 49: "De ordinario, la alusión proporcionada es a lo pasado".

[82]*Agudeza* Discourse 49: "Galantemente, un embajador de España, diciéndole el gran Enrico de Francia que pensaba con aquel numeroso ejército que tenía junto, poco antes de su infeliz muerte, ir a Italia, almorzar en Milán, oír misa en Roma, y llegar a comer a Nápoles,

The ambassador hinted at the "Sicilian Vespers," a massacre of the French which resulted in their expulsion from Sicily in 1282.[83]

Another example of allusion from *Agudeza* is the following:

> After returning from the sack of Cambrai and coming in to kiss the hand of Louis XI, Marrufine wore a luxurious golden chain set with a wealth of gems. When it was noticed and admired by the rest of the Messieurs, one of them stretched out his hand to touch it; then the King quickly reacted with much wit, though it ought to have been with more piety: "Ahem!, don't touch it, for that's a sacred thing." He alluded to a gossip that Marrufine had had it made from the monstrances and reliquaries of the churches he had dispoiled.[84]

Allusions can also be made by explicitly denying something while implicitly affirming another. The context provides the clue for the hinted meaning.[85] For example, as quoted in *Agudeza*, Martial thus answered Zoilus's snobbery:

> With a gorgeous and new robe, Zoilus, you laugh at my clothes.
> They are even worn, Zoilus, but they are mine.[86]

United with the equivocal use of language,[87] allusions are the foundation of

---

replicó el español: 'Sire, si tanta prisa ha de llever V. M., podrá muy bien, a ese paso, llegar a vísperas a Sicilia'".

[83]See Chambers 742, n. 5.

[84]*Agudeza* Discourse 49: "Entrando el Marrufino a besar la mano a Luis Undécimo, de vuelta de saquear a Cambray; traía un riquísimo collar de oro con mucha pedrería; reparando en él, los demás Mosiures, y alabándoselo, alargó uno dellos la mano para quererlo tocar. Al punto el rey, con mucha sal, que debiera con más celo: 'Tá, dijo, no lo toquéis, que es cosa sagrada', aludiendo a lo que se murmuraba, que lo había hecho de las custodias y relicarios de las iglesias que había despojado".

[85]See *Agudeza* Discourse 49.

[86]See *Agudeza* Discourse 49. Martial's epigram is the following:
Pexatus pulchre rides me, Zoilus, trita.
Sunt haec trita quidem, Zoile, sed mea sunt.

[87]See *Agudeza* Discourse 33.

ironies, and in general, of malicious wit.[88]   Moreover, the broad realm of judicious wit very often rests on implied terms, that is, contextual and not expressed circumstances, as I will amplify later.[89]

Gracián associated techniques of allusion with witty figurative language. Next after his treatment of allusions, he explained many figures as belonging to the unlimited number of possible types of concepts, for example, distribution, transition, gradation, epiphoneme, reflection, exception, etc.[90]   According to Gracián, figurative language only offers the materials; mind's ingenuity is the one in charge of squeezing the deviated meanings[91] by contrasting what the person plainly seems to say with contextual factors or with structural properties of the text.[92]   "Chuck's Conclusion" may be enough to illustrate this theory:

A small carafe of wine is illogical, immoral and inadequate.[93]

Concerning explicit concepts, it is enough to squeeze the substantive terms of the witticism, but in this case, *a small carafe of wine, to be, illogical, immoral,* and *inadequate* are not sufficient to reach by themselves the right meaning of the statement.   Following similar rules applied to allusions, the mind's wit should also pay attention to other assumed "contextual" elements, such as the implied structure of "Chuck's conclusion."   There is gradation,[94]

---

[88]See *Agudeza* discourses 26, 49, and 60.

[89]See, for example, *Agudeza* discourses 27 and 28.

[90]See *Agudeza* Discourse 50, but also the former edition of 1642: *Arte del Ingenio* Discourse 41, which offers a more diverse treatment of the subject, and a separate chapter on antithesis (Discourse 38).

[91]See *Agudeza* Discourse 50 and "Al Lector".

[92]See *Agudeza* Discourse 50, and *Arte de Ingenio* Discourse 41.   The many illustrations used by Gracián offer their deviated meaning implicitly.   The reader should be the one reaching the right understanding of the figurative language used.

[93]*1001 Logical Laws* 24.

[94]Note that if the mind's ingenuity does not assume gradation in "Chuck's Conclusion",

which, if matched with the terms, gives to *the inadequacy of scarce wine* a climactic and hyperbolic turn: as a culinary sin, it is worse than failing in logic and even morality! Moreover, the absolute *is* provides the ending hyperbole with a resolute, summarizing, and conclusive value, as happens with epiphonemes, that is, sententiae closing a piece of reasoning.[95]

The Number of Relationships Rendering One Idea

Correlations may be considered according to the number of correspondences contained in a simple idea or thought: either pure or mixed concepts.[96] Years ago, I received in Mexico some explanations of the relatively exotic kiwi fruit. One friend plainly told me that it was like lemon green strawberries. Another friend made all this explanation more detailed: for her, a kiwi also looked, tasted, and was shaped like the prickly pear; both fruits share a seedly flesh, and their flavors are enhanced if the fruits are chilled. My first friend offered a pure concept about the kiwi fruit. It rested on a single correspondence between the lemon color and strawberry taste. My second friend offered a mixed concept about the kiwi fruit. It rested on several correspondences established between the features of strawberries, lemons, and prickly pears. In any case, there was only one idea in question: the kiwi fruit. Independently of the informative success, the use of pure or mixed concepts only meant the number of correspondences squeezed to reach one single idea.

Indeed, it is not always true that the richer the correlation the better the squeezed concept. Juan Rufo almost purely, quickly, and very fittingly observed the disproportion between a murderer's motives and the effects of his crime:

---

the statement loses all its point, and becomes a cold and unwitty expression, probably just a simple enumeration.

[95]Note that considering several equally possible interpretations, the wit should choose the most befitting one for the case. Thus, the art of ingenuity is associated again with the art of rhetoric, in so far as both deal with the contingent and the appropriate.

[96]See *Agudeza* Discourse 3.

To shut one mouth he had opened seven.[97]

The same author dazzled Gracián with a mixed concept built over more, said Gracián, than one hundred relationships. Gracián was right in noticing its amazing, condensed, and almost endless interweaving of dissociations. Nonetheless, its twisted accumulation of correlations seems to me just coldly clever, and often irrelevant and unhappy, considering the many contrasts made between St Anne, the grandmother of Jesus, and the pagan gods:

Say, Anne, are you Diane? It is not possible,
for you are fecund and fairer.
Are you joyfully the Sun? Although unique,
being he is unbecoming to your sex.
Are you a beautiful Bellona? No, she was terrifying!
Neither Venus, for she was easy, though a goddess.
Miraculous image! Who, then, could you be
if being human and yourself is incredible.
You may be Diane, Anne, in purity;
Phoebus in the splendor and the joy;
in courage, Pallas, and Venus in beauty.
You are a woman who was given more
than what the heedful and liberal nature offers:
in making you, she made more than she knew.[98]

---

[97]See *Agudeza* Discourse 5: "...por cerrarle una boca, le había abierto siete." The disproportion is not completely pure since the seven new mouths refer both to the wounds and to the evidence denouncing the murderer and proclaiming his wickedness.

[98]*Agudeza* Discourse 16:
Di, Ana, ¿eres Diana? No es posible,
Que eres fecunda y eres más hermosa.
¿Eres, por dicha el sol? Tampoco es cosa,
Aunque sola, a tu sexo compatible.
¿Eres Belona bella? Fue terrible;
Ni Venus, que era fácil, aunque diosa.
Pues ¿qué serás, ¡oh, imagen milagrosa!,
Si el ser humana y tal es increíble?

Any way, as a chemist needs an elaborate compound—$C_{12}H_{22}O_{11}$—to make sugar sweet whereas he needs simple compounds—$12C$ and $11H_2O$—to make sugar's result—carbon and water—literally amorphous and tasteless, in the same way a wit should proceed with the chemistry of ideas. In some cases a pure concept may be enough to explain the case; in others, a person must use mixed wit. To give a quick account of a plain liar, a speaker may simply establish a pure and absolute relationship with the eighth commandment. But regarding special types of liars, for example, one who deceives to save his life from cruel murderers, a casuist, say, must include and dwell upon the many additional circumstances qualifying the case, if he wants to squeeze an appropriate concept. At the end, suggested Gracián, the complex case should be conceptualized by means of conglobated parallels in which the idea is neither just black nor just white, but ranging through all the colors and tones of the spectrum.[99] Moreover, a singular but complex thought may be conceptualized through a compound of all kinds of concepts: correlations, ponderations, ratiocinations, and inventions.[100]

> Serás Diana, Ana, en la pureza,
> Febo en el resplandor y en la alegría,
> En valor Palas, Venus en belleza,
>   Y mujer, a quien dio más que podía
> La atenta y liberal naturaleza;
> que en hacerte más hizo que sabía.

[99]See, for example, *Agudeza* Discourse 15: "Since conglobated parallels contain many terms in their correspondences, some of these terms are animate and others inanimate." ("En las paridades conglobadas, como son muchos los términos de la correspondencia, unos son animados y otros inanimados"). See also *Agudeza* Discourse 16: "A single act of understanding could contain many terms, in such a way that concerning one term, there is proportion with the subject in question, and concerning another term, there is disproportion..." ("En un mismo acto pueden entrar muchos términos, de modo que con el uno diga conformidad el sujeto comparado, y con el otro oposición...")

[100]Interpreting *Agudeza*'s different discourses is rather difficult because they discuss not only the pure varieties of the concepts specifically in question, but also the mixed varieties. For example, when addressing similitudes, Gracián did not refer just to pure types, but also to mixed types in which argumentation, ponderation, and specifically sententiae were

In short, and generally speaking, Gracián praised, blamed, and used plain as much as elaborate speech, depending on how well it rendered the idea in question.[101]

The Relationship of Ideas Within a Discourse

According to Gracián, discourses are witty either because they have independent jewels of ingenuity sprinkled throughout the text, or because the discourse itself keenly puts together the different ideas into a systematic and yet unexpected whole.[102] The first kind of wit in discourses is called loose or *minor art wit*. The second kind is called compound or *major art wit*.[103]

Examples of loose wit are some historical narratives with scattered and sharp clarifications of the diverse events narrated, some sapiential books collecting distinct and profound sententiae or aphorisms, like Gracián's *Oráculo*, some informative letters whose different issues are here and there enlightened through clever observations, or some freely written sermons which enrich the different doctrines and problems addressed with opportune and sharp remarks. Gracián thought that Spaniards were the greatest in the practice of loose wit. His preferred writers were the judicious Seneca and the acute Martial. Gracián believed the virtues of loose wit were its freedom (since it is not chained to a whole, it allows the mind its boldest adventures) and its greater simplicity which prevents it from being tiresome.[104]

In compound wit the subtleties are not disperse, as in loose wit, but interweaven in a coherent whole, which is either uncomplicated or complex. The first kind rises from simply correlating all the speech's ideas. The second kind

---

involved. See, for example, *Agudeza* Discourse 12.

[101]See *Agudeza* Discourse 61. There, Gracián considered the propriety of either laconic or rotund oratory.

[102]See *Agudeza* Discourse 3.

[103]See *Agudeza* Discourse 51.

[104]See *Agudeza* discourses 51 and 61.

does it by means of complex inventions, such as symbols.[105]

Uncomplicated compounds can be further classified either as metaphorical or as comparative, depending on the precision of the correlation made. These compounds are metaphorical if the compared sets of ideas assimilate each other into an imprecise but imaginative discourse.[106] For example, a speaker can explain the set of blessings enjoyed by an organized society if he uses the extended metaphor of beehives. Uncomplicated compounds are comparative if they rest on clear parallels which specify the circumstances grounding the concept.[107] For example, a jurisconsult may write a complete legal treatise by contrasting the federalist principles reigning in the United States and in Mexico. Or he may theorize about the philosophy of law behind the Mexican Constitution, by weighing the balance between the individual and the social rights specified in this supreme decree. Comparative compounds are harder to pursue than the metaphorical ones because of the precision the former requires in making the correlation.[108] Even so, Gracián found several methods to establish comparative compounds, for example, by connecting the parts of an hypothesis, by matching the parallel terms of several propositions, by gradation, by ponderation, by abstracting the universal, by grounding the association in sets of circumstances, by combining objections and ripostes, by paradoxes, or by simply explaining a text, etc.[109] Gracián believed that, in general, uncomplicated compounds were mothers of the arts and sciences, and particularly of eloquent speeches. He thought the Italians were the greatest in this kind of wit.[110]

Complex compounds rest on more than simple correlations—the mere matching of raw materials—and have recourse to inventions—especially

---

[105]See *Agudeza* discourses 51 to 57.

[106]See *Agudeza* discourses 9, 10, 53, and 54.

[107]See *Agudeza* discourses 14, 15, 16, 52, and 54.

[108]See *Agudeza* Discourse 54.

[109]See *Agudeza* Discourse 54.

[110]See *Agudeza* Discourse 51.

fictions—to bring forth a concept. The correlation which then is still made takes place between the invention and the set of ideas it symbolizes. Great and clear examples of complex compounds may be found in the Spain of Gracián's times, to name few, the first and best *Don Juan* ever written,[111] which fictionally addresses the theological issue of faith without works, and Pedro Calderón de la Barca's *El gran teatro del mundo* which dramatically gives an insight into the coexistence of God's omnipotence and human freedom. However, probably thinking about Homer, Gracián believed the Greeks were the greatest in complex compounds.[112]

According to Gracián, the value of literature and generally the fine arts rests mainly on their symbolic power as complex compounds. Gracián saw in these arts a way sweetly to squeeze difficult truths, and thus a way to combine the task of teaching with the task of pleasing. He particularly thought that complex compounds sweetened controversial ideas which it would be imprudential to state directly before an unprepared audience.[113] Gracián analyzed several complex types of wit, for example, apologues, parables, allegories, epopees, novels, drama,[114] metamorphoses, fables, tales, jokes, paintings, hieroglyphs, emblems, coats of arms, mottos, and coin inscriptions.[115] In any case, thought Gracián, they share in common their strong reliance on metaphorical correlations to squeeze out the concept.[116] Even so, their most striking character still rests on their being inventions, that is, the fourth great genre of concepts, which later will be explained.

---

[111]I mean, Tirso de Molina's *El Burlador de Sevilla.*

[112]See *Agudeza* Discourse 51.

[113]See *Agudeza* Discourse 55.

[114]Regarding drama, see *Agudeza* Discourse 45.

[115]On species of complex compounds, see *Agudeza* discourses 55, 56, 57, and also 35.

[116]See *Agudeza* Discourse 55.

Ponderations

The second great genre of concepts, said Gracián, "is that of judicious and subtle ponderations, and this subsumes *crises* [the witty conceptualization of judgments], paradoxes, exaggerations, sententiae, ripostes, etc."[117]

The essence of this genre is the discovery of the new or extravagant *in view of the ordinary and established.* For this purpose ingenuity must be assisted by judgment in order to recognize what is ordinary and what is extraordinary before rendering the witticism.[118]   Gracián even saw in some varieties of ponderation—for example, maxims—more judgment than wit, since they strongly express the dictates of reason.[119]   However, the interest shown in *Agudeza* is rather in the wit embodied by ponderations.   Thus some types discussed—for example, paradoxes—may be so bizarre that their exquisite subtlety can well appeal to ingenuity but hardly to sound judgment.[120]

Ponderations differ from correlations in that for the later it is enough simply to match terms for the squeezing of concepts, whereas for the former it is also necessary to ponder which correspondence—among many possible ones—exceeds previous standards of subtlety.[121]   Ponderations thus consist in trascending the common and the expected by squeezing previously unconsidered circumstances from the case in question—circumstances which strikingly modify the old view of such a case.[122]

---

[117]*Agudeza* Discourse 3: "La segunda es de ponderación juiciosa sutil, y a ésta se reducen crisis, paradojas, exageraciones, sentencias, desempeñós, etc."

[118]See, for example, *Agudeza* discourses 28 and 43.

[119]See, for example, *Agudeza* Discourse 43.

[120]See, for example, *Agudeza* Discourse 23.

[121]See *Agudeza* Discourse 4.

[122]See, for example, *Agudeza* Discourse 28. Let it be clear that correlations find something new because of introducing such a novelty into the mind for the first time in view of no other consideration, whereas ponderations find something new in view of the preexistent old. A correlation would be my purely new discovery that brown rice and lentils can mix. Bingo!

Ponderations are established on several foundations, and render a very interesting variety of subtleties:

The Subjective Foundations of Judicious Wit

A wit may display ingenuity if he trascends the established view of a case by associating it with circumstances which are then regarded as extravagant or rare, in as much as they have not been noticed before.[123] For example, consider Martial's answer to Sextus:

> I pleaded your cause, Sextus, having agreed to do so for two thousand [silver coins]. Did you send me that money? Only one thousand: what is it? "You did not plead anything," you tell me, "and you made me lose my case." You ought to give me as much again, Sextus, as I had to blush for you.[124]

Martial's reason may not be the best to secure sound judgment, but Gracián believed that it nevertheless was the wittiest:

I lacked any preconception about rules concerning the cooking of brown rice and lentils. A ponderation would be my discovery that I can beat steamed rice without turning it into a yucky paste. Heresy! This discovery strongly contrasts with the Mexican most orthodox cuisine which prescribes that one should never ever beat steamed rice. Ponderations also differ from argumentative wit. Ponderations discover unconsidered circumstances which make ingenuity see the case with a new and astounding light. In constrast, some types of argumentative wit—for example, mysteries, difficulties, and contrarieties—"prove" what is already seen as new or extraordinary, by advancing the "proofs" or circumstances which ground the novelty of the case. Despite their perceived soundness, by turning the novelty into something which fits into the mind's ordinary frame of ideas, these "proofs" become a token of the most powerful ingenuity, and produce the greatest astonishment in the audience who see the unexpected meet the expected. See, for example, *Agudeza* discourses 6, 7, and 8, and also 12.

[123]See, for example, *Agudeza* discourses 6, 9, 23, 24, 25, 28, and 29.

[124]*Agudeza* Discourse 25:
  Egi, Sexte, tuam, pactus duo milla, causam.
 Missisti nummos quod mihi? mille: quid est?
 Narrasti nihil inquis, et a te perdita causa est.
 Tanto plus debes, Sexte, quod erubui.

When the reason advanced is contrary to the one previously conceived, then it is very pleasing because it is unexpected and difficult.[125]

Moreover, the reason was relevant to the case.[126]

A wit may even display more ingenuity by reaching the unexpected and difficult, quickly and briefly.[127] Gracián quoted King Sebastian of Portugal replying to a dismal omen:

¡Eh, que no lo entendéis! Que el Cometa me está diciendo que acometa.[128]

Both promptness and brevity are signs of powerful ingenuity; promptness because it satisfies the urgency of a reply;[129] brevity because it satisfies the rule of efficiency:

The good, if brief, twice as good.[130]

Brevity itself is witty. Even the most frequently used common places acquire new life if the mind's wit discovers briefer and more condensed ways

---

[125]*Agudeza* Discourse 25: "Cuando la razón que se da es contraria de la que se concebía, tiene mucho agrado por lo impensado, y por lo dificultoso".

[126]That is, the reason was not something unrelated to the case. See *Agudeza* Discourse 25.

[127]See, for example, *Agudeza* discourses 18, 29, 48, and 45.

[128]*Agudeza* Discourse 18: "Hey!, you do not understand it! The *comet* is telling me to *attack*." King Sebastian's reply is grounded on an equivocation impossible to render into English.

[129]See, for example, *El Discreto* Realce 15, and *Agudeza* Discourse 45.

[130]*Oráculo* Aphorism 105: "Lo bueno, si breve, dos veces bueno". This may be one of the most famous aphorisms of Gracián. It certainly has become the coined expression ruling brevity in the Spanish language, and through Madame de Sablé's translation, it is also widely used in France. Cf. Arturo del Hoyo 179b, n.4.

of expressing them: the novelty of the expression rests purely on its brevity. For Gracián, sententiae are witty, if not for other reason, because of their power of condensing universal rules of morality into very brief expressions. Moreover, sententiae unite this density with depth of understanding.[131]

Behind the *extravagance* or *unexpected* aspects of witticisms, and also behind the *urgency* or *difficulty* of problems and the *efficiency* of the responses, requiring *prompt* and *brief* actions from speakers, there is a subjective element which reflects less the case in question than how the case is particularly perceived by those minds concerned about it. Or if not subjective, at least this element strongly indicates the peculiar relation of these minds to such a case. For example, Gracián celebrated the heliocentric theory less because it was judicious than because it was witty. In Gracián's times it still was extravagant and new for many to think differently than that the Sun revolves around the Earth. Gracián himself wondered whether the yearly seasons could be explained if the Sun remained fixed in Space. In any case, the novelty of the idea made it even more appealing to Gracián's wonderment.[132]

As said before, the new is a subjective property of *every* witticism. Ingenuity's effort in fact is *invention*, that is, to discover the previously unseen. However, this property has a special place within judicious wit, because the new could deliberatedly be used to startle audiences with extravagant propositions.[133] Consider for instance this prudential paradox from the sage Pittacus, challenging customary ways of thinking:

The half is larger than the whole.[134]

---

[131]See, for example, *Agudeza* Discourse 29, and *Oráculo* Aphorism 105.

[132]See *Agudeza* Discourse 23.

[133]In ponderations, the new is specifically new because it is extravagant, rare, inconceivable, and unexpected, if compared with the ordinary, common, conceivable, and expected.

[134]*Agudeza* Discourse 23: "...la metad es más que el todo."

By means of an equivocation, this Greek sage was contrasting the often grandiose figments of imagination with what the complete view of reality finally offers to persons. The sage also signified the prudence of always renovating people's expectations rather than disillusioning them with any definite result.

The Objective Foundations of Judicious Wit

The subjective properties, discussed above, imply a second general property of every "sound" ponderation (and every "sound" witticism): every ponderation should display witty propriety—it should be plausible, that is, it should apply at least in an understandable, if not certain way, to the case.[135] Responding to this need, Gracián believed that especially the most extravagant varieties of witticisms—many of them pertaining to judicious wit—should not just imply but always reveal the plausible circumstance which understandably grounds the novelty of the proposition.[136] Only if perceived, the witticism would make sense, shed new light to the mind, truly startle.[137] For example, although judgment rejects it,[138] it is still conceivable by the understanding that King Louis XI decapitated those who prevented his suicide, if an explanatory circumstance is given: nobody should oppose the king's will.[139] In fact, the extravagance of well

---

[135]See, for example, *Agudeza* discourses 23, 28, 39, and 44.

[136]On plausibility, see, for example, *Agudeza* Discourse 43.

[137]The need to establish the new on a plausible circumstance resembles Richard Whately's burden of proof as pertaining to those advocating changes. Cf. Richard Whately *Elements of Rhetoric* III, 2. However, for Whately, this requirement seems to satisfy a procedural rule of argumentation and judgment—the *presumption* belongs to the one pre-occupying the grounds of debate in the beginning of a controversy—or a psychological need of assuring proofs to win conviction to an idea. For Gracián, the need of "proofs" rather satisfies a more basic cognitive requirement: the reaching of perception or understanding of a case, considering that it was previously unknown or not conceived.

[138]The authoritarian Gracián nevertheless willingly celebrated King Louis XI's most vicious crime. See *Agudeza* Discourse 23.

[139]See *Agudeza* Discourse 23. Gracián regarded King Louis XI's "witty" reply a type of paradox embodied not in words but in actions.

known facts finally is grasped when a previously unseen circumstance renders understanding:

>   ....Apolo,
> such a prudent and sensible god
> that he himself is his own coach driver
> to prevent the pain of suffering one.[140]

The case is that if a proposition lacks foundation in any circumstance conceivably related to the case, it should not even be tested by judgment, but simply regarded as senseless by the understanding, and thus the most unwitty.[141] For example, if one hears for the first time, "let's go to the races and bet on the tortoise against the hare," one probably will find it extremely senseless, considering the speed ordinarily shown by each animal. Yet, this proposition may become palatable to the understanding, if not to reason, if one notices that tortoises are perseverant and hares inconstant. Or it may make sense to bet on the tortoise because of the high profit to be gained if by the slightest chance the tortoise wins the race. Or moreover, one may understandably, if not wisely, choose the tortoise because of a sentimental whim, such as "he is cute," or "it is very sad that most people do not have the heart to support a definite loser; I rather have a heart, therefore I go for the loser tortoise."[142] However, saying that

---

[140]*Agudeza* Discourse 25, which quotes Alonso Jerónimo de Salas Barbadillo's "Fábula de Dafne":

>   ....Apolo,
> dios tan prudente y tan cuerdo,
> que de cochero se sirve,
> para no sufrir un cochero.

[141]Here the lack of wit does not come, as in most cases, just from the lack of novelty in the idea. The lack of wit is rather the most extreme: the idea is senseless; in fact, the idea is not any idea at all, since nothing is truly presented to the mind in an understandable form.

[142]A whim may be witty, if clearly and surprisingly presented to the mind. Although unreasonable, some whimsical ideas still have their own type of meaning for the understanding. The wide criterion of the understanding—as compared with the one of judgment—may be illustrated by pure wordplays grounding paradoxes. Gracián quoted this

one goes for the tortoise because "the Martians founded a new settlement on Venus," simply does not make any sense at all, even when recalling the sweetest stories of mythology. What does that has to say, concerning the hare and tortoise case, to the understanding? The mind can not even consider such a proposition! Since the proposition is not grounded on any plausible circumstance relevant to the case, the proposition becomes a vacuous play on ideas, something impossible to test by judgment, but worse!, something meaningless!

The general principle of witty propriety may be best summed up by Gracián himself, as he did when talking about paradoxes:

> ...lacking any basis, [the extravagant witticism] is not appraised as a subtlety but as a flippancy....
>
> Paradoxes should be like salt: rare and plausible. Since they are opinions causing scruples and thus without credit, they can not win any reputation. Many indicate unsoundness of ingenuity, and if of judgment, they are worse.[143]

---

riddle:

En un medio está mi amor,
Y-sabe-él
Que si en medio está el sabor,
En los extremos la hiel.

[Middling goes my love
and it does know
that if the middle has the flavor,
its extremes contain the gall.]

The untranslatable Spanish version contains in itself the explanation of the riddle. Gracián lingered on it, saying: "The point rests in the name Isabel, in which, when divided, the first syllable, *I* and the last, *el* give *gall*, while *flavor* lies in the middle..." ("Fúndase en el nombre de Isabel, que, dividido, la primera sílaba, que es *I*, y la última, *el* dicen *iel*, y en medio queda el *sabe*...") *Agudeza* Discourse 1.

[143]*Agudeza* Discourse 23: "...si no hay razón, no se gradúa por sutileza, sino por ligereza." "Las paradojas han de ser como la sal, raras y plausibles, que como son opiniones escrupulosas, y así desacreditadas, no pueden dar reputación; y muchas, arguyen destemplanza en el ingenio, y si en el juicio, peor".

If every objective circumstance grounding a ponderation should attain witty propriety, that is, plausibility, circumstances nevertheless may vary in their class depending on the case. If one should trascend ordinary ideas grounded on the *substantial*, then one may attain the extravagant by introducing an *accidental* circumstance; if the *general* must be beaten, then a *special* reason may be brought forward; if a belief does not reach beyond the *surface* of events, then *profound* circumstances may be presented to enlighten the subject; and viceversa in either case.[144]　　Some immigrants from Asia have horrified Californians because the immigrants eat dogs. The Californians ponder, of course, the substantial: "It is inhumane!" The immigrants modify the case by transforming the circumstance into something accidental: "If so, it should be also inhumane that Californians eat beef, pork, and other domesticated animals; at least other peoples believe so, but Californians think of it as something simply accidental." The Californians may reply by noticing a special circumstance of the case: "But that's unAmerican!"　　The immigrants having recourse to a legitimate equivocation may in their turn answer with a very general precedent: "On the contrary, dogs along with turkey are the most American sources of protein; the other sources—beef, pork, chicken, and the like—were brought by the Europeans to this beautiful continent." Then one Californian may oversubtilize by raising a most special point: "But they ate my dog!," and so on. The view of the case may subsequently be modified by introducing new and unconsidered circumstances.[145]

---

[144]Concerning the substantial, see, for example, *Agudeza* discourses 15, 43, and 44; concerning the special, see, for example, discourses 12, 17, and 29; concerning the general, see, for example, discourses 27 and 28; concerning the accidental, see, for example, discourses 6 and 19; concerning the profound, see, for example, discourses 28 and 30. Many other types of circumstances are illustrated in *Agudeza*, for example, the deficient, the excessive, the contrary, etc. Even so, it is enough to study the few types of circumstances here mentioned, to understand that judicious wit consists in modifying ordinary views of things by introducing an unconsidered circumstance into the case.

[145]Notice that, according to Gracián's conceptism, the introduction of circumstances like the ones illustrated above is not an operation of inference in which from proofs a conclusion is inferred. This series of circumstances rather contributes to the prior operation of

As explained later, these distinctions among general, special, substantial, accidental, and profound circumstances are·important to identify the witty element of sententiae, maxims, and other types of judicious wit; moreover, they become part of Gracián's standards of judgment.

The Formal Foundations of Judicious Wit

The formal foundations of ponderations can be explained by answering two general questions: 1) what are the procedures for judicious witticisms?, and 2) what is the actuality of the witticism?

The procedures of judicious wit. The basic and general procedure judiciously to subtilize is to find and introduce an unexpected circumstance into a case, so that the ordinary may be turned into something extraordinary. This circumstance may be introduced into the case in different ways: disproportions, transpositions, and retorts.

It appears that the first and simplest procedure is *disproportion*. The wit may simply find the new and introduce it into the case. The disproportion between the previously accepted and the now plausibly proposed may then cause witty wonderment in view of a drastically changed case. Gracián quoted an example from Alexander the Great which contrasts the ordinary belief of Alexander's incompetence to organize and secure his empire for posterity with a new and plausible theory: he was too arrogant and wicked to suffer or imagine a successor greater than himself, governing such an empire.[146]

In the example above, the disproportion between the new and the old in fact causes wonderment. However, the wondermet only comes from the new being different to the old idea. The disproportion does not indicate any accidental or substantial opposition between the ideas; it does not deny either that such ideas

---

conceptualization. These circumstances serve as a framework facilitating the perception or apprehension of the case in question, and also its definition. When the concept has been properly delimited, and also tested by judgment, then, the third mental operation could follow: inference.

[146]See *Agudeza* Discourse 26.

may occur together. Thus far, Gracián called *mysteries*[147] the pondering of this degree of disproportion which only rises from the difference of the thoughts compared, and yet, from the extraordinary or new being suddenly thought as very possible by the mind, when there were many other plausible things more easily or ordinarily conceivable.[148]

A judicious disproportion does not need to rest on properly introducing the new or extraordinary into the mind—on clearly conceiving an idea differing from the old and ordinary. A judicious disproportion is sufficiently stunning by producing doubt when hinting at the plausibility of something other than the ordinary or established belief. Gracián illustrated *doubts* with these verses celebrating a woman warrior:

> She is as brave as she is beautiful,
> that the wounds she inflicted
> are in doubt concerning what hurt more,
> her sword or her countenance.[149]

Moreover, it is not necessary properly to introduce a new belief or a doubt in order to startle the mind. It suffices to reflect on the old itself, bringing it again to consciousness or noticing in it elements which were not attentively considered before, in order to produce wonderment. From Góngora, Gracián quoted this *reflection*:

---

[147]*Agudeza*'s use of the word mystery has a very technical meaning which does not apply to the sense given in Catholic theology.

[148]See *Agudeza* Discourse 6. See also discourses 11, 25, 39, and 44. Mysteries reach their highest level of subtlety when resolved. That however belongs to argumentative wit, as explained later.

[149]*Agudeza* Discourse 44:
> Tan valiente como hermosa,
> que en duda están las heridas,
> a cuál reconozcan más,
> a su espada o a su vista.

> Her eyes were the joy,
> **if they weren't the hope**
> that Spring wears
> on the greatest day of splendor.[150]

Furthermore, a wit may startle his audience by simply lingering on the well and attentively known. The listeners' surprise rests on the annoying—and thus, unconceivable—superfluity of the reflection, and, more importantly, on the listeners' experience of witty *suspense*, since their minds now expect something else to be said in order to justify such a lenghty abuse of words. This suspense is not just the emotional anxiety of expecting the unknown; it is also an intellectual act: if something else can be said about an issue, then the mind may skeptically suspend judgment about what now is well known through the overstated reflection; thus the mind may patiently wait for the new pieces of information.[151] An instance of suspense is the sermon of Ash Wednesday quoted above. It dwells for a good while on many high, authoritative, and accepted opinions about the dignity of human beings, and then "*ex abrupto*," as Gracián prescribed,[152] the preacher disrupts the overstated idea with something different and even contrary: the misery and nothingness of man. Another instance of suspense is "Peter's Perfect-People Palliative":

> Each of us is a mixture of good qualities and some (perhaps) not-so-good qualities. In considering our fellow people, we should remember their good qualities and realize that their faults only prove that they are, after all, human. We should refrain from making harsh judgments of people just because they happen to be dirty,

---

[150]*Agudeza* Discourse 44:

> La alegría eran sus ojos,
> **si no eran la esperanza,**
> que viste la Primavera,
> el día mayor de gala.

[151]See *Agudeza* Discourse 44.

[152]See *Agudeza* Discourse 44.

rotten, no-good sons-a-bitches.[153]

For Gracián, the use of suspense should not fail to reach its resolution, not betray the audience's expectations.[154] And though the ending disruption does not need to be contrary to the ordinary belief which has been overly reviewed, the disruption nevertheless should take the line of discourse on a different track, offering something profound, eminently judicious or critical, or emphatic and rare.[155] Consider the following narrative about the casuistic training received by a priest:

> When, as a new priest, I was released on the unsuspecting public 25 years ago, I had the benefit of an education geared to prepare me for the daily problems of life. I had been taught, for example, the circumstances in which a widower might marry his mother-in-law, that tortoise might be eaten on a day of abstinence, that fox hunting was sinful on a day of fasting, and—most fascinating of all—to whom the calf of a cow belonged when the cow's owner had allowed the cow to be taken advantage of by a bull without the bull owner's consent.
>
> And so I went to my first parish waiting for a fox-hunting widower to turn up to wed his mother-in-law on Ash Wednesday, to be followed by a tortoise buffet and nuptial fox hunt while his cow sought pastures new. No such person arrived.
>
> Instead, I was met with a seemingly endless stream of young Venuses and Adonises seeking marriage, their main worry being the choice of hymns.[156]

---

[153] *1001 Logical Laws* 217.

[154] I myself think that, in occasions, suspense may admit the lack of an explicit resolution. The bewilderment caused in the mind by not having found such a resolution then may lead this mind to squeeze out one. For instance, in her *Reply to Sister Philothea* (actually to the faultfinding Bishop of Puebla), Sister Juana Inés de la Cruz overstated her regards for Sister Philothea to such an excess, that the reader can not think but that there is much of sarcasm in Sister Juana: "...because I felt that considering the reverence I owe you, the title of Your Reverence would actually show very little reverence, replace my familiarity with any form of address you deem worthy of your merits, for I have not had the daring to exceed the limits of your style nor to infringe the margins of your modesty."

[155] See *Agudeza* Discourse 44.

[156] Richard Wilson, "A Priest Smiles Back on 25 Years," *Catholic Digest* (St Paul, MN:

The disproportion may not be between old and new ideas, but between situations themselves. Finding himself in a very tight spot, a wit astonishes the observers if he comes out from the problem quickly, easily, and rightly. Then, he achieves what Gracián called *ripostes in action* or *in word*. Consider this example quoted in *Agudeza*:

> Don Alonso de Aguilar in very courtier like fashion satisfied the Catholic King's objection, when he hosted the latter at his palace at Montilla. The King asked him why he had made the staircase so narrow in so august an edifice. He answered: "Sire, I never thought to have so great a guest."[157]

According to Gracián, the succession of suspense and quick ripostes is the structure which builds up most narratives.[158]

Disproportions may go beyond mysteries—that is, the discovery of alternative but noncontradictory possibilities—and rather imply opposition between the old belief and the new. Many Mexicans regard the PRI[159] antidemocratic because of its permanence in power for decades, and the alleged dishonesty of most of its politicians and members—characteristics which belie the *accidents* of honesty and alternation of power usually associated with democracies. However, a wit may notice that most Mexicans keep voting for the PRI, as happened in the last and unquestionable federal elections in August 1994. If the *accidentally repugnant* occurs, Gracián called its ponderation *difficulty*.[160]

University of St Thomas, September 1991) 60.

[157]*Agudeza* Discourse 26: "Satisfizo cortesanamente don Alonso de Aguilar al reparo del Rey Católico, cuando lo hospedó en su palacio de Montilla. Preguntóle cómo había hecho, en una obra tan augusta, una escalera tan angosta, y respondió: 'Señor, nunca pensé tener huésped tan grande'".

[158]See *Agudeza* Discourse 45.

[159]The PRI has been the governing political party in Mexico for more than six decades.

[160]See *Agudeza* Discourse 7. Difficulties are wittier if resolved. But that belongs to argumentative wit, as explained later.

Difficulties are harder to conceive than mysteries, and therefore, wittier. However, all of them are surpassed by disproportions in which the old belief and the new imply a substantial opposition. It is contrary to communist parties to acknowledge a Pope, because of their essentially militant atheism. Conceiving it otherwise implies a substantial opposition to the ordinary idea of communism. However, President Gorbachov astonished the world when in good will he visited John Paul II at the end of 1989. The event required either accepting a paradox, or the revision of the idea of communism in the public's mind, or the hypothesis that something else than ordinary communism was taking place in the Soviet Union. Actually, since then, President Gorbachov did not cease to astound the world with the many changes he brought to Eastern Europe and the Soviet Union. If the substantially repugnant occurs, Gracián called its ponderation *contrariety*.[161] If the contrariety is wittier in its resolution, then it is *ponderation by contrarieties*, and it is studied under the heading of argumentative wit.[162] If the contrariety is witty enough as such, then, there is a *paradox*.[163] An example of paradoxical contrariety is these verses from Jorge Montemayor:

> All is one for me,
> to be and not to be hopeful,
> that if today I would die to see her
> tomorrow, because I saw her.[164]

---

[161]See *Agudeza* Discourse 8. A contrariety is often wittier if resolved. But that belongs to argumentative wit, as explained later

[162]See *Agudeza* Discourse 8.

[163]Gracián used the word *paradox* in equivocal ways. Most times it meant just the rare or the extravagant. See, for example, *Agudeza* Discourse 23. Other times, it applied closer to what is a logical paradox: a statement in which something seemingly contradictory is affirmed and probably valid. See, for example, *Agudeza* Discourse 42. Here, I use the word paradox in the second sense.

[164]*Agudeza* Discourse 42:
> Todo es uno para mí,
> esperanza o no tenella,

Another instance is from Miguel Hernández:

> It is necessary to kill in order to live.[165]

Gracián believed that any kind of witty contrariety should not be real but only apparent. Either resolved by witty argumentation, or containing a hidden solution in paradoxes, the witty contrariety can only be accepted by the mind because there is such a solution. Their power to startle the mind rests on their contradictory presentation, which at the same time must at least hint at a plausible explanation.[166]

A second major procedure which renders a judicious witticism is *ingenious transpositions*. Here, the contrast between the old and the new is subtler. Rather than resting on a general disproportion, the case is turned upside-down by converting a definitional circumstance into its opposite. To do it, the wit does not simply introduce a new circumstance into the general case; the wit rather keenly introduces the new circumstance into the circumstance which still defines the general case.[167] Gracián illustrated transpositions with Caesar's promptness to turn a dismal omen into a presage of success:

> ...in Africa, Caesar fell on the ground as he leapt from the ship, but he quickly corrected the omen, and said: "**Teneo te, Africa** I did not fall, but took possession." He made an equivocation between falling and clasping the earth: and there lies the point of this kind of wit.[168]

---

que si hoy muero por verla,
mañana, porque la vi.

[165]"Es preciso matar para seguir viviendo". Quoted by Pelayo H. Fernández, *Estilística* (Madrid: José Porrúa Turanzas, S. A., 1972) 81.

[166]See, for example, *Agudeza* Discourse 23.

[167]See *Agudeza* Discourse 17.

[168]*Agudeza* Discourse 17: "...César, en Africa, cayó en tierra al saltar del bajel, pero corrigió pronto el agüero, y dijo: **Teneo te, Africa**; no he caído, sino que he tomado posesión. Equivocó el caer con el abrazarse con la tierra; y allí está el punto desta sutileza."

A third major procedure of judicious wit is *quick retorts*. They are ripostes defeating an interlocutor's opinions or actions, by applying to the interlocutor what he meant to apply to somebody or something else, either in scorn or praise. Retorts are very similar to a transposition, though they have their own peculiarity. The reversion occurs not so much in the positive or negative sign of the definitional circumstance of a case, as it occurs in the subject the circumstance is applied to.[169] The retort may make the proponent share what he meant to apply only to the respondent. Consider this example quoted in *Agudeza*:

> Cicero, asked by Pompey when he arrived at the military camp, where he had left his son-in-law Piso, the husband of Tullia, replied instantly: "He is staying in the camp of your father-in-law Caesar." Cicero found a parallel between Pompey and Pompey's very imputation, and Cicero squeezed it as a reply.[170]

The retort may be more radical and even make a complete reversion, turning back on the proponent the whole imputation, without the respondent sharing a bit of it. Consider this illustration from *Agudeza*:

> ...when Demosthenes said to Phocion, "Look out, the Athenians will kill you the day they lose their temper," Phocion replied, "And you, too, when they regain it." The retort triumphed because if the former said "lose their temper," the later, on the contrary, said "regain it," which is to say much more.[171]

The actuality of judicious wit. A new idea may be introduced in an *absolute*

---

[169]See *Agudeza* Discourse 18.

[170]*Agudeza* Discourse 18: "Preguntándole Pompeyo a Cicerón, cuando llegó a su campo, que dónde dejaba a su yerno Pisón, marido de Tulia, respondió pronto: 'Queda en el campo de su suegro César'. Halló la paridad de lo mismo que le oponía, y exprimióla por respuesta".

[171]*Agudeza* Discourse 18: "...Foción, diciéndole Demóstenes: 'Mira que los atenienses te han de matar el día que salieren de sí', respondió: 'Y a ti, si volvieren en sí'. Venció la retorsión, porque si aquél dijo cuando salieren de sí, éste, por lo contrario, cuando volvieren en sí, que es decir mucho más".

way.[172] For example, an ingenious gentleman boasted of his well known and celebrated promptness to versify before His Holiness Leo X, greatest and most happy patron of renaissance artists:

> The Archipoet writes as many verses as one thousand poets.[173]

Pope Leo replied in the most absolute fashion:

> And, for one thousand more, the Archipoet drinks.[174]

Sometimes introducing the new idea in an absolute way is not conceivable. Modifying the old idea may only be possible through an *exaggeration* or by emphasizing the extreme case as the exemplary one.[175] For instance, the Nobel laureate Octavio Paz replied to the belief that orthodox Catholicism is enjoyed by Mexicans, by presenting a meditation from a Chamula Indian, from Chiapas, mixing Christian Faith with preCortesian traditions:

> This one in the coffin is Our Lord Saint Emmanuel, who is also called Saint Savior...before Saint Emmanuel was born, the Sun was cold like the Moon. On the Earth, the *Pukujes* lived, who used to eat the people. The Sun started to be warm when Baby God was born, Who is the Son of the Virgin, and the Lord Our Savior...[176]

---

[172]See, for example, *Agudeza* Discourse 15.

[173]*Agudeza* Discourse 18: "Archipoeta facit versus pro mille poetis."

[174]*Agudeza* Discourse 18: "Et pro mille aliis Archipoeta bibit."

[175]See, for example, *Agudeza* discourses 4, 15, and 19 to 22. Exaggerations are also called "assisted" ("ayudado") method by Gracián, since the wit should supply an extra amount of materials to make the novel idea take shape.

[176]Octavio Paz, *El laberinto de la soledad*, (México: Fondo de Cultura Económica, 1989) 97: "Éste que está encajonado es el Señor San Manuel; se llama también San Salvador...antes de que naciera San Manuel, el sol estaba frío igual que la luna. En la tierra vivían los pukujes, que se comían a la gente. El sol empezó a calentar cuando nació el niño Dios, que es hijo de la Virgen, el señor San Salvador". Octavio Paz quotes

Echoing Gracián, Octavio Paz sees the extreme case (or the exaggeration) as the way to introduce the unconceivable idea into the mind:

> In the Chamula narrative—an extreme, and therefore, an exemplar case—the religious superposition and the indelible presence of Indian mythology are identifiable.[177]

An unconceivable and even impossible idea may also be introduced by means of a *conditional proposition*.[178] The Monster of Wits, Lope de Vega, wrote this elegy for Prince Charles:

> The heavens ruled he should live
> a succint and swift life,
> **so that a second Charles never exist**
> **to equal Charles the Fifth.**[179]

Lope de Vega meant the conditional—that if Prince Charles lived he would have surpassed the imperial feats of Charles V.

Moreover, an unconceivable or unspeakable idea may be introduced by means of a *fictional proposition*, which works as a symbol for what is meant to be said.[180] Gracián quoted this gallant ancedote:

Ricardo Pozas A., *Juan Pérez Jolote. Autobiografía de un tzotzil*, 5a. ed. (México: Fondo de Cultura Económica, 1965).

[177]Octavio Paz 97: "En el relato del chamula, caso extremo y por lo tanto ejemplar, es visible la superposición religiosa y la presencia imborrable de los mitos indígenas".

[178]See, for example, *Agudeza* Discourse 15.

[179]*Agudeza* Discourse 15.
    Término breve y sucinto
quiso el Cielo que viviese,
    porque otro Carlos no hubiese
    que igualase a Carlos Quinto.
Gracián called this example a non expressed conditional.

[180]See, for example, *Agudeza* discourses 15, and 55 to 57.

A lovely woman was once giving sweets to a little boy, and before putting them in his mouth she told him to close his eyes; since the boy refused her command, she repeatedly pressed him, urgently, to shut his eyes, and again he continued looking at her. The gallant and keen Rufo then remarked, "*Señora*, he would not want to lose Heavens for a trifle."[181]

Furthermore, an unspeakable idea may simply be introduced *indirectly* by properly applying it to something else, but similar to what is meant. Gracián quoted the poets' riposte to Apolo, who was condemning these artists to silence because of the lack of judgment and truth of their writings. Instead of recklessly offering a retort to Apolo, the poets willingly assented to him, by extending his godly command to all liars, such as lawyers, politicians, historians, and the like.[182]

The Varieties of Judicious Wit

Several varieties of judicious wit were studied by Gracián with special attention. Some of them may be grouped according to the type of statement rendering a new idea, and other varieties may be grouped according to the type of novelty or extravagance which is being stated.

The type of judiciously witty statements. A ponderation may just be stated as a *simple assertion*. Then, the extravagant is bluntly expressed by means of a proposition. Consider, for example, the faultfinding god, Momo, who censoriously commented about the not quite perfect completion of the first human being, because

---

[181]*Agudeza* Discourse 26. "Estaba dando una hermosa dama unos confites a un niño, y al ponérselos en la boca, le decía que cerrase los ojos; no obedeciendo el rapaz, volvió a instarle que cerrase los ojos, y él proseguía en estarla mirando. Dijo entonces el galante y agudo Rufo: 'Señora, él no quiere perder el cielo por una golosina'".

[182]See *Agudeza* Discourse 18.

...man lacked a little window in his chest to disclose the interior in his heart.[183]

Another example of a simple assertion is this paradoxical contrariety from a courtly lover in the age of the Catholic Kings:

> My life is lived dying;
> if it lived, it would die,
> for dying it would escape
> from the harm suffered by living.[184]

Novel thoughts may also be introduced by means of an *interrogative statement*.[185] In her diatribe against man's folly, Sister Juana keenly questioned:

> Who is more to blame
> though either one does evil:
> she who sins for the pay
> or he who pays to sin?[186]

Questions may be conceived in the form of *riddles*. Then the question asks something seemingly contradictory, making the finding of an answer very

---

[183]*Agudeza* Discourse 23: "...le faltaba al hombre una ventanilla en el pecho para descubrir lo interior del corazón". Gracián is quoting Lucian.

[184]*Agudeza* Discourse 24:
> Mi vida vive muriendo;
> si viviese moriría,
> porque muriendo saldría
> del mal que siente viviendo.

[185]See, for example, *Agudeza* Discourse 39.

[186]¿Y quién es más de culpar
aunque cualquiera mal haga:
la que peca por la paga
o el que paga por pecar?

difficult.[187] Gracián illustrated riddles with this example:

> Who are those sisters that the one once she leaves a place, never enters it again, and the other once entering a place, she never leaves it any more? The answer is Shame and Suspicion.[188]

Questions are not purely stylistic expressions. Rather, their very wit often rests on their power to discover, define, and point out a *problem* not seen before. A student of Aristotle asked the Philosopher:

> Why do we enjoy more meeting and talking with persons of beautiful faces?[189]

In Gracián's system, argumentative wit is in charge of solving mysteries, riddles, and problems, and of reducing the puzzlement they produce into something which makes pretty good sense.[190] However, sometimes the answers are more extravagant than the questions themselves, since they offer a completely unexpected turn.[191] Then *answers* belong to judicious wit, as Aristotle's response to his troubled student does:

> Your question could only be asked by a blind man.[192]

---

[187]See *Agudeza* Discourse 40.

[188]*Agudeza* Discourse 40: "¿Quiénes sean aquellas dos hermanas, que la una, de donde una vez sale, nunca más vuelve a entrar, y la otra, donde una vez entra, nunca más vuelve a salir? Respóndese ser la Vergüenza y la Sospecha".

[189]*Agudeza* Discourse 41: "...cuál sea la causa que gustamos más de tratar y conversar con las personas de buen rostro..."

[190]Although argumentative wit frees the mind from the puzzlement caused by judicious wit, argumentative wit still is a powerful cause of wonderment, since finding an answer of very difficult questions in fact is an amazing achievement.

[191]See *Agudeza* Discourse 41.

[192]*Agudeza* Discourse 41: "Esa pregunta sólo pudiera hacerla un ciego".

The type of extravagance stated. The extravagant conceptualizations best studied by Gracián are those assisting the moral judgment of people and their actions. In fact, his attention centered on those related to his art of prudence.[193] Their major types are what Gracián called 1) *crises*, 2) witty sententiae, and 3) witty maxims.

Gracián broadly included all moral wit under the heading of critical wit or *crises*. However, crises themselves refer in a more specific way to the apprehension of other people's thoughts and intentions. If serving the art of prudence, their specific function is to discover the many plausible motives behind people's behavior in order to have them present when judging people and events prudentially.[194] If serving the art of wit, their specific function is to discover the extravagant and unconceivable motives behind people's behavior, and to astonish with the extravagant but plausible finding.

Behind squeezing other persons' motives, there is the belief that human beings share one nature, and that they are free agents who follow, not univocal and necessary mechanisms of behavior, but different plausible motives. By recognizing a universe of plausible motives in himself, the wit may transpose his own self to that of his neighbor and may see the plausibility—not the necessity[195]—of those motives in the neighbor he observes.[196] It is this plausibility—meager as it may be—that allows the wit to conceive extravagant explanations for other people's actions. And this shared plausibility of the extravagant puzzles the wit in two ways: he somehow perceives—I think that if not consciously, at least unconsciously—that the most unspeakable motives exist

---

[193]See, for example, *Oráculo* aphorisms 13, 37, 131, 145, and 146; *El Criticón* 3, crises 3, 4, and 5.

[194]See, for example, *Oráculo* Aphorism 13.

[195]A principle of religious oratory strongly emphasized in the Spanish Golden Age was that the preacher should keenly and deeply recognize in his own soul both the springs of virtue and of vice, in order to be able to persuade properly audiences to be virtuous, and dissuade them from vice. See, for example, Luis de Granada, *Rhetorica eclesiastica* III, x–xii.

[196]On the plausibility of human actions, see, for example, *Agudeza* Discourse 28.

in his own soul, and moreover he sees those motives possibly and astonishingly being carried out by his neighbor.[197]

However, the initial artistic principle rendering the extravagant in crises is not a direct discovery of extravagant motives, but a previous discovery of what ordinarily is hidden in the minds or the hearts of people. For this, a ponderation is not necessary; but a plain correlation suffices, which establishes a correspondence between the simplest human motives self-known by the observer and the action of the subject observed.[198] Then the observer may become an ordinary "seer" of what is expectedly invisible, a common kind of "decypherer" who not surprisingly penetrates beneath the surfaces, and even a usual type of "foreteller" who predicts the predictable behavior of people.[199] For example, the observer may squeeze from his known motives and Anne's hard work that Anne may be enjoying her job or that she is looking for a promotion.

Thus correlations are the method for disclosing the simple-mindedness or the wickedness of our neighbor. If the neighbor's behavior is good, the observer may extract a good motive; the extracted motive is then called simple-mindedness.[200] If the neighbor's behavior is evil, the observer may extract a bad motive; then this extracted motive is called wickedness.[201] In both cases the wit

---

[197]In a more extensive way, a shared human nature and experience is assumed in all witty communication. If the listener's mind should wittily squeeze by itself what is told to through witticisms, then the speaker is implying that the listener indeed shares in human nature and the experience needed to decodify the sharp saying, without having to present the assumed explanation.

[198]See, for example, *Agudeza* Discourse 6 and 26.

[199]See, for example, *El Criticón* 3, crises 3, 4, and 5.

[200]In *Agudeza*, because of the equivocal meaning of simple-mindedness, Gracián often made this word a synonym of folly. See, for example, discourses 26 and 27. However, simple-mindedness also refers to the honest simplicity of apprehending the good from the good, and not twisting an analysis too much to discover dirt where there was not any.

[201]I derive *simple-minded wit* and *wicked wit* from their counterparts which Gracián explained with detail: *malicious wit* and *derisive wit.*

apprehends what Gracián called *first kind of intentions.*[202] However, if the wit does not straightforwardly associate good motives to good behavior, or bad motives to bad behavior, the wit then is getting into the realm of the extravagant, that is, the realm of judicious wit, the realm which trascends the ordinary. Then, the wit properly extracts *crises*—or what, in another place, Gracián called them *second intentions.*[203]

The first type of crises is called *malicious wit* by Gracián, since the wit associates bad motives to good behavior. This illustration in *Agudeza* is taken from Martial, and refers to a generous heir of Gaurus:

> The presents he gives you, rich and old Gaurus,
> if you see and understand him well, tell you: "Die!"[204]

Another instance is from Cicero, who censored Julius Caesar, explaining the dictator's restoration of Pompey's statues as Caesar's means of securing his own statues.[205]

A second kind of crises explains bad actions not on the ordinary grounds of wickedness, but on the less obvious grounds of well-intentioned folly. Gracián called these crises *derisive wit*, since their attention is centered on the ridiculous.[206] Consider this example about two misers quoted in *Agudeza*:

> 　Oh, self-captive fasters,
> who ever saw such blunders:
> to fatten dead cats,

---

[202]See *Oráculo* Aphorism 13.

[203]See *Oráculo* Aphorism 13.

[204]*Agudeza* Discourse 26:
Munera qui tibi dat locupleti, Gaure, senique,
si sapis, et sentis, hic tibi ait: Morere.

[205]See *Agudeza* Discourse 26.

[206]See *Agudeza* Discourse 27.

you starve living cats.[207]

According to Gracián, the soul of humor rests on malicious and derisive wit, since they combine the good and the bad in actions and intentions, offering a plausible mixture of sweet and sour to the ingenious mind.[208] Consider this example from Sister Juana which contains both malicious and derisive wit, and refers to an adulteress and her husband:

> In deceiving him you are so skilled,
> and in still looking good, you are so accustomed
> that what comes out of your womb
>   you have him understand, when he suspects,
> that to increase his wealth,
> you turned another's savings into his harvest.[209]

Among many other combinations of plausible intentions and actions studied by Gracián, *gallantry*,[210] or *third intentions*,[211] may be the most ingenious type

---

[207]*Agudeza* Discourse 27:
    ¡Oh ayunadores cautivos,
quién vio tales desaciertos!
Por engordar gatos muertos,
enflaquecer gatos vivos.
Gracián was quoting Juan Rufo, who refers to the misers' money sacks made of cat skins.

[208]See *Agudeza* Discourse 26.

[209]*Estás a hacerle burlas ya tan* ducha
y a salir de ellas bien estás tan hecha,
que lo que tu vientre desenbucha
    sabes darle a entender, cuando sospecha
que has hecho, por hacer su hacienda mucha,
de ajena siembra, suya la cosecha.

[210]See, for example, *Agudeza* Discourses 26 and 27, *Oráculo* Aphorism 131, and *El Discreto* Realce 4.

[211]See *Oráculo* Aphorism 13.

of crises. Here, the wit completely makes good both a bad action and a bad motive, by finding a circumstance which turns the wicked case into something praiseworthy. As quoted by Gracián, Pliny the Younger changed Trajan's image of disgusting hypocrisy—Trajan was seen as trying to cover up his cruelty with liberal bribes—into one of a most loving ruler, by noticing that Trajan's presents went randomly to the Roman people as a response to Trajan's love for his country.[212] When Louis XII finally seized power, the opponents who insulted him before as a Duke were then fearful of King Louis's bloody revenge. King Luis gallantly conquered their goodwill by saying:

> Hey!, the King of France does not avenge the affronts received by the Duke of Orleans.[213]

Gracián's attention to gallantry trascends the technical aspects of the art of wit, and reaches the discreet aspects of the art of prudence. He called it a most political perfection, and the regalia of the reason of state. In fact, Gracián strongly related gallantry to magnanimity, and to the peacemaker's role of opportunely and tactfully solving embarrassing or insulting situations.[214]

Crises do not always need to penetrate into the inner-self of people to pronounce wittily judgment on their actions. With *judicious crises*, it is enough that the observer discover something not noticed before in the scutrinized object or action, and make this new circumstance turn what could have been an ordinary verdict into an unexpected but plausible conclusion.[215] Quoting Andrea Alciati, Gracián told a story about a fox that, entering a sculptor's studio, examined the artist's new creation: the magnificent bust of a handsome young man. The fox then ruled that the bulk was beautiful, but that it lacked brains

---

[212]See *Agudeza* Discourse 26.

[213]*El Discreto* Realce 4: "¡Eh!, que no venga el rey de Francia los agravios hechos al duque de Orliens".

[214]See, for example, *El Héroe* Primor 4, *El Discreto* Realce 4, and *Oráculo* Aphorism 131.

[215]See *Agudeza* Discourse 28.

within, thus rebuking all vain beauty which, said Gracián, ordinarily is the throne of stupidity.[216]

Gracián defined *sententiae* as universal verdicts which often apply to moral situations common to all human beings. According to Gracián, sententiae become witty in two ways: 1) either the wit applies them so fittingly or in such a new way to a very special case, that the application fills the mind with wonder and unusual understanding, or 2) the wit passes such a profound or substantial judgment on a singular case that the judgment trascends the specificity of the case and becomes a new way of apprehending a universal moral principle.[217] Mourning the death of a boy who probably was among the most beautiful, honest, and beloved who ever lived in Rome, Martial very keenly and specially applied to the case a universal and well known sententia:

> Life is excessively short, and old age, extraordinary:
> whatever you love, make sure it does not please too much.[218]

Extremely sickened by some essays published in Mexico which approved of the last Persian Gulf War because its extreme competitive character might promote scientific and technological development, Alberto Domingo coined this sententia:

> A peculiar kind of contentment, in the very last instance: the whole life of a human generation turned into shit in exchange for one compact disc or one Nintendo.[219]

The power of this specific assertion trascends the case of the Persian Gulf

---

[216]See *Agudeza* Discourse 28.

[217]See *Agudeza* Discourse 29.

[218]*Agudeza* Discourse 29:
Immodicis brevis est aetas, et rara senectus.
Quidquid amas cupias non placuisse nimis.

[219]Alberto Domingo, "Aguila o Sol," *Siempre!*, (México).

War. It becomes universal—a new *sententia* which rebukes every attempt to justify war as a factor for progress.[220]

According to Gracián, the most excellent extravagances are *sublime observations* or *prudential maxims*. Their novel or astonishing element consists in proposing an unthinkable universal which challenges other universal beliefs which are ordinary. Their witty power is to expose the folly of some existing opinions, and to submit human understanding to the discomforting truths of disabuse.[221] Gracián could not have found a better example than Coheleth's:

> Vanitas vanitatum, dixit Ecclesiastes, vanitas vanitatum et omnia vanitas.

No less appropriate is this illustration that Gracián borrowed from Jorge Manrique:

> Let the sleeping soul be roused,
> good sense get sharp and wake up
> contemplating
>   how life is passing by,
> how death comes upon us
> and so silently.[222]

---

[220]From the universalization of *sententiae* follows the great importance of sapiential literature such as Gracián's *Oráculo*, *El Héroe*, and his other moral treatises which collect aphorisms and exemplary moral cases. Sapiential literature is not just a collection of fancy sayings reflecting on particular observations, but a repertoire of moral judgments plausibly applicable to a whole universe of cases by the rhetor. If no theoretical discussion of self-mastery and other rhetorical subjects were contained in the mentioned treatises, these books could still enjoy an inmense value for rhetoric in as much as they constitute an arsenal of arguments.

[221]See *Agudeza* Discourse 43.

[222]*Agudeza* Discourse 43
>   Recuerde el alma dormida,
> avive el seso, y despierte,
> contemplando
>   cómo se pasa la vida,
> cómo se viene la muerte,

As in other moral witticisms, a very impressive component of maxims is that they are truly plausible.[223]

Ratiocinations

The third great genre of concepts is ratiocination, and it embraces, said Gracián, "mysteries, objections, illations, proofs, etc."[224] It is also called argumentative wit.

If judicious wit astonishes the mind by conceiving extravagant ideas, argumentative wit goes a step further and astounds the understanding by conceiving solutions for these ideas. In this sense, argumentative wit presupposes the preexistence of puzzling ideas which startle the mind. It is only then that ratiocination can carry out its task of finding and identifying its species of new ideas—a possible proof, an objection, a line of argument—which may restore mental order and sound thinking.[225]

Argumentative wit can be studied under two general headings: 1) the solving of disputations, and 2) the solving of arguments.

Solving Disputations

Several of Gracián's most lively methods of being witty imply a disputation in which at least that two or more competing positions are weighed by the wit. Thus his task is to find, conceive, and advance proofs or objections which may

---

tan callando.

[223]See *Agudeza* Discourse 43. In the case of maxims, what we have is universal plausibility which should not be confounded with universal necessity.

[224]*Agudeza* Discourse 3: "La tercera es de raciocinación, y a ésta pertenecen los misterios, reparos, ilaciones, pruebas, etc."

[225]Note that neither judicious nor argumentative wit have yet to emerge from the task of conceptualization. Their task is not yet to judge or to prove, but to conceive a plausible judgment or to devise a potential proof. They are still dealing with concepts and by no means, in a full sense, with judgment or inference.

support or complicate the solution of either case. In doing so, he wittily searches for unexpected circumstances to make the case, as he sees it, more effective in producing wonderment and understanding, and he achieves it using disproportions, transpositions, retorts, conditionals, exaggerations, fictions, etc., as it has been exemplified before. The main difference between judicious and argumentative wit is that the former uses the mentioned methods to produce the extravagant, whereas the latter does so to restore, surprisingly, the ordinary belief. Admiring the beloved's dark eyes, Luis de Góngora challenged their beauty:

> But they are not so merciful.

However, Góngora immediatly restored his belief by transposing the objection; that is, he introduced a circumstance into the circumstance:

> Though, yes, they are, for we see
> **that dress deep mourning**
> **for all the souls they have slain.**[226]

A more attentive explanation of Gracián's disputations may notice that what is in play is a method of disposition which combines in the most effective way judicious and argumentative wit to startle the mind. First, a challange to the ordinary is almost insolently thrown by means of a ponderation—the extravagant. The wit then lingers on the challenge, raising a series of objections against the ordinary by finding as many circumstances as are needed to make the extravagant the most plausible case, and the ordinary, impossible, finally succeeding in instilling serious doubts about the previously most accepted belief. Next the wit *ex abrupto* introduces the most substantial, profound, or special,

---

[226] *Agudeza* Discourse 6:

> Pero no son tan piadosos;
> aunque, sí, lo son, pues vemos,
> **que visten rayos de luto,**
> **por cuantas almas han muerto.**

etc., circumstance which decisively turns—*solves*—the whole case back to the ordinary, restoring order and belief, even more strongly after succeeding against such a difficult challenge. A happy ending! What takes place is not only an argument, but also an intellectual drama where the protagonist is belief and the antagonist is doubt.

In spite of the dramatic effect, Gracián did not mean that his disputations would create a false sense of doubt, apparently later solving difficulties. For Gracián, that is false wit, built on smoke and empty words.[227] Objections to the ordinary should come as truly as possible in the shape of *problems*, *mysteries*, *difficulties*, and *contrarieties*.[228] Arguing both sides of the question should not be confounded with sophistry either. Proposing mysteries, difficulties, and contrarieties which in different degrees truly oppose unexamined existing beliefs, which later will be restated, does not mean that several irreconcilable truths are possible at the same time, but that truth is indeed complex, and that diverging circumstances somehow converge in the complex case, making it difficult to regard it just as either black or white. Thus, the purpose of disputations is not to protect wittily a stagnant belief, but to revive and enhance it by having it be appreciated with all its hues.[229]

Father Hennington from Holy Redeemer Parish, in Madison, Wisconsin, used a witty disputation as a means to structure and convey clearly the point he desired to make in his sermon. He started insolently, challenging what probably is one of the most important keys to read the Bible rightly, that is *Matthew* 22: 37–40:[230]

---

[227]On false wit, see, for example, *Agudeza* Discourse 61.

[228]See, for example, *Agudeza* discourses 6, 7, 8, 39, and 41. The definition of these terms has been already given under the section of judicious wit.

[229]My analysis of witty disputations goes beyond the discourses on mysteries, difficulties, and contrarieties found in *Agudeza* discourses 6, 7, and 8. It also includes the notion of conglobate concepts, mixed and compound wit, and plausible ideas and moral behavior. See, for example, *Agudeza* discourses 15, 28, and 51–57; *Oráculo* Aphorism 94.

[230]Cf. St. Augustine, *On Christian Doctrine* I, xxvi Translated, with an introduction, by D. W. Robertson, Jr. (Indianapolis: The Liberal Arts Press, Inc., 1958) 22–23.

> "Thou shalt love the Lord thy God..." This is the greatest and the first commandment. And the second is like it, "Thou shalt love thy neighbor as thyself."

Father Hennington denied that such commandments were *fully* Christ's doctrine. When we his parishioners were ready to report him to the Pope, he astonishingly and wittingly pointed out the final qualifier of these two supreme commandments, and he used it to support his challenge and to contest our standard belief:

> On these two commandments depend the whole Law and the Prophets.

"The whole Law and the Prophets, says the Gospel, but not the whole of Christ's doctrine," Father Hennington neatly observed, and his extravagance made plausible sense, throwing us into deep confusion.   Fortunately Father Hennington *ex abrubto* rescued us, and more than restoring our belief, he enriched and reinforced it by properly answering the objection. Christ's full, last and *very personal* commandment is found in *John* 13:34., said our Parish Priest, and was pronounced during the Last Supper:

> A new commandment *I give unto you*...that as I have loved you, you also love one another...

Explaining it, Father Hennington discreetly pointed to a not too vivid Christ on the Cross in front of the altar.[231]

---

[231]Hans Urs Von Balthasar refers to a similar meditation he found in the works of St Thérèse of Lisieux: "...she...detects a certain tension between the text in Matthew, 'Thou shalt love thy neighbour as thyself,' and that in John, 'Greater love than this no man hath, that a man lay down his life for his friends.' She sees that the latter represents an intensified love; it goes beyond the former, which completes the law of love in the Old Testament, by adding the specifically New Testament teaching." Hans Urs Von Balthasar, *Thérèse of Lisieux. The Story of a Mission*, trans. by Donald Nicholl, (New York: Sheed and Ward, 1954).

Solving Argumentations

Ingenuity strongly assists argumentation by helping the mind discover the implicit arguments which make the inference possible. To achieve it, ingenuity establishes a correlation between the explicit terms of the argumentation, makes the necessary arrangements, and extracts the missing premises to argue what is intended.[232]

Sometimes the extracted missing premise is a general line of argument, for example, *a fortiori* as in this concept quoted by Gracián from Saint Agustine, and which ponders the consternation of Herod at the news of the true King:

> What will the Last Judgment be like, says he, if the manger so terrifies evil people?[233]

Gracián called this squeezing of general lines of argument *conceptual arguments*. Camoëns begged to the sea which was taking away his beloved:

> If pity dwells in you, O waves,
> then carry away from me the tears I weep,
> as you thus bear away from me their cause.[234]

The request makes sense, said Gracián, if by means of conceptual argumentation the line of argument *a causis* is supplied.[235]

Many other general lines of arguments are exemplified by Gracián.

---

[232]See *Agudeza* Discourse 36.

[233]*Agudeza* Discourse 36: "¿Qué hará, dice, el Tribunal del Juicio, si así aterra a los malos el pesebre?"

[234]*Agudeza* Discourse 37, and *Arte de Ingenio* Discourse 37:

....

> mas se em vox, ondas, mora piedade,
> levai tamben as lagrimas que choro,
> pois assi me levais a causa dellas.

[235]See *Arte de Ingenio* Discourse 37. If the cause of the tears is gone, the tears should be gone as well.

However, sometimes the missing premises are not general but special to the argumentation in question; then the argument is called *illation*. As quoted by Gracián, Augustus once heard the prodigy that a palm tree had sprouted and grown on the altar that some people from Tarragona had dedicated to his health. Augustus arrived at this conclusion:

> From that I infer how frequent your sacrifices and incense offerings take place there, since not only grass but even palm trees sprouted on it.[236]

For Gracián, conclusions like this are not deduced from general lines of argument discovered by wit, but from the "circumstances and adjuncts" of the case, known, experienced, or accepted by the mind, and the power of ingenuity which makes the necessary connections—in Augustus's case, that no grass, let alone trees, grow on heavily used surfaces used for burning, leads him to deny the practice of sacrifices on his altar in Tarragona.[237]

If competing plausible circumstances and adjuncts are applied to the case, assisted by transpositions, or another witty method, very different conclusions may be reached by the illation. As stated in *Agudeza*, Caesar noticed that the face and the build of a foreign lad much resembled those of a well known gentleman in Rome, and so Caesar asked the youth whether his mother once visited the court. Observing Caesar's malice, the clever foreigner answered:

> Sire, not her, but certainly my father.[238]

Either assisting conceptual arguments or illations by supplying missing premises, ingenuity at the end makes the inference fit the structure of

---

[236]*Agudeza* Discourse 38: "De ahí colijo yo cuán frecuentes son vuestros sacrificios y el ofrecer incienso en él, pues no sólo nace yerba, sino palmas."

[237]*Agudeza* Discourse 38.

[238]*Agudeza* Discourse 38: "Señor, no; mi padre sí".

syllogisms.[239]

Gracián explained his belief that ingenuity is the art truly in charge of finding and supplying the missing premises by comparing what he called dialectical, rhetorical, and purely witty arguments:

> Wit has also its arguments, for if efficacy reigns over the dialectical, and eloquence over the rhetorical, beauty does so over them [witty arguments].[240]

By achieving beauty, Gracián meant that wit discovers harmonies between things seemingly lacking any type of association, proportion between objects initially perceived as isolate, consonance in what at first sight appears separate, correlation between the apparently unrelated, light where chaos reigned,[241] and even order, structure, plausibility—meaning—in what nonetheless may remain as extravagant.[242] And in the case of argumentation, wit finds missing premises.[243]

But dialectic syllogisms are posterior to the discovery or conceiving of ideas, and should go further: they should test the efficacy or solidity of the ideas

---

[239]Argumentative wit function is discovering the assumption implied by the case in question—the assumption which secures the perceived conclusion. This assumption can be either a universal line of argument (as happens with conceptual arguments) or a particular line of argument (as happens with illations, which are grounded in special generalizations from experience). In either case, the assumption leads syllogistically to the conclusion. And in any case, I think that wit's assistance in discovering the assumption behind an argument facilitates later judgment's criticism of the argument, not only on the necessary grounds of the valid structure of the syllogism, but also on the reliable grounds of the given assumption concerning its support by experience.

[240]*Agudeza* Discourse 36: "Tiene la agudeza también sus argumentos, que si en los dialécticos reina la eficacia, en los retóricos la elocuencia, en éstos la belleza".

[241]See *Agudeza* Discourse 2.

[242]See *Agudeza* discourses 23 and 24.

[243]See *Agudeza* Discourse 36.

discovered by wit.[244]   Rhetoric should even search for persuasiveness by lingering over honest, useful, and pleasant ideas.[245] Nonetheless pure wit, which conceives the argument, is satisfied enough by accomplishing such a feat well. Pure wit is indeed satisfied by merely letting the mind enjoy and wonder before an argumentatively novel harmony. Consider the example of a "girlish" ball game once played by my mother and her friends:

> *Simple Game,*
> without laughing,
> without moving
> from my place,
> with one hand,
> with the other,
> on one foot,
> on the other,
> and praying,
> and sewing,
> comes and goes,
> forwards,
> backwards,
> forwards, backwards,
> forwards, backwards, forwards,
> a small turn,
> a half turn,
> a whole turn,
> and the Sign
> of the Cross.[246]

---

[244]See *Agudeza* Discourse 1.

[245]See *El Criticón* I, Crisi 10. Contrasting with Gracián's common and explicit description of rhetoric as just stylistic ornament, it should be noted: 1) his placing of rhetoric among the practical arts (see *Agudeza* Discourse 47) and 2) his endorsement of Francisco Terrones's theory of rhetoric (Francisco Terrones del Caño, *Instrucción de Predicadores*, "Prólogo y notas" by P. Félix G. Olmedo, S. I., (Madrid: ESPASA-CALPE, S. A., 1946, from 1617 edition)). See *Agudeza* Discourse 58. In doing so, Gracián recognized that rhetoric indeed deals with some sort of argumentation: the persuasive one.

[246]My mother and Mrs. Sofia Oropeza de Ramírez agreed on this version of *Simple Game:*

Neither our syllogizing power nor our rhetorical faculty are the ones which directly reveal to us the presence of an argument in this game. It is ingenuity which let us discover that the proposition "simple game" is being refuted with the increasing complication of the match. It is wit that discerns an implied opposition between this proposition and the "girlish" tasks to be acomplished. Moreover, concerning ingenuity, there is an argument in such a game in so far as there are, I would say, many beautiful links, many missing premises, consciously or unconsciouly discovered by wit, rendering an inference.

However, concerning dialectic, the argument would only exist if it is sound, which is something difficult to demonstrate quickly, and concerning rhetoric, the argument would only exist if there is a persuasive end, which is something no less troublesome to specify since there may be none.

Yet, there is an argument, a witty one at least, and ingenuity is satisfied enough since what it directly seeks is the discovery of the missing premise. According to Gracián, the order established by wit provides its own legitimate degree of satisfaction for the mind: it is wonderment before the witty, or moreover, amazement before the poetically beautiful.[247] But more important, wit is the art of invention, the art of discovering and establishing order, and as such

---

"*Juego simple*, sin reír, sin moverme de mi lugar, con una mano, con la otra, en un pie, en el otro, rezando, cosiendo, va y viene, adelante, atrás, adelante atrás, adelante atrás adelante, vuelta chica, media vuelta, vuelta entera y la Cruz."

[247]See *Agudeza* discourses 2 and 36. Since it is wit that enjoys the "logic" empowered by poetic forms—for example, rhyme, parallelisms, and extended metaphors—, it may seem that argumentative wit consists in this "logic" only, as thought Pellegrini with his "figurative links" and suggested Tesauro with his "urbanely fallacious enthymemes". Certainly, poetic forms prompt the mind to anticipate or "infer" the development of a discourse regardless its dialectical and rhetorical soundness. Thus this "logic" strictly pertains to argumentative wit. However, argumentative wit is not limited to marvel at the discovery of these forms. Indeed, it properly refers to the discovery of any kind of argument, notwithstanding if this argument is poetic, dialectical or rhetorical. Moreover, although poetic enjoyment often is a result of wit, the only necessary outcome of a mind's ingenuity is an operation of understanding, particularly the apprehension of ideas. Thus, argumentative wit primarily renders conceptualizations; it specifically perceives, abstracts, and makes arguments understandable.

it is prior to dialectic and rhetoric.[248]

Invention

The fourth great genre of concepts is that of invention, but understood in a narrower sense than above: here it is the creation of new ideas or things, and according to Gracián, "it comprehends works of fiction, stratagems, inventions in action or speech, etc."[249]

Constrasting with the previous modes of concepts, invention does not discover or actually see correspondences, extravagant circumstances, or arguments in its studied and already existing object. Invention rather makes up a new object by putting together many pieces or circumstances which were never together before,[250] or, as implied in Gracián's doctrines, invention also creates new objects by separating the parts of a whole for the first time.[251] By adding wheels to a box, ingenuity invents a car, and by then adding to it an internal-combustion engine, ingenuity produces an automobile. By plucking and grinding the coffee beans from the bush, the most necessary ingredient for an invigorating drink is obtained; and by extracting from them the caffeine, their energizing power is purified into a jolting drug.

Gracián studied inventions according to the means used to render the novelty, and according to the types of novelty produced.

---

[248]See *Agudeza* Al Lector and Discourse 1.

[249]*Agudeza* Discourse 3: "...comprehende las ficciones, estratagemas, invenciones en acción y dichos, etc."

[250]See, for example, *Agudeza* discourses 35 and 45.

[251]In Gracián, if there are methods of associating, and introducing circumstances into a case, there should also be methods of dissociating, substracting, and transposing circumstances from a case.

The Means Rendering the Invention

Inventions can be rendered either through sayings (words or ideas) or through actions (things or behavior).[252] Lacking any symbol powerful enough to express his thoughts, Gracián invented this allegory to portray the idea of "wait":

> On a cart and on a throne made of tortoise shells—the cart pulled by remoras, Wait was advancing through the spacious fields of Time to the palace of Occasion...[253]

Ingenuity may not find any other answer to the most difficult problems than to contrive a specific action which trascends the limits of actual reality. Consider this illustration quoted in *Agudeza*:

> Other kinds may occur through stratagem and through rare and extravagant invention. Such was the heroic plan of the never sufficiently admired Don Fernando, illustrious Infante of Castile, when he saw himself, concerning his invincible fidelity, in the most urgent peril, and he found the means for a greater crown when all the kingdom was forcing him to be its king. Beneath the purple—not royal, but loyal—on the day of the coronation, he carried the true king in diapers, and revealing him suddenly, he enthroned him on his own head, proclaiming: "Here is your king, Castilians!" Heavens rewarded his great virtue with the heraldic bars of Aragon, in mysterious recognition of what he in his loyalty had thrown away.[254]

---

[252]See *Agudeza* discourses 35, 45, 47, 55, 56, and 57.

[253]*El Discreto* Realce 3: "En un carro y en un trono, fabricado éste de conchas de tortugas, arrastrado aquél de rémoras, iba caminando la Espera por los espaciosos campos del Tiempo al palacio de la Ocasión".

[254]*Agudeza* Discourse 45: "Otros hay por extratagema, y por una rara extravagante invención. Heroica traza fué la del nunca asaz admirado don Fernando, ínclito infante de Castilla, cuando viéndose en el más urgente riesgo de su invencible fidelidad, pues le obligaba todo el reino a ser su rey, halló medio superior para mayor corona. Llevóse el día destinado para la coronación, debajo de la púrpura, no real, sino leal, al verdadero rey en pañales, y descubriéndolo de repente lo entronizó sobre su cabeza, diciendo: 'Este es vuestro rey, castellanos.' Premió el Cielo tanta virtud con las barras de Aragón, en misterio de lo que él la había tirado en su lealtad".

The Type of Invention

According to Gracián, there are two major types of inventions. The wit may create new symbols to mean something else, or he may create new inventions as such.[255] Gracián's allegory of the Wait is an example of symbolic inventions. Don Fernando's stratagem is a new invention as such.

According to Gracián, symbolic inventions rest on the similitude they keep with the thought signified.[256] They differ from simple similitudes because the term assimilated is invented and not just discovered. Sometimes the symbol is invented because using the ordinary one may be too impudent for the audience.[257] Consider this symbol used by a most pious abbot:

> Such was the prudent and wary teaching of that abbot who, drawing his shears from their sheath, began to trim the myrtle hedge, lopping off the projecting sucker shoots.[258]

The abbot was answering Ramiro the Monk's concern about the way to suppress the rebellion of the nobility of Aragon.

Likewise symbolic inventions are created because the case in question is so complex that it needs a new and special symbol powerful enough to comprehend, or to contain in a nutshell, all the observed or conceived circumstances of the case.[259] Gracián tended to include all literature and fine arts into the class of symbolic inventions. He specifically analyzed masquerades,[260]

---

[255]See *Agudeza* Discourse 47.

[256]See *Agudeza* discourse 47 and 55.

[257]See *Agudeza* Discourse 55.

[258]*Agudeza* Discourse 47: "Tal fué la prudente y cauta enseñanza de aquel abad, que sacando las tijeras de su estuche, fué igualando el arrayán y descabezando los pimpollos que sobresalían..."

[259]See, for example, *Agudeza* Discourse 35.

[260]See *Agudeza* Discourse 47.

apologues, parables, allegories, epopees, novels, dramas,[261] metamorphoses, fables, tales, jokes, paintings, hieroglyphs, emblems, coats of arms, mottos, and coin inscriptions.[262]

Inventions as such are themselves the answer to a practical problem.[263] The scornful Gracián might laugh at the little squirt coming out from Juanelo's fountain in Toledo;[264] nevertheless Gracián could not conceal his marvel at the sight of the complex machinery ingeniously drawing water from River Tajo up to the fountain.[265] Practical arts such as rhetoric, painting,[266] cooking, gardening, architecture, and warfare are mentioned in *Agudeza* as examples of this class of invention since they contrive new artifacts either in words or in deeds to solve practical problems.[267]

---

[261]Regarding drama, see *Agudeza* Discourse 45.

[262]On species of symbolic wit, see *Agudeza* discourses 55, 56, 57, and also 35. Tesauro beat Gracián: Tesauro also studied tombstone inscriptions.

[263]See *Agudeza* Discourse 47.

[264]See *El Discreto* Realce 20, and *El Criticón* I, Crisi 7.

[265]See *Agudeza* Discourse 3, and *El Criticón* I, Crisi 8.

[266]Concerning practical inventions, "painting much appreciates them in order to duplicate perfections." ("...estímalos la pintura para duplicar la perfección"). *Agudeza* Discourse 47. By painting as a practical invention, Gracián probably meant the creation of techniques and materials which allow the painter a greater range of artistic possibilities.

[267]See *Agudeza* Discourse 47. It is surprising to find in Gracián this understanding of rhetoric as a practical art after knowing his common description of it as an art purely concerned with ornamental style. We may still wonder whether he meant by rhetorical practical inventions the new ends or *solutions* conceived by a rhetor for a problem, or he just meant by them the *persuasive instruments* or means devised to pursue an already given end. Either case might be possible since he acknowledged the persuasive force of orators (See *Agudeza* Discourse 36) and the creative decision-making role of politicians (See, for example, *El Discreto* realces 3, 10, and 15, *El Héroe* primores 5–11). However, I somewhat doubt Gracián believed in rhetoric as an art to conceive solutions to problems. A pure notion of conceiving persuasive intruments accords better with Gracián's most common idea of rhetoric, since the ornaments of style might suffice for what seemed to be the duties of eloquence, that is, persuading about an end—style being the means to amplify eloquently the

Review of the Different Methods of Artistic Wit

An extended example may help to perceive the distinctions of the four different major methods of artistic wit more clearly. Let's consider the story about Indiana Jones and his quest for the Holy Grail. At the end of the movie, Indiana Jones is inside the chamber where the Holy Grail is. Problem: the chamber also contains several thousand other chalices; which one is the Holy Grail? By means of correlations, Indiana establishes the similarities and distinctions concerning the chalices. He discovers that, although all are chalices which had contained the most precious Blood, they differ in their degree of piety, beauty, and richness of materials used to honor the Sacrament; moreover, only one can be the chalice that the Lord used during the Last Supper. By means of a ponderation, Indiana challenges preconceptions concerning the honor due to the Eucharist, and discovers that only a poor and ordinary chalice could have been used by Jesus then: it is the wooden chalice, since he was a humble carpenter! By means of ratiocinations, Indiana secures his ponderation; his choice for a wooden chalice is warranted by discovering and syllogistically applying this assumption to the case: a person's utensils (and the Lord's utensils are here included) are a mirror of a person's personality. Finally, by means of inventions—especially, stratagems—Indiana Jones was able to overcome the many obstacles which blocked his entrance to the Holy Grail Chamber; for example, he could discover and cross the invisible bridge by throwing sand on it: the sand made the bridge visible.

---

sight of such an end. Thus, the politician's decision-making would be transferred to what Gracián called first the art of wit, and second, and more important, the art of prudence.

A Chart of Gracián's Four Modes of Wit

Correlations	**Ponderations**	**Ratiocinations**
A. Grounded on the direction of the relationship: proportions and disproportions.	A. The subjective foundations: the new, the rare, the extravagant, the unexpected, the difficult, the brief, the prompt resolving the urgent.	A. The solving of disputations: (of mysteries, difficulties, contrarieties, and problems).
B. On its matter: things or actions, ideas, and words (quotations); logos, pathos, and ethos.	B. The objective foundations: supplying or suppressing different classes of circumstances to change the case. Subtleties vs., flippancies.	B. Discovering and solving argumentations: *1. Conceptual arguments.* *2. Illations.*
C. On its precision: similitudes and comparisons; tropes and topics.	C. The formal foundations: *1. The procedure:* (a) Disproportion: with an opposition grounded on mere novelty (mysteries, doubts, reflections, suspense, surprise, ripostes in action or in word, ironies, narratives); with accidental opposition	
D. On its explicitness: declared concepts and allusions; literalness and figurativeness.	(difficulties); with substantial opposition (paradoxes, and ponderation of contrarieties). (b) Ingenious transpositions. (c) Prompt retorts (simple or complete ones).	**Inventions** A. The means rendering the invention: *1. Words* *2. Deeds.*
E. On the number of relationships: pure and mixed wit (conglobate concepts).	*2. The degree of actuality conceived:* (a) Absolute. (b) Limited: exaggeration, conditionals, fiction, and indirect concepts.	B. The type of inventions: *1. Symbols.* *2. Inventions themselves.*
F. On the relationship of ideas within a discourse: loose wit and compound wit (uncomplicated and complex compounds).	D. The varieties of judicious wit. *1. The modes of ponderation:* simple assertion, interrogative statement, riddles, problems, answers. *2. The extravagances conceived:* (a) Crises or conceiving particular judgments: concerning the motives of persons (simplicity, wickedness, malice, folly, gallantry); concerning their actions (judicious crises). (b) Conceiving general judgments: sententiae (from the general to the particular, and viceversa); sublime and prudential maxims (general concepts vs., general concepts).	

11   Judgment

COMMENTING ON GRACIÁN'S ACCOUNT OF UNDERSTANDING as a union of ingenuity and judgment, Hidalgo Serna says:

> In the third chapter of *El Héroe*, "The Greatest Quality of the Hero," Gracián says nothing about judgment but emphasizes the importance of *ingenium* and *agudeza*.[1]

Hidalgo Serna thus expresses his disappointment because of the lack of an explicit and systematic theory of judgment in all of the Jesuit's books.

Even so, Gracián already was working within a theory of judgment. In spite of his special interests, emphases, and turns, this Spaniard was a scholastic. His doctrines of human nature, understanding, reality, society, nay, wit, in their own way were assimilated to the Aristotelian-Thomistic tradition of logic, physics, metaphysics, ethics, and politics strongly endorsed by Jesuit colleges. Therefore, this Aristotelian-Thomistic tradition should be placed together with Gracián's theories of wit and his doctrines on prudence, in order to obtain a view of what would be the complete logical system and complete theory of human understanding for Gracián.[2]

I mean, Gracián's theory of judgment should be "squeezed out" from his works and their context. And although it may quite be Aristotelian and Thomistic, it should be peculiar in itself considering the Spaniard's special insights and contributions to scholasticism.

---

[1]Hidalgo Serna 250.

[2]Gracián studied the methods for the apprehension of ideas because, in contrast with the other operations of the understanding, this one lacked rules and methods. (See, for example, *Agudeza* Discourse 1). It would follow that he did not discuss the methods for the two other operations of understanding because he was satisfied with the current methods in practice for this purpose. Thus Gracián would have endorsed the methods of judging and inferring as taught in Jesuit colleges, and strongly fashioned after Aristotle's *Organon*.

Judgment as Seen Through an Understanding of Wit

Gracián's theories of wit in fact respond to a very fundamental problem of scholasticism, and of all the history of philosophy: the universals. On the one hand, human beings rationally think with abstract ideas. On the other hand, their ideas are learned from and refer to concrete experience. Acknowledging truths implies that rational thinking in some way can agree with the sensual data it predicates.[3] Judgment rests on this possibility of agreement between experience and ideas—and so does truth.[4]

Gracián theorized on wit to explain how we grasp abstract ideas from a concrete reality (or from words or other ideas). His theories refer to the first act of understanding: the apprehension of ideas. They do not explain the methods of judgment: either testing the ideas by observing their agreement with the object of understanding (second act of understanding) or validly inferring these ideas from an accepted premise (third act of understanding). Nevertheless, Gracián's emphasis on the abstract character of ideas and on the necessary precedence of their apprehension over their judgment or inference[5] says much about what judgment or inference should be like. Judgment's and inference's functions should necessarily consist in judging abstract ideas already apprehended and in inferring new abstract ideas from abstract ideas already apprehended by wit and endorsed by judgment.

---

[3] Cf. Rafael Gambra Ciudad, *Historia Sencilla de la Filosofía*, (Madrid: Ediciones Rialp, S. A., 1981) 132. Gambra Ciudad believes that the problem of universals was often posed for Greek philosophers by noticing first the rational experience of the mind, and then by marveling at the constant change of individual things; and that, concerning the medieval scholar, the problem was often seen inversely: the scholar first enjoyed the immediate experience of senses and then wondered about the universal character of ideas.

[4] Here the classical scholastic definition of truth should be remembered: "The agreement of the mind with reality".

[5] See *Agudeza* discourses 1 and 2.

Wit, Induction, and the Advancement of Learning

Even so, Gracián sometimes seemed to explain the primal learning of abstract ideas through induction. For example, apparently proposing principles of generalization, he addressed the need for diverse and abundant information from all times and places of the world. Suggesting the requirement of spread in the data, he required that the well informed person be acquainted with news from all corners of the Earth, comprehending the words and deeds of the most different peoples.[6] This experience of facts should be enriched with the person's own observations in real affairs through public life, travels, and friendly relationships.[7] The marvels of the world could be contained and condensed in museums and other experimental centers, and there studied.[8] This fresh experience is often of greater use, said Gracián, than the liberal arts themselves all together.[9] Suggesting the frequent experience that secures the solidity of observations, he often doubted that, even in a life span, this experience could be enough of a test to warrant the certainty of a belief.[10] His peculiar doctrines of disabuse pointed out the extensiveness of unwarranted beliefs which frequently are crushed during the last minute before death.[11] In testing either the recurrence or the spread of ideas on observed objects the person should rely on direct experience or on testimonies, the latter being the most common source of data, and yet, the most dubious.[12]

Nonetheless, for Gracián, being a well informed person without the light shed by wit would not be more than only enjoying an elephant-like memory.

---

[6]See *El Discreto* Realce 5.

[7]See, for example, *Oráculo* Aphorism 229; *El Discreto* Realce 25.

[8]See *El Criticón* II, Crisi 2.

[9]See *El Discreto* Realce 5.

[10]Without excluding the problem of generalization, Gracián's skepticism went deeper and was rooted in the complexity of the process of intellecting universals.

[11]See, for example, *El Criticón* III, Crisi 5, *Oráculo* Aphorism 110, 230.

[12]See, for example, *Oráculo* Aphorism 80.

The data itself would be meaningless, and thus useless for any posterior operation of the mind.[13] This belief has its consequences: if the well informed person aims at a generalization, then he should be sure that his erudition supplies *clearly delimited observations* which rightly measure the data needed to test the spread or the recurrence of an idea. This means that if the idea to be tested and the test cases are not well defined, then, the generalization does not proceed since it is not clear if the same object is the one observed and tested in several times and places. Wit should necessarily assist generalization not only by proposing the general idea to be tested by experience, but also by clearly defining the test cases—that is, the class of experience—which will secure the generalization.[14]

Hence, a concern prior to generalization should be conceptualization. As discussed before, Gracián saw that the mind must deal first with *raw sensual data* as vague and unclear as images, feelings, or hunches could be. The mind should find clarity in its experiences before proceeding to any posterior operation of the mind, such as a generalization. Thus, the task of conceptualization is to allow reason to shed light on things, discover their order, their being, their meaning, and so reach clear intellectual representations of these things by means of ideas or, let's say, Gracián's concepts.[15] Conceptualization thus transforms pure and vague sensations into clear-cut intellections. The mind performs an act of understanding by recognizing and abstracting the intelligible experience from the sensual experience. This act itself is called *simple apprehension* by the men of schools. Gracián took this mental operation to the level of art. Truly, he found an intellectual method to illuminate the senses: his structures of correspondences which, more than representing, present the idea

---

[13]See *Agudeza* Discourse 1.

[14]Today, in theory of science, the design of the experiment to test an hypothesis implies a task of conceptualization. Only the clear definition of test cases secures the reliability of the generalization.

[15]See, for example, *Agudeza* Discourse 1–2.

to the mind.[16]

The distinction between conceptualization and generalization may become clearer by observing how each one differently advances learning.

Conceptualization implies a task of discernment.[17] It proceeds from the most universal predicates which can be recognized in a thing, for example, "is",[18] to the most specific, subtle, nay, rarified ones, for example, identifying not only the individuating traits of such a thing, but its very particular variables depending on the occasion. Following a systematic philosophical procedure, discernment would carefully descend the Porphyrian tree and gain detail in the perception of an object.[19] Some philosophers of science, like Thomas S. Kuhn, would see the development of theories from general explanations to more specific answers[20] entailing, at the same time, the discovery of many new problems whose solving should start anew from formulating general explanations to be developed into

---

[16]See *Agudeza* discourses 1–5. Marc Fumaroli, somehow scornful of this Jesuit theoretical achievement, would relate the method of *presenting* ideas to the mind to the Jesuit —Catholic—devotion to the *Real Presence*. See Marc Fumaroli, *La Age de L'Eloquence. Rhétorique et «res literaria» de la Renaissance au seuil de l'époque classique,* (Genève: Librairie Droz, 1980).

[17]See *El Criticón* I, Crisi 1. Cf. Aristotle, *Physica* I, 1; and St Thomas Aquinas *Summa Theologica* I, Q. 85, Art. 3.

[18]This apparently vague predicate "is"—its meaning and its implications—is the foundation of the trascendental principles of methaphysics and logic, which, because of their utmost universality, apply to all reality and sciences.

[19]In Gracián's system, even the Porphyrian tree should be comprehended by the most general principles of artistic wit, since Gracián's correlations—he believed—explain every apprehension of ideas. A possible understanding of the Porphyrian tree under Gracián's conceptism would be that we descend the tree and perceive the genres and differentiae by means of the basic conceptist process: establishing comparisons and contrasts which discover similarities and distinctions between things.

[20]In doing so, Kuhn seems to endorse the old Aristotilian-Thomistic, and also Gracianean paradigm: the advancement of learning consists in going from the most universal to the most specific, in going from the most vague to the most keen understanding of things. In doing so, Kuhn also seems to oppose to the Baconian paradigm which sees learning as going from the most specific to the most general. See Francis Bacon, *Advancement of Learning*.

specific answers.[21] For a number of baroque artists, to beat the serene models of the renaissance meant exhausting the themes' many possible variations, daring to capture the most minute, and sometimes itemizing trifles to a sickening excess.

Thus far, Gracián could spare Porfirian trees[22] and baroque filigree. He rather proposed the shortcut of artistic wit to discernment: "Quintessences bring about more than jumbles."[23] Consider, for example, how Ramón López Velarde detailed Cuauhtémoc's special place in Mexican hearts. López Velarde avoided burdensome volumes explaining the littlest aspect on the life of the last, glorious, and yet teenage Emperor of the Aztecs. Rather, López Velarde wittily said: "Young grandfather..."[24]

Gracián's quick and artistic structures of correspondences squeeze the thinnest residues. By swiftly apprehending the subtlest circumstances these structures do not only serve discernment. They also may turn a case up-side down, if needed, and thus they may do a good service to the truth, as an honest casuist intends.[25]

The process of generalization at first sight seems to follow precisely the reverse order of conceptualization—of discernment—, since a generalization inquires if the specific can be generalized—or, more exactly, if an idea trascends a singular case and widely comprehends a class of cases. However, generalization can not entirely be the reverse order of discernment.

---

[21]See Thomas S. Kuhn, *Structure of Scientific Revolutions*, 2nd. enlarged ed. (University of Chicago, 1979).

[22]Although Porfirian trees as a method of apprehension of ideas is included in the whole comprehensive method of correlations, nonetheless Gracián most common application of ingenuity would be the use of pointed sayings, which spare long processes of specification and reach clear detail by means of quick flashes of wit.

[23]*Oráculo* Aphorism 105: "Más obran quintas esencias que fárragos".

[24]Ramón López Velarde, *Suave Patria*: "Joven abuelo..."

[25]Similarly, a rhetor strives to observe in the given case the available means of persuasion. Cf. Aristotle, *Rhetoric* I, 2.

Generalization does not proceed from particulars to universals, but, as exactly said, from a singular and well defined case, to a generality of cases of the same species. Moreover, one may argue that a generalization is an additional specification of the case in question—an additional piece of discernment: it details that the idea in question is general enough to apply to many cases. As indicated, a generalization can not proceed if the idea being measured has not been discovered, mentally abstracted, apprehended, and specified before.

To sum up, discernment is what leads one to discover, specify, and clarify the ideas which may apply to raw data. Accordingly discernment is what originally leads to the advancement of learning. Meanwhile, the function of a generalization or induction is simply to infer the special applicability of a subtle property discovered by wit—and tested by judgment—to a whole class. Thus, a generalization can not be by itself the means for discovery or invention—the opening means for the advancement of learning. It is discernment that frees the mind from vagueness and identifies or discovers the subtle realms of knowledge which the mind has not yet learned—realms which may apply later, if secured by judgment, and inferred by induction, to a whole class.

Rational Judgment and Wit

For Gracián, having ideas in the mind is a precondition to judging them.[26] This distinction between simple aprehension and judgment, as acts of understanding,[27] is sharply explained by St Thomas Aquinas:

---

[26]See *Agudeza* Discourse 1.

[27]Concerning judgment, let's apply to this subject the same warning advanced about Gracián's approach to wit: his attention was on the mind's acts to reach understanding, not on the posterior language used to criticize such acts, as studied by formal logicians. Thus, for Gracián, judgment would be an act of understanding assenting to or asserting ideas, and not rules of logic prescribing a formal criticism of ideas (probably already endorsed by the mind) by means of their neat representation by propositions. Actual judgment could be expressed in more diverse forms than such propositions, and would include simple terms, propositions, inferences, discourses, or even pure actions, omissions, and meaningful silence (see, for example, *Agudeza* Discourse 49, on allusions) which embody some sort of assent from the mind. Judgment would be the mind's act which endorses the harmonious

The first operation considers the whatness of a thing; the second operation considers its being.[28]

This recognition of the order followed by the three operations of the mind is relevant to an appropriate understanding of judgment. Neither the raw experience itself which should be illuminated by conceptualization nor the ultimate conclusions about this data reached through the rules for generalizations are the primary foundation of judgment. Judgment does not make sense of raw experience—that is conceptualization's duty. Nor does it generalize a well defined and proven piece of data to a whole class of cases—that is the task of inference. In the middle of these first and third operations of the mind, the second operation makes *intelligible observations* which secure or reject a previously not warranted idea, and, if the idea is secured, then judgment offers its results to generalization, which on such grounds would determine how extensively the idea applies to a whole class.

Gracián acknowledged that judgment sometimes skips intelligible data and is legitimately persuaded more by pure hunches:

> **Believing the heart**. The more so when it is unyielding. Do not contradict it, since it often is a forecast of the most important—a domestic oracle. Many people perished through what they feared the most; but, what was the use of this fear without the remedy?...It is not prudent to go forth to accept misfortunes, but it indeed is good sense to go forth to confront and surmount them.[29]

---

correspondence that the concept keeps with reality, (see *Oráculo* Aphorism 96) or with any other standard that the concept implicitly claims to refer. Concerning standards different than experience, we may consider, for example, a concept whose propriety rests on pure logical validity. Then the mind should act and pass judgment by checking whether this concept satisfies its claims to meet the rules of validity of terms, propositions, and inferences, as prescribed by formal logic.

[28]"Prima operatio respicit quidditatem rei; secunda respicit esse ipsius." St Thomas Aquinas' *Comm. in I Sent.*, 19, 5, 1 ad 7, as quoted by Umberto Eco, *The Aesthetics of Thomas Aquinas* Trans. Hugh Bredin (Harvard University Press, 1988) 198.

[29]*Oráculo* Aphorism 178: **"Creer al corazón. Y más cuando es de prueba. Nunca le**

However, judgment should regularly proceed under the light of intellection[30] in the making of observations. This means, as said before concerning induction, that wit should assist judgment by defining the idea to be tested and the test cases which will prove an idea. Unless the attesting data is clearly perceived,[31] reason can not venture any judgment at all about an issue at stake, since a raw feeling is something still too undetermined to speak about it seriously with precision and certainty.

Contemporary sciences may help to illustrate my point.[32] Physics is assisted by the light of mathematics whose formulas and equations not only permit accurate observations but exact predictions. The mathematical formula is the instrument to observe, not the intelligible observation. Nonetheless, the formula is necessary to observe rationally, since, in Gracián's system, pure and vague sense data do not mean anything to the understanding. Using a formula to screen the data may suggest the risk of distorting the data by imposing a preconception. However, if the formula does not agree with the observation, then judgment actually can discard the formula and can search for a new one that is better suited to screen the data. Also, in communication research, conceptualization not only proceeds in supplying hypotheses, but also intervenes in defining the sample, the questionnaire, the survey, in short, the instruments that specify the

---

desmienta, que suele ser pronóstico de lo que más importa: oráculo casero. Perecieron muchos de lo que más se temían, mas, ¿de qué sirvió el temerlo sin el remediarlo?...No es cordura salir a recebir los males, pero sí el salirles al encuentro para vencerlos."

[30]See, for example, *Agudeza* Discourse 1, *Oráculo* Aphorism 35. Cf. Jaime Balmes, *Filosofia Elemental*, (México, Editorial Porrúa, 1973) 53-69; Jaime Balmes, *El Criterio*, 3ª ed. (Buenos Aires: Espasa-Calpe Argentina, 1943) 219.

[31]Judgment of course can reach conclusions not just through direct intelligible observations, but from *a priori* notions. Even so, the grounds of judgment and the departing point of an inference, for a realist, in one way or another should be traced to intelligible observations.

[32]Experimental research can not proceed if the working concepts, test cases, and hypotheses have not been defined; otherwise confusion can only arise from the data analyzed. Cf. Mario Bunge, *Scientific Research* (Berlin, Heidelberg, New York: Springer-Verlag, 1967).

kind of data which may make the hypothesis reliable. These instruments are not the observation itself which makes the hypothesis reliable, but they still are necessary to make the observation intelligible, precise. Researchers are aware of some bias risks concerning the design of the experiment; for example, careless wording in questionnaires may distort the collection of data. Even so, researchers try to achieve the best conceptualizations to avoid such a bias. And, in any case, they should use some instrument to observe the data. At the end, the instrument itself will prove its efficiency or defficiency depending on its power to collect data consistently.

A rhetorical illustration may also help to see how wit assists judgment. Consider Pope Paul III's fervent defense of the Americans against the threat of slavery and extermination brought by the Europeans:

> We consider...that they really are men, and not only capable of understanding Catholic religion but according to our information exceedingly desirous of embracing it.[33]

---

[33]Paul III's Bull *Sublimis Deus* (1537), as quoted by Jean Dulumeau *Catholicism between Luther and Voltaire: a new view of the Counter-Reformation*, (London: Burns & Oates, 1977) 70. By means of this bull, Pope Paul publicly condemned not only the slavery which currently was being imposed on the Americans, but also all types of slavery which could be imposed at any time on any people. Since all peoples were capable and had the supreme right of being Christianized, it a fortiori followed that all peoples were capable of and deserved all the remaining rights which pertain to them as human beings. Although his grounds were eminently theological, Pope Leo strongly relied on the pressing news of slavery he received from missionaries in the New World. His authoritative pronouncement served to condemn officially, before Renaissance scholars and entrepreneurs, the then fashionable Aristotelian thesis which justified slavery over "barbarian" peoples. It also served to reaffirm the Imperial decrees of Spain, banning slavery in her territories. Cf. Ezequiel A. Chávez, *Apuntes sobre la Colonia II, La Reeducación de Indios y Españoles*, (México: Editorial Jus, 1958) 89–91. Of course, enacting laws and decrees is not the same thing as enforcing them. In any case, it is interesting to notice as well, that the Indians also found their strongest assertion of their own humanhood in their capacity to embrace or reject a faith. See "Contra los doce misioneros franciscanos enviados por el papa Adriano VI en 1524," *Omnibus de poesía mexicana*, ed. Gabriel Zaid, 11 ed. (México: Siglo Veintiuno Editores, S. A., 1984) 47–48.

Pope Paul is able to conceptualize a clear-cut frame to observe intellectually if the Americans were full human beings: their capability of embracing Catholic religion. His analytic frame is not the test to which judgment assents, but the intelligible observation the Pope was able to make *through the concept*. After explaining the concept, he confirms the idea through an intelligible observation, saying "according to our information..." Even so, the conceptual frame is what empowered Paul III to screen and intellectually attest the information. Without this conceptual frame, judgment could not proceed since it would lack well defined test cases. If the conceptual frame is defective, then it should be replaced by a better one which actually allows the testing of the humanity of the Indians. In any case, judgment cannot proceed without any light from intellection.

All this means, if applied to artistic wit, that Gracián's structures of correspondences assist judgment by screening raw data and making it intelligible.[34] The structures of correspondences are not the rational experience which wins the assent of judgment. But these structures are necessary to observe rationally. These structures are the light by which the mind gets hold of such an experience. These structures do not mean to distort the perception of the data by imposing a preconception. If the mind does not get hold of any fitting data, then judgment discards the witty structure and searches for a new one which in a better way uncovers reality. It is not raw data, or the simple apprehension making sense of that data, but the *intelligible observation* that provides the grounds for judgment. Even so, the conceptualization shedding light on the data is what makes the observation intelligible. Latter, according to the rationally observable results, inference may proceed and make generalizations.[35] In short, for Gracián, "every skill begs for guidance," and

---

[34]The structures of correspondence not only allow the mind to observe rationally quantitative patterns, as through Mathematics, but also to recognize substances, qualities, relations, and the other array of categories as present and existing in things. Cf. *I Fonti dell' Ingegno* chapters 5, and 8–19; *Cannocchiale* 107–111.

[35]See, for example, *Oráculo* Aphorism 49.

concerning the powers of the mind, this guidance is wit.[36]

Artistic Concepts and Listeners' Judgment

Intelligible observations acquire a special place when performed through artistic wit. A witticism is not a declarative assertion.[37] It does not merely state and transmit to, or even impose on, listeners an observation which has already been made—for example, that American culture is attached in such a way to English measurement units that it would be almost impossible to persuade people to use the metric system. A witticism is rather a structure which offers both the speaker and the listener a means to "squeeze" and make by themselves an observation, either directly on things, or on the experience they save in memory or in their words in use. By means of this witticism, Murphy does not state but let us observe his impossible "Metric Recommendation":

We should go metric every inch of the way.[38]

Wit, the Abstraction of Universals, and Deduction

In scholasticism, a judgment is lucid since it rests on intelligible observations. This intelligibility makes judgment abstract since the observation itself is intelligible by means of the abstract terms of the idea to be tested—every idea involves an abstraction. Moreover, this judgment is universal since, in making sense and rationally experiencing a thing through the screen of a concept, the mind filters many individuating characteristics.[39] Thus the idea

---

[36]See *Agudeza* Discourse 1: "Mendiga dirección todo artificio..."

[37]See *Agudeza* Discourse 60. Cf. Margarida Vieira Mendes, "Apresentação, crítica, selecção, notas e sugestjões para análise literária," *Sermões do Padre António Vieira* (Lisboa: Editorial Comunicação, 1987) 32: "The language is not there to transmit the ideas; it is there to make them *visible*, imitating them in their configuration, as if in a material simulacrum."

[38]*1001 Logical Laws* 124.

[39]Simple apprehensions proceed from the most universal to particulars. However the mind will never be able intellectually to capture all the extensive number of particulars which not

conccived and later tested trascends the individual thing originally observed and reaches universality. For example, by filtering the differentiating traits of things as diverse as Mexican *tamales*, Italian ravioli, German potato dumplings, and Puerto Rican *pasteles*, I keep in mind what is a universal cooking procedure: the boiling of dough with some filling inside for a tasty dish. Then the intelligible observation's results extend to whatever thing later fits into the abstract description. For example, I may dare to cook rice or even rye dumplings. In fact, this universality of an observed idea is what makes its generalization possible, and its deductive application to new specific cases appropriate. Gracián said:

> Having seen a lion means having seen all lions, and having seen a lamb, all...[40]

Today—through the lens of scholasticism—I can say that the universal principles of genetics discovered and tested in fruit flies generally apply and deductively extend to any creature possessing genes, either algae, lobsters, rats, or human beings, since these principles trascend flies by prescinding what is specific of flies, and more so since these principles only observe what is universal in all genes, for example, possessing some type of acid such as DNA or RNA.

Indeed, the apprehension of universals can also stimulate a very creative and judicious use of deduction for technological progress. James Watt's genius was not simply to invent a steam engine which automatized the manufacture of textiles. More importantly, his genius was to ignore the particularities concerning the manufacture of textiles, and to "squeeze" truly the universal principle behind the steam engine. Thus this principle could deductively and creatively apply to the most specific new tasks—the locomotive, the printing press, the steam boat, the assembly line—and introduce humanity into the

---

only individuate a thing, but also make it variable according to occasions, places, and other circumstances.

[40]*El Criticón* I, Crisi 11: "Visto un león, están vistos todos, y vista una oveja, todas..."

Industrial Age.

Wit, the Judgment of Unique Cases, and Casuistry

As said above, the universality of the judgment reached under the light shed by a general idea may lead to many deductive and practical applications to many singular cases. However, the "light" of abstractions on judgment or posterior deductions becomes questionable when the abstraction itself, from one singular case, starts to be specified, or more, when it is specified so much that it refers to individuating and even circumstancial characteristics difficult to apply to other singular cases. Gracián warned about this problem:

> ...having seen one man means no more than having seen only one, and even such a man is not well known.[41]

The knowledge of the individual is so specified that it can not be generalized and applied in block to other cases:

> ...one should not act by example, because it usually lacks some of the circumstances.[42]

There are not two equal cases—not even my two pupils—since the individual is unique in its own class. The series of circumstances and individuating traits appear in such a way combined in the case that they make it be unrepeatable—the case even may be seen in such a fashion in just a single

---

[41] *El Criticón* I, Crisi 11: "...visto un hombre, no está visto sino uno, y aun ésse no bien conocido". This *sententia* of Gracián not only refers to the impossibility of generalizing what is individual. It also refers to the extreme contingency of our knowledge about people on the grounds of their free agency which takes people away from the fixed rules of necessity to the always open possibilities of choice.

[42] *Agudeza* Discourse 23: "...no se ha de obrar por ejemplo, por faltar casi siempre alguna de las circunstancias". Even though this quote does not come as part of the body of theories in *Agudeza*, but as an illustration of an extravagant opinion, the passage nevertheless strongly reveals what is involved in Gracián's method of conceptualizing the uniqueness of a given case.

occasion. Gracián prescribed:

> **Knowing and discerning things at their right point, in the right time, and then knowing how to achieve them.**[43]

Even so, Gracián's structures of correspondences still aim to shed light on and intellectually capture the unique case through the universalities it shares with other cases. The trick is that these structures "squeeze" the proportions and disproportions which the case's circumstances separately may share with other cases:

> The subject of reflection and pondering...is like a center from which a discourse develops lines of thought and subtlety to the surrounding entities, that is, the adjuncts which crown it, such as the causes, the effects, attributes, qualities, contingencies, circumstances of time, place, mode, etc., and any other correlative term...[44]

After tracing the lines of correspondences, Gracián's conglobate concepts and compound wit should find the unique combination of differently shared circumstances, and only then be able fully to conceptualize and test such a singular case.[45]

Thus, since the unique case appears as a composite, it divergently shares universality through its particles as they are shared by other cases. Mexicans, for example, are unique, and yet, they share many characteristics with other peoples of the world, for instance, their piety toward the dead is similar to the

---

[43]*Oráculo* Aphorism 39: **"Conocer las cosas en su punto, en su sazón, y saberlas lograr"**. This aphorism is among the best ones describing the nature of prudence.

[44]*Agudeza* Discourse 4: "Es el sujeto sobre quien se discurre y pondera...uno como centro, de quien reparte el discurso, líneas de ponderación y sutileza a las entidades que lo rodean; esto es, a los adjuntos que lo coronan, como son sus causas, sus efectos, atributos, calidades, contingencias, circunstancias de tiempo, lugar, modo, etc., y cualquiera otro término correspondiente..."

[45]See, for example, *Agudeza* discourses 15, and 51-57.

Chinese, and their gravity of spirit is similar to the Spaniards'. In fact, what is known of the Chinese and Spaniards may shed some light and assist a restricted judgment of Mexican piety on one hand, and Mexican gravity on the other.

But the unique case is also a unity. Through compound or conglobate wit, the person should observe how an otherwise separate set of universal ideas meet and apply to the concrete case in the most singular and unified way. The person should recognize that the whole is more than the sum of the parts. For example, the commonality found in some Mexican characteristics with other peoples does not discard the uniqueness of Mexicans, which is not perceived but through the whole comprehending and still abstracting power of wit. It is only by "squeezing" this unique wholeness of the case that wit can fully assist judgment. It is only by having a unified vision of Mexican traits that reason can render a unified judgment of Mexicans.[46]

Apparent Circularity and Compound Wit

There is a composite way that a person may come to learn and observe an idea—the person may pay heedful attention to at first apparently different events. Later, his mind's wit may discover connections between these events, for example through illation,[47] and realize and *judge* that what he observes is a single event. Consider this report from a plane crash:

> Eleven minutes after Flight 629 took off from Denver at 6:52 p.m., November 1, 1955, it crashed on farmland north of Denver. Wreckage was strewn over an area five miles long and two miles wide. The tail section and nose section were found virtually intact, far apart, but the engines, wings, and main cabin section were destroyed. Many bits of metal looked like shell fragments. Some remnants of the plane had the acrid smell of gunpowder. A thorough investigation turned up no indication of malfunction of the plane or of the crew. Farmers in the area told of

---

[46]Today, sciences try to predict the development of a case by measuring precisely every variable involved—every factor determining the course of the thing. But only by considering the variables all together through factor analysis, the scientist can advance a unified prediction of the case.

[47]See *Agudeza* Discourse 38.

hearing loud reports just before the crash. Officials of the Civil Aeronautics Board and the F.B.I. properly concluded that a bomb had been placed in the luggage compartment and that its explosion had caused a crash.[48]

Gracián explained this process of judgment saying:

> **The judicious and heedful man**...keenly notices, subtly conceives, judiciously infers: he discovers, recognizes, reaches, and comprehends all.[49]

Often this process of discovering and observing the unity of what at first appears as separate to the mind—if interpreted not by wit but by inference—looks like a fallacy of circularity.[50] The reason is that the parts of the composite are taken not as different events from which the idea rises as a mosaic through wit, but different premises which in a linear and circular way depend the one on the other. Consider these propositions:

---

[48]This example is quoted in Monroe C. Beardsley, *Thinking Straight*, 4th ed. (Englewood Cliffs, New Jersey: Prentice-Hall, Inc., 1975) 24. Beardsley cites this report as an example of an induction. He calls induction any argument which rises from weighing the evidence. In Gracián's system, the report would not be an induction, since it does not rise from singular cases to a generalization to a class. It rather would be an observation of very different pieces of evidence which, put together by wit—by an illation—, allow judgment to advance a verdict about a singular case—not a whole class.

[49]*Oráculo* Aphorism 49: **"Hombre juicioso y notante**...Nota acre, concibe sutil, infiere juicioso: todo lo descubre, advierte, alcanza y comprehende."** Cf. *El Discreto* Realce 19.

[50]Cf. Vieira Mendes 20-21. In her analysis of António Vieira's sermons—the Brazilian Jesuit who was the greatest preacher consciously practicing the rules of conceptism during the baroque era—Margarida Vieira Mendes recognizes many textual instances of what some people may take as circularity. The Jesuit's sermons evolve through a series of images and concepts. Their succession seems to make the images and concepts reciprocally support each other in a circular way, in an apparently inferential and fallacious pattern—when what truly is being presented is a mosaic of structures of correspondences which shed light on and integrate the series of images. Thus the mind intellectually learns and observes ideas on these images through the structures of correspondence.

1) God exists.

2) The Bible says it.

3) The Bible is the true revelation from God.

If inferential, these statements suffer from circularity since the existence of God follows from the veracity of the Bible, which in its turn is attested by the revelation from the existing God. However, under the lens of wit, these statements are not "proofs" from which the mind deduces a conclusion in a linear way, but different observations to be made as when one recognizes the pieces of a mosaic:

1) The existence of God.

2) His revelation.

3) His truthfulness.

From these separate observations, wit rises. Then it grasps a different sort of learning. It is about a unified object. What resembled pieces of a mosaic is next perceived by the mind as a whole, in this example, God, the ineffable One.

Thus, circularity cannot be blamed on wit since observations made through wit are not the result of a deduction. Observations are *observations*, not conclusions which follow from previous knowledge. Observations cannot be demonstrated but just seen.[51] Thus, the failure which could be attributed to wit is not the lack of demonstrative power, but the lack of explanatory power (the power of making sense of raw data) or that the witticism does not allow the mind to make any true intelligible observation on reality (judgment then rejects the idea since the idea does not agree with reality.)[52]

---

[51]Cf. Aristotle, *Nicomachean Ethics*, Bk. VI: Ch. 5. Aristotle described intellections as first principles which do not follow from any other knowledge, and which can not be demostrated but just grasped by intuitive reason. They are either seen or not.

[52]In science, the more powerful a theory is to explain and predict a whole universe of events, the more acceptable it is to judgment. In the same way, the more comprehensively a structure of correspondence—such as a conglobate concept—is able to make intelligibly observable a whole universe of events, the more appealing this structure of correspondence is to judgment.

Use of Many and Alternative Concepts for Learning

Aware of a possible failure of a given structure of correspondence concerning its power to shed light on judgment, artistic wit strives to use as many means as possible—as many structures of correspondences as available—to facilitate the observation, if the object is difficult to perceive by the mind. I remember some teachers in elementary school instructing me about seemingly self-evident truths, that is fractions, first by slicing cakes, then by separating oranges in their segments, next by tearing paper into pieces, and so on. Consider this other example from the Mellifluous Doctor:

This queenly maiden[53]...radiant with this perfect beauty[54] of spirit and body, renowned in the assembly of the Most High[55] for her loveliness and her beauty,[56] so ravished the eyes[57] of the heavenly citizens that the heart of the King himself desired her beauty[58] and sent down to her from on high a heavenly messenger...Make haste,[59] mothers and daughters...Gather round this virginal chamber and, if you can, enter your sister's[60] chaste inner room.[61] Behold, God has sent down for the Virgin. Behold, Mary is being spoken for[62] by the angel. Put your ear to the door,[63] strain to listen to the tidings he brings.[64] Maybe you will hear soothing words to confort

---

[53]*Song* 7:1.

[54]*Esther* 15:5.

[55]*Sir* 24:2.

[56]*Ps* 44:5.

[57]*Judith* 16:9.

[58]*Ps* 45:11.

[59]*Sg* 8:14.

[60]*Sg* 8:8.

[61]*Wis* 17:4.

[62]*Sg* 8:8.

[63]*Sir* 21:24.

[64]*Sg* 8:13.

you.[65] Rejoice...[66]

St Bernard apparently found insufficient all the Scriptures themselves for the purpose of properly penetrating into the mystery of St Gabriel's wondrous salutation to the Virgin—*"Hail, full of grace"*—announcing the coming of the Savior. St Bernard advanced one concept, and then another, and next a different one as an effort to shed light on what is extremely difficult to discern with our tiny minds.

These recurrent efforts by artistic wit to illuminate the yet to-be-observed object give a seemingly repetitive character to many pieces of baroque oratory, which once, and again, and yet another time, come with the same idea through the whole speech. Seemingly misunderstanding the enlightening purpose of artistic wit, José Miguel Oltra Tomás criticizes Baltasar Gracián for being repetitious in *El Político*:

> Gracián's procedure is...too monotonous, without a narrative development which could justify the number of pages devoted to the subject...The issue is synthetically presented in the first paragraph of the work...the rest of the text being variations of the same theme. If the musical comparison be permitted, it could be said that we are before Mussorgski's *Pictures from an Exhibition*'s equivalent.[67]

And yet, not surprisingly, artistic wit implicitly is praised as serving the most magnificent pieces of philosophical inquiry. Concerning St Thomas

---

[65]*Est* 15:8.

[66]Bernard of Clairvaux, "Homily II in Praise of the Virgin Mother," *Magnificat, Homilies in Praise of the Blessed Virgin Mary by Bernard of Clairvaux and Amadeus of Laussanne*, Introduction by Chrysogonus Wadell, OCSO (Cistercian Publications Inc., 1979) 16. The Scriptural concordaces of this text are from the translators: Marie-Bernard Saïd and Grace Perigo.

[67]José Miguel Oltra Tomás, "Conformación de un texto de Gracián: El Político Don Fernando." *Gracián y su época*, (Zaragoza: Institución Fernando El Católico, 1986) 164.

Aquinas' "Five Ways,"[68] Miguel Benzo Mestre says:

> Really, all valid demonstrations of the existence of God are no more than diverse pedagogical methods for leading the student to the twofold and basic intuition of the finiteness of the internal world beings, and of the impossibility that finite existence be the foundation of itself. But the terms «finiteness» and «foundation» may be understood with diverse degrees of depth, whose intuition is always possible to us, since it is always close to us, in ourselves, and in the world.
>
> He who limits himself only to understanding the meaning of such terms, but does not dare to submerge himself in the intuition of ontological finiteness, is scarcely able to glimpse the proving value of the demonstrations of God's existence. That is what has happened with those following the new logical positivism.
>
> On the contrary, there are countless human beings who, unable to articulate a logical argumentation, have a profound conviction of God's existence for having deeply penetrated into the intuition of the finiteness of men and the world.[69]

Even so, if enlightened through multiple and diverse concepts, the object observed richly emerges, appearing before the mind not as a "monotonous" idea, but as one with the most delicate distinctions and with many facets, as if it were a diamond. St Thomas's argument for the existence of God may be summarized by the need of a foundation for the finite beings. Nevertheless, the "Five Ways" are not repetitious. They keenly discern different forms in which this problem could be apprehended from experience: 1) the movement of finite beings, 2) their causality, 3) their contingency, 4) their degree of being, and 5) their purpose. In the same way, Gracián's *El Político* may be summarized as a eulogy to Ferdinand the Catholic, which repeatedly presents him as the exemplar of kingship. However, the speech is not a humdrum. Although apparently Gracián repeats the ideas and even the enlightening witticisms, he developed the subject by finding very subtle and important variations of the same topics: 1) the essential achievement of Ferdinand is stated: he founded the Spanish Monarchy; 2) the conditions which brought about his exemplary kingship are considered;

---

[68]See *Summa Theologica* I, Q. 2, A. 3.

[69]Miguel Benzo Mestre, *Teología para universitarios*, 6ᵃ ed. (Madrid: Ediciones Cristiandad, 1977) 134.

3) the specific kingly and personal endowments of Ferdinand are detailed; 4) it is shown that Ferdinand's endowments were reflected and generalized in his deeds; 5) the conclusion is the universality of Ferdinand as a model of kingship.[70]

A Single Concept for Different Observations

The distinction between the structures of correspondence which allow the mind to observe, and the observation itself made by the mind, can be better appreciated by noticing that a single structure of correspondence may shed light on very different observations. The same conceptual frame may be repeatedly applied to shed light on the same group of objects, but the attention to some slight situational circumstances may bring very different observations. Consider the correspondence between tomatos and potatos. Of course, there is this song, which anchors the observation on a linguistic circumstance:

> We say *tomayto*, they say *tomahto*;
> we say *potayto*, they say *potahto*;
> *tomayto, tomahto, potayto, potahto*...

Yet, if the circumstance pertains to botany, the correspondence reveals that *Lycopersicon esculentum* and *Solanum tuberosum* belong to the same family *Solanaceae*. If geography and history of agriculture, the observation is that tomatos and potatos are American crops. If cuisine, perhaps some gentlemen may judge that French fries and catsup harmonize. However, farmers know well that these plants hate each other to death, and must not be sown in the same furrow; thus the correspondence turns from a proportion into a disproportion.[71]

---

[70]Cf. Miguel Batllori and Ceferino Peralta, "Indice General," Baltasar Gracián, *Obras Completas* I, (Madrid: Ediciones Atlas, 1969) 442. Batllori and Peralta explain the structure of *El Político* there. Moreover, their edition of the speech (pages 274–302) reveals the structure found by these critics, by separating in parts what normally is edited as an undivided text.

[71]There are important examples in Gracián's writings of one concept applied to different objects of understanding and thus producing different observations. For instance, in *El Criticón*, Gracián screens the character of different nations, the ages of man, the social

Repetitive Light from Wit and Assent to Experience

Here is a most important remark: even if artistic wit is truly repetitious, for the same reason it will better serve judgment in gaining certainty about an idea. Through its repetitions, its use of even different squeezing concepts, through its many routes to observe the very same event, artistic wit makes judgment increase its belief in its perceptions, and leads judgment to assent to what is rationally experienced.[72]

Wit and Prudence

According to Gracián, judgment should also be responsive to the urgency of a situation to advance a verdict. Decisions which imply deep and long term consequences require delay from the statesperson to give time for the most careful examination and testing.[73] However, when the most pressing events are in play, then the purest wit must be sufficient, without any posterior substantiating observations, as happens during battles with military leaders.[74] Thus, for Gracián, the exemplar of prudent judgment is the statesperson and the exemplar of witty judgment is the military leader during the most pressing battle.

Wit and Rhetorical Judgment

However, urgency is just the surface of the type of judgment that is humanly

---

classes, and other topics, through the conceptual frame of the faculties of the mind; each observation produces interesting variations in the results obtained. In *Agudeza*, Gracián constantly reintroduced the special techniques of correlations (proportion, disproportion, pure or mixed concepts, comparisons or similarities, etc.) into the analysis of the three other major genres of witticisms (ponderation, ratiocination, and invention), and in doing so, he obtained significant variety in the learning.

[72]See *El Discreto* realces 5, 29, and 25.

[73]See *El Discreto* realces 15 and 3.

[74]See *El Discreto* Discourse 15; *El Héroe* Primor 3.

contingent.[75] On a deeper level, there is human *free agency*[76]—the Jesuit dogma, or, as Chesterton put it, the truth disputed[77]—which is at least twofold: 1) the freedom enjoyed by the master judging,[78] and 2) the freedom enjoyed by masters being judged, whose simplicity, wickedness, malice, folly, and, yes, gallantry,[79] if diversely probable, are nevertheless equally possible. Then, pure wit, judgment, or inference may fall short. Then—Aristotle might have said—we must dare to put into practice our faculty of rhetoric.

The True, the Good, and the Beautiful

Gracián's views on the true, the good, and the beautiful—supreme values and standards of judgment—are separately treated in his books and, thus far, in this study. Some of the important points about his views on these values should be summarized next to be better appreciated.

The True

A most important consideration is the ordinary attitude Gracián prescribed for the person who is in search of the true: *prudence*. Through prudence, the person weighs the measure of assent to be given to the often deceptive and malicious experiences in which he is immersed and becomes part. Through prudence, the person heedfully calculates the means to secure for himself the valuable amid a hostile environment. Through prudence, the person may wake

---

[75]In scholasticism, necessity is only reserved to God. Anything else is contingent. However, human beings are twice contingent because of their free agency.

[76]See *El Héroe* primores 1 and 2. Cf. Jaime Balmes, *Filosofía Elemental* (México: Editorial Porrúa, 1973) 61-63.

[77]"Truths turn into dogmas the moment they are disputed." See G. K. Chesterton, *Heretics.*

[78]See *El Héroe* primores 1 and 2.

[79]See *Agudeza* discourses 26–29; *Oráculo* Aphorism 13.

up and finally reach disabuse.[80]

Prudence is conditioned by the many contingent factors which are present in human judgment: the pressing force of events, the contingency of human nature and affairs, the *señoril* freedom enjoyed by the judge and the judged, etc. Moreover, prudence is a response to the possibility that, in the progress of learning, a new specification could be apprehended on the way, qualifying previous ideas with unexpected and disabusing turns. Depending on the occasion, the mind may have some havens to anchor its certainty, following what judicious wit grasps as the substantial, or the accidental, or the general, or the specific, or the profound, and so on.

However, grasping truths often is a task which trascends simple knowledge, and rather involves conscious living. Truths are lived through their practice in life. Aging itself is a process revealing the most vital truths in a painful and disabusing fashion. Only with maturity, a person may claim to master public affairs and, with old age, really experience the futility of wordly concerns and finally open himself to the everlasting. And yet, age is not self-sufficient in bringing such truths to the person. He should willingly embrace virtue and live with thoroughly good habits. He should be Aristotle's "person of practical wisdom," Cicero's "commander" or "statesperson," Quintilian's "person of virtue." But moreover, he should be Gracián's "disabused person," "hero," "master," or even "saint." The most meaningful truths otherwise cannot be really experienced, known, communicated, or persuaded, thus appearing as senseless to the fool, the wicked, and the vulgar—the hard cases of rhetorical interaction.

The Good

In Gracián's scholastic environment, the good is an objective value present in things, rooted in the degree and the actualization of being which occur in the

---

[80]The whole of Gracián's treatises are a meditation on prudence. Even so, on specific references to prudence, see, for example, *Oráculo* Aphorism 243; *El Discreto* Realce 23. Cf. Arturo del Hoyo clix.

things' becoming.[81] Both in things and in human beings, the degree and the actualization of being may be richer or poorer, and in that sense things and people may be better or worse.[82] In fact, nothingness is the most radical opposite of the good, since it is the complete absence of being.[83]

As an objective aspect of reality, the good can be apprehended by reason as any other observable event. Gracián assigned to *taste* the discriminating capacity of identifying, appreciating, and enjoying what is good. The extensive and eminent realizations of the good is what enables taste to have keen discernment of its objects.[84]

As mentioned before, Gracián identified in *choice* the judgment discriminating, determining, and contriving practical matters.[85] Good choice rests on good taste and the right dictates of prudence.[86]

Gracián's "goods" are the scholastic triad of the honest, the useful, and the pleasant. From these goods, only honesty is an end in itself, whereas usefulness and pleasure are subordinate instruments to achieve such an end.[87] The reason for honesty's preeminence is that this good consists in the actual and integral possession of the perfections of being, in the case of people, their mastery.[88]

---

[81]The degree and the actualization of being were studied by Aristotle as two of the four universal rhetorical lines of arguments: degree and possibility. See *Rhetoric* II, 18–19. These lines indeed serve to judge the goodness of things.

[82]Cf., for example, *Nicomachean Ethics* Bk. X: Ch.5; *Summa Theologica* I, Q. 5.

[83]See *El Criticón* III, Crisi 8. In one of his most chilling texts, Gracián astonishingly portrayed—made visible to the understanding—the worst of evils: nothingness.

[84]See, for example, *El Héroe* Primor 5.

[85]See, for example, *El Héroe* primores 6, 7, and 8; *El Discreto* realces 3 and 10; *Oráculo* Aphorism 283.

[86]See, for example, *Oráculo* Ahporism 51.

[87]See *El Criticón* I, Crisi 10.

[88]See, for example, *El Discreto* Realce 24. Cf., Aristotle, *Nicomachean Ethics* Bk. X: Chapter 6.

Through eloquence, rhetoric[89] may unite the pleasant and the useful[90] to attain the integral good: honesty.

It appears that Gracián's strong emphasis on the honest is applied to the triad of rhetorical goods—the just, the honorable, and the expedient[91]—, and that this emphasis may probably subordinate all ends to the honorable, making the practice of justice a mark of honesty, and the choice of the expedient a means to secure and enhance the integrity of the person.[92]

The Beautiful

The school philosophers often defined beauty as the *splendor formae*. Beauty shines on the objects if their sight splendorously reveals the underlying intelligible forms with such a novel and unexpected clarity that minds are moved with awe before the wondrous discovery. For example, through its proportionate arranging and the harmony of its elements, a work of art may aptly capture and embody an intelligible notion uncovering the integrity and clarity of an apparently chaotic reality.[93]

Similarly, Gracián found in proportions, harmonies, consonances, correspondences, etc., the foundations of beauty.[94] It is through these structures of corresponcences that the intelligible is disclosed. It is through wit that sensual experience becomes clear and unified to the mind, producing wonderment and unusual understanding. Thus, wit can not be content with truth, like logical

---

[89]See *Agudeza* Discourse 36.

[90]See *Agudeza* Discourse 55.

[91]See Aristotle, *Rhetoric*, I, 3.

[92]See, for example, *Oráculo* aphorisms 97, 120, 165, and 234.

[93]Cf. Eco 64–121. St Thomas Aquinas' formal criteria of beauty comprehends the notions of consonance, integrity, and clarity of the beautiful object, which together make intelligible forms shine and be experienced with awe and unusual understanding by the observer.

[94]See *Agudeza* Discourse 2.

judgment. Wit also strives for the beautiful.[95] Wit strives to contemplate and enjoy its intelligible discoveries which astound the mind.

The wondrous revelation may be given—as Giambattista Vico studied—through an imaginative universal,[96] that is through an image which fittingly embodies, screens, and uncovers an intelligible form, for example, a renaissance sculpture or painting like *La Pietà*.[97] But the splendorous vision disclosing universals does not always need to be imaginative for Gracián. The imaginative is only the material aspect of tropes identifiable in the branch of wit he called similitudes.[98]   Many other varieties of awesome and beautiful discoveries arise from contemplating the consonance of pure ideas. Remembering Pythagoras, Gracián cited the music perceived in the proportionate movement of the celestial bodies.[99] Gracián prescribed this kind of wit to such a degree that Menéndez Pelayo bewailed:

> *Agudeza y arte de ingenio*...[is] a treatise on literary rules whose error consists in reducing all virtues of style to a single one; all faculties producing an artistic work are one as well. It is a code of poetic *intellectualism*.[100]

Concerning Gracián's literary practice, Jorge Luis Borges abhorred the labyrinths, quibbles, stratagems, and emblems to which he thought Gracián had reduced all poetry.[101]

---

[95]See *Agudeza* Discourse 2.

[96]See Mooney 227–228.

[97]Cf., Mooney 104–105.

[98]See, for example, *Agudeza* "Al Lector", and discourses 10, 11, and 19. Cf., for example, with *Agudeza* discourses 14–16, which address witty comparisons. This kind of concepts are founded not on the imaginative terms, but on precise ideas.

[99]See *Agudeza* Discourse 23.

[100]Menéndez Pelayo 582.

[101]See Ramos Foster 70. Being blind, Borges was more able to perceive the music of the celestial bodies, and yet he missed it in Gracián's works.

Even so, Gracián's aesthetics and its practice to some degree is older than this Jesuit, and highly appreciated. It is found, for example, in St Thomas Aquinas' theories,[102] and in their correlative application to the composition of religious hymns still in use, for instance, St Thomas's *Office of the Blessed Sacrament*:

> Tantum ergo Sacramentum
> Veneremur cernui
> Et antiquum documentum
> Novo cedat ritui;
> Praestet fides supplementum
> Sensuum defectui.[103]

In a multi-dimensional structure of correspondences, St Thomas proportioned all: sacramental life, revelation, theology, philosophy. The harmonious novelty and clarity of these few stanzas rival the intellectual order and rigor of his bulky *summae*, and there lies the beauty perceived.[104]

For the purposes of rhetoric, Gracián's aesthetics of wit imply the possibility of fusing the pleasant with the useful in speech, as ancient authors prescribed.[105]

---

[102]Cf. Eco.

[103]There is this version of the hymn, as heard in church, and translated by Melvin L. Farrel:
> Humbly let us voice our homage
> For so great a sacrament;
> Let all former rites surrender
> To the Lord's New Testament
> What the senses fail to fathom,
> Let us grasp through faith's consent!

Philosophy's sensual grounds of truth, the old testament of law, and the human toils present in bread and wine, respectively and in a parallel way recede before theology's supernatural grounds of faith, the new testament of grace, and the Divine Presence which is true food and sustenance for the everlasting life.

[104]Cf., Walter J. Ong., S. J. "Wit and Mystery: A Revaluation in Mediaeval Latin Hymnody" *Speculum* 22 (1947) 310–341.

[105]See, for example, Horace, "On the Art of Poetry" *Aristotle/Horace/Longinus*

Truth is both pleasant and useful through wit, since new and unusual knowledge is presented to the mind, and the mind enjoys the splendorous sight of such a piece of knowledge. Thus, Gracián placed wit among the most fundamental means of eloquence.[106]

Style

Gracián included a brief discussion of style in his *Agudeza*. Gracián's emphasis on giving rules for judging stylistic propriety subordinates style—a usually separate part of rhetoric—to the faculty of judgment.[107] This discussion contributes much to clarify style's relation with and distinction from wit.[108]

Reviewing some ordinary characterizations of style, Gracián distinguished two broad and polar categories: the *rotund* and the *concise* styles. He noticed that their use is advocated on the respective grounds of the Asians' and the Lacedaemonians' authority.[109] The first style is usually prescribed for rhetorical eloquence; the second is often required for precise philosophical inquiries; a mixture of these styles is preferred by historians. Yet, Gracián believed that the propriety and perfection of either style rested on its fitness for the case and the occasion. Styles should not just be indiscriminately chosen or condemned in mass without considering the specific circumstances at hand addressed in the different stages of a discourse. Moreover, diverse styles should usually meet in

---

—*Classical Literary Criticism* trans. T. S. Dorsch. (Penguin Books, 1965) 90–91.

[106]See, for example, *Agudeza* 55.

[107]Gracián's system of rhetoric does not follow the classical scheme of the parts of oratory: invention, disposition, style, memory, and delivery. Gracián's system follows the structure of human understanding: ingenuity, judgment, and imagination/memory. Since Gracián's main concern on style is about its propriety, then style seems to link best not to memory or ingenuity, but to judgment.

[108]See *Agudeza* discourses 60–62.

[109]Thus the one is the Asiatic style, and the other is the laconic style.

a single work to provide enjoyable variety in its pages.[110]

In any case, the soul of style is not in the length or the texture of its sounds but in its contents. Either *declarative,* transmiting already understood data, or *conceptist,* extracting new understanding, style should not be a flaky accumulation of voices, but should consist in the unending richness of "pregnant" words.[111]

Gracián's distinction between declarative and conceptist style is very important for perceiving the nature of wit. If no new understanding is involved in a discourse, declarative style is fitting, since, managerially, it only transmits already known ideas, without any effort of conceptual invention. Declarative style often communicates new information. But even loads of new information do not necessarily add any new understanding about the nature of reality. For example, a friend could come with the richest and most incredible narrative about her last social adventure, and yet she would not always add something new to my understanding or expectations of her personality. It is wit, through the conceptist style, which rises above the mass of information. It is wit which, like rare gems, appears here and there to shed light on the mountain of data.[112] It is not just a concern for appropriate composition that requires that witty language appear sparsely in discourses, like stars in heavens,[113] salt in dishes, and the sun in skies.[114] "Invention is arduous,"[115] discovery is difficult, and new understanding unusual, and thus in the same proportion conceptist style should be applied to a text. Otherwise conceptist style produces false wit—void structures of correspondences with the pretense of new knowledge, as noisy and

---

[110]See *Agudeza* discourses 3 and 61.

[111]See *Agudeza* Discourse 60.

[112]See *Agudeza* Discourse 60.

[113]See *Agudeza* Discourse 60.

[114]See *Agudeza* Discourse 3: "Wit is rare like the sun and pleasant like salt." ("Soles por lo raro, sales por lo agradable").

[115]*Agudeza* Discourse 1: "...arduo el inventar..."

void as empty vessels.[116]

The measure of artistic resources applied to a text allowed Gracián to propose a new classification of styles.[117]

Natural style is the one which plainly transmits well understood data. Interpreting Gracián, I think this style satisfies the simplest attempts at communication. It may be an ordinary enumeration of particulars or a plain narrative of events not offering any complexity to the understanding. An example is a letter from Gracián to Francisco de la Torre, charmingly informing him with the utmost simplicity about the most diverse news: from having ministered the Holy Oils to an extremely sick parishioner, to the recent sack of Flanders by the French.[118]

An enhanced natural style is the one used by educated people. It does not consist in a careless account of any fact, but in a conscious selection of the best and most fitting words and pieces of knowledge acquired through long years of schooling and urbane erudition.[119] An illustration of this style is Gracián's letter criticizing his friend Manuel Salinas's Latin grammar.[120] The concision, circumspection, and good sense achieved through this style also makes it the best for the austere office of kings and princes.[121]

Gracián recognized a middle style between the fully plain and fully artistic.[122] It happens when a plain discourse starts introducing structures of

---

[116]See *Agudeza* discourse 60 and 62; *El Criticón* III, crises 7 and 10.

[117]See *Agudeza* Discourse 62.

[118]See Baltasar Gracián, "Epistolario: A don Francisco de la Torre, Zaragoza, 16 de septiempre de 1655," *Obras Completas*, ed. Arturo del Hoyo 1157–1159.

[119]See *Agudeza* Discourse 62.

[120]See Baltasar Gracián, "Epistolario: A Salinas, Marzo de 1652," *Obras Completas* ed. by Arturo del Hoyo 1147–1150.

[121]See *Agudeza* Discourse 62.

[122]See *Agudeza* Discourse 62.

correspondences here and there as the conterpoint added to plain melodies.[123] An elementary illustration is Gracián's letter to a Jesuit in Madrid, informing him of the Succour of Lérida. The letter is a vivid and yet almost plain news report from a direct witness of the battle. Even so, there is one single and deeply sad correspondence casually placed in the text. Gracián briefly mentioned that his offering of extreme unction was rejected by some French soldiers. The sight of their pale and dying bodies, previously mentioned, thus becomes a chilling insight of heretics embracing eternal death.[124] The middle style is often used in a fuller way by historians. They do not reduce their task to a simple account of events, but also squeeze out some interpretations by means of artistic wit in sporadic and strategic points in the narrative.[125] In *Agudeza*, most of the stylistic models analyzed by Gracián come from historians, for example, Tacitus, Valerius Maximus, and Lucius Florus. Other of Gracián's highly appreciated models of middle style are moral philosophers, like Seneca. Among the orators, Gracián studied illustrations from Cicero and Pliny the Younger.[126] For Gracián, all these authors share the mastery of dense and substantial phrases offering new avenues of understanding to the mind.[127] A consideration of the baroque literary schools in Spain would show that conceptist writers are mainly the practitioners of the middle style. In fact, most of Gracián works could be placed in this genre: *El Héroe, Agudeza, El Discreto, El Político*, and *Oráculo*. This last work takes the middle style to its most extreme concision.

Beyond the middle style, Gracián identified a fully artistic style: the ornate one,[128] or, considering the baroque schools, the style used by the Gongorists.

---

[123]See *Agudeza* Discourse 61.

[124]See Baltasar Gracián, "Epistolario: A un jesuita en Madrid, Lérida, 24 de noviembre de 1646," *Obras Completas* ed. Arturo del Hoyo 1130–1136.

[125]See *Agudeza* Discourse 61 and 62.

[126]See *Agudeza* Discourse 61.

[127]See *Agudeza* Discourse 62.

[128]See *Agudeza* Discourse 62.

Here not only witty structures of correspondences, but also the material resources of rhetorical figures and tropes are applied to the text, to make it not only richly dense, but also embellished. Gracián illustrated this style with the daring oratory of Hortensio Paravicino, the current model of Gongorist preaching.[129] Gracián's *El Criticón* and *El Comulgatorio* may also be placed in this stylistic genre, although considering that, in these works, the dense contents predominate over ornate artifices.

According to Gracián, ornate style should only be used exceptionally because it is extremely dangerous. Its artistry may be just a flaky display of words, or a void and noisy pretense of eloquence, if the orator does not meet and convey proportionally elevated contents and situation. Then, said Gracián, what is practiced is the false wit and false rhetoric of many pulpits of his contemporary Spain.[130]

In any case, Gracián believed that his different methods of wit could provide specific and opportune stylistic turns to a discourse:

> One must strive to make propositions beautify style, contrary views enliven it, mystery make it pregnant; ponderations, profound; exaggerations, prominent; allusions, disguised; challenges, stinging; transmutations, subtle; that ironies provide the salt; that crises provide the bite; paronomasias, poise; sententiae, seriousness; that similitudes make it fecund and that comparisons enhance it.[131]

And yet, beyond pure style, the various resources of artistic wit expand and aim at the vast horizons of the mind's ingenuity.[132]

---

[129]See *Agudeza* Discourse 62.

[130]See *Agudeza* discourse 60 and 62; *El Criticón* III, crises 7 and 10.

[131]*Agudeza* Discourse 60: "Hase de procurar que las proposiciones lo hermoseen, los reparos lo aviven, los misterios lo hagan preñado, las ponderaciones profundo, los encarecimientos salido, las alusiones disimulado, los empeños picante, las trasmutaciones sutil, las ironías le den sal, las crisis le den hiel, las paronomasias donaire, las sentencias gravedad, las semejanzas lo fecunden y las paridades lo realcen."

[132]See *Agudeza* Discourse 3.

12   Erudition

AN ACCOUNT OF GRACIÁN'S THEORIES AND THEIR RELEVANCE TO RHETORIC
would be severely incomplete if the issue of erudition were absolutely neglected.
This subject itself is different than wit and judgment, implies another major
power of the mind, memory,[1] and thus deserves separate consideration.

For Gracián, erudition entails a wide, extensive, keen, and eminent learning
of the most diverse subjects. He also defined it as follows:

> ...a universal learning of deeds and sayings, to enlighten with them the matter which
> one reasons about, and the doctrines one is asserting.[2]

In spite of its reliance on an elephant-like memory, erudition is not a
collection of trivial facts. It is rather the ever handy experience which triggers
ingenuity with new insights, clarifies ideas with explanatory cases, calls attention
to important facts, grounds reason in its judgments, and seasons conversation
with the spice of the old, the new, the near, and the far.[3] The more learning a
person has, the more linking-points for correspondences are provided to the
inventive mind;[4] the more information, the richer and more useful to the heedful
mind;[5] the more cases appreciated, the keener the taste;[6] the more knowledge,

---

[1] In *The Spiritual Exercises*, the Ignatian scheme of faculties is presented as follows:
memory/imagination, ingenuity, and judgment. As a Jesuit, Gracián not only endorsed this
scheme strongly, but also used it as the major conceptual frame structuring his theories of
human understanding.

[2] *Agudeza* Discourse 58. "...consiste en una universal noticia de dichos y de hechos, para
ilustrar con ellos la materia de que se discurre, la doctrina que se declara."

[3] See *Agudeza* discourses 58–59.

[4] See *Agudeza* Discourse 59.

[5] See, for example, *El Discreto* realces 5 and 18.

[6] See, for example, *El Criticón* II, Crisi 4. Poetry and the Fine Arts have a special place
in the education of taste, and its discriminating power.

the more solid judgment.[7]

Erudition is not a collection of frozen facts either. It is rather the pasture of the mind,[8] from which are extracted the needed spiritual nutrients with unending novelty by means of the most different methods of artistic wit.[9] Memory is a storehouse[10] and true words are pregnant.[11] Either one is waiting to release enlightenment through a happy correspondence which squeezes out an apt and opportune idea.[12] Either one at first is a reservoir of experience whose vagueness equals an obscure feeling.[13] Through wit, discernment is gradually gained in an unceasing search for luminous specificity.[14]

Erudition is not a nostalgic contemplation of the past Golden Age,[15] as it was for some Renaissance men. It also relishes the fresh, welcomes the extravagant, adapts to the fashionable, seeks out new problems, provides discoveries, searches for objections to the established, admits unconsidered pieces of evidence, turns previous judgments up-side down, stimulates inventions, sharpens taste, solidifies choice, acts in public affairs, and solves practical matters.[16]

---

[7]See, for example, *El Discreto* realces 3 and 15; *Agudeza* Discourse 58; *El Criticón* II, Discourse 4: A wide acquaintance with the sciences provides rich and handy evidence which reason uses to judge cases.

[8]See *Agudeza* Discourse 58.

[9]See *Agudeza* Discourse 59.

[10]See *Agudeza* Discourse 58.

[11]See *Agudeza* Discourse 60.

[12]See *Agudeza* Discourse 59.

[13]Erudition is not "luminous" by itself. Its experience may simply be a vast collection of sensual and meaningless data. Wit always is what discloses the nature of things and leads the mind to abstract ideas.

[14]See *El Criticón* I, Crisi 1.

[15]See, for example, *Oráculo* aphorisms 1, 109.

[16]See, for example, *Oráculo* aphorisms 20 and 22; *El Discreto* 5, 6, 7, and 18.

Concerning wit, erudition is indispensable because it provides the needed terms to extract new ideas. A wit does not simply transmit ideas, but reveals them through lines of correlation established between many facts. It is from extensive acquaintance with terms that a wit can speak about something wittily.[17] G. K. Chesterton explained it clearly:

> I cannot talk about anything without talking of everything.

But the growth of erudition should not make it so rarified that it becomes mute. There is a degree of erudition which should be shared by groups of people. The fact is that wit, like jokes, looses all its grace if explained. Wit can simply present a structure of correspondences, and then it abandons itself to the listener's use of the concept, who applies it to a piece of common experience. Indeed, the possibility of communicating wit rests on the shared experience from which both the speaker and the listener simultaneously extract the ideas.[18]

I think that so-called cultural literacy can be identified with the erudition that keeps the lines of communication in a society open. On occasions, among strangers, the common knowledge of a television series, baseball, or songs may suffice to break the ice. However, interpreting Gracián, I believe that the deepest grounds of communality should not be sought outside, but inside, in the human condition shared with every neighbor.[19]

Here lies the important place Gracián gave to the humanities as a source of erudition. These studies are a mirror of our common nature. Their timely and concrete dimensions are transcended by their universal contents. The *Odyssey* is not valuable because it is Greek, but because it is a moral portrait of the toils and wisdom of humanity.[20] Lines of communication with every people are thus opened by this kind of erudition.

---

[17]See, for example, *Agudeza* Discourse 4.

[18]See, for example, *El Discreto* realces 5–9, and 18.

[19]See, for example, *Agudeza* Discourses 26–30.

[20]See, for example, *El Criticón* I, Crisi 11.

Literary fictions are particularly valuable to ingenuity because they create exemplary cases which richly capture the complexities often found in ordinary human life. They offer infinite points of linkage to trace witty correspondences with real cases in the world.[21] History adds reality to the exemplar. Thus its myriad contingencies trigger not only ingenious parallelisms, but also grounds for judgment.[22] Sapiential literature seizes pieces of the common moral experience in brief gems such as sententiae, emblems, anecdotes, and fables.[23]

This humanities project is the one developed by Gracián in his works. He searched for the universal hero, the exemplary politician, the paradigmatic wit, the model of discretion, the oracle of prudence, the mirror of disabuse, the master, and the ideal recipient of grace.

---

[21]See, for example, *Agudeza* discourses 35, and 55–58.

[22]See, for example, *El Criticón* II, Crisi 4.

[23]See, for example, *Agudeza* Discourse 58; *El Criticón* II, Crisi 4.

Part Three

The Eloquence of Wits

13   The Embarrassment of Wits

MANY PEOPLE DO NOT REGARD THE SEVENTEENTH CENTURY as a fortunate period for oratory. They may admit it to be an age of eloquence and splendor; and yet, by "eloquence," they mean a derogatory term applied to bombastic style and to dramatistic delivery.[1] Scholars sometimes recognize genuine embellishments in baroque expression, but these embellishments are, they think, just expression and a deviation from the correct use of language.[2] More often, such speech is seen as deprived of its logical foundations and abandoned to unrestrained emotions,[3] if not to error, conceit, buffoonery, flattery, trifling, and, alas!, superstition. In brief, the seventeenth century is thought of as being one of those lost ages in which orators surrendered themselves to sophistry[4]—as is said happened in pre-Socratic Greece and postclassic Rome. A modern cliché is that the enlightenment, of course, had to come and rescue oratory from the last manifestation of the Dark Ages suffered during the Baroque. What else could be expected from this darkest period, when the most absolutist despots ruled, when speech was just meant to pronounce flatulent assent to the king's whims, when religion was the means to spread ignorance and impose fear on the oppressed masses, and when the most militant arm of the Romish Church were the Jesuits, with their cunning and their Jesuitry? Must the age of eloquence be understood differently than a problem, considering that it was followed by a solution: the ages of Reason and Science?[5]

---

[1] Cf., for example, Mooney 51–68; Marc Fumaroli, *L'Age de L'Eloquence. Rhétorique et «res literaria» de la Renaissance au seuil de l'époque classique*, (Genève: Librairie Droz, 1980). It should be noticed that, in the English tradition, eloquence produces the term elocution, which in its turn means only the artificial delivery of the elocutionist schools of rhetoric.

[2] Cf., for example, Curtius.

[3] Cf., for example, Conley 151–162; Mooney 60–62.

[4] Cf., for example, Fumaroli 223–423.

[5] Cf., for example, Conley 162–234.

Snubbing Wit

The specific contempt for baroque eloquence may be just a derivation from the general repudiation of rhetoric made fashionable by some "modern" and "scientific" minds:[6] the ordinary and, yet, wrong view of rhetoric as an instrument of deceit and the display of empty words—the idea of it as just "pure" rhetoric. John Locke deplored:

> ...all the art of rhetoric, besides order and clearness; all the artificial and figurative aplication of words eloquence hath invented, are for nothing else but to insinuate wrong ideas, move the passions, and thereby mislead the judgment; and so indeed are perfect cheats...I cannot but observe how little the preservation and improvement of truth and knowledge is the care and concern of mankind; since the arts of fallacy are endowed and preferred. It is evident how much men love to deceive and be deceived, since rhetoric, that powerful instrument of error an deceit, has its established professors, is publicly taught, and has always been had in great reputation: and I doubt not but it will be thought great boldness, if not brutality, in me to have said thus much against it. Eloquence, like the fair sex, has the prevailing beauties in it to suffer itself ever to be spoken against. And it is in vain to find fault with those arts of deceiving, wherein men find pleasure to be deceived.[7]

If by reducing logic to geometrical reasoning, judgment to clear facts, and style ideally to mathematical symbols with univocal meaning, rationalists and empiricists could not recognize the most basic and genuine problems of rhetoric, such as contingent reasoning and value judgment, it may follow that these modern thinkers could more easily ignore, dismiss, and even condemn the very complex problems of the current baroque eloquence they witnessed—the problems of invention through wit and its subtleties. If rhetoric generally had a

---

[6]Contempt for rhetoric is not necessarily a modern phenomenon. It has been recurrent through different ages of humanity. The classical indictment of rhetoric is Plato's *Gorgias*. Yet, many of the contemporary clichés condemning rhetoric can be directly traced to the enshrining of science and mathematics as the foundations of the new age of Reason which humanity enjoys today.

[7]See John Locke, *Essay Concerning Human Understanding* III, x, 34.

bad name, it may follow that the more specialized and directly experienced oratory—that of the seventeenth century—could easily have received a worse depiction.[8]

Yet, the rebuff of baroque eloquence—and specifically wit—might have come from more modest circumstances than the rise of new philosophies. Seventeenth century oratory's infamous reputation could also be a result of the rising ideological, religious, and nationalistic interests of that time. With a desire of legitimatizing themselves by means of something new and renowned, these just out interests would conveniently embrace some new philosophy and accordingly dissociate themselves from an art of discourse strongly based on "old-fashioned" theories of wit.[9] To what degree were rationalism, empiricism, neo-scholasticism, and neo-Ciceronianism simply philosophies, instead of also ideologies useful for rival nations, groups, and churches? To what degree were Pascal's disdain of Jesuitical choices of expression[10] and Fénelon's love of simplicity[11] purely a question of eloquence, or were they rather attached respectively to Pascal's general enimity towards the Jesuits and Fénelon's

---

[8]As seen before, the philosophies of the Age of Reason are irreconcilable with the very notion of wit, let alone baroque eloquence. Cf., for example, Fumaroli 681–682.

[9]Cf., for example, Fumaroli 673–706. Concerning ideological biases depending religious, nationalistic, and group disputes, Cf., for example, McSorley, *An outline of History of the Church by Centuries (From St Peter to Pius XII.)* (B. Herder Book, Co., 1947), 630–699; Maurice Braure, *The Seventeenth and Eighteenth Centuries* (London: Burns & Oats, 1963).

[10]See Blaise Pascal, *The Provincial Letters*, for example, Letter XI. Pascal's rebuke against Jesuitical use of maxims, raillery, and other witty resources did not prevent him from using the same kind of clever methods in his letters. Indeed, Pascal needed the use of wit, and specifically of maxims, to reach the highest expression of his humanism: the *Pensées*.

[11]See François Fenélon, "The First Dialogue, against the affectation of fine wit in sermons..." *Dialogues on Eloquence*, trans. Wilbur Samuel Howell (Princeton, New Jersey: Princeton University Press, 1951). Fenélon's criticism of witty fashions did not prevent him from recurring to the format of a dialogue to expound his theories—a format which was regarded as the wittiest for the exposition of sciences during the baroque period. See Pallavicino's *Trattato dello Stile e del Dialogo* chapters 32 to 38.

tendencies towards Quietism?[12] To what degree was the not uncommon blame of Spain as the source of bad taste,[13] and of Gracián as the theorist of sick eloquence,[14] the results of an impartial assessment, or of a biased and summary judgment against the common enemy of all other European countries during the sixteenth and seventeenth centuries?[15]

Regardless of the motives, baroque eloquence should not be condemned in mass,[16] at least because "all sorts make a world." Examining published sermons

---

[12]Cf., for example, McSorley.

[13]Cf., for example, Arturo del Hoyo cc–cci; Father Isla, *Fray Gerundio de Campazas* (Madrid: Espasa-Calpe, S. A., 1960), for example, 1: 39–60. Concerning the publicity presenting Spain as the source of bad taste in rival European countries, Father Isla reported false collections of Spanish sermons published in countries like Holland, advertised with titles like *Dialectical eloquence from the European savages* (Isla 1:47). Not even the Italian theorists of ingenuity were free from anti-Spanish biases. Pallavicino (*Trattato* Chapter 4, p. 34) and Tesauro (*Cannocchiale* Chapter 9, pp. 501–540) singled out the Spaniards as the main practitioners and theorists of the vices of wit. However, some Portuguese have stayed away from blaming Spain for witty oratory. They rather claim that witty eloquence was a Portuguese accomplishment. Conceptist preaching is indeed the "*método português de pregar.*" (Cf., for example, Margarida Vieira Mendes 35). These Portuguese probably take pride in their generation of baroque preachers, which includes figures such as Fr. António Vieira.

[14]Cf., for example, Arturo del Hoyo cc–cci; Menéndez Pelayo 581–585.

[15]Concerning biases or summary judgments from other European countries against Spain, Cf., for example, Isla 1:57; Gambra 177–178; G. Marañon, "La literatura científica en los siglos XVI y XVII," *Historia General de las Literaturas Hispánicas*, (Barcelona: Editorial Vergara, 1953) 933–966; José Mª López Piñero, *La ciencia en la historia hispánica*, (Barcelona: Salvat Editores, S. A., 1982); Gregory Cerio, "The Black Legend: Were the Spaniards That Cruel?" *Newsweek*, (Special Issue, Fall/Winter 1991).

[16]If the motives behind a summary contempt are truly philosophical because of the new thought's incompatibility with seventeenth-century theories of wit, baroque eloquence should not be seen as a failure on the grounds that it is associated with these theories. On the one hand, the oratory of any period is not necessarily the complete result of a fashionable theory (more often, and particularly in the case of baroque theories of wit, the rhetorical system rather comes as a result of inquiring into some features of the current fashions of oratory: Sarbiewski, Pellegrini, Gracián, Pallavicino, and Tesauro were not proposing a new system

from the late sixteenth to the late seventeenth centuries, Miguel Herrero García found that in the "golden age" of Spanish eloquence there were preachers like Baltasar Arias whose evangelical simplicity could be "almost boring."[17] Herrero García also found that by the end of the seventeenth century—the "age of decadence"—he could nevertheless identify astounding preachers like Manuel de Guerra:

> To speak of Fr. Manuel de Guerra and evaluate his accomplishments in style, I do not find expressive words, because all of them seem to me worn and faded...Let's suppose that one Gracián, enhanced a third and a fifth, has risen to the pulpit, and we may start to have an idea of this magnificent tongue given to the sacred platform. The holy has never been treated in a holier way, and the highest evangelical mysteries with greater sublimity and decorum. His style is majestical, marmoreal, chiselled (rather than cutting), sharp, often animated with flashes of

---

of oratory, but trying to understand some features of speech—wit—which were particularly emphasized in the eloquence of their times.) Indeed, practices of oratory can evolve very independently of the contemporary rhetorical systems. On the other hand, baroque theories of wit aimed at explaining subjects of broader scope than baroque eloquence, and even broader than eloquence. In the case of Gracián, the theories explain an act of understanding. In this sense, the association of theories of ingenuity with seventeenth century oratory could only be generic, and could not apply directly to the species. And if it applied directly and completely to the species—if this application were possible—baroque theories of wit are not enough of a reason to regard the correlative oratory as doomed to failure. Considering my analysis of baroque theories of ingenuity—particularly Gracián's—I think that some critics may legitimately question whether these theories are insufficient, (granted these theories' innovative concern for giving method to conceptual invention, it might be said that they nevertheless are still in their childhood and that they are still in need much of development) uneven in their treatment of rhetorical issues (these theories might be accused of overemphasizing and even reducing all reason to wit), and even wrong in their answers to the problems they address (for example, some people may disagree with Baltasar Gracián's philosophical assumptions, such as his scholastic realism). But I believe that critics cannot hastily blame these theories—and hence the correlative eloquence—for being inherently irrational, immoral, or in bad taste, without having at least recognized that such theories give plausible and detailed answers to the function of wit in rational discourse.

[17]Miguel Herrero García, "La literatura religiosa," *Historia General de las Literaturas Hispánicas*, ed., Guillermo Díaz-Plaja (Barcelona: Ed. Vergara, 1953) 3:20.

fantasy, and at every step full of discretion and wit. Undoubtedly each page is a work of goldsmithery. There is not a single line in Manuel de Guerra which is not a gem as much of ingenuity as of patience...Fr. Manuel de Guerra y Ribera has been one of the most gifted natures among all whose channel of expression has been the Spanish language.[18]

Stressing the strong diversity of sermons during the reign of Philip III,[19] Hilary Dansey Smith says:

Again and again one becomes aware of the different currents which flow together in the formation of each preacher, if not each sermon, and which all demand to be followed back to their source. These include the Pauline and patristic tradition of preaching to which sermons in the Spanish Golden Age belong, regardless of more ephemeral fashions; the special character and traditions of each of the major preaching orders; the movement of spiritual renewal...orientated to different aspects of the Christian life...a legacy of wisdom, *sententiae* and *exempla*, which preaching has received and holds in trust from the medieval micellanies. Printed sermon literature in the Spanish Golden Age ...proposes, as a defining principle, to be *Para Todos* [for every kind of person]...

The sermons represent a vast repository of ideas, scriptural glosses, social observations, art theory, humanistic erudition, and *conceptos*...[20]

Opposing the Decadence theory which throws all Spanish baroque sermons into the same basket,[21] Smith explains:

---

[18]Herrero García 26.

[19]Philip III reigned during the peak of the Spanish Golden Age (1598–1621), particularly the times when the most famous writers of Spanish baroque literature were creating their works (for example, Cervantes), and when very famous baroque preachers delivered their sermons, (for example, the Trinitarian Fray Hortensio Paravicino).

[20]Hilary Dansey Smith, *Preaching in the Spanish Golden Age* (Oxford University Prress, 1978) 158.

[21]Another example of a study opposing clichés in religious oratory is John O'Malley's survey of the sermons preached at the Papal Court from 1450 to 1521. Contradicting Erasmus's indictment of religious oratory for being reduced to humanistic fashions, and his yearn for evangelical contents in the sermons then listened to by the popes, Malley's identifies

I feel it is more accurate to consider coincidences of style and taste rather than conscious emulation or "contamination"...[22]

Smith in fact resists advancing to a summary judgment of Spanish preaching:

An initial survey of so vast an area as preaching in Spain, even within the limiting framework of a single reign and a handful of preachers, must of necessity be inconclusive.[23]

Perhaps, the belief describing baroque oratory, and especially Spanish preaching, as decadent, corrupt, irrational, and in bad taste, might deserve Father Isla's reply to an eighteenth century "enlightened" critic of all Spanish culture:

Thus, with the greatest humility, it is begged Your Most Reverend, that next time you do not mess with what you do not understand; that you do better justice (since you deny love) to the Spanish nation; that when you intend to correct abuses, you speak with less universality...and in conclusion, that you do not forget this little Spanish adage: "People who live in glass houses should not throw stones."[24]

The Pretense of Wit

And yet, although pharisaic, summary, and biased judgments are what deserve to be snubbed, great dissatisfaction was nevertheless felt by many people who, enthusiastically immersed themselves in the very fashions of baroque eloquence, still found in such fashions something smelly, if not rotten.

---

a great variety of orations serving the most diverse evangelical purposes, and accordingly grounded in the most different ways on the Sacred Scriptures. See John W. O'Malley, *Praise and Blame in Renaissance Rome*, (Durham, North Carolina: Duke University Press, 1979).

[22]Smith 159.

[23]Smith 158.

[24]Isla 1:57. *El Criticón* II, Crisi 11, is a complete meditation on the cited proverb.

Father Isla himself has been one of the greatest critics of baroque oratory. His bitter scolding makes him resemble the self-righteous censors who dissociated themselves from every baroque fashion. However, Isla very much appreciated good baroque oratory, and, among the models for imitation, he proposed some of the most eminent preachers of that era, for example, the Brazilian Apostle António Vieira.[25] Through the judicious Fr. Prudencio, Isla appraised Vieira:

> The novelty of issues, the ingenuity assisting the proofs, the exquisiteness of thoughts, the opportunity of places, the vividness of expression, the fluency of eloquence which rule over all Father António Vieira's sermons perhaps made him deserve the title, who many give to him, of Monster of Wits and Prince of Our Orators.[26]

Even so, Isla had to create his satire *Fr. Gerundio de Campazas* in order to denounce, through a negative exemplar (the character of Fr. Gerundio), all the abuses which had affected the eloquence of his own country—Spain—during the baroque age.[27] His novel is said to have been a "complete success"[28] in eliminating the vicious preaching fashions of the seventeenth century, and in making religious orators return to the evangelical simplicity of the Scriptures, in the eighteenth century.

Notwithstanding Isla's success, he was not the only critic who denounced baroque abuses from an inside position. Many authors preceeded him in this

---

[25] Vieira's accomplishments as an orator go beyond ordinary homiletics. He engaged in bitter political controversies concerning the destruction of Indian peoples and slavery in Brazil, and the Inquisition and the Jewish converts in Portugal. After being censored and silenced in his own country, the Jesuit appealed to the Pope who backed Vieira and suspended the Portuguese Inquisition from all activity. Cf. McSorley 682.

[26] Isla 2:189–190.

[27] See Isla 1:16: "[It is] the only aim of this work to eliminate, from the Spanish pulpit, the intolerable abuses which have been introduced in it, especially from a century ago till now..."

[28] Emiliano Diez–Echarri and José María Roca Franquesa , *Historia de la Literatura Española e Hispanoamericana,* (Madrid: Editorial Aguilar: 1979) 718.

task, to name a few: Pellegrini, Pallavicino, Tesauro, and, yes, Gracián. The theorists of ingenuity were not unaware of the many dangers of applying wit to eloquence. In fact, their theoretical works respond to the need to regulate the then fashionably extensive use of wit in preaching.

In 1623, strongly alarmed, Superior General Muzio Vitelleschi denounced a fashion of preaching among the Jesuits:

> I have been recently informed that there are some [preachers] who rise to the pulpit to make display of their language and ingenuity, and that their sermons are intended to this purpose, and not to move the wills of people to abhor and flee from the vices...[29]

In 1631, Father Vitelleschi deplored again that "all is wasted on witty concepts, and not a few of them very extravagant".[30]

Echoing Vitelleschi's alarm, Matteo Pellegrini opened his treatise *Acutezze* by identifying the abuse of wit as the worst and most extensive malady then suffered by eloquence. He particularly lamented ten very frequent and pervasive vices of wit: 1) *frigid wit* takes place when a witty hyperbole is so out of proportion that it leaves the audience cold since the subtlety does not make any sense; 2) *farfetched wit* consists in too distant comparisons which deprive subtleties of any legitimate linkage between the extremes; 3) *childish wit* reduces a subtlety to mere wordplay; 4) *empty wit* lacks content since the subtlety is unable to express anything, or the subtlety does not make any point at all related to the speech; 5) *tasteless wit* does not require from the audience any effort of discovery since the middle term is easily found, and the point made and its expression is well known; 6) *inept wit* mistakenly renders subtleties by means of wrong associations and misapplication of the circumstances; 7) *silly wit* surrenders an orator to the lust of expressing a subtlety regardless of whether it is contrary to the true ends of the speech; 8) *wicked wit* stirs up malicious

---

[29]P. Vitelleschi, "Letter to the Provincial of Aragon, June 9, 1623." Quoted by E. Correa Calderón, *Baltasar Gracián. Su vida y su obra*, (Madrid: Ed. Gredos, 1961) 51.

[30]Quoted by Arturo del Hoyo cxiii.

thoughts; 9) *dishonorable wit* revolves on the obscene; and 10) *buffoonesque wit* turns the orator into a clown since a) his subtlety is ill-timed (*sluggish wit*), b) he establishes relationships contrary to reason (*superstitious wit*), c) his speech only aims at the boastful display of acuities (*boastful wit*), d) he often supposes grounds to distrust other people (*suspicious wit*), and e) his speech contains abuses of jests and jokes (*foolish wit*).[31]

Even though more briefly than Pellegrini, Tesauro and Pallavicino sternly warned orators against the epidemic abuse of ingenuity. Grounded on Aristotle,[32] Tesauro banned *improper, ridiculous, swollen,* and *farfetched* forms of wit.[33] More systematically, Pallavicino reduced wrong concepts to three major types: 1) sometimes a true but simple subject-matter is falsely presented as startling, new, or wondrous by means of a needless and bombastic structure of correspondence; 2) at other times what the structure of correspondence highlights truly is revealed as wondrous but it is grounded on false subject-matter; 3) finally, the concept can be falsely apprehended if a fallacious structure of correspondence is used—that is, one which cannot be reduced to a perfect syllogism.[34] However, Pallavicino did not limit his strictures to false concepts only. He also condemned some forms of true concepts if they are expressed through hyperboles or antitheses which are particularly unbecoming in the sciences.[35]

Although in 1575 Fr Luis de Granada had already warned against the abuse of wit,[36] and although many critics continued to decry this fashion, the malady

---

[31]See *Acutezze*, Chapter 11. Pellegrini's ten types of vicious wit are: *fredde, stiracchiate, fanciuilesche, vuote, insipide, inette, stolte, niquitose, sfacciate,* and *buffonesche*, which in its turn is divided into *morosum, superstitiosum, suspiciosum, gloriosum,* and *stultum.*

[32]See *Rhetoric* 3, Chapter 3.

[33]See *Cannocchiale* Chapter VII, 273–274.

[34]See *Trattato dello Stile* Chapter 17.

[35]See *Trattato dello Stile* chapters 18 and 19, which refer to *esagerazione marauiliosa* and to *contrapposti*.

[36]See, for example, *Los seis libros de la Rhetorica Eclesiástica* V, iii, 9.

was perceived as getting worse among preachers throughout and beyond the seventeenth century. In fact, in 1770, Josef Climent reedited Granada's *Ecclesiastical Rhetoric* hoping that its sound doctrines might help to fight the still common fashion among theologians and preachers of replacing the Scriptures and the Church Fathers with formulas to display ingenuity.[37] In 1758, Father José Francisco de Isla certainly regarded the misuse of wit as very frequent and extensive. In his novel *Fray Gerundio de Campazas*, he comprehensively satirized some bad practices preferred by Spanish orators. Russell P. Sebold thus sampled Isla's relation of this diseased oratory, and associated it with the most controversial Spanish preacher of the baroque age:

> Exaggerated to the point of insanity, the Gerundian sermon has remote stylistic precedents...the style of Fr. Hortensio Paravicino y Arteaga (Trinitarian and Royal Preacher, 1580–1633) for the first time offered all the features which later would be characteristic of all *culteranist-conceptist* preaching: surprising dogmatic doubts purposely schemed to gain the audience's interest, but later resolved on ingenious but superficial theological arguments; Gracianesque wit turned into pure wordplay and puns; mythological epithets to refer to biblical characters; metaphors, allegories, paradoxes, antitheses, hyperbaton, and parallelisms whose grammatical and significant relationships are increasingly fading; a metrical style of octosyllables and other feet, which make the titles of sermons be very close to turning into rhythmical titles of comedies, for example, *A muertos y a idos ya no hay amigos*;[38] and, finally, unending references to the Writ, the Church Fathers' works, and to profane books to ground the sermon's arguments, or emphasize its occasion, such as a concrete baptism or the taking of vows of a nun, all which later was reduced to a ritual display of skills concerning the "review of the circumstances" external to any sermon, that is, to find in old and revered texts as if there were there a prophetic

---

[37]See "Don Josef Climent, por la gracia de Dios, y de la Santa Sede Apostolica Obispo de Barcelona, del Consejo de Su Magestad, &c. Al Clero Secular, y Regular de mi Diocesis, salud, y bendición de nuestro Señor Jesucristo," Fray Luis de Granada, *Los seis libros de la rhetórica eclesiástica* (Barcelona: 12 de mayo de 1770) v.

[38]A literal translation could be:
For the dead and the gone,
the count of friends is none.
The proverb in English is: "Once dead and buried, nerry a friend."

sign predicting the date of the sermon to be preached, the parish church where it would be delivered, and the specific parishioners who would be listening the sermon.[39]

Isla's satire not only ridicules the Spanish orators who turned Gracián's theories of ingenuity into a caricature. The satire also magnifies the contempt many rhetoricians had during the whole baroque age for bad wit and the unrestrained search for novelties: these vices polluted the entire realm of eloquence. For example, erudition ceased to be solid grounds for judgment and became a pure display of exotic and pointless learning.[40] A pretense of ingenuity promoted a profuse display of language and rational skills around the most inane piece of information, thus making words skeletons, thoughts soulless, and all senseless.[41] The pure display of ingenuity revealed that the preacher vainly sought to establish his own reputation as subtle instead of proclaiming the Gospel.[42] Finally, the public participated in this corruption of eloquence by

---

[39]Russell P. Sebold, "Introducción y notas," José Francisco de Isla, *Fray Gerundio de Campazas* 1:xlvi–xlvii.

[40]For example, Fray Gerundio preached Christian penance on the grounds of Aztec mythology and bloody sacrifices. See Isla 2:279–298. On vicious erudition, Cf., for example, António Vieira, *Sermão da Sexagésima* V–VII; Cf., also, "Don Josef Climent, por la gracia de Dios, y de la Santa Sede Apostólica Obispo de Barcelona, del Consejo de su Magestad, &c. Al Clero Secular, y Regular de mi Diocesis, salud, y bendicion en nuestro Señor Jesucristo," Fray Luis de Granada *Los Seis Libros de la Rhetórica Eclesiástica* (Barcelona: 12 de mayo de 1770), xv: Bishop Josef Climent denounced the use of mythological florilegia, emblems, and anthologies of symbols as preaching aids which had replaced the true erudition which preachers needed, that is, reading the Church Fathers and the Scriptures.

[41]See, for example, Fray Gerundio's deranged sermon at Campazas, Isla 3:67–88. On empty formalisms, Cf., for example, António Vieira *Sermão da Sexagésima* V, VII, and IX. The corrupted use of wit ignores that Gracián understood the structures of correspondences not as an end in itself, but as a means to screen a true object of understanding and thus squeeze the concept. See, for example, *Agudeza* "Al Lector", and Discourse 63.

[42]Concerning the corruption of the ministry of the preacher, see, for example, Isla 2:40–56; Vieira's *Sermão da Sexagésima*; and D. Gregorio Mayáns i Siscár, "Dedicatoria" and

considering preaching to be a source of novel entertainment and startling experiences, as if the pulpit were the stage of comedies or a hall of parties.[43] Gracián himself summarized the problem:

> The same happened in the classroom as in the pulpit, with great diversity...[In a short time, Critilo and Andrenio had] identified twelve different fashions of speaking. [The orators] abandoned the substantive study of the Sacred Text, and preferred cold allegories, tired metaphors, making the saints eagles and suns, the virtues vessels, and keeping the audience entertained for a whole hour, thinking about a bird or a flower. They abandoned this and [then] turned to petite descriptions and delicate pictures. [Next,] the humanities were strongly in fashion, mixing the sacred and the profane, and other orators started their sermons with a quote from Seneca, as if there were not Saint Paul; either with a pattern or without it, with bound or free structure the speech; the text either incorporating the references or placing them as footnotes; sometimes wasting all on little phrases and little modes of expression, itching the ears of four impertinent freshmen; abandoning the solid and substantive doctrine, Golden Mouth's true method of preaching, and the great prelate of Milan's sweet ambrosia and profitable nectar.[44]

"Diálogo Primero," *El Orador Christiano ideado en tres diálogos*, 2nd. ed. (Valencia: Joseph I Thomas de Orga, 1776) (first published in 1773). Christian rhetoricians find sacrilegious the use of the pulpit for the pursue of worldly fame. Instead of a famous leader, the preacher should be a humble servant; instead of displaying his own knowledge and genius, the preacher should be a vehicle of God's wisdom; instead of gaining the audience's good will, the preacher should gain the audience's salvation; instead of aiming at the applause of the public, the preacher should aim at the glory of the Lord. See Fr. Luis de Granada's *Rhetorica Eclesiastica*, I, iii–viii and VI, xi and xiv.

[43]See, for example, Isla 4: 227–247; Correa Calderón, *Baltasar Gracián* 50, who quotes Bartolomé Jiménez Patón, *La Eloquencia Española en Arte* (Toledo 1604), Book 4, Chapter 2; Vieira, *Sermão da Sexagésima*, III.

[44]*El Criticón* III, Crisi 10: "Lo mismo que en la cátedra sucedía en el púlpito con notable variedad...notaron una docena de varios modos de orar. Dejaron la substancial ponderación del sagrado texto y dieron en alegorías frías, metáforas cansadas, haciendo soles y águilas los santos, naves las virtudes, teniendo toda una hora ocupado el auditorio, pensando en una ave o una flor. Dejaron esto y dieron en descripciones y pinturillas. Llegó a estar muy valida la humanidad, mezclando lo sagrado con lo profano, y comenzaba el otro afectado su sermón por un lugar de Séneca, como si no hubiera San Pablo; ya con trazas, ya sin ellas, ya discursos atados, ya desatados, ya uniendo, ya postillando, ya echándolo todo en frasecillas y modillos

The most pathetic effect perceived on the use of mock wit in preaching was that the pulpit became fruitless. Critics believed moral decadence was extensively spread in their nations. This decadence was a paradox since the number of preachers had increased in the century. The critics solved the paradox by saying that the pulpit was ineffective because preachers did not spread the all powerful Word of God, but their whims of wit.[45] Even the most acclaimed preacher of the age, António Vieira, now and then was charged with putting his own inventions before the solid doctrine of Saint John Chrysostom, Saint Augustine, and Saint Thomas Aquinas.[46] From Saint Paul, critics[47] often quoted the *Second Epistle to Timothy* (4:3–4) as fittingly applying to current religious oratory:

> For there will come a time when they will not endure the sound doctrine; but having itching ears, will heap up to themselves teachers according to their own lusts, and they will turn away their hearings from the truth, and turn aside rather to fables.

Three years after having published *Agudeza*'s second edition, Gracián recognized that his treatise had turned into something "more subtle than

---

de decir, rascando la picazón de las orejas de cuatro impertinencillos bachilleres, dejando la sólida y substancial doctrina y aquel verdadero modo de predicar del Boca de Oro y de la ambrosía dulcísima y del néctar provechoso del gran prelado de Milán." Cf., with the history of baroque eloquence as related by Marc Fumaroli's *L'Age de L'Eloquence*.

[45]See, for example, António Vieira, *Sermão da Sexagésima*, 1655 (ed. Margarida Vieira Mendes); D. Gregorio Mayáns i Siscár, *El Orador Christiano ideado en tres dialogos* 2nd. ed. (Valencia, 1786, first edited in 1733).

[46]See for example, Sister Juana Inés de la Cruz, *Carta Atenagórica* 1692, which denounces António Vieira's *Sermão do Mandato*.

[47]See, for example, Tesauro's *Cannocchiale* Chapter 9: 503; António Vieira, *Sermão da Sexagésima* IX; D. Gregorio Mayáns i Siscár, *El Orador Christiano*, Diálogo Primero 9; Isla 2:303. Although Tesauro recognized that the Pauline text was often applied to baroque oratory, he disagreed in finding that witty preachers taught fables: they rather taught truths by means of fables, following the Scriptural tradition of revealing the Divine through symbols and parables.

profitable."[48]

A Clinical History

In 1654, Emanuele Tesauro wrote about Italian eloquence:

> ...in the last century, which was the first one of very famous preachers, Cornelio
> Muffo, otherwise known as Bitonto, conceived a new style of sacred speech, by
> means of a swift torrent of eloquence more copious than elaborate, mixed with
> infinite arguments, both lofty and humble, with doctrine more often than subtly
> considered, with more quotations from the Writ than from its commentators, with
> more literal and plain interpretations than clever and difficult, and if it made resource
> of symbols and figures, which the Old and New Testament are full of, their use was
> prudent and solid, sounder than witty and unexpected; and all these things with such
> an affluence, and with so many memorized materials, that from a single sermon
> could be made ten, not ending the preaching until the proposed subject-matter has
> been exhausted completely.[49]

The historian Miguel Herrero García[50] refers to similar developments in
Spain during the sixteenth century. This is the age of the great and holy
reformers, such as St John of Avila, St Thomas of Villanueva, St Peter of

---

[48]*El Criticón* I, "A quien leyere": "...más sutil que provechosa..."

[49]*Cannocchiale* Chapter IX, 502: "...nel Secolo pasato, che fù il primo de' famosissimi
Predicatori: formò Cornelio Muffo, detto il Bitonto, vn nouello stile di Oration sacra, per
modo di vn rapidissimo torrente di eloquenza più copiosa ch' elaborata: mista di Argomenti
infiniti, alti, e bassi; di Dottrine frequentemente più che sottilmente toccate; di citationi più
de Scrittura, che di Scritturali; d' interpretationi letterali e piane, più che argute e scabrose:
& se pur si seruia di Simboli, e Figure, delle quali è piena la vecchia e nuoua Legge, le
applicationi eran sauie & sode, più tosto che acute & inopinate: & queste cose con tanta
affluenza, e tanta opera di memoria; che di vna Predica sola sene sarian fate diece: non
finendo di predicare, finche non hauesse finito di euacuare tutta la proposta materia."

[50]See Miguel Herrero García 3: 18–26. I interweave Herrero's history of Spanish baroque
preaching with Tesauro's account of Italy's, because of the parallelisms which one and the
other observe in their narratives.

Alcántara, and St Francis Borgia. Their eloquence is spontaneous, says Herrero, and flows like a torrent, not constructed by art, but driven by the richness of the divine Word. This "heroic age" of oratory culminates with Fr Luis de Granada: the Spanish Cicero, who balanced the conscious application of rhetoric and the sacred character of his ministry. Granada thus opened the "golden age" of Spanish preaching, which included figures such as Fr Diego Murillo, Fr Basilio Ponce de León, Fr Diego de Arce, and Fr Pedro de Valderrama.[51]

Artistic eloquence also flourished in Italy in that time. Tesauro praised Panigarola, who started preaching with the evangelical force of his teacher Cornelio Muffo, but also with an increasing assistance of substantive and rhetorical studies.

> Since he united his teacher's exquisite doctrine...with a refined expertise in rhetoric...and moreover, the grace and beauty...the propriety, ease, natural eloquence, and sweetness of tongue, he produced not a less toilsome preaching than his teacher, but a more learned, more ordered, and smooth.[52]

In Italy, said Tesauro, preachers imitated Panigarola's serious and rich speech well into the seventeenth century. However, the elaborate contents and form of sermons could become tiresome to less sophisticated audiences. Thus, explained Tesauro, preachers tried to gain the audience's attention and prevent tediousness by introducing dramatic effects and other startling tricks into their orations.

> They started to act the clown on the sacred pulpits, with mimic performances...and vulgar sayings, renovating the same corruption deplored by Dante in his century that

---

[51] See Miguel Herrero García 3: 18–23.

[52] *Cannocchiale* Chapter 9: 502: "Peroche, hauendo congiunta vn' esquisita Dottrina de gran Maestro...con vn' esquisita peritia delle Retoriche...& sopra totto, la gratia & leggiadria...la auuenenza, la facilità, la natural facondia, & la dolcezza della lingua; formò le sue Prediche non men faticose, ma più culte, più ordinate, & soaui, che il suo Maestro."

was prolific of every vice.[53]

But in Spain, noticed Tesauro, preachers were more prudent and becoming, since what they introduced into difficult speeches was wit to startle audiences. Thus they appropriately prevented tediousness, and succeeded because Spaniards were "naturally clever, and very perspicacious in scholastic doctrine."[54]

Herrero García says that this change to baroque preaching was quite controversial in the Spanish nations. From 1612 to 1633, the age of Fr. Hortensio Paravicino, the new fashion found strong opponents, and caused heated debates among theologians and critics. Even so, this fashion finally made its way and became the established form of preaching. This triumph, from 1633–1664, allowed orators to produce the best sermons of the baroque age. As suggested by Herrero García, these sermons could stress different features according to current *culteranist* or *conceptist* trends. Some preachers appealed to the imagination, with flashes of light, colorful surprises, and sensuous invention, as did the dazzling Paravicino and the Peruvian Juan Caballero de Cabrera. Others astonished the understanding by properly using wit, with its novel and subtle concepts, and the bold strikes of ingenuity, as did the keen Manuel de Nájera and the limpid Gonzalo de Arriaga. In any case, the baroque fashions could increase the complexity of sermons and still keep the audience attentive to a doctrine which was both entertaining and sound. According to Herrero García, everybody in different degrees enjoyed the method by which orators would "lengthen the way leading to the truth, putting it far away, or hiding it," because listeners found pleasure in surmounting many obstacles to

---

[53]*Cannocchiale* Chapter 9: 502: "...incominciarono à buffoneggiar sopra i Pulpiti sacri, con mimiche rappresentationi...& motti scurrili, rinouando la medesima corrottela deplorata dal Dante nel suo secolo di tutti i vitii fecondo."

[54]*Cannocchiale* Chapter 9: 502: "...naturalmente arguti; & nelle Scolastiche Dottrine perspicacissimi..."

learn this truth.[55]

Herrero often praises baroque oratory for renovating both the form of preaching and the range of understanding of Christian doctrine.[56] However, suggests Herrero, a renewal always grounded on the pursuit of novelties through wit had its limits. In order to be newer and more astonishing, witticisms had to beat former ones with more and more extreme correlations till the lines of correspondence became farfetched.[57] Moreover, he also suggests, the sacred platform turned extremely decadent when preachers increasingly reused expressions with the hopes of exhausting their possibilities of meaning. During the reign of Charles II the Bewitched (1665–1700), preaching often consisted in merely revolving over clichés or trying to revive carcasses by means of vulgarities disguised as wit.[58]

As a witness of these developments, Tesauro noticed that, since the early seventeenth century, the recycling of witticisms turned fashionable among the preachers who wanted to enliven dense sermons with the charm of sallies.[59] Collections of "preaching concepts" were published particularly in Spain, facilitating the finding of materials for preachers' subtleties.[60] These florilegia let religious orators save much of the time which they formerly invested in the Holy Writ.[61] They had to apply simply their ingenuity to find connections

---

[55]Herrero García 24–25.

[56]See Herrero García 23–26.

[57]See Herrero García 26.

[58]See Herrero García 25–26.

[59]See *Cannocchiale* Chapter 9: 502.

[60]See *Cannocchiale* Chapter 9: 538.

[61]See *Cannocchiale* Chapter 9: 503–504. Tesauro observed that even great preachers, such as Montolmo, found convenient replacing the direct study of the Holy Writ for the easier consultation of digests and anthologies. However, Josef Climent disagreed that the witty study of florilegia really saved time for preachers, concerning the composition of sermons. Josef Climent noted that a witty preacher could easily invest two months to prepare and memorize his sermon since it lacked the evangelical simplicity and the clear wisdom directly

between these digested materials and thus build up their sermons.[62] The problem was that they turned these preaching aids into their whole arsenal of Christian doctrine, philosophy, and sciences. The Scriptural and scholastic studies were left to theologians, whereas orators felt they could do well by just expanding a metaphor from an anthology to its exhaustion, depending on the persuasive end. For, according to Tesauro, the ease of this method led preachers to turn wit from the seasoning of speeches to the main and unique dish for the audience.[63] As quoted before, Gracián confirmed Tesauro's narrative:

> [The orators] abandoned the substantive study of the Sacred Text, and preferred...keeping the audience entertained for a whole hour, thinking about a bird or a flower.[64]

Florilegia and the methods of ingenuity combined to misquote the Writ. Vieira observed that error could resemble Christian doctrine by using Scriptural quotations out of their complex context.[65] Indeed, this was the greatest danger of florilegia, which took quotations out of the original text, and placed them

---

learned from the Scriptures. See "Don Josef Climent, por la gracia de Dios..." Fray Luis de Granada *Los seis libros de la rhetórica eclesiástica* (Barcelona: 12 de mayo de 1770), vi. In any case, these florilegia should not be regarded as a seventeenth century fashion. Preachers have used them in many centuries with different success, varieties, and purposes, till today. In fact, our modern encyclopedias resemble the florilegia in their function of digesting subject-matters and sorting them under different headings. Encyclopedias are certainly very resourceful works of reference; yet they can not replace a direct and thorough study of a specific subject. That was the problem in the baroque use of florilegia; it is also a risk in every age's use of reference books.

[62]See *Cannocchiale* Chapter 9: 538–540.

[63]Cf. *Cannocchiale* Chapter 9: 503.

[64]*El Criticón* III, Crisi 10: "Dejaron la substancial ponderación del sagrado texto y dieron en...teniendo toda una hora ocupado al auditiorio, pensando en una ave o una flor".

[65]Vieira illustrated his point with Satan misquoting the Writ to tempt Jesus, and with the false witnesses who missapplied Jesus's teachings when they accused him before the Sanhedrin. See António Vieira, *Sermão da Sexagésima*, IX.

under abstract headings. The preacher could later restructure the abstract data as he wished in speeches, assisted by methods of ingenuity—the structures of correspondence—but not assisted by methods of judgment. In fact, Matteo Pellegrini acknowledged that methods like his *Fonti* could prompt fluent and astounding speech without true learning from thorough studies.[66] A speaker could expand the most inane subject and astonish unsophisticated audiences if he linked this subject to the parts, the species, the antecedents, the concomitants, the subsequents, etc., as suggested by his "mind's wit" and the simplified—not rarely pointless and exotic[67]—information contained in florilegia. Ingenuity degenerated from a strenuous art of discovery to a lazy whim of fancy.

However, as Mayáns i Siscár indicated, an orator could startle audiences by cleverly misusing, not only wit, but any artistic method, if the pretense of systematically expounding a subject is the only purpose in mind. Mayáns complained that, regardless of the orator's knowledge of a subject, not only the methods of ingenuity, but also every rule from the liberal arts could be shrewdly misused to contribute to an appearance of scholarship.[68] Isla illustrated this deceptive use of methods for pretense in his *Fray Gerundio*, and he included not only wit, but also grammar,[69] philology,[70] scholastics,[71] poetics,[72] rhetoric,[73] eru-

---

[66]Pellegrini confessed that his *Fonti* were requested by a patron who needed a method to speak fluently without having to undergo the pain of studying. See *I Fonti Dell' Ingegno* "L' Avtore A' Lettori:" 10.

[67]See, for example, Isla 2: 220–237.

[68]See, for example, Mayáns I Siscár, *El Orador Christiano ideado en tres diálogos* "Diálogo Primero," 12–14.

[69]See, for example, Isla 1: 97–172.

[70]See, for example, Isla 3: 170–194.

[71]See, for example, Isla 2: 9–41.

[72]See, for example, Isla 2: 57–75.

[73]See, for example, Isla 3: 19–44, 108–127, 170–194; 4: 22–84, 136–168.

dition,[74] piety,[75] and even the rational and empirical criticisms[76] which were in fashion in Isla's times. In fact, his strongest satire is not against the pretense of wit[77] but against the pretense of historical criticism. He exposed the former with the most ridiculous sermons, but he denounced the latter with his whole novel, a pretense of meticulous and objective accumulation of facts to authenticate an insignificant and rather false event.[78] For no formalistic training, no sectarian allegiance can replace the integrity of Christian doctrine,[79] a subject-matter irreducible to pieces of knowledge or mere logical structures since it even transcends the richness of a way of life.[80]

Remedies to the Malady

The ills of wit were treated with correctives for ingenuity itself, for judgment, and for the character of the orator. These correctives implied the classical instruments of education: theory, imitation, and practice.

---

[74]See, for example, Isla 3: 146–169, 170–174; 4: 22–37, 193–226.

[75]See, for example, Isla 4: 169–191.

[76]See, for example, Isla 2: 57–179.

[77]A great extenuatory and paradox of Fray Gerundio's attack against wit, is that Isla's novel strongly and consciously relies on wit itself to achieve this critique.

[78]It is not through historical criticism but through wit that the reader can discover some truth, meaning, and relevance in Isla's narrative.

[79]I believe that there are many more subject-matters than Christian doctrine which are reduced to pieces of knowledge or logical structures without really achieving understanding.

[80]One of Isla's antidotes for intellectual sectarism and formalism was the training of orators through models, since models could more easily keep the integrity of eloquence. See, for example, Isla 2: 180–200. Moreover, Vieira clearly subsumed the imitation of great Christian orators into the imitation of exemplary sermons, since preaching and living the Word of God should not be separate models. See, for example, António Vieira, *Sermão da Sexagésima*, particularly, I, VII, IX, and X.

Empowering the Formulas

Many believed that orators abused wit because they did not know how to hold the reigns of their own ingenuity. They just let it go wild. A theoretical education could provide a remedy. Easy to use formulas should be facilitated. Orators should receive accessible answers about what wit and its proper use in eloquence are before they apply wit to their speeches.

Pellegrini believed that by learning to recognize the types of vicious wit, orators could also learn to avoid their use.[81] He also warned orators against the misuse of several kinds of good wit. A quick review of his many precepts reveals that he cautioned against farfetchedness in the linking of extremes (orators should rather compare close things), against cryptic subtleties (if cryptic, the subtlety should be explained),[82] against misapplication of the different valid witticisms to wrong persons, times, occasions, genres of discourse, subjects, etc., and, among other things, against the frequent use of wit, or even its moderate use if subtleties are jokes or mere wordplays. Although Pellegrini admitted some occasions in which the bold use of wit might be appropriate, even so his rules can be summarized to require moderation, clarity, and decorum.[83]

Pallavicino's listing of wrong types of subtleties reveals a view very similar to Pellegrini's: education can correct the ignorance leading to the misuse of wit. Moreover, in spite of his intellectualism, Pallavicino attached wit—like Pellegrini—strongly to stylistic questions.[84] He related its misuse to its faulty

---

[81]See *Acutezze* Chapter 11.

[82]Gracián reproved specific types of cryptic speech common in his social milieu, for example, the inside talk and false appearances of different circles at the Court. However, rather than solving these problems by restricting wit, the prudent listener—believed Gracián—should increase the heedful use of wit to make sense of what is going on around him, and thus prevent any harm conspired by the malicious courtiers. See, for example, *El Criticón* III, crises 4 and 5.

[83]See *Acutezze* Chapter XII.

[84]There is not any contradiction between Pallavicino's intellectualism and his finding of remedies to wit in style. Pallavicino believed that true style springs from true contents, and not from preconceived empty formats. See, for example, *Trattato dello Stile* Chapter VI.

placement in texts. For example, sententiae do not fit the sciences,[85] but some poetic allegories[86] and witty dialogues may facilitate the exposition of philosophical matters.[87] Even so, Pallavicino's remedies transcend the issue of defective wit and comprehend the most diverse questions concerning the misuse of style in sciences. His doctrine could be summarized by saying that he found neither forceful eloquence nor dry scholastic style, but discreet elegance to be the language appropriate for the sciences.[88]

Tesauro's *Cannocchiale* does not seem to join this effort of proposing restraint to wit. Rather his book appears to promote the swagger of ingenuity—a faculty which Tesauro unblushingly called "the Intellect's utmost effort."[89] Nevertheless, Tesauro's understanding of wit should be enough of a restraint since he reduced ingenuity to the symbolic power of the mind—to the creation of meaning.[90] Tesauro's nominalism regards ideas as pure meanings—as something produced and created by wit rather than discovered. An idea's value is pragmatic, not epistemological. Ideas are useful in so far as they enable people to think succesfully rather than to know truthfully.[91]

---

[85]See *Trattato dello Stile* Chapter 6.

[86]See *Trattato dello Stille* chapters 30 and 31, especially pp. 294–295. Pallavicino's discussion of poetic allegory for sciences is particularly interesting because, as he acknowledged, through it, he became aware of the distinction between poetic imagination—a lower form of poetry—, which produces literary texts and consists in rich imagery, and poetic judgment, which is assisted by strict wit and serves the sciences.

[87]See *Trattato dello Stile* chapters 32–38.

[88]See *Trattato dello Stile*, especially, chapters 4, and 20–29.

[89]*Cannocchiale* Chapter One, 1. "...vltimo sforzo dell' Intelletto..."

[90]Contrastingly, Gracián regarded symbolic subtleties as a small branch of wit. Moreover, Gracián never reduced symbols to the expression of pure meanings; they could properly refer to reality. See, for example, *Agudeza* Discourse 47.

[91]For Tesauro, and nominalism in general, the mind never closes the gap between concrete data and abstract meanings. Ideas are good in so far they let people to use things successfully, rather than to know them truthfully. The consequences of nominalism in thinking can be illustrated—according to George Sim Johnston—with the "Galileo Affair".

Consequently, the *Cannocchiale* restricted wit to symbolic activities, such as heraldic symbols, mottos, emblems, medals, coin inscriptions, and masquerades,[92] and estranged its use from rational or factual inquiries such as science and philosophy.[93] Although witty sermons could more powerfully symbolize Christian doctrine before popular audiences, only religious facts and strict scholastic reasoning properly lead one to know the doctrines embodied in theology.[94]

Apparently keeping alive Gracián's legacy, some eighteenth-century Spaniards did not deny an epistemic function to wit. Although in a brief chapter,[95] Gregorio Mayáns i Siscár discussed invention of thoughts as a prerequisite to rhetorical inference. Inferences cannot proceed if the ideas involved have not been previously discovered, apprehended, and defined, either by means of absolute apprehensions,[96] or by means of sayings or other witty

---

The "Geocentric Theory" was the preferred one—says Johnston—not because scholars expected it to be true, but because it made easier for them to describe what they seemingly saw concerning the movement of celestial bodies, while the "Heliocentric Theory"—not expected to be true either—did not help much because as a "name" or "symbol" did not make things easier to be thought of. See George Sim Johnston, *The Galileo Affair* (Scepter Publishers, 1994).

[92]See *Cannocchiale*, especially, chapters 13 to 19.

[93]Tesauro's doctrines should not be regarded as reducing wit to pure style. Wit produces—invents—symbols, which are not pure expression, but a blend of the signifier and what is signified: a meaning. Although meanings resist factual judgment due to their origin in fallacious urbane enthymemes, these meanings still produce understanding and pragmatic applications which poetically lead to rationally valid inferences. Wit indeed lets "truth beam as if through a veil." ("...il vero vi traspaia come per vn velo...") *Cannocchiale* Chapter Nine, 494.

[94]See, for example, *Cannocchiale* Chapter 9, 503.

[95]See "Libro Primero. De la invención rhetórica. Capítulo X. De la invención de los pensamientos retóricos," *Rhetorica de Don Gregorio Mayáns i Siscár* 2nd edition (Valencia: Josef i Thomas de Orga, 1786) (1st. edition: 1757).

[96]Here, it may be useful to recall Pallavicino's distinction between absolute and comparative apprehensions. The latter is the only kind which is witty and which rises from

methods.[97] Reviewing the circumstances—that is, Gracián's lines of correspondence[98]—was still a valid method of analyzing an issue, admitted bishop Josef Climent, who was a great reformer of the sacred platform in Catalunia.[99] Nevertheless, both Mayáns and Climent also believed that limiting wit was the means to avoid wrong and extravagant conceptualizations. For example, Mayáns banned true concepts if squeezed from false material, such as fables, allegories, and the like.[100] And Climent confined the method of reviewing circumstances to what is "*circa*," that is, "near" the issue, in order to avoid farfetchedness.[101]

With friends like these, wit did not need enemies such as the empiricists who only admitted close sensual resemblances between associated ideas, the rationalists who did not think about wit at all since valid ideas already existed in the mind, and the censorship officials, like Superior General Vitelleschi, who believed that the easiest way to correct the abuses of wit was to ban its practicioner from speaking: "...take him away from the ministry of preaching..."[102]

---

raw data to abstract knowledge. See *Trattato dello Stile* Chapter 7, 79–80. Mayáns i Siscár distinction is rather between pure concepts—ideas or words which lack a predicate—and sayings—sentences which provide a definition to the idea. Either kind implies an effort of discovery, and accordingly, either kind could be witty—new.

[97]For example, sententiae, adages, aphorisms, axioms, and popular sayings.

[98]See *Agudeza* Discourse 4.

[99]See "Don Josef Climent, por la gracia de Dios, y de la Santa Sede Apostólica Obispo de Barcelona, del Consejo de su Magestad, &c. Al Clero Secular, y Regular de mi Diocesis, salud y bendición en nuestro Señor Jesucristo," Fray Luis de Granada, *Los Seis Libros de la Rhetórica Eclesiástica* (Barcelona: 12 de mayo de 1770) xxiii.

[100]See *Rhetorica de Don Gregorio Mayáns i Siscár*, 2nd. ed. (Valencia: Josef i Thomas de Orga, 1786) (1st. ed: 1755), Chapter 10, 27.

[101]See "Don Josef Climent, por la gracia de Dios..." Fray Luis de Granada, *Los seis libros de la rhetórica eclesiástica* (Barcelona: 12 de mayo de 1770), xxiii.

[102]Father Muzio Vitelleschi, "Letter to the Provincial Father of Aragón, June 9, 1623," as quoted by Correa Calderón, *Baltasar Gracián*, 51. Father Isla and Gregorio Mayáns were

The case is that, by limiting wit to close correspondences, because of the fear of farfetchedness, the friends of wit revealed that they did not understand what wit is. Discovering close resemblances does not need strenuous ingenuity. Rather, wit is necessary in order to find subtle, small similarities or distinctions between extremely distant objects. Gracián clearly stated that wit consists in "a harmonious correlation between two or three cognizable *extremes*,"[103] for novel ideas tend to be wittier if squeezed from extreme correspondences: "when the correspondence is recondite... then, it is subtler since it demands more from the mind."[104]

Rather than losing precision by using "farfetched" subtleties, the orator gains it, since it is on the subtle distinctions and thin—difficult to perceive—similarities discovered from comparing extreme cases that wit reveals its sharp edge and leads discernment to its keenest limits. As Aristotle believed that bold wit provided wings to the highest philosophical flights,[105] in the same way Gracián regarded the swagger of ingenuity essential to reach the depths of prudence and the detail of casuistry.[106] An unembarrassed Gracián praised paradoxes as "monsters of truth,"[107] since from daring to ponder apparent impossibilities, the orator squeezes out plausible, new, and the most astonishing ideas.

We should not mistakenly infer that Gracián was an enemy of moderation and decorum concerning wit. But he did not see in true ingenuity any abuse:

---

among those supporting censorship as a means to stop the abuses of wit. See Isla 4: 211–226; Gregorio Mayáns i Siscár, *El Orador Christiano ideado en tres diálogos* 2nd. ed. (Valencia: Joseph i Thomas de Orga, 1786) (1st. ed: 1733) "Diálogo Primero."

[103]*Agudeza* Discourse 2: "...una armónica correlación entre dos o tres cognoscibles extremos..."

[104]*Agudeza* Discourse 4: "Cuando esta correspondencia está recóndita...es más sutil, cuanto más cuesta..."

[105]See *Rhetoric* III, 11.

[106]See, for example, *Oráculo* aphorisms 35, 182, 245, 250, 253, 269, and 283.

[107]*Agudeza* Discourse 23: "monstruos de la verdad".

reaching true discoveries is so difficult that we should expect that wit rarely presents them in speeches.[108] Thus the remedy to sick wit was to be found elsewhere. Learning more about good methods of wit was insufficient. If anything, the formulas were already too many. Formalism rather turned into another ailment of wit. What speakers urgently required was a spoonful of judgment: "Better a gram of good sense than a thousand pounds of subtlety."[109]

Empowering Judgment

As Father Isla understood it clearly, good judgment would not follow from learning additional empty formulas of thinking, whether they were from theories of wit, rhetoric, logic, mathematics, grammar, empirical criticism, etc.[110] Rather than just thinking well, orators needed to know their subject thoroughly. They needed to study, to experience, to observe the reality at hand. And even for thinking well, Gracián saw in substantive studies—in erudition—not just the necessary materials leading to judgment,[111] but also the stuff which creative thinking is made of, in order to be truly productive.[112] Giambattista Vico made a distinction between cleverness and true wit: the former rested on the tricks given by formulas, whereas the latter came from keen experience of the civic life.[113] Even Pallavicino, who was strongly interested in rules of composition, warned against learning pure forms of expression as if they warranted the force found in true style:

---

[108]See *Agudeza* Discourse 3. According to Gracián, true subtleties are "suns since they are rare and salt because they are pleasant." ("Soles por lo raro, sales por lo agradable...")

[109]*Oráculo* Aphorism 92: "Más vale un gramo de cordura que arrobas de sutileza".

[110]See José Francisco de Isla, *Fray Gerundio de Campazas*.

[111]See, for example, *El Discreto* realces 3 and 15; *Agudeza* Discourse 58; *El Criticón* II, Crisi 4: A wide acquaintance with the sciences provides rich and handy evidence which reason uses to judge cases.

[112]See, for example, *Agudeza* discourses 58–59.

[113]Cf., for example, Mooney 158.

He who writes of philosophy with pompous dreams calls himself Platonic; who embitters it with abstruse technicisms regards himself peripatetic; who writes either coordinatedly or loosely, but without wit, labels himself either Vergilian or Ciceronian; *who rides a hack without many embellisments*, instead of the Pegasean steed, glorifies himself of being another Ovid; the reckless and obscure sets up as an underling of Statius; and among the Italians, a melancholic and sometimes cadenced versifying is boasted of as Petrarchan.[114]

Concerning the revival of religious oratory, most critics agreed on the need to return to the basics: preachers should thoroughly read the Scriptures and the Church Fathers.[115] The zeal for assuring the essentials led some authors, like Mayáns,[116] to propose banning any attempt to interpret the Scriptures, unless the student had become well acquainted with every book of the Writ literally, because wits cannot pretend to interpret something if they are not informed of it yet.[117] More often, studying the Church Fathers was seen as an antidote against the chopping of Christian doctrine into pieces in florilegia without

---

[114]*Trattato dello Stile* Chapter 6, 77–78: "Chi di sogni pomposi compon la filosofia, si chiama Platonico: Chi di scabrosi termini la inasprisce, s' appella Peripatetico: Chi scriue ò legato ò sciolto senza acutezza, s'intitola Virgiliano ò Ciceroniano: *Chi caualca un ronzin non molto adorno* in cambio del destrier Pegaseo, gloriasi d' esser vn altro Ouidio: Il temerario ed oscuro spacciasi per sguace di Stazio: E frà gl' Italiani il verseggiar malincolico, e talor cadente si vanta di Petrarchesco."

[115]This remedy has been continuously prescribed in the Iberian Peninsula through the centuries. See, for example, Fr Luis de Granada, *Rhetórica Eclesiástica*, (1575) II, vi, 2; António Vieira, *Sermão da Sexagésima* (1655); Baltasar Gracián, *El Criticón* III (1657), Crisi 10; Gregorio Mayáns i Siscár, *El Orador Christiano ideado en tres diálogos* (1733) Diálogo Primero; Isla *Fray Gerundio de Campazas* (first edited in 1758) Sebold's edition: 2: 279-317; and "Don Josef Climent, por la gracia de Dios..." (1770).

[116]See Gregorio Mayáns i Siscár, *El Orador Christiano ideado en tres diálogos* 2nd ed. (Valencia: Joseph i Thomas de Orga, 1786; first edited in 1733) Dialogo Primero.

[117]Cf., for example, Fr Luis de Granada, *Rhetórica Eclesiástica* I, viii: "Preachers immediately want to pour doctrine in spite of not having been filled of it before."

coming to know it in its integrity.[118] The Church Fathers were the exemplars who embodied the most complex cases concerning the ministry of preaching. Their continuous imitation would lead the student to transcend the concrete model and assimilate it in its whole complexity as his own, according to the different new needs of the sacred platform:

> ...imitation consist in reading so often an Author that one finishes naturalizing in oneself the modes of thinking, propounding, ordering, proving, amplifying, refuting, speaking, and moving, without ever coming again to the same configuration of the model, but certainly to a similar appropriateness, fluency, smoothness, majesty, splendor, and grace...[119]

In short, by imitating the evangelical simplicity of the Church Fathers—it was believed—preachers could learn the sound doctrine to be preached and the method to accomplish this end, all in one. Other preaching resources may be occasional aids but never a substitute to the basics.

But, although the Church Fathers—not to mention the Scriptures—always enjoyed a strict authoritative standing both for their doctrine and the method, there were authors who pointed out some problems in using them indiscriminately for the training of preachers. For example, the Church Fathers' simplicity might mean only that they offered an *integral* model of preaching, but not that they necessarily spoke simply about simple matters. Vieira noticed that, in fact, many of the Church Fathers were closer to the richness of the culteranist-conceptist fashions of the seventeenth century than to the unvarnished preferences of the sixteenth century:

---

[118]See, for example, Isla 2: 180–200; "Don Josef Climent, por la gracia de Dios..."

[119]Gregorio Mayáns i Siscár, *El Orador Christiano ideado en tres diálogos*, 2nd. ed. (Valencia: Joseph i Thomas de Orga, 1786; first edited in 1733) Diálogo Primero. Cf., for example, with Fr Luis de Granada, *Rhetórica Eclesiástica*, Prólogo, also I, ii, and II, vii; also, an extensive and critical discussion about imitation as a method of learning can be found in Pallavicino's *Trattato dello Stile* chapters 11–15, where he established distinctions between plagiarizing, imitating, and emulating.

...concerning studiedness and embellishments, *culteranist* preachers defend themselves with the great Nazianzen, with Ambrose, with Chrysogonus, with Leo; concerning obscurity and hardness, with Clement of Alexandria, with Tertullian, with Basil of Seleucia, with Zeno of Verona, and others...[120]

Vieira also found St John Chrysostom, St Basil the Great, St Bernard, St Cyprian, St Gregory Nazianzen, St Gregory the Great, and St Augustine very complex because they often preached multiple and intertwined subjects at the same time, resembling more the fashions of the baroque age than those of the renaissance.[121] The problem was that a freshman of the sacred platform might not be able to distinguish the gold found in the Church Fathers from the fool's gold which was common in the seventeenth century, and thus take the latter practices as a valid form of preaching.[122] Moreover, the Church Fathers did not speak any modern language, but Greek or Latin. Their sensible imitation could not be accomplished without the necessary adaptations to the national language used in preaching; otherwise, believed Pallavicino, Latin or Greek could do violence to the syntax spoken.[123] This problem of language could be solved, thought several authors, if the models of eloquence were carefully selected from the great and pristine national orators, for example: Fr Luis de Granada, St John

---

[120]António Vieira, *Sermão da Sexagésima*, V: "...os cultos pelo polido, e estudado, se defendem com o grande Nazianzeno, com Ambrósio, com Crisólogo, Com Leão; e pelo escuro, e duro, com Clemente Alexandrino, com Tertuliano, com Basilio de Selêucia, com Zeno Veronense, e outros..."

[121]See António Vieira, *Sermão da Sexagésima*, VI. Vieira did not deny unity and fruits to the Church Father's sermons—rhetorical virtues which he saw as deficient in many baroque sermons. But, he noticed, the contemporary sermons and the ones from the Church Fathers shared the display of erudition and textual complexity.

[122]Cf. António Vieira, *Sermão da Sexagésima*, V, VI, and IX.

[123]See *Trattato dello Stile*, for example, Chapter V. Cf. Gregorio Mayáns i Siscár, *El Orador Christiano ideado en tres diálogos* 2nd. ed. (Valencia: Joseph i Thomas de Orga: 1786; first edited in 1733), Primer Diálogo.

of Avila, St Thomas of Villanueva, and Fr António Vieira.[124] In any case, as a critic, Vieira warned that there were students unable to naturalize the models imitated, and who would undiscriminatedly repeat as parrots the materials they learned, regardless of the situation.[125] These models did not contain in themselves explicit instructions concerning the specific new cases where the exemplars and the doctrine assimilated could be applied: here the preacher should rely on his own wit and judgment. Furthermore, if the imitable in models is what can be generalized to other cases, then the model itself cannot shed light on what is strictly particular—unique—in the new case. Let's remember what Fr Luis de Granada said of moral laws. It can be applied to any generalizable learning:

> ...the laws...do not contemplate the particulars, but the common and general...not what is experienced by particular persons, but what generally applies to what is common of everybody...[126]

This problem certainly summarizes the most heated controversy of the casuists, who debated about preferring the safest over the sufficiently safe opinion—who disputed about the weight of general moral principles as compared to the particulars unique to the case.

To some degree, Gracián proposed a solution to the problem of shedding light on very uniquely new cases, by means of being acquainted with many and diverse previous cases. As discussed before, Gracián's conglobate and mixed concepts would break down the new case in many thinny and tiny aspects, and

---

[124]See, for example, Isla 2: 181–200; Gregorio Mayáns i Siscár, *El Orador Christiano en tres diálogos*, 2nd edition (Valencia: Joseph i Thomas de Orga, 1786; first edited in 1733); see, also, "Don Josef Climent, por la gracia de Dios..."

[125]See António Vieira, *Sermão da Sexagésima*, VII.

[126]Fr Luis de Granada, *Guia de Pecadores* (1567) "Prólogo Galeato." If seen through the casuistic controversy concerning safe and safest opinions, Granada should be placed among those favoring the safest opinions, that is, the general rule rather than the exceptional but safe opinion.

then analyze each through lines of correspondence as established with parallel aspects of already known things. Next, wit would rebuild the case as at such point seen under the light of the multiple set of the established correlations. Thus the person would be able to discern, understand, and finally judge.[127] However, by definition, the extremely new cannot be learned from just thinking about previous data, but requires also observing the event directly.[128] Moreover, regardless of the person's acquaintance with previous cases or his direct observation of the event, he cannot just count on learning—even if assisted with methods of wit and other formulas—as a sufficient means properly to judge the case at hand. There are occasions when the urgency of judgment deprives him of sufficient learning: there is not enough time to accumulate it.[129] Nevertheless, he still needs to make a competent judgment. Thus where can the orator ground

---

[127]On conglobate concepts, see *Agudeza* Discurso 15; on mixed concepts see *Agudeza* Discurso 3; on complex concepts, see *Agudeza* discourses 3 and 51–57.

[128]Cf., for example, *Agudeza* discourses 1–4, 15, and 47; *Oráculo* Aphorism 283; *El Criticón* I, Crisi 1.

[129]See *El Discreto* Realce 15. Something more radical than the urgency of judgment is what I call the *leap of discernment*. Gracián believed that the advancement of learning consisted in discernment, that is, going from the most universal and vague perception of things to a more particular and detailed one. (See *El Criticón* I, Crisi 1; cf., Aristotle, *Physica* I, 1; St Thomas Aquinas *Summa Theologica* First Part Q. 85, Art. 3.) However, reason does not proceed to specify all details until reaching their exhaustion: such a process could be endless since smaller details can always be specified. And even if an end were possible in discernment, reaching it would be needless since reason does not require the exhaustion of discernment to pass judgments. The American Consulate did not need to know all, say, that I lack the vermiform appendix in order to issue an F-1 visa to my benefit; but it needed to know that I was Mexican and that, at that time, I studied in the University of Wisconsin-Madison. Thus the leap of discernment consists in this: that reason does pass judgment before exhausting the process of discernment. It is like the leap of induction: reason makes a generalization before having exhausted all the cases comprehended under the generalization. However, the leap of discernment is more radical than the leap of induction because the former precedes the latter, as operations of understanding. And the leap of discernment is more radical than the urgency of judgment because the first is characteristic of whereas the second is accidental to human reason. Only God can discern perfectly.

his competence if formulas and the accumulation of learning are not enough?[130] The answer is on mastery.

Remedies Focused on the Character of the Orator

The most comprehensive remedy against deficient eloquence was found in the formation of a good character. Gracián's theories of mastery include objective learning as a component of the master's competence, either in the knowledge of methods or of rich information.[131] But this competence should go beyond mere pieces of learning and be centered on the person's good habits of learning and all the other virtues which an eloquent master must possess. In fact, Gracián believed that "the authority earned with reputation, and the mastery achieved through exercise"[132] were the grounds of the person's lordliness concerning words and deeds.

Concerning this mastery of eloquence achieved through exercise, Gracián tought that:

> It is not enough the greatest speculation to give this mastery; required is the continuous exercise of the specific duties, so that the assiduous action is what generates the masterly habit.[133]

Thus, explained Gracián, the habit of kingly deeds was what made Alphonsus The Magnanimous superior to Alphonsus The Sage who was just a book worm.[134] The person's active familiarity with his responsibilities is what

---

[130]Cf. *El Criticón* III, Crisi 10.

[131]See, for example, *El Discreto* Realce 5.

[132]*El Discreto* Realce 2: "...la autoridad conseguida con el crédito, y el magisterio alcanzado con el ejercicio". A mastery grounded on exercise, thas is, practice, is more properly described as one grounded in the *habits of life*—virtue.

[133]*El Discreto* Realce 2: "No basta la mayor especulación para dar este señorío; requiérese el continuado ejercicio en los empleos; que de la continuidad de los actos se engendra el hábito señoril".

[134]See *El Político*.

empowers him with dazzling ease (*despejo*) when he speaks of and performs his duties.[135] Thus mastery "ministers words and even *sententiae* to the person who speaks".[136]

This training in performing actions previews and finds answers to *new events* since action is what takes into realization anything that is potential:

> Thus an uncommon skill is to invent new ways to excellence, to discover modern paths to fame. Multiple are the routes which lead to singularity, not all for the first time tracked. The newest, though arduous, usually are shortcuts to greatness.[137]

How preeminent this mastery is in Gracián's doctrines can not be emphasized and detailed enough. He remarked: "This crowned and enhancing perfection... is the king of all the others."[138] But it may suffice to say that all his books are directed to making the reader achieve this perfection. Even Gracián's most theoretical book—*Agudeza*—trains a person in ingenuity less through learning the types of concepts there listed than through strenuously making him apply his mind's wit to decipher the purposefully obscure examples and configuration of the book.

Thus, in his peculiar way, Gracián shared one of the central teachings of classical rhetoric: that eloquence springs less from mere knowledge than from virtue—less from the accumulation of methods and information than from the practice of good habits, which become the second nature we acquire, similar to the muscles grown from going to the gym. For eloquence's seat, as Cicero proclaimed, is the Orator, and not the theories of rhetoric; it is the commanding

---

[135]Cf. *El Héroe* Primor 13; *El Discreto* Realce 2.

[136]*El Discreto* Realce 2: "Ministra palabras y aun sentencias al que dice..."

[137]*El Héroe* Primor 7: "Es, pues, destreza no común inventar nueva senda para la excelencia, descubrir moderno rumbo para la celebridad. Son multiplicados los caminos que llevan a la singularidad, no todos sendereados. Los más nuevos, aunque arduos, suelen ser atajos para la grandeza".

[138]*El Discreto* Realce 2: "Este coronado realce...es rey de los demás..."

power enjoyed by those experienced in statesmanship.[139] Its reasons are supplied by practical wisdom, specified Aristotle, an ability "to deliberate well about what is good and expedient".[140] Rhetoric, then, is not an art but a faculty, the Philosopher concluded,[141] the virtue of a virtuous speaker, summarized Quintilian.[142]

According to Gracián, the mastery of words and deeds also springs, from among other sources, the authority earned from reputation.[143] This component of ethos is also specified by classical authors, such as Aristotle, who called it good moral character.[144] However, probably influenced by the Spanish ticklish sense of honor, Gracián took the authority enjoyed from reputation to gigantic proportions. Words are powerful not just because they are spoken well, but also because they have been *given* well. They embody the commitment of a dutiful person. They contain the reliable promise of accomplishing a good action. And although these words may not be the ones presenting the best choice, if the audience purely analyzes the options, these words nevertheless are the best alternative in so far as the speaker's character makes them not just credible but possible through action.[145]

Concerning preaching, the religious correlative of secular mastery is holiness. As Gracián said it, the person of mastery is, "In one word, saintly."[146]

Holiness, though a gift from God, requires the recipient's acceptance, in a careful balance of grace and works. According to Gracián, in paying attention and responding to God, a person practices all virtues. Thus, holiness "makes a

---

[139]See *De Oratore* I, ii, 8.

[140]*Nichomachean Ethics* VI, 5.

[141]See *Rhetoric* I, 2.

[142]See *Institutio Oratoria* XII, i, 1.

[143]See *El Discreto* Realce 2.

[144]See *Rhetoric*, II, 1.

[145]See, for example, *Oráculo* Aphorism 116.

[146]*Oráculo* Aphorism 300: **"En una palabra, santo..."**

subject prudent, heedful, sagacious, sensible, wise, brave, controlled, integral, happy, plausible, true, and a universal hero."[147]

Iberian ecclesiastical rhetoricians who also were eloquent preachers agreed on the preeminence of holiness over all other virtues taken to the sacred platform. Quoting the parable of the sower,[148] Vieira pondered that the sower was not just one of name, but one who truly sowed the word of God, that is, one seriously commited to his mission:

> *Ecce exiit, qui seminat, seminare.* Between the sower and him who sows, there is much of difference. One thing is the soldier, and another thing is the one who fights. One thing is the governor, and another he who governs. In the same way, one thing is the sower and another thing he who sows. One thing is the preacher and another thing he who preaches. The sower and the preacher are names. He who sows and he who preaches are actions. And the actions are what give its being to the preacher. Having the title of a preacher or being a preacher by name is worth nothing. The action, the life, the example, the works are what convert the world.[149] The best concept taken by the preacher to the pulpit—which one do you think it is? It is the concept that the listeners obtain from his life. In ancient times it was common to convert the world. Why isn't anybody converted today? Because words are preached, and also thoughts, but in antiquity words were preached, and also works. Words without works are like discharges without bullets: they stun but do not wound.[150]

---

[147]*Oráculo* Aphorism 300: "...ella hace un sujeto prudente, atento, sagaz, cuerdo, sabio, valeroso, reportado, entero, feliz, plausible, verdadero y universal héroe".

[148]See *St Matthew* 13: 3. English translations of the parable do not permit Vieira's subtilizing over the differences between the sower and he who sows; these translations just talk about a "sower." The *Vulgate*—used by Vieira—makes the distinction possible by translating *"qui seminat,"* that is, "he who sows."

[149]Vieira's ethical standards of preaching express the most comprehensive remedy proposed for the maladies suffered by baroque eloquence. Cf. *El Héroe* Primor 14: Gracián recognized in full mastery the awsome virtue which, if recognized by the audience, does not need to express itself to be persuasive—a virtue whose wise and tested honesty easily commands without wasting time in wordy persuasion, and even could win listeners' wills silently.

[150]António Vieira, *Sermão da Sexagésima*, IV: «*Ecce exiit, qui seminat, seminare.* Entre

Fr Luis de Granada believed that holy life was the greatest and the primary form of persuasion that missionaries should use before the heathens.[151] Moreover, as the greatest reformer of the sacred platform during the late sixteenth century, Granada relied less on the theories of his *Ecclesiastical Rhetoric*, and his moving, eloquent, and very abundant writings, than on the living and achieving of holiness.[152]

From Gracián's understanding of mastery and Granada's understanding of holiness as the primary and often sufficient grounds of persuasion, and from the most ordinary view of sixteenth-century Iberian preachers as superior than seventeenth-century preachers, it follows that sixteenth-century eloquence was less a result of the preachers' artistry than of their holiness.[153] Their grounds of

---

o semeador, e o que semea há muita diferença: ua cousa é o soldado, e outra cousa o que peleja: ua cousa é o governador, e outra o que governa. Da mesma maneira, ua cousa é o semeador, e outra o que semea: ua cousa é o pregador, e outra o que prega. O semeador, e o pregador é nome; o que semea, e o que prega é acção: e as acções são as que dão o ser ao pregador. Ter o nome de pregador, ou ser pregador de nome, não importa nada: as acções, a vida, o exemplo, as obras, são as que convertem o mundo. O melhor conceito que o pregador leva ao púlpito, qual cuidais que é? É o conceito, que de sua vida têm os ouvintes. Antigamente, convertia-se o mundo; hoje porque se não converte ninguém? Porque hoje pregam-se palavras, e pensamentos: antigamente pregavan-se palavras, e obras. Palavras sem obras, são tiros sem bala; atroam, mas não ferem.»

[151]See Fr Luis de Granada, *Breve Tratado en que se declara de la manera que se podrá proponer la doctrina de nuestra Santa Fe y Religión Cristiana a los nuevos fieles.* (Madrid: Biblioteca de Autores Españoles, 1945) 2: 598–611. Granada suggested that virtue itself is what, at first, converts people to Christianity. In his treatise, words seem to be vain and wasted if they have not been formerly established by virtue itself.

[152]See, for example, Granada' *Guía de Pecadores, Memorial de la Vida Cristiana, Introducción al Símbolo de la Fe*, etc. Cf. Granada's grounds to reform the sacred platform with Baltasar Gracián's grounds to reform the public life: both authors relied less on their artistic theories or knowledge of sensible doctrines than on actual *mastery* or holiness as the medicine to revitalize the religious, public, and moral life of Spain. Cf. *Rhetorica Eclesiástica* Book One.

[153]We should recall, here, that for Gracián, holiness—the whole comprehensive practice of human and supernatural virtues—is a sign that a person practices the habits of wisdom, attentiveness, prudence, perseverance, etc., to their highest degree. Cf. *Oráculo* Aphorism

persuasion were not as much words as virtue:

For out of the abundance of *the heart* the mouth speaks.[154]

All of them are saints: St John of Avila, St Thomas of Villanueva, St Francis Xavier, St Bartholomew of the Martyrs, Bl Alonso de Orozco, St Francis of Borgia, St Peter of Alcántara...! Their eloquence sprang less from their studies than from their fidelity to the reformed and stricter rule of their religious orders, leading them to a holier life.[155] For in the Church of all ages—it follows from Gracián's radical concept of mastery—religious eloquence comes from holiness. It was the Apostles' single asset. It was the persuasiveness of the Martyrs. It provided Monica with stronger arguments than the ones of philosophers to bring the rebellious Augustine to the faith. It helped Bernard to rebuild Europe more from the seclusion of the Cistercium than by influencing in the Crusades or recommending the appointment of popes. It made Aquinas's ecstatic dumbness before the Eucharist more convincing than all his summae. Thus, Little Thérèse is the patron saint of all missions, although she never set foot outside the nunnery. Mary only uttered seven words in the Writ, and so did her Son on the Cross—seven words more enlightening of His mission than the Sermon on the Mount. But eloquence could not be greater than when Innocence proved himself through the silence of the Lamb.

---

300. As such, holiness is more than the potential wisdom contained in books, but rather, it is the actual wisdom exercised in the life of the saint.

[154]*Luke* 6: 45.

[155]Cf. McSorley 538-629; Herrero García 18–19.

14   Wit and Criticism

THE PERVASIVE FAILURE TO SEE IN WIT AN ACT OF REASON strongly impoverishes the criticism of texts. Then, critics seemingly appreciate witty texts through some enchanting and alternative view of wit: a stylistic device, an emotional effect, its degree of whim concerning fancy, its power of imagination, its comprehensiveness of vision provided for the world, etc. But such a view, in any case, is limited: it fails to see the rational component of wit, and, if wit is what predominates in the text, then the text should consequently be seen as predominantly *reasonless*. Not surprisingly, baroque eloquence is thus tritely described, because of its rich use of wit.

The tragedy of failing to see reason in wit is less the biased reputation of baroque eloquence than condemning ourselves to fail in our understanding of witty texts of any age. For example, if we coherently hold the "modern" beliefs that only clear facts or self-evident truths are grounds of reason, witticisms should necessarily be condemned as a species of folly, since witticisms by definition are unclear—that is, they do not declare clear facts or self-evident truths; the most that they do is to hint at these facts or truths; the reader should be the one who, by applying his ingenuity to the text, discovers the point made by the subtlety, but that is a step some distance removed from the immediate clarity of facts or self-evidence of truths endorsed by modern minds, on whose view witticisms should be reasonless.

These tragic mistakes can be avoided if the reader of witty texts keeps in mind the rational character of wit. For that purpose, the critic may find helpful the following seven rules I have "squeezed out" from Gracián's books.[1]

---

[1]To make the most of my discussion, I sometimes illustrate these rules with some controversial examples of witty or baroque oratory that modern minds not seldom decry as models of sophistry or bad taste. If my rules do not free these models from their notoriety, I hope at least that they free the models from gross misunderstanding.

Establish the Concept

The most exceedingly simple failure concerning the analysis of witty texts is not meeting the most basic responsibility of a listener, that is, listening—that is, trying to understand, trying to realize what is being said.

This most basic mistake not seldom consists in the failure to squeeze out the idea insinuated by the subtlety. Then, the audience only takes the text literally, or regards wit as merely imagery or a stylistic embellishment, or simply searches the emotional in the subtlety, etc. But, in any case, the result is not identifying the subtlety's points and lines of correspondence, the result is not establishing the correlation, and, on that basis, alas!, the result is not extracting the idea—not understanding at all what is said.

The reader can avoid this mistake by doing the opposite: he should *establish the concept*, which is the first rule; the reader should draw the lines of correspondence, and so, squeeze them to extract the idea.

As easy as it may seem, this rule can be ignored even by a complete parliament, with very undesirable results. In 1746, the Parliament in Pamplona[2] commissioned Father Francisco de Isla to write a speech to commemorate Ferdinand VI of Castile's accession to the Throne of Navarre. Yet, the Parliament still wanted to assert its own autonomy by proclaiming the King as Ferdinand *II of Navarre*—this kingdom should not be less important than *Castile*, or than any other territory of the Spanish Empire.[3] Moreover, to emphasize the occasion and *the importance of Navarre*, Isla was requested to use *culteranist* style, that is, something more inflated than bombastic style, as Isla believed it to be, and hated. Even so, Isla seemingly accomplished the commission: his speech was celebrated, officially approved, printed, and widely published by the Parliament.

---

[2]Pamplona is the capital city of the Kingdom of Navarre, and where people still run for their lives while being chased by bulls.

[3]The line of Ferdinands ruling Navarre started with Ferdinand the Catholic, the Second of Aragon, the Third of Naples, the Fifth of Castile, and who was the First of Navarre, after its annexation to Aragon by this shrewdest Catholic King.

But what Isla actually accomplished was probably the greatest prank of his life. He mastered the *culteranist* style so cleverly that he both stridently pleased the chauvinist whim of the provincials and sotto voce made of them the laughingstock of Europe.[4]

Referring to *the Kingdom of Navarre*, Isla quoted a Latin poem which "in brief and elegant clauses makes the most discreet apology of *nothing*."[5] The deputies "are not always men of schools, but always are the school of men,"[6] and, in them, "nobility is the least;[7] for the least that they are is what their grandfathers were;[8] and the most is what they are themselves."[9] Thus, Isla said that "a kingdom where there is so much to choose from, or where there is not anything to choose from since everything is chosen, it is not known what is chosen..."[10]   Referring to concrete deputies, Isla mentioned Don Antonio de

---

[4]Cf. Russell P. Sebold, "Introducción y Notas," José Francisco de Isla, *Fray Gerundio de Campazas* (Madrid: Espasa-Calpe, S. A., 1960) xxxiv.

[5]José Francisco de Isla, "Día Grande de Navarra," *Obras escogidas,* (Madrid: Biblioteca de Autores Españoles XV, 1945) 8. The concept is produced by establishing the correlation between "Navarre" and "nothing."

[6]Not being men of schools means that the deputies lacked school education. Being school of men then means that the uneducated deputies became example to other people concerning the undesirable consequences of not going to school.

[7]If the least identifiable quality of the deputies is nobility, then, they are not noblemen, but plebeians.

[8]Therefore, the deputies are not grandchildren of noblemen, but probably the bastard product of a shameful affair consumated by their grandmothers or their mothers.

[9]Isla, "Día Grande de Navarra," 10. If the deputies have just been defined as bastards, then bastards is the most that the deputies can be themselves.

[10]Isla, "Día Grande de Navarra," 10. This wordplay seemingly starts praising the people of Navarre, by noticing that they deserve to be chosen among the best, because they are the best. Then Isla introduces a paradox: if all of them are the best, why should one choose at all if everybody is equally preferable? On the grounds of this paradox, Isla finally denies to the people of Navarre—and thus to the deputies—the possibility of making choices, and even of knowing to choose at all. Hence the conclusion radically denies human nature to these people; it denies to the deputies the very nature of their responsibility—to make choices; and,

Ozcariz:

> ...although all the powers of the world were at war, the powers of this gentleman
> would remain in an Octavian peace...[11]

Seemingly praising the regalia of the carriages during the occasion, Isla
identified women of Navarre saying: "I wish I were a horse!"[12] In brief, Isla
enchanted the deputies with the pleasant sound of his words, and succeeded in
insulting them without being noticed, or risking punishment.

Russell P. Sebold reports that the Navarrean finally realized the prank and
requested from Isla a public retraction. But the Jesuit freed himself from
this—says Sebold—in the most ingenious possible way: Isla warned the
Parliament that by retracting himself from what the Parliament publicly praised
would be like the Parliament made scorn of itself.[13]

Thus, the rule is to establish the concept, make sense of the text or the data,
lest we are ridiculed like the Navarrean Parliament.

Consider the Possibilities Which Make Sense

Texts, and even facts, may suggest many possible interpretations, and we should

---

concerning the current political situation, the paradox could be pointing out that deputies
actually could not have any choice to make, since they were mere subjects of the Spanish
King—Navarre, just a Castilian colony. It should also be noted that Isla never specified what
made the people of Navarre the best—the best in not knowing how to make choices?, the best
in being abject to the Spanish King?...

[11]Isla, "Día Grande de Navarra," 12. Isla was not referring to Ozcariz's armies, but to
Ozcariz's mental faculties.

[12]Isla, "Día Grande de Navarra," 21. This rebuke applies less to the simplicity of these
women than to the offensive vanity of the occasion.

[13]See Russell P. Sebold, "Introducción y notas," José Francisco de Isla, *Fray Gerundio
de Campazas*, (Madrid: Espasa-Calpesa, S. A., 1960) xxxv.

not forget about it. Remember these illustrations:

Caesar quickly had to proclaim his conquest of Africa—*"Teneo te, Africa,"*[14]—since his soldiers could possibly interpret his falling when he leapt from the ship to the African ground as an ominous omen. A young and provincial lad had to bet—among several possibilities—that Caesar was malicious when, after comparing the lad with a Roman gentleman, the ruler questioned the lad if his mother had visited the Roman court: fittingly, the lad answered that "not her, but certainly my father."[15] This answer could be a truthful assertion of a simple-minded countryboy, a resentful retort from a not at all naive lad, or probably both a truthful and a resentful reply.[16] Concerning the palm tree sprouting from Augustus's altar, the Emperor could spare some modesty and wonder whether he indeed had some godly powers instead of explaining the event with the lack of cult he suffered at Tarragona.[17]

These examples show that different ideas may fit as explanations to a series of things or words. Judgment may test these ideas later as better or worse. But the testing can not proceed if these ideas are not apprehended and sharply perceived by the mind first. Thus, the rule is that the reader should look for and supply different possible interpretations for the text at hand, if he latter wants to choose the most appropriate interpretation.

However, this attention to alternative understandings also responds to the possibility that several different ideas cohabit in the same analyzed text. For instance, Gracián wrote this meditation on St Peter, which evolves by means of a series of contrasts with St John the Apostle:

> Consider that if John deserved so many favors from the Divine Master because of being virgin, Peter received them because of being humble. John was the beloved

---

[14]*Agudeza* Discourse 17.

[15]*Agudeza* Discourse 38: "...no; mi padre, sí".

[16]Cf. Gracián's theories of crises, *Agudeza* discourses 26–28.

[17]The lack of cult to Augustus was complete, he thought: not only grass but even palm trees sprouted on his altar at Tarragona. Cf. *Agudeza* Discourse 38.

disciple, Peter the humiliated one...[18]

The series of contrasts suggest to the mind this other reading:

> Consider that if John deserved so many favors from the Divine Master in spite of not being humble, Peter received them in spite of not being virgin. Peter was not the beloved disciple, John was not the humiliated one...[19]

More ideas come to mind not only by discovering and comparing different alternative interpretations, but also by squeezing further the alternatives already given. In doing it, the understanding of one interpretation becomes richer by digging deeper into the potential meanings of a text. But this can be better perceived with this other example, which is a typically Gracianean acrobatics of wit:

> Soul, prostrate you at the feet of this Baby God. After having received Holy Communion, put forward your three powers to Him: the incense of contemplation, the gold of affection, and the myrrh of remembring his sorrows; offer him a living faith, an enthusiastic hope, and a burning charity; grant him the incense of your obedience, the gold of your poverty, and the myrrh of your chastity; serve him the prayer to God, the alms to the neighbor, and the mortification of yourself.[20]

---

[18]*El Comulgatorio* Meditación IX, i: "Considera que si Juan mereció recibir tantos favores de su Divino maestro por lo virgen, Pedro los consiguió por lo humilde. Juan fué el discípulo amado, Pedro el humillado..."

[19]If one abandons pure wit, that is correlations, and recurs to judicious wit, that is ponderations, by introducing preconceptions in the analysis of this text, one may reject the idea that Jesus did not love Peter—that does not make sense with one's preconception of an all loving Christ. Thus, another idea arises: John is the beloved disciple by antonomasia, but not exclusively.

[20]*El Comulgatorio* Meditation XXVII, iii:
"Alma, póstrate tú a los pies deste Dios Niño. Después de haber comulgado, preséntale tus tres potencias: el incienso en contemplaciones, el oro en afectos y la mirra en las memorias de sus dolores; ofrécele una fe viva, una esperanza animosa y una caridad abrasada; franquéale el incienso de la obediencia, el oro de la pobreza y la mirra de la castidad; sírvele

At first, the meditation seems to be overpowered by the lust of rhythmical composition,[21] searching for anything that sounds like a waltz or a minuet: the three gifts of the three wise men—gold, incense, and myrrh; the three faculties of the mind—understanding, will, and memory;   the three theological virtues—faith, hope, and love; the three religious vows—obedience, poverty, and chastity; the three works of penance—prayer, alms giving, and mortification (fasting). Yet, why shouldn't this lust enhance and turn into a Pythagorean orgy, say, the three Persons of God, the three groups of angelic choirs,[22] the three branches of the Church,[23] the three ages of persons, the three tempters of man,[24] the three bodily orifices...? Probably Gracián found that it was enough of a lust for word architecture. Or probably Gracián did not go on because he wanted us to squeeze from his words more than ternary periods. He probably wanted us to abstract particular ideas.

Traditionally the gifts of *incense, gold,* and *myrrh* respectively have stood as symbols of Baby Jesus's essence: *eternal God, all powerful King,* and *mortal Man.* Gracián extended these lines of correspondence to the communicant's faculties of the mind: the communicant should offer them as presents to Baby Jesus in the Eucharist; thus, after having received Holy Communion, the communicant should *contemplate* in It the mystery of His *Divinity,* should surrender his *will* to the *King's* grace, and should make *remembrance* of Jesus's sorrows then reenacted in the Eucharistic *sacrifice.* Gracián went further. He stretched the correlations to the theological virtues. After communion, the communicant enjoys *faith* in Baby Jesus's *Divinity,* puts all his *hope* on the *all powerful King,* and burns with a *love* whose measure is the *sacrifice* then

---

la oración para con Dios, la limosna para con el prójimo y la mortificación para contigo."

[21]This word architecture was something that Voltaire and Borges hated from Gracián.

[22]The direct servants of the Godhead, the angels taking care of the universal principles governing material creatures, and the angels who take care of particular material creatures.

[23]The glorified Church in Heavens, the penitent Church in the Purgatory, and the militant Church on Earth.

[24]The Devil, the Flesh, and the World.

reenacted. But Gracián did not stop at this point. He expanded the comparisons to the religious vows, by means of contrasts. The communicant renders better cult and adoration to God than *incense: obedience*. The communicant can not give Him, who is infinitely rich, *gold*, but just acknowledge his nothingness by presenting before Him his *poverty*. The communicant truly responds to Him, who is incorruptible but accepted the corruption of *death* for the sake of men, if the communicant puts away his many corruptions of sin, and accepts the incorruptibility of *chastity*. Gracián crowned these series of proportions and disproportions by including the works of penance. The communicant's self-discipline towards God is adoring Him with the *incense* of *prayer*. The communicant's self-denial, by surrendering his *gold*, is requested but not needed by God who is infinitely rich; thus it turns into *alms* and love to the neighbor. The communicant's self-awareness of his nothingness and *mortality* increases by means of *mortification*,[25] such as fasting.

We could continue squeezing out this concept by establishing cross correlations among the different points of correspondence. But that is enough. Besides, Gracián's laconism is fuller for the ingenious reader than any fixed explanation I could render here.

Thus, the rule is that, when trying to understand a text, or an event, the critic should consider the many possible interpretations that make sense—and desirably rich ones—so that these interpretations can lead to a powerful testing of ideas by judgment.[26]

---

[25]Here the concept between mortification and mortality is by no means simply grounded on paronomasia.

[26]Contemplating many possible explanations of events is essential to prudence. For example, the survival of the disabused critic within a hostile world rests on his mindfulness concerning the great variety of motives possible in persons. His prudence should be heedful of the potential simple-mindedness, wickedness, malice, folly, or gallantry of people's actions; his prudence should even be cautious about the possibility that all these motives coincide in the same person. Nevertheless, contemplating multiple explanations of people's behavior, of events, or of texts should not turn critics' mindfulness into suspiciousness. A most honest speech may be found wicked by malicious minds, by grounding the analysis on a stupid ambiguity of language. Critics who confuse their mission of disabuse with faultfinding would

Do Not Dismiss Extravagant Ideas Hastily

At first, we may think that the rule should be the opposite: if things or texts bewilder our mind because they appear contradictory, or are too extravagant, too paradoxical, we may simply dismiss their consideration, and remain within the safest boundaries of what is seen as clear and sound by us,[27] as rigorist casuists did. Rigid thinkers may only tolerate these bewildering ideas in lyric poetry,[28] whose authors are thought as stung by the madness of passion, and thus suffering contradictions such as hating and loving at the same time. Consider this sonnet from Sister Juana Inés de la Cruz which addresses the possibility of remembrance and oblivion as occurring at once in lovers:

> You say that I forget you, Celius, and you lie
> in saying that I remember to forget you,
> for, in my memory, there is not a place
> that you present yourself even as forgotten.
> My thoughts are so different
> and completely alien to considering you,
> that neither they know if they can forget you,
> nor, if they forget you, they know if you resent it.
> If you were capable of being loved,
> you would be capable of oblivion, and that would well be glory,
> at least, the potential of having been so [forgotten and thus loved].

---

wrongly be suspicious of every text and event. Watch out: *Como el león, los cree a todos de su misma condición.* (He, like the lion, regards others of his same condition.) Ultimately, these critics forget not only to contemplate the possibilities of simple-mindedness and gallantry, but also the duty of appropriately testing ideas by judgment. Cf. *El Criticón* III, Crisi 6.

[27]But if we decide to do that, we should not only dismiss paradoxes, but also every subtlety—or even every puzzling event—because by definition subtleties, or puzzling events, are not immediately clear, but require an effort of understanding.

[28]See, for example Kames. Surprisingly, a liberal thinker such as Gracián is rigid enough to exemplify most of his paradoxes and extravagances with lyric poetry, specifically poetry from courtly *cancioneros*. See *Agudeza* discourses 23–25.

But you are so far away from that victory
that this not remembering is not oblivion
but an abscense of any memory.[29]

Sister Juana was aware that Celsius could reply in this way:

You say that you do not forget, Clori, and you lie
in saying that you forget of forgetting,
for, in your memory, you well grant a place
where, as forgotten, you remember me.
   If your thoughts are different
from Albirus's, you will permit to be considered,
since you yourself pretend to take offence
by wanting to persuade that you do not resent.
   It is denied to me to be capable of being loved,
and you yourself grant me this glory;
thus, your argument has turned back to you;
      for if, to achieve such great victory,
you remember to forget forgetting,
you do not experience an abscence of memory any more.[30]

---

[29]Sister Juana Inés de la Cruz:
   Dices que yo te olvido, Celio, y mientes
en decir que me acuerdo de olvidarte,
pues no hay en mi memoria alguna parte
en que aun como olvidado te presentes.
   Mis pensamientos son tan diferentes
y en todo tan ajenos de tratarte,
que ni saben si pueden olvidarte
ni, si te olvidan, saben si lo sientes.
   Si tú fueras capaz de ser querido,
fueras capaz de olvido; y ya era gloria,
al menos, la potencia de haber sido.
   Mas tan lejos estás de esa victoria
que aqueste no acordarme no es olvido
sino una negación de la memoria.

[30]Sister Juana Inés de la Cruz:

Contradictions like these, in poetry, reveal less a mad heart or a wordplay than an act of the intellect,[31] such as a hurting memory conscious of its lasting presence through the effort of forgetfulness, an event not at all uncommon in our daily life. At first, contradictions may seem nonsensical to the mind, but if they continue to come up and secure our attention, they may be asking for additional consideration and understanding, rather than for their hasty dismissal. Probably, if they at the end do not make sense by themselves, they nonetheless may throw light on something else. Paradoxes, said Gracián, are "monsters of truth."[32] By reflecting on the concurrence of memory and oblivion, we have learned that our suppression of hurting thoughts is in fact a reaffirmation of these thoughts by our memory.

Indeed, difficulties,[33] if not paradoxes, abound in politics, and we can commit a big mistake if we hastily dismiss them. The United States humanely

---

Dices que no te acuerdas, Clori, y mientes
en decir que te olvidas de olvidarte,
pues das ya en tu memoria alguna parte
en que, por olvidado, me presentes.
    Si son tus pensamientos diferentes
de los de Albiro, dejarás tratarte,
pues tú misma pretendes agraviarte
con querer persuadir lo que no sientes.
    Niégaseme ser capaz de ser querido,
y tú misma concedes esa gloria;
con que en tu contra tu argumento ha sido;
    pues si para alcanzar tanta victoria
te acuerdas de olvidarte del olvido,
ya no das negación en tu memoria.

[31]Sister Juana is indeed considered the most genuinely intellectual poet from the baroque age in all Hispanic nations, including Spain. See, for example, Octavio Paz, *Sor Juana Inés de la Cruz, o las Trampas de la fe*, 1ˢᵗ ed. (Barcelona: Seix Barral, 1982).

[32]See *Agudeza* Discourse 23.

[33]Concerning difficulties, I am using the technical meaning used by Gracián in *Agudeza* Discourse 7.

dropped atomic bombs on Hiroshima and Nagasaki to prevent additional loses of human lives. Mexicans keep voting—and seriously—for the PRI. Puerto Ricans do not want either the full status of independence or the full status of statehood; they rather want to remain in the wishy-washy colonial status. Algerians democratically voted to kill the democratic regime in their country; champions of freedom—such as the Peruvian Vargas Llosa[34]—defend the Algerians' decision since it is one expressing their sovereign will; and Western democracies discreetly show relief after knowing that the Algerians' democratic decision to kill democracy has been killed by an undemocratic (of course) coup d'état whose purpose is to preserve democracy. Not only human actions but also the sciences abound in paradoxes. The Heisenberg principle postulates that the greater the certainty in the one measurement of a parameter, the greater the uncertainty in the measurement of another parameter in quantum mechanics. Scientists still try to reconcile the wave and corpuscular theories—contradictory, but equally powerful in explaining what light is. Biologists flirt with the idea of abiogenesis—as Aristotle did—when bacteria are generated in unpredictable and inconceivable fashions. My father ponders that even the most momentous fields bewilder his mind with enigmas: in cuisine, if something is good, more of it is not necessarily better.

Admitting the conceptualization of the paradoxical is not yielding to the nonsensical. If the object studied exceeds full comprehension, grasping it, at least, in a veiled or puzzling way rather is reaching the limits of human understanding as sharply as possible.[35] Then artists enter into the realm of the sublime. Fr Luis de Granada offered this example:

> It is said of a famous painter that having painted the death of the king's virgin daughter on a wooden panel, and drawn the relatives with extremely sad counte-

---

[34]See Mario Vargas Llosa, "¿Dios o la espada?" *El Norte* (Monterrey, México: 16 de febrero de 1992) 2A.

[35]Gracián's theory of paradoxes often requires from the wit the ability to find a reason which either solves the paradox or plausibly and awesomely reasserts the contradiction. See *Agudeza* Discourses 23–25.

nances around her, and much more sadder the mother, the painter then proceeded to draw the father's countenance, and skillfully hid it by a shadow, to give understanding that any art was insufficient to express a thing of such a deep sorrow.[36]

Exerting the powers of the mind to its limits is probably not experienced more intensely in any other situation than religion. Human understanding hits its *non plus ultra* in the face of mystery.[37] For example, it recognizes the evidence for an omniscent God and also for human free will, but at the same time this understanding shrinks when perceiving that these coexisting facts seem to contradict each other. And so does the mind shrink with the knowledge available about an all good and powerful Creator, and the actuality of suffering and evil. Having an idea of God is in itself a mystery since the idea refers to a Being which exceeds the possibility of human comprehension.[38]

Christians go beyond this philosophical puzzlement before the Ineffable, and are bewildered with the long list of mysteries known through Revelation: the Creation, the Fall, the Chosen People, the Incarnation, the Redemption, the Church, the Final Judgment... To these central mysteries should be added the many obscure portions found in the revealed texts, which—to give a concrete example—seemingly portray Jesus as a bad boy with his mother.[39]

---

[36]Fr Luis de Granada, *Guía de Pecadores*, I, iv.

[37]Here, I use the term mystery in its theological sense, and not as Gracián meant it to be in *Agudeza* Discourse 6.

[38]This mystery extends to all knowledge. The inexhaustible richness of any concrete being is beyond the comprehending powers of the human mind. Reason, because of its limitations, operates with abstract knowledge, not with full knowledge (like God). It is in this sense that our advancing of learning goes from the most general to the most specific. But the most specific is always waiting to be understood, because there is always something beyond which was left to know. Thus human understanding should be resigned to what I already called *the leap of prudence*: the judgment that what has been known is enough for the exigence of human action.

[39]See, for example, *Luke* 2:41–52, which narrates the mistery of the Lost Child.

Baroque oratory was mainly preaching, and preaching in all ages has had the duty of teaching and reflecting on the revealed mysteries. Rather than failing in his eloquence, the preacher somehow exerts his duty, and his understanding to its limits, by pondering these religious paradoxes in full perplexity. Fr Luis de Granada exclaimed:

> Should I remain silent or should I speak? Neither I should remain silent nor I can speak. How could I be silent about such great mercies?, and how could I express such ineffable mysteries? Silence is ingratitude, and speaking seems recklessness.[40]

Grace and wit granted, the preacher's effort sometimes helps to penetrate further into the mystery. Fr Luis de Granada thus spoke of the Incarnation and Redemption:

> Such a great friendship developed between God and man, that it culminated not only with God forgiving man, restoring him into grace, and becoming one with him in love...but also in person. Who would imagine that these two things...would come to meet together, not in a house, or at the table, or in grace, but in a single person?...It was so close this union and so loyal, that when it came the time of breaking apart, which was the time of the Passion...death could separate the [man's] soul from the [man's] body...but it never could take God away, either from the soul or from the body which were in union with the divine person; since what He once took for our love, He never left it at any time.[41]

In fact, Gracián ascribed to wit the function of providing new glimpses of solution to paradoxes.[42] The power of the mind is measured according to its skill in surmounting difficulties and solving them by keeness of perception.[43] Numerous baroque sermons display this Gracianian passion for intellectual

---

[40]Fr Luis de Granada, *Guia de Pecadores* I, iv.

[41]Fr Luis de Granada, *Guia de Pecadores* I, iv.

[42]See, for example, *Agudeza* discourses 23–25, and 39–42.

[43]In Gracián's system, this effort expresses itself in form of witty ratiocinations. See, for example, *Agudeza* discourses 6–8.

gymnastics.

However, there is also wit in purely acknowledging and presenting the paradox. For example, the very discovery and awareness of a problem is in itself an advancement of learning even when the solution is not found.[44] By means of a paradoxical sermon, Vieira succeeded in convincing the King of Portugal to let him go back and preach in the Brazilian missions—a return which was seriously questioned before. In the *Sermão da Sexagésima*,[45] this Jesuit reviewed all the possible things which do go wrong in preaching, because preachers fail to be good preachers and fail to practice sound rhetoric. Nevertheless, Vieira apparently contradicted himself in every point. He illustrated each different type of flaw with superbly *successful* examples of *flawed* preaching. If the fault is in an audience with rock-hard ears or acute faultfinding minds, such hard things as rocks nevertheless witnessed the death of Jesus and were rent to confess Him as Lord, while such acute things as thorns crowned Him as King on Good Friday.[46] If the fault is in the preacher because he is wicked, Jonas nevertheless could convert Ninive:

> Jonas, God's runaway, disobedient, stubborn, and still after having been swallowed and spewed out, angry, impatient, little charitable, little merciful, and more zealous and friend of his own reputation than of God's honor and the salvation of souls, eager for watching Ninive subverted, and for watching it subverted with his own eyes, being it populated by so many thousands of innocents: even so this same man, with one sermon, converted the greatest king, the greatest court, the greatest kingdom of the world, and not of faithful men, but of masses of idolaters.[47]

---

[44]Cf., for example, *Agudeza* discourses 39–42.

[45]This sermon is probably one of the most important ones in the seventeenth century defining the role of rhetoric and the rhetor in preaching, as compared with the role of grace and God.

[46]See António Vieira, *Sermão da Sexagésima*, III; cf. *Matthew* 27:51 and 27:29. This illustration strongly requires from the reader to establish the concept.

[47]António Vieira, *Sermão da Sexagésima* IV: "Jonas fugitivo de Deus, desobediente, contumaz, e ainda depois de engolido, e vomitado, iracundo, impaciente, pouco caritativo, pouco misericordioso, e mais zeloso, e amigo da própia estimação que da honra de Deus, e

Vieira also noticed: the abuse of embellishments do not belie the religious eloquence of St Ambrose, St Leo, or St Clement;[48] the lack of extensive studies and personal naturalization of learning did not make St John the Baptist less convincing when repeating Isaiah's prophecies and teachings on penance;[49] Moses lacked a powerful voice and still led his people...[50] And so on. Vieira was not denying the need of proper training and virtue for preachers; he certainly required it. But Vieira also presented the paradox that both good and bad preachers are equally poor instruments for an all powerful God.[51]

Acknowledging paradoxes is more than a display of wit: it is practicing humility,[52] a virtue which speaks more of the sanctity of a preacher than the

---

salvação das almas, desejoso de ver suvertida a Ninive e de a ver a suverter com os seus olhos, havendo nela tantos mil inocentes: contudo este mesmo homem com um sermão converteu o maior Rei, a maior Corte, e o maior Reino do mundo, e não de homens fiéis, senão de gentios idólatras."

[48]See António Vieira, *Sermão da Sexagésima*, V.

[49]See António Vieira, *Sermão da Sexagésima*, VII.

[50]See António Vieira, *Sermão da Sexagésima*, VIII.

[51]Gracián had years before summarized Vieira's paradoxical instruction on the training of preachers by means of this aphorism: **"Resort to human means as if there were not divine means, and to divine means as if there were not human means."** (**"Hanse de procurar los medios humanos como si no hubiese divinos, y los divinos como si no hubiese humanos"**).

[52]See Fr Luis de Granada, *Los seis libros de la rhetórica eclesiástica*, I, iii-viii; IV, xi. See also Pope Pius XII's Encyclical Letter *Divino afflante Spiritu*: Concerning the proper "attitude to be taken toward unsolved difficulties," Pope Pius XII taught: "...no one will be surprised that all difficulties are not yet solved and overcome; but that even today serious problems greatly exercise the minds of Catholic exegetes. We should not lose courage on this account; nor should we forget that in the human sciences the same happens as in the natural world; that is to say, new beginnings grow little by little and fruits are gathered only after many labors...if the wished-for solution be slow in coming or does not satisfy us, since perhaps a succesful conclusion may be reserved to posterity, let us not wax impatient thereat, seeing that in us also is rightly verified what the Fathers, and especially Augustine, observed in their time, viz: God wished difficulties to be scattered through the Sacred Books inspired by Him in order that we might be urged to read and scrutinize them more intently, and,

dangerous—almost satanic—pride which the preacher could suffer in lasciviously exerting the powers of his mind before the Ineffable. During Lent of 1622, St Francis de Sales recognized his inability to explain the mystery of the Cross. Moreover, he was unashamed to display this incompetence by resorting to superstitions in order to expound this mystery:[53]

> I must tell you what happened to me once when I was about to preach on the Passion of Jesus Christ...I needed some appropriate symbol to describe my subject more clearly. Not finding any elsewhere, I found one in a book...
>
> This symbol, then, is the bird called the oriole in French and *icterus* in Latin. This bird is entirely yellow, but not because of jaundice. It has this special property: from a treetop, it cures those afflicted with serious jaundice, always at the expense of its own life. When the jaundiced person and this bird exchange glances, the oriole, as it were, so pities man, his good friend, that he draws to himself the man's jaundice. Then the bird's whole body turns completely yellow. His wings, which were already yellow, become more so; then his stomach, feet, all his feathers, and his little body. Meanwhile man, his great friend, becomes white, clean and completely cured. This poor bird then flies away, sighing and singing a song pitifully loving for the delight he experiences in dying to save his human friend. A truly admirable phenomenon! This bird is never afflicted with jaundice, yet he dies of it when curing a man so afflicted. Indeed, it takes pleasure in dying to save him.
>
> Our Lord is certainly this divine Bird of Paradise, the divine Oriole, attached to the tree of the Cross to save and deliver us from the serious jaundice of sin. To be cured, however, man must look at Him on this Cross...Though our Saviour was innocent, He died for our iniquities. Indeed, He died with a holy joy at our cure, even though this was at the cost of His own life.[54]

St Francis's incompetence[55] to teach mysteries paradoxically is the best

---

experiencing in a salutary manner our own limitations, we might be exercised in due submission of mind."

[53]One of the most criticized aspects of baroque sermons is that they often applied profane materials—even mythology—to the explanation of religion.

[54]St Francis of Sales, "Sermon for Good Friday, March 25, 1622," *The Sermons of St. Francis de Sales for Lent given in the year 1622*, as edited by Father Lewis S. Fiorelli, O.S.F.S., trans. by Nuns of the Visitation. (Tan Books and Publishers, Inc., 1987) 186–187.

[55]A "competent" preacher would not let himself be intimidated when trying to explain the

teaching concerning mysteries. His confessed and displayed incompetence teaches that humility is the right attitude before the Ineffable—and, I think that, by extension, before any object of understanding.[56]

Consider if the Context Enriches the Concept

All witty discourses require from the critic some effort of discovery. Their meanings are not explicitly declared word by word, but extracted from the different relationships perceived between the points or "extremes"—as Gracián called them—of the speech, either contained clearly by the text or simply implied by the context.

Sometimes all the elements which render meaning are contained in the text itself. Then, to squeeze out the concept, one needs only to establish the lines of correspondences between these expressed elements. Consider this description of Little Thérèse—a nineteenth century saint[57]—of her Little Way:

---

mystery of the Cross. Rather he would face his duty, and ably cite appropriate texts ranging through all the Scriptures. And of course he would never use superstition.

[56]St Francis's "incompetence" strongly establishes his virtuous character before the audience. His incompetence springs from his perplexity, and his perplexity speaks of his spiritual childhood, his humility, and his awe before the divine mysteries; for Gracián indeed identified in children—the little ones—the greatest capacity of wonderment (see *El Criticón* I, Crisi 1); and the degree of wonderment reflects the degree that wit remains open to the amazement of discoveries (see, for example, *El Criticón* I, Crisi 1; *Acutezze* Chapter Three, 36; *Cannocchiale* Chapter Nine). Thus, spiritual childhood—as a virtue—suggests a mind's wit that remains open to be amazed by discoveries—a mind ready to experience awe before the divine mysteries. St Francis's openness to the Christian mysteries is now strongly recognized by the Church since she sees in him one of her doctors.

[57]Little Thérèse is an illustration which helps me to address the common cliché describing post-reformation Catholic writings as blindfolded by dogmatism, and thus mechanically practicing devotions, and finding a substitute for true religion in sentimentalism. Though not specifically from the baroque age, for many critics, Little Thérèse is the embodiment of the whole post-reformation sentimentalism. Rather I think she is among the wittiest saints.

> Alas, I have always noticed, in comparing myself with the great saints, the same difference between them and myself as we see in nature between a mountain whose summit is lost in the clouds and an obscure little grain of sand trampled underfoot by passers-by...it is impossible for me to grow great...But we live in an age of inventions: nowadays there is no need to go to the trouble of climbing a stairway step by step; this is now done amongst rich people by means of a lift. I also wished to discover a *lift* to take me up to Jesus; because I am too little to climb the steep stairway of perfection...[58]

Though self-sufficient, this text can still be enriched and even specified in meanings if confronted with other similar texts. If this happens, then the search for points of correspondence trascends the original text, and considers contextual explanatory factors. For example, this letter of Thérèse to Abbé Bellière very much contributes to a better understanding of the former illustration:

> More than ever I realized the degree to which your love is sister to mine, since it is called to go up to God by the lift of love, not to climb the rough *stairway* of fear.[59]

Sometimes, the search for elements outside the original text responds less to the possibility of enriching its understanding than to the necessity of avoiding wrong interpretations. Here, Thérèse seemingly professed quietism—seemingly

---

[58]Quoted by Hans Urs Von Balthasar, *Thérèse of Lisieux. The Story of a Mission*. Trans. by Donald Nicholl, (New York: Sheed and Ward, 1954) 182. Here, Thérèse is explicitly establishing a disproportion between the great saints who can climb the mountain stairway of virtue and the little Christians who would rather want to go to God by means of a lift because of their own weakness.

[59]Quoted by Hans Urs Von Balthasar 182. By associating this illustration with the former one, we can identify that, now, the points of correspondence are, on the one hand, the "great" saints and their great way to sanctity—the mountain stairway, that is, reliance on their own virtue, which springs from fear, and, on the other hand, the "little" saints and Thérèse's little way—the lift, that is, her complete surrender to the love of God. Though apparently sentimental by emphasizing her "littleness," weakness, and surrender to love, Thérèse rather is daring to challenge some distorted and pervasive views concerning the doctrine of "faith and *also works*" as the way to salvation.

did not see in her will the responsibility of offering at least a personal assent to God:

> Oh, how I should like to be hypnotized by Our Lord!...Yes, I want Him to take over all my faculties so that I no longer perform human and personal actions but utterly divine ones, inspired and directed by the spirit of love![60]

Apparently, Thérèse searched in God for a rapist, not a lover. Seemingly, she did not want to be wooed but possessed, without having been even asked about it—just hypnotized! Hence the theologian Hans Urs Von Balthasar perceived the smell of heresy on that passage:

> ...the image is obviously incomplete since hypnotism eliminates the subject's personal freedom whereas grace preserves and intensifies it.[61]

Von Balthasar confronted the image with other Thérèsean texts. He thus found a new understanding of the passage:

> The point is that man cannot be hypnotized by grace apart from his own will and self-surrender, but that once he is in the power of this higher will then he carries it out without knowing its laws and purposes...The lover's stake in God's play is himself; he throws himself into it for God's sake. He does not care to know whether he will be multiplied a hundredfold, sixtyfold, or thirtyfold, for the sum of his winnings no more belongs to him than the ear of wheat belongs to the seed that died...love, in a sense, is magic: it produces what was not there and spirits away what was there. "The principal plenary indulgence, and one which everyone may obtain without the customary conditions, is the indulgence of *charity which covers multitude of sins.*"[62]

---

[60]Quoted by Hans Urs Von Balthasar 183.

[61]Hans Urs Von Balthasar 183.

[62]Hans Urs Von Balthasar 184, who at the end quotes Thérèse of Lisieux, quoting St Paul. Here, far from sentimental dogmatism, Thérèse again challenged distorted and pervasive views of Catholic religion; this time, she addressed the issue of indulgences, which she asked to find their foundation in the rule of charity rather than on mechanical devotion.

If Thérèsean writings are read isolated, they often seem to be among the most sentimental and childish from Catholic writers of the romantic century—for example, her choice of nicknames such as the "Little Flower of the Child Jesus."[63] But by searching and putting together the disperse elements of her writings, her life, and her mission, she arises as one of the great reformers and most profound religious thinkers of the Church.[64] Thus, drawing lines of correspondence between the text and the context can enrich the understanding of a discourse and prevent wrong interpretations.

Moreover, texts out of their context could simply not make any sense at all. "I die because I do not die" may sound like gibberish if the critic ignores who pronounces that. If spoken by Great Teresa, then the words suggest the spiritual death she experienced by not surrendering herself quickly enough to the love of God. If the words come from a courtly gentleman, then the death and love enjoyed are rather profane.

Allusions particularly acquire meaning from their context. They do not specify the terms to be related and squeezed out, but just imply them from situational factors.[65] Praising a dish of mushrooms, Nero called them "food for gods." Nero's companions well understood that Nero cynically was confessing the murder of Claudius with poisonous mushrooms, and mocking the recent placement of Claudius among the Roman gods.[66]

The need for drawing lines of correspondence with the context may not be

---

[63]Catholic iconography does not help much to dispel this sugary image of Thérèse: she is usually represented with her head graciously leaning on her shoulder.

[64]One of her most puzzling insights challenges the simplistic picture of Heaven as a place of happy glee. She presents it as essentially a place of love—a love which is the most real, and thus the most fraternal with the sufferings of the militant Church still on Earth. Thérèse's promise that she would do more in Heaven for Catholic missions than she had already done in the Carmel has led her to be regarded as the patron saint of world missions. This insight into Heaven reveals her less as a sentimental writer abandoned to passivity, than a person engaged in the strongest activity: love. See Balthasar.

[65]See *Agudeza* Discourse 49.

[66]See *Agudeza* Discourse 49: "Al fin son comida de dioses".

obvious when the text intentionally and successfully omits meaningful information concerning situational factors surrounding the discourse. Consider, for example, Fr Luis de Granada's *Sermon on the Sin of Scandal*.[67] At first, it appears as a forthright doctrinal explanation of the nature, causes, and remedies of this sin. Granada particularly referred to the seriousness of religious scandals directly confusing people about their faith and the authority of the Church. A great enthusiast of Christianity, Granada especially aimed to strengthen the audience in a faith, a hope, and a love more powerful than any scandal or sin. Though not concrete in its references to the speech's circumstances, the text itself is very rich and extensive, and a reader can understand much from it concerning situational factors, for example, what audience Granada meant to address, what kind of people Granada meant the audience to become, what character Granada portrayed of himself, what issues Granada meant to set before the audience's consideration, etc. If the text does not explicitly inform us with additional detail about the concrete situation, the critic can justifiable see that the sermon did not mean to remain within the limits of the unique occasion, but aimed to trascend the occasion and to preach eloquently to all peoples and all ages.[68] Even so, the text lacks some information which can be found in any standard biography of Granada: the sermon specifically was an answer to a notorious scandal committed by several religious people, including Granada himself at the age of 84.[69] This information may not change at all the essential

---

[67]Fr Luis de Granada, *Sermón en que se da aviso que en las caídas públicas de algunas personas ni se pierda el crédito de la virtud de los buenos ni cese y se entibie el buen propósito de los flacos.* (Lisboa: Antonio Ribero, 1588), as included in Fr Luis de Granada, *Obras*, ed. by Fr Justo Cuervo, (Madrid: 1906) Vol. 14.

[68]A critic of baroque oratory would indeed praise Granada's classicism, that keeps the sermon within the essential; and he would contrast this classicism with the seventeenth-century fashion of excessively reviewing the circumstances—lingering over as ridiculous points as the hidden meanings to be discovered from the name initials of an applicant to the nunnery. Cf. Isla, *Fray Gerundio de Campazas.*

[69]Apparently moved by credulity rather than careful study and sound judgment, Granada defended as true some stigmata allegedly suffered by a nun. A thorough investigation later proved that the stigmata were false. See John A. Moore, *Fray Luis de Granada*, (Boston:

character of the speech. Still, the few details enrich the text's meaning. Granada was indeed silent about the concrete scandal in which he was involved. But it was not because of cowardly shame, a cover-up, or an irresponsible avoidance of the issue: he in any case spoke about scandals in the very moment he himself was the scandal. Granada's silence responds to other reasons. First, he owed the other scandalizers love, or at least finesse, since charity reserves the correction of particular sinners to the privacy of the confessional, and not to the publicity of the pulpit. Second, he owed God humility, since Granada's own penitential acts should be performed in private, and not in public with vain displays of repentance concerning the scandal. Third, he owed his subject authenticity, since preaching against scandals becomes virtue with reserve, not with more notoriety exhibited from the sacred platform. Finally, he owed his listeners not the trash of tabloids but a good sermon: the uplifting doctrine that the Church is holy regardless of the scandals of the past, the present, or the times to come. Thus, Granada's silence is meaningful. Yet, to grasp this meaning, the critic must have at least an idea of the facts on which Granada silenced—a piece of information to be found outside than the silent text.

Finally, sometimes the search for information different from the text itself responds to the elementary need of starting with easy materials in order to understand difficult ones later. Baltasar Gracián is often blamed for obscurity, when he might be just difficult. In fact, it is possible to make sense of his writings through the aid of extensive reviews of literature on his works and his life, and the comparison of his theories to simpler ones prepared by authors like Pellegrini, Pallavicino, Tesauro, etc.

Consider the Communicative Process of Wit

Very often some witty texts—for example, Gracián's—are blamed for snobbery because of their difficulty to communicate. But their difficulty is legitimate:

Twayne Publishers, 1977) 37.

witty discourse does more than transmitting existing ideas to passive listeners; witty discourse also requires from listeners the effort of apprehension of ideas. Ideas should be well understood first, and only then can the speaker aim at their clear exchange with the audience.

Despite of this perceived snobbery, many baroque texts are also condemned as vulgar because they adapt themselves to the ways of ordinary people in order to facilitate an already difficult communication. In fact, this summary contempt to reach the populace is what is true snobbery. Father Isla thus addressed the enlightened "public" of his times:

> You thought convenient to call wise those who knew certain subjects, and to regard ignorant those who ignored them, in spite that they knew other arts probably more—or at least equally—useful to human life. And you succeeded on accomplishing it. All around the world, theologians, canonists, lawyers, philosophers, physicians, mathematicians, critics, in a word, the scholars, are esteemed wise, and farmers, carpenters, masons, and blacksmiths are labeled ignorant.[70]

Isla's *Fray Gerundio de Campazas* is a satire especially attacking snob preachers whose sermons pretend scholarship to impress the ordinary people. Even so, Father Isla could not save himself of the snobbery of often portraying these people as vulgar. He certainly ridiculed many of their religious practices such as allegorical processions and plays in which the whole community is involved. Fray Gerundio is finally censored not when he is snobbish, but when he decides to adapt his preaching to the audience, by integrating his sermons of Holy Week into several traditional representations of the Passion the villagers practiced.[71]

Besides snobbery, Isla here seems ignorant of the communicative process of wit. As said, wit does not declare or simply transmit information. Wit suggests or points to it. Wit does not simply supply experience to a passive audience.

---

[70]José Francisco de Isla, *Fray Gerundio de Campazas*, "Al público, poderosísimo señor".

[71]See Isla 4: 227–247.

Rather wit relies on the common experience which both the speaker and the listener share, and which both persons together and actively analyze to make sense of it, according to the lines of correspondence proposed by each. Effective communication occurs when both reach the same idea.[72] It takes place not by explicitly expressing the idea, but by silently gazing at it during an intimate, often enjoyable, complicity,[73] as happens with something as ordinary as jokes, much of our conversation with friends, and frequently in politics. For instance, George Bush's "Read my lips!" was not simply a trope for "No more taxes." Regardless of our sympathy for him and his policies, the expression serves as a conceptual frame which recalls the experience many of us have had of answering impertinence with a grave and silent glance at those who already know what our answer to their question is. The expression also defined Bush's character as firm and grave towards impertinence. Thus, to reach communication, wit requires not only the same analytic frame—the expressed witticism—but also the same set of data to analyze—usually, the common and internal experience stored in memory.

The implied understandings reached through wit help people become aware of their own commonality, which at its highest level is a self-awareness of their shared humanity. Gracián thus described Andrenio's first encounter with another man:

> Critilo, you ask me who I am, and I wish to know it from you. You are the first man who I have ever seen until now, and in you I see myself mirrored more lively

---

[72]Nonetheless, reaching the same idea does not mean reaching the same judgment. See *Agudeza* discourses 1–4. Even though the speaker and the listener share a common experience, a common frame of analysis, a common perception of the data through the witticism, and reach the same idea, that does not mean that they reach the same judgment. They may disagree in judgment by simply noticing that the frame of analysis is improper.

[73]Concerning the communicative process of wit, see, for example, *El Criticón* I, Crisi 1 (Gracián particulary referred here to the common experience which is discovered and enjoyed through conversation.); see also *Oráculo* Aphorism 68 (Gracián here described the best process of communication not as one which refers to facts, but as one which makes sense of these facts.)

than in any of my mute reflections in a spring...[74]

Communities stir up this awareness through the intimacy of wit rather than through explicit declarative communication which somehow marks their distance from strangers. But since wit rests not only on an analytic frame, but on a common experience, communities much search this experience in their common activities, which set the initial grounds to explore, perceive, and assert their more inner commonality. Dances, dinners, singing, parties, parades, masquerades, popular representations, allegorical processions come not just as opportunities of socializing, but as opportunities of raising inner self-awareness. Then the greatest feast is wit.[75]

Sometimes baroque preaching was not just an oration. On occasions it was a complex spectacle, which strongly involved the audience. Unashamed, Gracián called the Royal Hospital of Saragossa "playhouse of the greatest talents,"[76] which the best preachers used as a pulpit. Hilary Dansey Smith reports sermons like this from Valderrama:

> Fray Pedro de Valderrama...much extolled by biographers, was responsible for a very elaborate show in Saragossa in the early 1600's. He first blacked out the church and concealed two torches...behind the pulpit. Then he placed 'cantores y músicos de Cornetas...a cuatro coros en los ángulos de la Iglesia' [singers and musicians with cornets...in four choirs at the corners of the church], to be brought into action at a given signal. These preparations made, 'con todo secreto' [in complete secrecy] he was ready to preach his sermon on the Conversion of St. Mary Magdalene. Half-way through he suddenly broke off and, 'dando una voz con fuer-

---

[74]*El Criticón* I, Crisi 1: "Tú, Critilo, me preguntas quién soy yo y yo deseo saberlo de ti. Tú eres el primer hombre que hasta hoy he visto y en ti me hallo retratado más al vivo que en los mudos cristales de una fuente..."

[75]Masquerades and other symbolic inventions which enliven social events are an important type of wit discussed in treatises of ingenuity. See, for example, *Agudeza* Discourse 47; *Cannocchiale* Chapter 18.

[76]*El Criticón* III, "A Don Lorenzo Francés de Urritigoyti, Dignísimo Deán de la Santa Iglésia de Sigüenza:" "...palenque de los mayores talentos..."

za extraordinaria' [exclaiming with an extraordinarily powerful voice], said: 'Señor mío, Jesu Christo, parezca aquí vuestra divina Magestad, y vea este pueblo el estrago que con sus pecados han hecho en su Santa persona, tan digna de respecto y veneración' [My Lord, Jesus Christ, present here your Divine Majesty, and let this people see the damage that with their sins they have made in your Holy person, so much deserving of respect and veneration]. No sooner had he finished speaking than there suddenly appeared 'la santa imagen de Christo, puesto en Cruz, y a los lados las antorchas' [the holy image of Christ, set on the Cross, and the torches at his sides]. We have no record, unfortunately, of whether the 'heavenly choirs' and trumpeters intervened at this point, or what they played, but the effect on the congregation, taken by surprise, was truly dramatic. Shrieks, wails, and lamentations rent the air. The 'mujeres perdidas' [lost-minded women]...flung around in an agony of remorse, tearing their hair and beating their breasts, 'como gente de veras convertida' [as if they certainly were people converted]. The biographer, full of admiration, comments that the confusion inside the church 'parecía una pintura o representación del juicio final' [seemed a picture or representation of the final judgment].[77]

This narrative provides a good picture of the spectacular character which preaching sometimes had in Spain during the baroque age. However, I think the story is to some degree misleading. Probably drawn by the not uncommon sentimentality of hagiographies, the narrator took for granted the secrecy of the special effects as if churches had not richly exhibited statues and images for centuries, which the parishioners were not accostumed to see, or which they themselves had not made with their own hands.[78] The hagiographer also took the emotional response of the audience as "lost-minded"—surprisingly, he seemingly was happy about this reasonless response. But this hagiographer completely missed the strong and very conscious sense of decorum kept by Valderrama's audience. They carefully listened when Valderrama was speaking, and appropriately kept silent. But when Valderrama showed the Crucified to them, then they realized that it was the time to indulge themselves with shrieks,

---

[77]Smith 66–67.

[78]Today, the special effects used in richly decorated churches are enhanced by means of electricity.

wails, and the beating of breasts. This audience's wit was manifest in their knowing the time to refrain and the time to indulge.[79]

As Smith notices,[80] António Vieira reported a similar case in which a preacher was failing to move the audience with a verbal account of the trial of Jesus, but that thereafter:

> A curtain was then opened, and an image of *Ecce homo*[81] appears. Behold, everybody postrated to the ground; behold, everybody beating their chests; behold, the tears; behold, the shrieks; behold, the wails; behold, the blows. What's all this? Did He appear again in this Church? Everything that was uncovered from that curtain was already spoken by the preacher...if all this did not move then anybody, how does it accomplish so much now? Because then it was a heard *Ecce Homo*, and now it is a seen *Ecce Homo*.[82]

It should be noted that Vieira was not particularly arguing then about the effectiveness or propriety of special effects on the sacred platform. His point was remarking that, rather than confining preaching to a hollow exposition of doctrines, the preacher should let the people see the actuality of these doctrines

---

[79]Concerning self-awareness and the discharge of the passions, I have these examples: Great Teresa was once rebuked by a nun because of the saint's indulging in eating partridges at the bishop's table. Teresa replied: "When penance, then penance; when partridges, then partridges." My mother ran to give my 86 year old grandmother a posthumous letter from the last of her sisters. My grandmother was watching a very interesting TV program and ignored her daughter until the program was finished. Then my grandmother indulged herself in reading the letter with deep weeping and mourning from the bottom of her heart.

[80]See Smith 66.

[81]This image is one of Christ as presented by Pilate to the Jews during the trial: "Behold, the man!" *John* 19:5.

[82]António Vieira, *Sermão da Sexagésima*, IV: "Corre-se neste passo ua cortina, aparece a imagem do *Ecce Homo*: eis todos protrados por terra; eis todos a bater nos peitos, eis as lágrimas, eis os gritos, eis os alaridos, eis as bofetadas: que é isto? Que apareceu de novo nesta Igreja? Tudo o que descobriu aquela cortina, tinha já dito o pregador...Pois se isto então não fez abalo nenhum, como faz agora tanto? Porque então era *Ecce Homo* ouvido, e agora é *Ecce Homo* visto".

through exemplars: the wooden image of Christ on the Station of the Cross, or, more important, the living image of Christ as embodied by the preacher himself in living a holy life.

A further step is allowing the people to gaze at the actuality of a doctrine, as embodied in themselves when dramatized, imitated, or lived. In many Catholic churches, while reading Good Friday's Gospel, parishioners play the role of the Jews shouting: "Crucify him! Crucify him!" As simplistic as it may be, this dramatization helps parishioners to make sense of the Nicene Creed's severe confession—"for our sake he was crucified"—and to trascend the literalness of the Gospel saying that Jesus was handed to the Jews to be crucified[83]—a literalness which not rarely has led to serious distorsions of Christian doctrine, and also to the most abhorrent "redressing" persecutions against the Jews.

Father Isla disliked and ridiculed Fray Gerundio's adaptation of his Holy Week sermons to the villagers' plays and allegorical representations.[84] Isla seemingly perceived this adaptation to the popular taste as vulgar, and displayed a contempt similar to the one he showed to the provincial deputies of Navarre.[85] Not in a novel, as Fray Gerundio, but in real life (Valencia, December 8, 1644), Father Baltasar Gracián suffered the censorship of one of his sermons because he at the same time attempted to dramatize receiving a letter from Hell.[86] I have already said that this attempt probably was a childish trick to startle and entertain his audience. But who knows if Gracián's sermon rather was as keen minded, enlightening, and profound as his writings.

I know, though, that the many popular religious traditions which survive from centuries, and are often framed by keynote sermons,[87] are very witty,

---

[83]See *John* 19:16.

[84]See Isla 4: 227–247.

[85]See José Francisco de Isla, *Día Grande de Navarra.*

[86]See Smith 66.

[87]The integration of popular religious festivals with solemn liturgies and sermons has not been exclusive to the seventeenth century, but has been common to many different ages and has survived till today in different forms. See, for example, G. R. Owst, *Preaching in*

enjoyable, and enlightening about the faith, rarely vulgar, and far away from the manipulative or rashly emotional. For instance, *las posadas* recreate Joseph and Mary in search of an inn before the Nativity; sermons, prayer, and meditation are combined with playful songs, clever versifying, and the breaking of *piñatas*. Another example is *las pastorelas*, when families or neighbors join together to represent the haste—or delay—of shepherds to adore Baby Jesus; it is time for agile comedy and innuendo, witty improvisations and debates, but also the most limpid poetry:

> But look how thirsty the fish drink in the river,
> but look how thirsty they drink to see the God born![88]

The most complex expression of these traditions is reached with the *autos sacramentales*, plays which allegorically expound the Christian mysteries. In spite of the intellectual difficulty of their subjects, and the refinements of language, these mystery plays continue to attract large publics. But more important, they continue to serve as keen instruments to advance the understanding and to communicate the faith.[89]

Medieval England, an introduction to sermon manuscripts of the period, (London: Cambridge University Press, 1926).

[88] ¡Pero mira cómo beben los peces en el río,
pero mira cómo beben por ver a Dios nacido!

[89] An excellent example of mystery plays is Pedro Calderón de la Barca's *El gran teatro del mundo*, which almost philosophically inquires about the non contradiction between God's omnipotence and human free will. Another instance is *Don Juan*, with its many versions and its parade of specters, that is on stage during All Souls' Day, and reflects on the importance of both works and faith to reach salvation. The many different versions emphasize, among other things, either faith or works; an easy way to identify this preference is if Don Juan goes to Heaven or to Hell.

Use Wit to Identify the Proper Grounds of Judgment

For Gracián, judgment should follow understanding, and not viceversa;[90] moreover, judgment can take place only after the idea to test has been clearly defined and the testing grounds have been sharply identified through the assistance of wit. Without the clear understanding gained through wit, judgment could only face the meaningless, and judgment would be impossible. However, there are critics who, ignoring the rational character of wit and thus failing to understand witty texts, nevertheless dare to judge these texts, as if they could judge something that for their minds appear meaningless. Doing this is nonsense.

Consider for instance Adolphe Coster. He strongly expresses disgust at what he defines as bad taste fashionable in Gracián's times and most notorious in this Jesuit's works. Referring to *El Comulgatorio*'s style,[91] Coster says:

> Although [this style is] less deformed than [the one] in his other treatises, we find in this one [book] traces of bad taste which remind us of the listeners he thought of in his «Letter from Hell»...Meditation 16 is the perfect model of lack of taste. The author compares the Eucharistic banquet to a feast with a menu where the guests can select the dishes...using a method not to be disdained by Fray Gerundio...[92]

Coster then illustrates his belief with this passage from that meditation:

> Here is served a lamb fed with virginal[93] milk, warmed up[94] by the fire of His[95] love:

---

[90]See *Agudeza* Discourse 1–2.

[91]*El Comulgatorio* is a collection of fifty meditations on the Eucharist fitting to consider by the communicant in every religious feast of the year.

[92]Coster 80.

[93]A "cordero de leche" means a sucking lamb, and it literally translates as a "lamb fed with milk." The Lamb of God was fed with "virginal milk" because of his Mother.

[94]It should be noticed that "sazonado" here means both: "warmed up" and "seasoned."

[95]The pronoun "su" is ambiguous. It may mean "His," that is Jesus's love, or "her," that

Oh, what a vast[96] entrée! Here is a heart in love of souls: Oh, what a delicious meal! Here is a tongue: although milk and honey flows from it, it nevertheless was soured with bile and vinegar:[97] look that you eat it with good taste,[98]　for some hands and some feet pierced with nails[99] are not to be left-over: continue pondering what you eat in this fashion, and sorting[100] your devotion.[101]

Coster nauseates and says that "This «gastronomic» piety is repulsive."[102] If so, this other passage should also be revolting for him:

...those who eat...linger over that that they taste: "not with haste," they say, "let's

---

is the Mother of God's love. Rather than impoverishing, this ambiguity enriches the passage.

[96]"Regalado" is both "vast" and "free."

[97]The text suggests both: Jesus's torture of vinegar during the Crucifixion, and "lengua a la vinagreta," a dish of tongue soured in vinaigrette.

[98]Here "de buen gusto" may be better translated as "with enthusiasm." However, I still prefer the literal translation of "with good taste," since, associated with Gracián's doctrines of good taste, this choice of translation also emphasizes a request to use our faculty of keen discrimination to appreciate the banquet we are enjoying.

[99]It should be noticed that "clavos" means both "nails" and "cloves." As far as I remember, cloves are used to prepare pork feet in vinaigrette.

[100]In saying that the communicant should "sort his devotion," Gracián cleared this meditation from the potentials of a doctrinal error. It is not the Body of Christ which is sorted in parts in the Eucharist, as if here were the hands, and there were the eyes, but the communicant's devotion, which, meditating can contemplate all these aspects as present *substantially* in the sacrament: Christ's body, blood, soul, and divinity, and yet one unified and whole person.

[101]Coster 80, who quotes *El Comulgatorio* Meditation 16: "Aquí se sirve un cordero de leche virginal, sazonado al fuego de su amor: ¡Oh qué regalado plato! Aquí un corazón enamorado de las almas: ¡Oh qué comida tan gustosa! Una lengua, que aunque de sí mana leche y miel, pero fué aleada con hiel y con vinagre: mira que la comas de buen gusto, pues unas manos y unos pies traspasados con los clavos, no son de dejar: ve desta suerte ponderando lo que comes, y repartiendo la devoción."

[102]Coster 81.

ruminate slowly, let's chew well and it will be good for us"...[103]

A most tolerant Coster excuses Gracián because of his irrational Spanish race:

> ...we should not forget that what results irritating for us in these excessively material images by no means would capture the attention of the author's countrymen, whose temperament hardly accomodated to pure abstractions.[104]

What shall we say to this criticism? I do not agree with Coster. For the "temperamental" Spaniards and for any other person, the greatest power of abstraction—the greatest power of wit—is necessary to understand that Gracián's meditation was not inflaming primitive minds with toothsome images, and not even aiming at rendering, through those images, only mere ideas—pure thoughts—as if these ideas did not have any real reference; the greatest ingenuity is needed to see that Gracián's concept is here referring to a most concrete and mysterious reality: the Real Presence. Moreover, according to many Catholic exegetes like Gracián, this reality is supposed to be a shocking dogma. When Jesus revealed the Eucharistic dogma, He said:

> For my flesh is food indeed, and my blood is drink indeed.[105]

Many thousands of followers[106] rejected this revelation:

> Many of his disciples therefore, when they heard this, said, "This is a hard saying.

---

[103]*El Comulgatorio* Meditation 16: "...los que comen...se van deteniendo en aquello que van gustando, 'no vamos aprisa', dicen; 'rumiemos a espacio, masquemos bien y nos entrará en provecho'..."

[104]Coster 81.

[105]*John* 6:56.

[106]These events followed the multiplication of the bread by Jesus to feed thousands of followers. See *John* 6:1–15.

Who can listen to it?"[107]

Only Twelve disciples remained:

> Jesus therefore said to the Twelve, "Do you also wish to go away?" Simon Peter
> therefore answered, "Lord, to whom shall we go?..."[108]

I think that in Meditation 16 Gracián wanted to capture the tension between this shocking element of the Eucharist and faithfully receiving this sacrament. This meditation moves the communicant faithfully to request many particular graces as he receives the sacramental banquet, but it also reminds him about how distressing and challenging to faith the eating of this Real Flesh and Real Blood could be. Gracián achieved his goal by associating the Eucharist[109] to the most real foods[110] and by savoring communion with gusto.

Coster's disgust about Gracián illustrates how judgment can go wrong if the critic, lacking the assistance of wit, consequently fails to identify the proper grounds of testing. Coster should not expect a sanitized scholarly exposition of what the Eucharist is since Gracián was doing something else: meditating on one of the darkest aspects of the night of faith. Similarly many other texts regarded as exemplars of the Spanish "lack of taste" may not be so. The truly gruesome

---

[107]*John* 6:61.

[108]*John* 6:68–69.

[109]It seems a doctrinal error that Gracián compared perishable dishes with the Eucharist, which is the food sustaining people to eternal life. However, at the end of Meditation 16, and in many other places of *El Comulgatorio*, Gracián took care to specify the unperishable character of the Person present in the sacrament: "...each of these entrées deserves a complete day, and even all eternity." ("...cada plato destos merece todo un día, y aun toda una eternidad").

[110]The shocking effect is strengthened by making some of these real foods to be more than entrées: they are entrails.

narratives found in the *Lazarillos, Guzmanes,* and *Quevedos*[111] do not seek pleasure on contemplating feces; these narratives seek disabuse[112] for those self-deceived persons who do not recognize the immorality[113] they are immersed in.

One of the oldest tenets of scholasticism is that a well-regulated will moves itself to specific choices by being informed by a clear understanding.[114] In the Spanish tradition of oratory, this being informed by the understanding is achieved either by wit which squeezes out sharp concepts,[115] or by amplification

---

[111]I am referring to picaresque novels—about rogues—typical of the Spanish tradition. The *Lazarillo de Tormes,* and Mateo Alemán's *Guzmán de Alfarache*—along with some works of Francisco de Quevedo—are the best models of this genre of literature which strove for the grotesque, caricatures, and the ugly. To some degree, Gracián's *El Criticón* belongs to this literary trend: it often uncovers very disagreeable aspects of the human condition, and it lingers over them to disabuse the reader. Cf. José F. Montesinos, "Gracián o la picaresca pura," *Cruz y Raya,* 4 (Madrid, 1933).

[112]Here disabuse may be a closer synonym of enlightenment. In any case, in Gracián's theories, disabuse liberates people from deception, and thus allows them to start their journey into virtue. See *El Criticón.*

[113]Picaresque narratives usually overtly portray the immorality of the lower classes. But the real target—if the concept is squeezed out—is the upper classes.

[114]Let's recall that Fr Luis de Granada—both a great Spanish neoscholastic and a great orator—described the will as a blind faculty, which is not moved to any affection if the understanding does not present the motives and causes for which it should be moved in such a direction. See Fr Luis de Granada, *Guía de Pecadores,* "Prólogo Galeato." The perceived goodness or badness in objects is not a sentiment or an internal emotion. It is something objective which the understanding grasps from the things analyzed: the degree and actualization of being identified in objects. Cf., for example, *Nicomachean Ethics,* Bk. X: Ch. 5; *Summa Theologica* I, Q.5. A well-regulated will accordingly responds to the goods or evils perceived by reason. If in doing it, the will feels emotions and pleasure, that is just an accompanying goodness gained from the pursuing and accomplishing of the choices made, but it should not be necessarily confused with the chosen good itself. See, for example, Plato's *Gorgias; Nicomachean Ethics,* Bk. VI: Ch.11–14, Bk. X: Ch.1–5.

[115]Wit is the method theorized by Gracián in his *Agudeza,* and exemplified by his Eucharistic meditations as contained in *El Comulgatorio.*

which strengthens the detailed perception of objects.[116] The Spanish preachers' sharp or detailed presentation of bad objects to the understanding, and thus to the will, is not necessarily an instance of bad taste if, for example, this discourse becomingly informs the understanding and prevents the will from evil. And presenting good and nice objects to the mind—as Spanish oratory often did, too, sharply or with detail—is not necessarily an instance of good taste if this task and its ends are not becomingly undertaken. Moreover, the grounds from which judgment should arise are not necessarily the good or bad taste of the piece of discourse. Sometimes it is its Scriptural fidelity; other times, its historical accuracy; often, its moral adequacy and force; in many occasions, its theological soundness; not rarely, its spiritual and mystical keenness; not seldom, the logical correction; frequently, its rhetorical eloquence and decorum; and there are situations in which even the geometrical precision and coherence are the significant factor which grounds our judgment.[117]

I should repeat that wit precedes judgment,[118] at least in two ways. First, wit sharpens the concept so that this concept later can be tested with precision by judgment. Second, wit discovers the proper grounds of judgment. Though rarely a text explicitly prescribes the grounds of its testing, if the text is squeezed out enough, it will clearly speak of its referred objects and many other related things. Then judgment can test the idea by checking if it *precisely* fits these referred objects and related things (whatever they may be: factual truths, practical actions, moral values, a beautiful artistic form, etc.) Not wit, but

---

[116]This method was studied in detail by Fr Luis de Granada in his *Rhetorica Eclesiástica*. There, he devoted a whole book to the subject—the third one. Granada also accomplished the greatest exemplars of this method in oratory, as identifiable in his sermons and meditation books.

[117]St Augustine included the most diverse sciences and arts assisting the study of the Scriptures, for example, philosophy, dialectics, mathematics, rhetoric, grammar, music, history, natural sciences, astronomy, arquitecture, cookery, medicine, agriculture, navigation, and even gymnastics. See *De Doctrina Christiana*, Book Three.

[118]Cf. *Agudeza* Discourses 1–2.

judgment is what abhors farfetchedness.[119]   If the idea's testing is made with something of the same species, then the proof is an example. If the idea's testing is made just with something similar, then the proof is an analogy. If the testing is made with something remotely resembling the idea, then prudence very often dictates dismissing the proof as such.

By squeezing out Gracián's meditation on St Peter's humility, addressed to those receiving communion, we may recall events mentioned by the Writ (and other authoritative texts):

> Consider that if John deserved so many favors from the Divine Master because of being virgin,[120] Peter received them because of being humble. John was the beloved disciple,[121] Peter the humiliated one,[122] for he had to become the head of the Church,[123] and superior of all in dignity,[124] even so he had made himself feet of everybody because of his humility.[125] As fervor enraptured him in occasions,[126] in the same way abasement restrained him.[127] He did not dare to question the Lord,[128] and thus he was the one questioned by the Lord.[129] When the others disputed the

---

[119]Judgment's repugnance for farfetchedness is the very reason of wit's farfetchedness. The more extreme a witty comparison is, the subtler the similarities that ingenuity can discover. Thus, the keener the concept that is abstracted, the sharper the idea which can be tested by judgment with exact precision is.

[120]St John's virginity is a belief traceable to the Patristic tradition.

[121]Cf., for example, *John* 21:20–24.

[122]Cf., for example, *Luke* 22:31–32.

[123]Cf., for example, *Matthew* 16:13–20.

[124]Cf., for example, *John* 21:15–19, *Acts* 1:15, 15:7–14.

[125]Cf., for example, *John* 13:6–19, 20:3-10, 21:7.

[126]Cf., for example, *Matthew* 14:27–33; *Luke* 24:12; *John* 18:10–11, 21:7, 6:67–69.

[127]Cf., for example, *John* 13:7.

[128]Cf., *John* 13:24.

[129]Cf., *Matthew* 17:24–27.

best seats,[130] he did not consider himself worthy of being present before his Master.[131] Pleased the Lord by this abasement,[132] leaving the other boats,[133]   He comes into the one of him,[134] He preaches from it,[135] and He rests on it.[136]   Peter received the reprehensions,[137] but he enjoyed[138] the special favors.[139]

This analysis reveals the extensive aquaintance Gracián had of the Scriptures, and his amazingly condensed use of these texts to construct his discourse—a discursive pattern which may remind us of St Bernard's.[140] The analysis also enriches the understanding of the meditation by informing the mind about the concrete details there condensed. But not even a more detailed and complete study of the Scriptures could provide the best grounds of judgment for

---

[130]Cf. *Mark* 10:35–37.

[131]Cf. *Luke* 5:8, *John* 13:6–8.

[132]Cf. *John* 13:9–10.

[133]Cf. *Luke* 5:2.

[134]Cf. *Luke* 5:3.

[135]Cf. *Luke* 5:3.

[136]Cf. *Luke* 5:3; *Matthew* 16:13–20, 8:23–24.

[137]Cf. *Matthew* 14:31.

[138]Cf., *Matthew* 17:24–27; *Mark* 1:29–31; *John* 21:18.

[139]*El Comulgatorio* Meditación IX, i: "Considera que si Juan mereció recibir tantos favores de su Divino maestro por lo virgen, Pedro los consiguió por lo humilde. Juan fué el discípulo amado, Pedro el humillado: había de ser cabeza de la Iglesia y superior de todos por su dignidad, pero él se hacía pies de todos por su humildad. Lo que le arrebataba el fervor en las ocasiones, le detenía su encogimiento; no osaba preguntar al Señor, y así el Señor le preguntaba a él; cuando los otros pretendían las primeras sillas, él no se tenía por digno de estar delante de su Maestro. Agradado el Señor deste encogimiento, dejando las otras barcas, entra en la suya, desde ella predica y en ella descansa; llevaba Pedro las reprehensiones, pero gozaba de los especiales favores."

[140]Cf. Arturo del Hoyo cxc, who compares Gracián's *El Comulgatorio* with the Church Fathers' conceptism.

the meditation. The critic should not forget that the meditation is not properly on St Peter's humility, but on the abasement which communicants should observe when approaching communion. Moreover, the meditation intends to inspire in the communicant this abasement. Thus, it is in the power present in the text to ignite a well-informed humility where the critic should identify the decisive test for the meditation.[141] Using this standard of well-informed devotion, Arturo del Hoyo summarized his judgment about *El Comulgatorio*:

> Partisan—as he who is the most [partisan]—of a fruitful devotional literature, [Gracián] nevertheless does not stop being conceptist in *El Comulgatorio*, but there he is so in an adequate manner. In this sense, he follows an ancient tradition, the one of some Church Fathers whose conceptism he abundantly demonstrated and illustrated in *Agudeza y arte de ingenio*.
>
> The result of this Gracián's position is a book almost unique among Spanish devotional literature. Its beautiful and appropriate parallelisms, and its energic contrasts, give to it quick and flashing iridiscences and, at the same time, a fruitful persuasiveness.[142]

Thus, the rule is that the critic should use wit in discovering the proper grounds of judgment. Otherwise, he risks testing the ideas in a wrong way. For example, he may be barbarian enough to condemn chivalry novels to the fire—as the Canon of *Don Quixote* did[143]—because they do not report factual truths, or he may regard Hernán Cortés's conquest of the Aztec Empire as impossible, because his story is more amazing than any work of fiction—as Diego Ortuñez

---

[141]António Vieira believed that the most decisive test of sermons is their power to reform the lives of the listeners to virtue and away from vice. Moreover, a sign of the failure of a sermon is that listeners leave the church remembering the excellence of the sermon rather than the reform of their lives. See *Sermão da Sexagésima*, X.

[142]Arturo del Hoyo cxc.

[143]The drama of chivalry novels being thrown to the fire is reenacted today but in the public attitude towards television. The fear of the unknown effects of unspeakable books at the dawn of the printing press has been transferred to television at the dawn of the mass media.

suggested.[144]

Keep in Mind: Wit is Important but not Everything

As said above, judgment often rushes and skips understanding in its haste to reach a conclusion. Recently, for example, a friend shared with me his indignation about a Chilean student who, on the grounds of expediency, expressed strong approval of Augusto Pinochet's coup d'état, which threw away the legitimate government, killed the constitutional President Salvador Allende, and in a bloody frenzy murdered several thousands supporters of democracy and human rights in the early 1970's, aided by the United States Government. Without giving to the Chilean's opinion further thought, my friend quickly concluded that this South American was "necessarily an idiot" by holding such opinions. But a stronger shock to his sense of indignation still awaited my friend: I told him to allow further thought to the Chilean's position, in order that he understand it better.

I meant it. Yet, understanding something well does not mean approval, but means possessing a well-informed mind and a keen conceptualization of the object being considered. This understanding can indeed generate a richer and deeper judgment. Hannah Arendt did not speed up in pronouncing judgment about Nazi Germany and its horrors. Rather, she carefully gazed at these horrors,[145] trying to grasp in detail the complexities of totalitarian societies, and the intricate modes of thinking of totalitarian minds.[146] Arendt's reader thus can

---

[144]See Diego Ortuñez de Calahorra, *Espejo de Príncipes y Caballeros*, Edición, introducción y notas de Daniel Eisenberg, (Madrid: Ed. Espasa-Calpe, S. A., 1975) Prólogo.

[145]Following another train of thought, here I recall the puzzling speculation of theologians about the beatific vision which the elected will have of the condemned in Hell. It is only through this vision that they will be able to *understand* the unquestionable Divine justice, and thus will be able to participate and enjoy this Divine perfection, in eternal unity with God.

[146]See Hannah Arendt, *The Origins of Totalitarianism*, (New York: Harcourt, Brace & World, Inc., 1966; first edited in 1951).

appreciate that, rather than being simple idiots, Nazis possessed powerful and most monstrous minds. Moreover, the reader can go beyond a simple moral judgment concerning Nazi wickedness. The reader then can better inform his prudence about taking appropriate steps to prevent Nazism or any other form of totalitarianism from ever occurring again.[147]

This illustration may help to explain how important wit is as a prerequisite of judgment. It is through rich and clear ideas that the mind can reach rich and clear judgment. Therefore, the mind should exercise its faculty of wit before applying to objects its faculty of judgment.

Even so, having rich and clear ideas through ingenuity does not warrant that the ideas themselves deserve judgment's assent, or that they themselves inform of appropriate reasonings to valid conclusions. There is a time when ingenuity should retreat and give place to the other operations of the mind—judgment and inference—in order properly to reason about reality, lest we act like Don Quixote, who did not care to check if the wind mills were evil giants or not. Gracián disliked persons who followed any idea that suddenly popped into their minds:

> They have a sense and a will of wax; what is the last seals and deletes anything else. They are not an asset because equally easily they are a liability. Everybody can dye them with his colors. They are bad as confidents, children all their life. Thus, with a variety of judgments and affections, they go on always fluctuating, lame of will and judgment, leaning to the one and the other position.[148]

---

[147]Referring to the nature of her work, just finished after the defeat of Nazi Germany, but before Joseph Stalin's death, Hannah Arendt explains: "With the defeat of Nazi Germany, part of the story had come to an end. This seemed the first appropriate moment to look upon contemporary events with the backward-directed glance of the historian and the analytical zeal of the political scientist, the first chance to try to tell and to understand what had happened, not yet *sine ira et studio*, still in grief and sorrow and, hence, with a tendency to lament, but no longer in speechless outrage and impotent horror." Arendt vii.

[148]*Oráculo* Aphorism 248: "Tienen el sentir y el querer de cera; el último sella y borra los demás. Estos nunca están ganados, porque con la misma facilidad se pierden; cada uno los tiñe de su color. Son malos para confidentes, niños de toda la vida; y así, con variedad en los juicios y afectos, andan fluctuando siempre, cojos de voluntad y de juicio, inclinándose a una

What I want to state clearly is that the rules of judgment and the rules of inference are not to be found in theories of ingenuity like Gracián's. Moreover, different ideas may require different specialized methods of judgment and inference. This Aristotle believed when he warned that the generality of rhetoric and dialectics' lines of arguments are not yet responding to the specificity of particular fields of science.[149] Furthermore, Gracián's theories of ingenuity can be too general to satisfy specific needs of conceptualization in very specialized fields of knowledge.[150] For instance, theory construction in the different scientific fields requires the most specialized kind of training, and often the use of artificial languages such as mathematics.[151] Even the most traditional realm of wit—humor—may be better guided with specialized methods for subtleties.[152]

Summarizing the seven rules I propose for using wit to understand witty texts, I should say that wit is important to understand and criticize a text. It helps the understanding to perceive its objects sharply and richly. But wit frequently is not enough. Then, criticism should be completed with specialized efforts of conceptualization—if needed—and with the appropriate operations of judgment and inference applicable to the case.

---

y otra parte."

[149]See *Rhetoric* I, ii; Cf. *Topica* I, i.

[150]Although very general, Gracián's theories of ingenuity are somehow specialized to study contingent moral cases (Cf., for example, *Agudeza* discourses 26–30) and, moreover, they fundamentally rest on the use of natural languages to reach the concepts (Cf., for example, *Agudeza* Discourse 31.) In this sense, their generality is constrained to those special cases, and to their study through natural languages.

[151]Concerning specialized methods of conceptualization in science, see, for instance, Mario Bunge, *Scientific Research*, (Berlin, Heidelberg, New York: Springer-Verlag, 1967); Jerald Hage, *Techniques and Problems of Theory Construction in Sociology*, (New York: J. Wiley, 1972).

[152]Cf., for example, Melvin Helitzer, *Comedy, Techniques for writers and performers. The HEARTS theory of humor writing*, (Athens, Ohio: Lawhead Press, 1984); Michael Mulkay, *On Humor. Its Nature and Its Place in Modern Society*, (Basil Blackwell, Inc., 1988).

15 The Realm of Wit

"ROUND CIRCLES: A CULTURAL ASPECT OF EUCLIDEAN GREECE," "Gregor Mendel's discovery: the *pea* laws of heredity," "Persons with emotions: the Mexican liquor smugglers at the Bajo Rio Bravo during the Prohibition," "The rhetorical Parliament: a style of doing politics in Victorian England," "An affirmative universal: a proposition contradictory to its negative particular proposition in times of the mediaeval alchemist Peter of Spain," all these would be sound phrases only if their expression figuratively intend a special emphasis. As general and matter-of-fact statements they talk nonsense, since they characterize the timeless as dated, the ubiquitous as restricted to a place, the universal as confined to one of its cases.

Thus far, I have tried to dispel such an error as it has reached not few accounts of Gracián's theories on wit: "Prompting ideas through wit: a minor literary trend of the Spanish Baroque Age." If up to this point I have failed in my rectifying purpose, I should repeat Gracián's invocation:

> And you, O Book, although what is new and tasteful guarantees you the good will if not the praise of your readers, nevertheless you still pray for the good fortune of coming across someone who understands you.[1]

And, in a last point, I should recall Gracián's radical main thesis, that *wit and its structures of correspondence are the springs of every discovery or production of new ideas*:

> This kind of correspondence is generic to every concept, and it embraces all the art of ingenuity.[2]

---

[1] *Agudeza* "Al Lector". "Y tú, ¡oh, libro!, aunque lo nuevo y lo exquisito te afianzan el favor, si no el aplauso de los lectores, con todo deprecarás la suerte de encontrar con quien te entienda".

[2] *Agudeza* Discourse 2: "Esta correspondencia es genérica a todos los conceptos, y abraza todo el artificio del ingenio."

Moreover, it ushers all art of reason, since no person can reason without concepts:

> Understanding without wit and concepts is a sun without light, without rays, and the many that shine in the celestial luminaries are material compared to those of ingenuity.[3]

Let *the swagger of ingenuity* shed again its glimmering beams on this finding—a final sparkle about the realm of wit—that the time is coming to close these pages.

Wit and Humor, Minor Literature, the Baroque, and the Fine Arts

Overlooking the vastness of wit's realm, and restricting it to humor and minor literary trends is easy because of the overwhelming exemplarity of such clearest cases.

Certainly, humor is the prototype of wit for most scholars of all ages. They first or more easily have found explanation of the power of wit in the funny. Thus happened to Quintilian and Cicero, who there identified the principles of mind's wit,[4] and in doing so tended to reduce all wit to the jocose. Gracián himself relied on the sallies of Martial as the most accessible and useful source of illustrations for *Agudeza*.

Even so, the conspicuous wit of humor should not be a denial, but a confirmation of other varieties of wit. Humor results from the amusing discovery of coexisting incoherences in human nature;[5] but somehow every original

---

[3]*Agudeza* Discourse 1: "Entendimiento sin agudeza ni conceptos, es sol sin luz, sin rayos, y cuantos brillan en las celestes lumbreras son materiales con los del ingenio".

[4]Cf. *De Oratore* II, 217-290; *Institutio Oratoria* IV, iii.

[5]Gracián explained the humorous on the discovery of harmony in the incoherence between the intentions and the actions of people. See *Agudeza* discourses 27–28, on malicious and ridiculous wit. Pellegrini also explained humor on discovering harmony between incoherent

conceptualization also rests on the insight of relations between the odd.[6]

Not without puzzlement, we may thus exclaim that there lies a mystery: our godlike understanding faces its own nature by gazing at the levity of laughter. Doubting and bewildered, like Aristotle, we nonetheless would perceive in the discovery of the joke in jests an explanation of the surmounting of philosophy to the ethereal region of ideas.[7]

There is another paradigmatic form of acuteness: the brief sayings distinctly studied by Aristotle when addressing the subject of style in rhetoric; the flashes of wit enjoyed by deranged geniuses, and captured in quick expressions, as eighteenth-century English theorists would say; the urbane and yet fallacious "syllogisms" of Tesauro, and also the courtly nosegay of the *cancioneros*; furthermore, the gems of wisdom, as keenly worded in laconic phrases—in aphorisms and sententiae—, among whose greatest and universal models shall always outshine Baltasar Gracián's writings; but, in short, such pieces of penmanship's "minor literature," as Correa Calderón calls them,[8] which reduce all literary form to an affected "intellectualism," as characterized by Menéndez Pelayo.[9]

Certainly, witty sayings are not the least striking illustrations of the power of ingenuity. Their brevity and freedom—in so far as "loose wit"—, perhaps

---

things, but he meant by that the seemly presentation of the ugly. See *Acutezze* Chapter 5.

[6] See *Agudeza* Discourse 4.

[7] Cf. *Rhetoric* III, 10, 11, and 18, where Aristotle glimpsed in wit a power to grasp ideas, and also *Posterior Analytics* I, 34, where Aristotle defined quick wit as "the faculty of instantaneously hitting upon the middle term." Elsewhere, Aristotle seemed to ignore any method for the apprehension of ideas from reality. On the one hand, the *Categories* supply a method for the analysis and criticism of ideas, but not for their discovery. On the other hand, Aristotle assigned the discovery of ideas to "intuitive reason" (*Nicomachean Ethics* VI, 6), which he also called "induction" (*Posterior Analytics* II, 19). In doing it, Aristotle apparently proposed that ideas are either simply seen in data or pre-existent in the mind, but not apprehended.

[8] See Correa Calderón, *Baltasar Gracián* 281.

[9] See Menéndez Pelayo 355–356

their easiness as Correa Calderón would rather believe,[10] would make these sayings the mind's instruments for its boldest adventures.[11] Their surprising novelty, and yet quick, common, use in suave conversation[12] would make them the most obvious exemplars of acuteness in our everyday life. And since at one time or another these sayings take recourse to words as their materials,[13] these expressions could well be described as "literature," moreover, as "minor literature" for their concision, and furthemore, as "baroque literature" because of being very fashionable in that age.

However, ingenuity is not only prominet in brief and "loose wit", but also outstanding in its compound forms,[14] "running with even flow through a speech," as Cicero explained.[15] And acuteness is not literary or baroque only, but extends to all the other fine arts of any age, whose novel harmonies, proportions, and consonances establish exquisite structures of correspondence[16] through which we can grasp not just the hollow artistic *forma* of the art for the art's sake,[17] or the dull *splendor* of pamphletary pomp.osities,[18] but the whole *splendor formae*[19]—the presence of the eternal and sublime ideas, as experienced in and

---

[10]See Correa Calderón, *Baltasar Gracián* 281.

[11]See *Agudeza* Discourses 51 and 61.

[12]Cf. *El Criticón* I, Crisi 1.

[13]Cf., *Agudeza* Discourse 31.

[14]See *Agudeza* discourses 51 to 57.

[15]*De Oratore* II, 218.

[16]Cf. *Agudeza* Discourse 2.

[17]This art would just appeal to the senses, without attempting to convey any meaning or appeal to the intellect. For instance, bad *culteranist* style. Cf. *Agudeza* Discourse 60.

[18]This art suffers from an authoritarian transmission—or attempt of imposition—of ideas to others by pure declarative language, without having a dialogue with the mind of the audience.

[19]Conceptist art could fit this category if it accomplished its goal of providing a frame—or concept—to squeeze out an idea.

revealed with unending novelty by the few master pieces.

Wit and the Making Sense of Facts: Science, Philosophy, and the Media

Science, philosophy, journalism, and some television genres pay attention to and claim to give an objective account of facts. They may differ, however, in their power to appeal to our understanding and judgment concerning these facts. In Gracián's system, facts—that is, sensual data—are not self-explanatory. "Pure information" can only acquire meaning and be pondered by reason until it is conceptualized, that is, until an idea of the facts is abstracted and specified through wit.

The sciences necessarily appeal to the understanding. Their data does not remain raw as it appears to the senses, but it is already conceptualized, and thus appropriate for their thinking and testing with precision. In fact, the power of scientific knowledge lies in it being abstract. By detaching itself from the irrelevant concreteness of singular things, science reaches a generality which comprehends a whole universe of objects.

It is true that the apprehension of this generality is achieved today, not through basic methods of wit, but through specialized methods of conceptualization and testing. However, many original ideas still seem to hatch when scientific minds exercise the most basic operations of ingenuity—that is, when they find meaningful connections between apparently unrelated things. If some stories about moments of productive puzzlement are not historical facts, these stories nevertheless have turned into archetypical accounts of how the scientists reach their key discoveries: Archimedes's lever,[20] his overflowing bathtube,[21] Columbus's egg,[22] Galileo's pendulums,[23] his feather and lead cannon

---

[20]It helped Archimedes develop the ancient science of mechanics.

[21]It helped Archimedes not only to device methods to measure volumes, but also—"Eureka!"—to define the concept of volume.

[22]Columbus's originality concerning the western route to the Indies was once questioned

balls,[24] Newton's apple,[25] Foucault's pendulum,[26]   Carlos Finlay's window screens,[27] August Kekulé's snake nightmare,[28]   Ernest Rutherford's diminute planetary system,[29]   Madame Curie's extra glowing ores,[30] Einstein's deceptive

---

by skeptics. He then challenged the skeptics to make an egg stand on its point. Only Columbus was able to do so after breaking and flattening the egg's point. The skeptics complained that such a method was too easy; any one could do it. Colombus's answered: "But it was I who did it first." The story does not illustrate Columbus's getting the idea to travel to the West, but does show Columbus's own understanding of what it means to be original and a discoverer.

[23]Their equal swinging rate suggested to Galileo that this movement did not depend on the pendulums' weight but on the unknown force he then called gravity.

[24]These are Galileo's test cases that he conceived for the demonstration of gravity. Galileo let the balls fall from the Tower of Pisa, says the story, and he observed their equal acceleration in their fall, independent of their weight, and thus caused by gravity.

[25]Although a myth, the story of Newton conceiving the universal laws of motion after contemplating the fall of an apple still illustrates the strange paths the scientific minds could follow in making discoveries.

[26]In 1851, Léon Foucault conceived a test case for the rotation of our planet. By interpreting the motion of a pendulum, he proved that the Earth rotates about its axis. Such pendulum always swings in the same vertical plane, but on a rotating Earth, this vertical plane slowly changes, at a rate and direction depending on the geographical latitude of the pendulum.

[27]In Cuba, Carlos Finlay noticed that the miasmas should poison houses either with or without window screens, but that only those houses without screens actually had a high incidence of yellow fever. He then had the idea that not the miasmas but the mosquitoes trapped in the window screens were the cause of the disease. He could thus contribute strongly to the opening of a great new field of medicine: epidemiology.

[28]In 1865, August Kekulé discovered benzene's structure during an almost demonic nightmare: he dreamed of snakes biting their tails, and thus he related this image to the hexagonal structure of the chemical.

[29]Ernest Rutherford could conceive the structure of ther atom by picturing it as resembling the planetary system. Though his model is wrong today, it still serves to symbolize atoms in popular culture.

[30]Marie Curie found that the ores of pitchblende were glowing more than the ordinary ores

trains,[31] and, say, the Syrian-leaping-hectic goats.[32]

As indicated, Aristotle was bewildered of the fact of philosophy's relying on ingenuity for its conceptualizations. He had, after all, the insight that philosophy, for being the most abstract and general field of knowledge, should strongly rely on wit—"brief sayings" and "jests", in his *Rhetoric*—to apprehend the quintessential forms embodied in the material world. He should not have been unsuspecting that Plato's dialogues would hardly lead to the apprehension of the ideas if Plato had not relied on poetry for intellectually apprehending these ideas—notwithstanding Plato's different opinion.

This bewilderment does not seem to jolt a tradition of journalism and media genres which, although sharing with the sciences the commitment to give an account of facts, nonetheless, contrasting with the sciences, claims to refer to these facts objectively seemingly meaning that the simple presentation of "pure information" to the mind suffices for their rational consideration.

"Just the facts" may be a valid standard for rational thinking under the lens of classical empiricism,[33] but not under the lens of Gracián's conceptism, and not even under the lens of contemporary sciences,[34] which require the assistance of concepts and other acts of understanding as the means for rationally considering any data. For Gracián, saying that just the facts or pure sensual data

---

of uranium and thorium. She then suspected the pitchblende contained unknown and more radioactive elements. She thus discovered both polonium and radium.

[31]An immobile train seems to move if another train at its side starts to move in the opposite direction to the one felt in the first train. This story has served to popularize Einstein's theory of relativity.

[32]Though not a scientific finding, coffee is enough of a discovery. According to a legend, coffee was first found by a Syrian shephard whose goats got crazy after eating coffee beans.

[33]Among rhetoricians, Richard Whately was the first attacking the classical empiricist assumption of "just the facts." In his *Elements of Rhetoric*, Whately noted that people cannot sensibly argue by just presenting the facts; people should also use arguments.

[34]The sciences never claim to give an accurate account of facts by "just presenting the facts." The sciences also require the conceptualization of data by means of theses and test cases. Only then reason can ponder the data rationally.

are sufficient for reason would be as if an encyclopedic erudition or an elephant-like memory were sufficient for enjoying an understanding of the data.[35] For conceptist scholars, not even the most massive supply of information is sufficient for understanding,[36] let alone for judging. The mind should function, and thus go beyond pure data. It should reach at least one meaningful idea, about the perceived facts, if aiming at thinking rationally of something.[37]

The "just-the-facts" belief implies another belief: "the media are a fair mirror of facts". A conceptist theorist would disagree and say that the media, willingly or unwillingly, often frame the information by means of some sort of "concept." The media often go beyond pure facts and insinuate ideas to the audience by framing the data with words or with "squeezable structures of correspondence." A small human settlement is differently understood with the words "slum" and "neighborhood"; and a small and autonomous locality is differently perceived with the words "tribe," "village," or "town."[38] Moreover, the mere choice of information may suggest a sense of relevance, and the structure of the message may produce a conceptual frame which favors a way to understand the facts

---

[35]See Chapter 12 that I devote to erudition. Erudition is the pasture of the mind, but not the ideas enjoyed by the mind after digestion.

[36]An acquaintance of facts is important but not sufficient for understanding. Through the most diverse information publicized, the media help audiences with the materials their minds need to make sense of the world they live in. However, pure media information is not yet a well-framed conceptualization. Media's "objective" facts may appear to the mind to be as sensuous and vague as any other chaotic glance directly obtained from the objects. These facts need to be interpreted, since in moving from facts to ideas the mind should perform the operation of conceptualization. Responsible media and publics should at least be aware that some conceptualization should be accomplished through wit in order to secure the grounds of understanding prerequisite in any rational thinking.

[37]See, for example, *Oráculo* Aphorism 68.

[38]It seems to me that the American press tends to call "slums," "tribes," or "villages" those human settlements or peoples that are colored or from "third" world countries, whereas "town" and "neighborhood" are applied to societies of a clear European background. Their word usage may respond more to a European bias than to a fair application of these words with their many connotations.

publicized. I often find that television news follow this order: first, the international news such as a bloody war in Yugoslavia or a famine in the Sudan; second, the national news such as a politician's flirting too much or a President failing to keep decorum and his food in place at the Imperial table; finally, the weather and the sports. In spite of the media's claim of offering just the news, this or any other format is not free from providing an order, a structure, and a choice of what is news. And all these are concepts,[39] and thus they deserve to be tested by judgment.[40] As strange as it may seem, the kind of newscast that I have just described has a structure which may suggest to some minds—either consciously or unconsciously—an urbane enthymeme, as Tesauro understood it, in which the audience, finding that everything in the nation appears much better than abroad, then conclude that the real news to worry about are the weather and the sports. What is at work is a squeezable structure of correspondence that may favor a point of view and of understanding.

Rather than denying the use of conceptual frames for their messages, advertising firms are very conscious of the power of structures of correspondence to suggest ideas to the public—advertising theories even fancy about "subliminal language." A dubious number of unclothed legs unclearly interwoven may make an audience squeeze the idea that "Ecstasy Jeans" are the sexiest in the market. Either true, false, or with a legitimate symbolic value,[41] ads render ideas which favorably define their products, targeting the consumer's needs.

In any case, either as news, as ads, or as any other form of squeezable format,[42] media's concepts like any other concept should be tested in order to

---

[39]They are not simply facts, but structures which facilitate it for the mind to see the facts.

[40]If an analytical structure has been chosen to apprehend the facts, then it needs to be judged whether it is appropiate for such an analysis.

[41]For instance, McDonald's and Coca-Cola may legitimately attach to their products the symbolic value of being as American as Sara Lee's apple pie.

[42]For example, the speed of modern communication leads politicians to rely much on witticisms—in the most Aristotelian sense—in order quickly to render their ideas to the

deserve assent. And if, after all, we truly face "pure information", then, we, the public, should make sense of the raw data before attempting any meaningful discussion of such facts. From facts to ideas, the mind should perform the operation of conceptualization. And from ideas to sound ideas, reason should perform the operation of judgment.

Wit and the Extensions of Man: Society, Culture, and Technology

Cicero identified in speech the power of assembling disperse people into societies:

> To come, however, at length to the highest achievements of eloquence, what other power could have been strong enough either to gather scattered humanity into one place, or to lead it out of its brutish existence in the wilderness up to our present condition of civilization as men and as citizens, or, after the establishment of social communities, to give shape to laws, tribunals, and civic rights?[43]

Under a conceptist point of view, this power is more than a verbal appeal to congregate. It is also a power to discover the hidden potentials of people to join in societies, and a power to conceive and design what sort of congregation will be such that associates the scattered humanity. It is the power of ingenuity to lead people into the most sophisticated levels of civilization.[44]

---

public. Thus Ronald Reagan's amazing capability to ignore responsibilities by either playing or being actually a fool was denounced with the saying "Teflon head" and George Bush's promise not to raise taxes was coined into a "Read my lips" phrase.

[43]*De Oratore* I, 33-34: "Ut vero iam ad illa summa veniamus; quae vis alia potuit aut disperos homines unum in locum congregare, aut a fera agrestique vita ad hunc humanum cultum civilemque deducere, aut iam constitutis civitatibus, leges, iudicia, iura describere?"

[44]Ingenuity is the concept which allowed Giambattista Vico to reconcile the development of different civilizations with his awareness of a natural and eternal law. By discovering the natural potentials of societies, ingenuity gradually leads people to different levels of actualization of these potentials—to different stages and varieties of civilization which in different degree accomplish the embodiment of the eternal and natural law. Cf. Peter Burke,

If ingenuity leads people from brutish isolation to civilized societies—from not being to being—, ingenuity as well transforms human beings from naked apes to culture and technology bearers.[45] Moreover, ingenuity not only creates culture and technology to satisfy physical, social, and spiritual needs of persons. Ingenuity also discovers these needs and establishes the relationship of these needs with the cultural or technological remedies to be created. Furthermore, ingenuity can make of culture and technology symbols of social understanding to foster additional discoveries and creation of artifacts, and to further social learning through people's common analytical frame for reality.[46]

Wit and Rhetoric: the Making Sense and the Bringing Forth of Actions

Certainly, wit serves to make sense of facts and to create the new facts which enrich the civilized world. But wit also understands and gives shape to the acts of people. These acts trascend the necessity, probability, and forcefulness of facts, and reach the free agency, possibility, and persuasibility of actors—that is, what Gracián called masters. Wit thus assists rhetoric, the faculty of persuasion—not of coercion—in its branch of invention.

Gracián's theories of ingenuity have a special relevance to rhetoric. Gracián often applied them to concrete cases, which were contingent and complex, requiring from the orator not just managerial skills to process information, but also invention: the capacity of seeing the just, the honorable, and the expedient which no one had seen before, and persuasively proposing this new view to fellow human beings.

Vico, (Oxford, New York: Oxford University Press, 1985) 32–88.

[45]Here I would recall that Vico's theory concerning the development of nations was preceded by *El Criticón*'s analysis of the developement of different nations in terms of cultural childhood, adulthood, and wise old age.

[46]Gracián classified inventions into practical—artifacts which help people satisfy a need—and symbolical—forms of language created to empower the human mind with additional instruments for understanding. Cf. *Agudeza* Discourse 47.

Gracián's emphasis was not like Pallavicino's that devoted wit to the service of science and philosophy's conceptualization.[47] *Agudeza* rather tends to help conceptualize singular cases such as Caesar's malice and the answer it found in the simplicity of a foreign lad,[48] Juan Rufo's gallantry towards the lady offering sweets to a child,[49] the two misers' folly in making dead cats fat,[50] the wickedness of Herod concerning the manger,[51] Alexander's solving of the Gordian knot,[52] Prince Fernando's stratagem to preserve his loyalty to the Infant King of Castile,[53] the Ambassador of Spain's subtle warning of the Sicilian Vespers to Henry the Great of France,[54] etc.

Gracián's system also addresses the contingency of human action, which springs from the freedom enjoyed by people, and which is exercised by each person choosing and making real the different sets of possibilities appealing to his individual interests:

> **Self-moderation in one's inclination.** Each one conceptualizes according to his own convenience and abounds in reasons to support such form of apprehension...It happens that two persons contradictorily meet, and each one presumes to hold reason on his side...May the sage proceed with caution in such a delicate matter, and thus self-criticism will reform his judgment of the counterpart's behavior; may he sometimes place himself on the other side; should he examine the counterpart's motives; then, he won't condemn him, or justify himself so overwhelmingly.[55]

---

[47]See *Trattato Dello Stile*.

[48]See *Agudeza* Discourse 38.

[49]See *Agudeza* Discourse 26.

[50]See *Agudeza* Discourse 27.

[51]See *Agudeza* Discourse 36.

[52]See *Agudeza* Discourse 45.

[53]See *Agudeza* Discourse 45.

[54]See *Agudeza* Discourse 49. Peace and war are among the main subjects pertaining to political oratory. Cf. Aristotle's *Rhetoric* I, 4.

[55]*Oráculo* Aphorism 294: "**Moderarse en el sentir**. Cada uno hace concepto según su

Wit's insightful understanding of individual choice paves the way for rhetorical hypotheses on past human actions, and for rhetorical negotiation permitting the accomplishment of future social enterprises.[56]

Gracián's theories of wit describe the mind as properly apprehending complex events not just by doing it analytically but also synthetically. Pure wit dissects a mosaic into its composing stones, but it is not but through conglobate, compound, and mixed concepts rebuilding the mosaic that the mind perceives the whole picture—which is more than its parts.[57] Thus Gracián's theories may appeal to some contemporary styles of policy making in public and corporative bodies which encourage an interdisciplinary and systemic vision for the solving of problems, rather than the partial views and predictions made by isolate technicians.[58]

Gracián also cherished what is extravagant, paradoxical, shocking to good sense and established reason, and he saw this daring form of thinking as a manifestation of the boldest ingenuity. This theoretical attitude may be relevant to innovation, a value strongly appreciated in the modern world of politics and corporations.

Extravagant minds may conceive unthinkable actions, and even undertake them to completion. James B. Stenson thus describes Columbus's unsound plan to reach the Indies through the West:

> Far from being superstitious ignoramuses, Columbus' critics included professors from the University of Salamanca (one of Europe's four great universities) as well

---

conveniencia, y abunda de razones en su aprehensión...Acontece el encontrarse dos contradictoriamente, y cada uno presume de su parte la razón...Proceda el sabio con reflexa en tan delicado punto, y así el recelo propio reformará la calificación del proceder ajeno; póngase tal vez de la otra parte; examínele al contrario los motivos; con esto, ni le condenará a él, ni se justificará a sí tan a lo deslumbrado."

[56]Here we may recall the judicial and deliberative rhetorical genres.

[57]Cf., for example, *Agudeza* Discourse 3.

[58]I am referring to general system theories as proposed by authors like Ludwing Von Bertalanffy and Jay W. Forrester.

as the most knowledgeable cartographers and geographers of Iberia—at that time the world's leaders in oceanic travel. Salamanca was firmly in the camp of Copernicus, more than a century before Galileo. These people, more than anyone else in Europe, knew what they were talking about.

Columbus claimed that only 2,400 miles separated Spain from Japan, the tip of Asia.

> The critics profoundly disagreed...By their expert calculations, the distance between Spain and Japan, sailing westward, was more like 10,000 miles—four times as great. [Columbus'] journey would take years... [It] was "uncertain and impossible to any educated person"... They were right, of course... What saved Columbus in this venture...was that he bumped into an unknown continent sitting right about where he thought Asia would be... What prompted Isabella, in the face of this sound scientific advice, to back Columbus anyway?... her royal treasurer, Luis de Santangel, urged her to give the expedition a try. Being a venture-capitalist entrepreneur by temperament, he sized up Columbus and judged him personally trusthworthy: "What have we got to lose—three small ships? Let's give the man a chance to prove himself."[59]

Here, the brilliantly extravagant thinker was not Columbus but Santángel, who could see a possibility in human action in spite of what scientists prescribed.[60]

Innovation does not rest only on conceiving new actions but on creatively rethinking them through new frames of mind.[61] Tom Sawyer turned the white washing of a fence from an unpleasant chore to a delightful game. We northern

---

[59]James B. Stenson, "A triumph of intuition over science," *Chicago Tribune* (Monday, October 10, 1988).

[60]Under the lens of Gracián's theories, Santángel made use of a transposition in which a circumstance ("What have we got to lose?") is introduced to redefine the definitional circumstance (science) of the whole case. Under the lens of Pellegrini's theories, Santángel made a shift of ingenuity, in which the category of science was replaced by the category of action to analyze the case.

[61]Under Gracián's theories, this rethinking is achieved through ponderations, whereas under Pellegrini's theories, this rethinking is achieved by shifts of ingenuity.

Mexicans believe that our relative lack of a profound and distinctive cultural life should be reinterpreted as pragmatism, of course. The story says that, threatened by the formidable Spanish Armada, the English turned their small and feeble boats into a swift and victorious navy, and the inmense invading battleships into clumsy and elephantine coffins. McDonald's reinvented the industrialized and impersonal feeding of the masses by changing it into a cheap, clean, and happily standarized-to-satisfy-everybody fast food service. One sees the donut and another sees the hole. And some neither see the glass half-empty nor half-full, but just dirty.

Wit is a particularly powerful tool for rhetoric in many ways. First, wit provides the orator with an arsenal of novel ideas to build up a persuasive case. Second, structures of correspondences make speeches very persuasive, since these structures invite listeners themselves to supply the ideas and proofs, rather than having to suffer their imposition from an orator who speaks declaratively. Unlike syllogisms which explicitly state all the premises, enthymemes rely on the audience to complete the argument. As Gracián demonstrated, the finding of missing premises is not an inference but an operation of ingenuity.[62] Finally, I think that wit allows the mind to conceive the most general lines of rhetorical argument: the ones of possibility, past fact, future fact, and degree.[63] These arguments can not be conceived by just looking to an isolated fact. For example, the idea of the possible rises from comparing different levels of actualization in things. The idea of a past or a future fact may come from comparing the evidence with other past and present facts. And the idea of degree—which lets the mind make value judgment concerning the just, the honorable, and the expedient—also rises from comparing qualities found in different things.

The complexity of the modern world has made the realms of social action to be highly dependent on technocracies. Politicians and corporate leaders strongly rely on a specialized staff to conceptualize reality, justify and choose options, and follow courses of action. Gracián's theories of mastery may challenge these

---

[62]See *Agudeza* Discourse 36.

[63]Cf. Aristotle, *Rhetoric* II, 18.

technocratic tendencies by considering that the different areas of competence and authority rest more on the persons than on their external skills.[64] Moreover, Gracián's theories of ingenuity should remind these professionals that what holds them together as civilized societies—respectful of the freedom and dignity of each member—is the human nature that everybody shares, with such basic faculties as wit and rhetoric making possible common ideas and argument, that rise above professional sects. Indeed, the more specialized are the members of a society, the more they have to return to the basics if they intend to think comprehensively and appeal to the common grounds of everybody. It is only then when we can truly share a common life and be rescued from Babel.

Wit and Mastery: Prudence and Concupiscence

What we do is what we are. If that adage strongly applies to social action, it more profoundly fits personal life. But how far can we really claim that we are architects of our destiny rather than destiny being an architect of ourselves?

Gracián's theories of wit are directed to make possible his conception of mastery.[65] Wit should provide enlightenment so that the person becomes lord of his choices rather than vice versa. A heedful mind's discoveries make the

---

[64]Technocratic emphasis on external facts or skills instead of personal mastery makes technocratic decision-making also differ, in its premises, from rhetorical decision-making. Social scientists, for example, would predict tendencies of *social behavior* by means of complex use of statistics and calculation of chances. On these grounds, a technocratic decision-maker would plan alternative policies which respond to the most probable forecasts. A rhetor would not simply predict, but he would also invennt and propose a particular *social action*, trusting in his own ingenuity to devise new solutions, going beyond pure tendencies or existing patterns, and aiming at new possibilities whose likelihood depends less on trends than on the reason, will power, freedom, social accord, and motivation of the public, as stimulated by persuasion. Although both kinds of decision-makers are necessary to the public, only the rhetor can truly be regarded as a leader.

[65]Wit is only one faculty which the master exercises, among many others. But wit is essentially important: it is the faculty which provides understanding.

person prudent so that he can prevent deception or be disabused from error. Moreover, it is through wit that a person conceives his vocation in youth, achieves excellence in adulthood, and understands his human limitations in old age.[66] It is through wit that a person realizes his own self and his possibilities. Wit informs prudence, taste, and choice in their judgments with the precise distinctions obtained from sharp conceptualizations. It is through wit that a person distinguishes the choices of self, and through wit that he determines whether these choices are or not actualized.

But self-conception is more than irascibly[67] contriving the sort of self to be accomplished. In a probably deeper sense, self-conception is self-awareness, nay, self-enjoyment; it is the keen and concupiscent[68] consciousness of the accomplished self. Wit is smart in letting people scheme their paths to the heights of love, the plains of play, or the abysses of lust. But wit is bliss—or damnation—in letting us consciously live each atom[69] of this love, this play, or this lust of being.[70]

---

[66]See *El Criticón*.

[67]By irascible, men of schools referred to the movements of the soul to accomplish an end.

[68]By concupiscent, men of schools often referred to the enjoyment of the accomplished ends.

[69]Here I recall the Brainy Monster of *El Criticón* III, Crisi 6, who was made of brains in every particle of his being.

[70]Love, playful games, and lust are different forms in which people, more than actualizing, consciously enjoy their actual being. Wit lets people contrive these forms of being. Moreover, wit lets them intellectually be aware of and enjoy their realization. But, again, wit is not judgment yet, and, though intellectual, the joys of wit could turn lascivious and blind the mind if it does not open itself to judgment. In any case, this concupiscence of wit may justify forms of speech from wordplays and pure rhetorical display to epideictic speeches, if in them what matters is not instrumental but just the enjoyment of one's own reason and speech abilities, as it occurs in sports and gymnastics, when one enjoys one's physical skills and their development for their own sake. When this enjoyment—this celebration—is judged by the mind as legitimate for a given public, then, what wit provides as a concupiscent idea may turn into an epideictic resolution: the speech and ideas proposed deserve consciousness now, celebration, and actual enjoyment through an epideictic speech. The speech is not

Wit, Religious Eloquence, and the Holy

Gracián warned those on their way to mastery: "If mortal excellence springs from greed, the eternal one should spring from ambition."[71] For wit may succumb to intellectual lust if just satisfied and dazzled with transient dishes, and if it does not respond to its call to contemplate in awe the most excellent and eternal Truth. And as the navigator cruises not rivers or lakes but the sea to assert his own greatness, in the same way the mind's wit is not aware of its own dignity and possibilities except when immersing itself in the ocean of God.[72]

As said before, religious practices of all ages strongly rely on wit to accomplish their purposes. Scriptural studies often consist in establishing concordances between different places of the Writ. From the contingency of transient beings, theologians have an insight of the necessity of God. Prayer and meditation frequently imply the consideration of connections between the contents of the Faith and the personal life and conversion of the faithful.[73] Preachers of all ages not seldom explain the Gospels by finding correspondences of their contents with the moral behavior of parishioners. From Gracián's illustrations we know that his theories directly explain not only baroque witty sermons but the wit found in the greatest exemplars of religious eloquence of all centuries, as he noticed in St Ambrose, St Augustine, St Leo, St Clement of Alexandria, St Basil, St Peter Chrysologus, St Gregory the Great, St Gregory Nazianzus, St John Chrysostom, and other Church Fathers. Though shyly, Gracián dared to point out something that he knew well: Jesus's taste for

---

debating about an end to accomplish. It rather invites and provides the means to enjoy an already accomplished end. That is the reason why epideictic speeches refer to what is present. They refer to what can be enjoyed now, through the speech.

[71]*El Héroe* Primor 20: "Si la excelencia mortal es de codicia, la eterna sea de ambición".

[72]Cf. *Oráculo* Aphorism 300.

[73]A method of prayer as traditional as the Rosary requires from the faithful reflecting on fifteen mysteries of Jesus's life by interconnecting them in the most complex structures of correspondence.

subtilizing even with puns. Gracián quoted Christ's words to Peter:

Tu es Petrus, et super hanc petram aedificabo ecclesiam meam.[74]

Beyond His numerous aphorisms and parables—I think—Jesus accomplished the most perfect extravagance: the folly, the scandal of the Cross.

According to Tesauro, ingenuity is such a lofty faculty that its supreme practitioner is God.[75] Echoing many religious traditions, Gracián saw in Creation a book expounding the providence, the power, and the wisdom of the Lord.[76] The book of *Wisdom* summarizes this belief:

If charmed by their beauty, they have taken things for gods, let them know how much the Lord excels them, since the very Author of beauty has created them...since through the grandeur and beauty of the creatures we may, by analogy, contemplate the Author.[77]

However, if wit often fails to uncover the most ordinary things' being, it may seem hopeless to aim at grasping the Being defined as inexhaustively rich and ineffable. Even so, there is hope, since, now, it is not our mind that alone understands but the all powerful God who speaks. Thus our mind's wit should humbly listen, as Søren Kierkegaard reminds:

In the true prayer relationship, it is not God who hears what is asked, but the one who prays, and who continues to pray until he or she has heard what God wishes.[78]

Baltasar Gracián thus conclusively acknowledged and proclaimed:

---

[74]As quoted in *Agudeza* Discourse 31. This pun is present in the original Aramaic as well.

[75]See *Cannocchiale* Chapter 3: 59–66.

[76]See *El Criticón* I, crises one to three.

[77]*Wisdom* 13:3,5.

[78]Søren Kierkegaard, as quoted in "Words for Quiet Moments," *Catholic Digest* (September 1991) 78.

Being hero of the world is little or nothing; being hero of Heaven is much, to whose great Monarch be the praise, be the honor, and be the glory.[79]

---

[79]*El Héroe* Primor 20; the book's last sentence: "Ser héroe del mundo, poco o nada es; serlo del Cielo es mucho, a cuyo gran Monarca sea la alabanza, sea la honra, sea la gloria".

Bibliography

PRIMARY SOURCES ARE TEXTS WHOSE DOCTRINES OR ILLUSTRATIONS are directly the object of consideration. Secondary sources are texts whose contents are relevant because of their reference to the primary sources here considered.

Primary Sources on Baltasar Gracián

Gracián y Morales, Baltasar. *Obras Completas*. Ed., and "Introducción, recopilación y notas" by E. Correa Calderón. Madrid: M. Aguilar, 1944.

—————. *Obras Completas*. Ed., and "Estudio preliminar, edición, bibliografía y notas" by Arturo del Hoyo. Madrid: Ed. Aguilar, 1960.

—————. *Agudeza y Arte de Ingenio*. Ed. by E. Correa Calderón. Madrid: Editorial Castalia, 1969. 2 vols.

—————. *El Discreto. El Criticón. El Héroe*. Ed. by Isabel C. Tarán. 2nd ed. México: Editorial Porrúa, S. A., 1986.

Chambers, Leland Hugh. "Baltasar Gracián's 'The Mind's Wit and Art'" Diss., U of Michigan, 1962.

The Critic: written originally in Spanish; by Lorenzo Gracian, One of the Best Writers in Spain, and Translated into English, by Paul Rycaut, Esq. London: printed by T. N. for Henry Brome at the Gun in St. Paul's Church-Yard, 1681.

General List of Primary Sources

1,001 Logical Laws, Accurate Axioms, Profound Principles, Trusty Truisms, Homey Homilies, Colorful Corollaries, Quotable Quotes, and Rambunctious Ruminations for All Walks of Life. Compiled by John Peers. New York: Fawcett Gold Medal, 1988.

Ad C. Herennium De Ratione Dicendi. Trans. by H. Caplan. Cambridge: Harvard University Press, 1981.

Alemán, Mateo. *Guzmán de Alfarache*. Ed Benito Brancaforte. Madrid: Ed. Cátedra, 1979. 2 vols.

Aquinas, St Thomas. *Summa Theologica*. Trans. Fathers of the English Dominican Province. London: Burns Oates and Wahsbourne, 1918–1930.

—————. *Summa Contra Gentiles*. México: Ed. Porrúa, S. A.

Aristotle. *The Basic Works*. Ed. by Richard McKeon. Random House, 1941.

—————. *The Rhetoric and The Poetics*. Ed. by Friedrich Solmsen. New York: Random House, 1954.

Aristotle/Horace/Longinus—Classical Literary Criticism. Trans. T. S. Dorsch. Penguin Books, 1965.

Augustine, St. *On Christian Doctrine*. Trans. by D. W. Robertson, Jr. Indianapolis: The Library of Liberal Arts, 1983.

Bacon, Francis. *Advancement of Learning*. (1605).

—————. *Novum Organum*. (1620).

Balmes, Jaime. *El Criterio*. 3ª ed. Buenos Aires: Espasa-Calpe Argentina, 1943.

—————. *Filosofía Elemental*. México, Editorial Porrúa, 1973.

Basevorn, Robert of. *Forma Praedicandi*. (1322). As found in *Three Medieval Rhetorical Arts*. Ed. James J. Murphy. University of California Press, 1971.

Boethius. *De topicis differentiis*. Trans. by Eleonore Stump. Cornell University Press, 1978.

Boncampagno. *Rhetorica Novissima*. As found in *Scripta Anecdota Glossatorum*. Ed. Augoto Gaudenzi. Bologna: Pietro Virano, Bibliotheca Juridica Medii Aevi, 1892. vol.2.

Burke, Edmund. *The Sublime and the Beautiful*. (1757).

Burke, Kenneth. *A Grammar of Motives*. University of California Press, 1974.

Campbell, George. *The Philosophy of Rhetoric*. Ed. Lloyd F. Bitzer. Southern Illinois University Press, 1988.

Capellanus (Andreas). *The Art of Courtly Love*. Trans. John Jay Parry. New York: Frederick Ungar Publishing, Co., 1959.

Cicero. *De Inventione*. *De Optimo Genere Oratorum*. *Topica*. Harvard University Press, 1976.

————. *De Oratore*. Harvard University Press, Vol. 1, 1979, Vol. 2, 1977. 2 vols.

Clairvaux, Bernard of. "In Praise of the Virgin Mother." *Magnificat, Homilies in Praise of the Blessed Virgin Mary by Bernard of Clairvaux and Amadeus of Lausanne*. Trans. Marie-Bernard Saïd and Grace Perigo, introduction by Chrysogonus Waddell, OCSO. Cistercian Publications, Inc, 1979.

Cruz, Juana Inés de la. *Obras completas*. México: Editorial Porrúa.

Dante Alighieri. *La Divina Comedia*. Ed. Francisco Montes de Oca. México: Editorial Porrúa, S. A., 1973.

Descartes, René. *Rules for the Direction of the Mind*. (1637).

————. *Meditations*. (1641).

Domingo, Alberto. "Aguila o Sol." *Siempre!* México. April, 1991.

Duff, William. *An Essay on Original Genius* (1767). Ed. John Mahoney. Florida: Scholars' Facsimiles & Reprints, 1964.

Essays on Wit. The Augustan Reprint Society. 1st ser. 1–3. (1946–1947).

Fénelon, François. *Dialogues on Eloquence*. Trans. and Introduction, Wilbur Samuel Howell. Princeton: Princeton University Press, 1951; first published in 1718.

Gerard, Alexander. *An Essay on Genius* (1774). Ed. Bernhard Fabian. Wilhelm Fink Verlag München, 1966.

Gorner, Peter. "Blood from a stone." *Chicago Tribune*. Tempo. November 15, 1990: 6

Granada, Fr. Luis de. *Los seis libros de la rhetórica eclesiástica.* Ed. por Josef Climent, Obispo de Barcelona. Barcelona, 1770.

――――. *Obras.* Ed. by Fr Justo Cuervo. Madrid: 1906. 14 vols.

――――. *Breve Tratado en que se declara de la manera que se podrá proponer la doctrina de nuestra Santa Fe y Religión Cristiana a los nuevos fieles.* (Madrid: Biblioteca de Autores Españoles, 1945). As found in *Obras.* Ed. by Fr Justo Cuervo. Madrid: 1906, 14 vols. Vol. 14.

――――. *Sermón en que se da aviso que en las caídas públicas de algunas personas ni se pierda el crédito de la virtud de los buenos ni cese y se entibie el buen propósito de los flacos.* Lisboa: Antonio Ribero, 1588. As included in Fr Luis de Granada. *Obras.* Ed. by Fr Justo Cuervo. Madrid: 1906. Vol. 14.

――――. *Guía de Pecadores.* As found in *Obras del V. P. M. fray Luis de Granada.* Prólogo y la vida del autor por don José Joaquín de Mora. Madrid: Ediciones Atlas, 1944–1945. 3 vols. Vol 1.

The Home Book of Quotations Classical and Modern. Selection of Burton Stevenson. 5th. ed. 1934, New York: Dodd Mead & Company, 1947.

Horace. "On the Art of Poety." *Aristotle/Horace/Longinus—Classical Literary Criticism.* Trans. T. S. Dorsch. Penguin Books, 1965.

Hume, David. *An Enquiry Concerning Human Understanding.* (1748).

――――. *Of the Standards of Taste.* As found in *Four Dissertations.* (1757).

Isla, P. Francisco José, S. I. *Historia del famoso predicador Fray Gerundio de Campazas alias Zotes.* Primera edición entera hecha sobre la edición príncipe de 1785 y el manuscrito autógrafo del autor por D. Eduardo Lidforss, Catedrático del Número en la R. Universidad de Lund. Leipzig, 1885.

――――. *Fray Gerundio de Campazas,* ed. Russell P. Sebold. Madrid: ESPASA-CALPE, S. A., 1960, first edited in 1758. 4 vols.

――――. "Día Grande de Navarra." *Obras escogidas.* Madrid: Biblioteca de Autores Españoles XV, 1945.

Kames, Lord Henry Home. *Elements of Criticism.* (1762).

Lives of Saints, with excerpts from their writings. Introduction by Father Thomas Plassmann, OFM. Introduction by Father Joseph Vann, OFM. (New York: Johb J. Crawley and Co., Inc., 1954.

Locke, John. *Essay Concerning Human Understanding.* (1690).

López Velarde, Ramón. *Suave Patria.* As found in *Ómnibus de Poesía Mexicana.* Ed. Gabriel Zaid. México: Siglo XXI, 1984.

Machiavelli, Niccolò. *The Prince.* Penguin Books, 1961.

Mayáns i Siscár, D. Gregorio. *El Orador Christiano ideado en tres diálogos.* 2nd. ed. Valencia: Joseph I Thomas de Orga, 1776. First edited in 1773.

————. *Rhetorica de Don Gregorio Mayáns i Siscár.* 2nd edition. Valencia: Josef i Thomas de Orga, 1786. 1st. edition: 1757.

Morris, Corbyn. *An Essay towards Fixing the True Standars of Wit, Humour, Raillery, Satire, and Ridicule* (1744). The Augustan Reprint Society 1st. ser. 4, 1947.

Nebrija, Antonio de. *Artis Rhetoricae compendiosa coaptatio ex Aristotele, Cicerone et Quintiliano.* 1515.

————. *Gramática de la Lengua Castellana.* Estudio y edición de Antonio Quilis. Madrid: Editora Nacional, 1980.

El Norte. Monterrey, México: Spring 1991.

Ómnibus de poesía mexicana. Ed. Gabriel Zaid, 11 ed. México: Siglo Veintiuno Editores, S. A., 1984.

Pallavicino, Cardinal Pietro Sforza, S. I. *Trattato dello Stile e del Dialogo.* Roma: Giovanni Casoni, 1662; first edited in 1646.

Pascal, Blaise. *Provincial Letters.* (1657).

————. *On Geometrical Demonstration.* (1658).

————. *Pensées.* (1688).

Paz, Octavio. *El laberinto de la soledad.* México: Fondo de Cultura Económica, 1989.

Pellegrini, Matteo. *Delle acutezze.* 1639.

————. *I fonti dell'ingegno ridotti ad arte.* 1650.

Perelman, Ch., and L. Olbrechts-Tyteca. *The New Rhetoric. A Treatise on Argumentation.* Trans. John Wilkinson and Purcell Weaver. University of Notre Dame Press, 1969.

Las poéticas castellanas de la Edad Media. Prologus Baenensis. Proemio y Carta del Marqués de Santillana. Arte de Poesía Castellana de Juan de Encina. Ed. by Francisco López de Estrada. Madrid: Taurus Ediciones, S. A., 1984.

Platón. *Diálogos.* México: Ed. Porrúa, S. A., 1979.

Quevedo y Villegas, Don Francisco de. "A una nariz," *Obras Completas.* Estudio preliminar, edición y notas de Felicidad Buendía. Madrid: Aguilar, 1988. 2 vols.

Quintilian. *The Institutio Oratoria.* Harvard University Press, 1980. 4 vols.

The Rhetorics of Thomas Hobbes and Bernard Lamy. Ed. John T. Harwood. Southern Illinois University Press, 1986.

Sales, St Francis de. *The Sermons of St. Francis de Sales for Lent given in the year 1622.* Edited by Father Lewis S. Fiorelli, O.S.F.S. Trans. by Nuns of the Visitation. Tan Books and Publishers, Inc., 1987.

Sherlock, Thomas. *Trial of the Witnesess.* (1729).

Soarez, Cypriano (or Cipriano Suárez, S. I.) *De Arte Rhetorica libri tres, ex Aristotele, Cicerone et Quintiliano praecipue deprompti* (1569)

Stenson, James B. "A triumph of intuition over science." *Chicago Tribune.* Monday, October 10, 1988.

Terrones del Caño, Francisco. *Instrucción de Predicadores.* "Prólogo y notas" by P. Félix G. Olmedo, S. I. Madrid: ESPASA-CALPE, S. A., 1946, from 1617 edition.

Tesauro, Emmanuel. *Il Cannochiale Aristotelico*. Turin: 1670; first edited in 1654.

Toulmin, Stephen. *The Uses of Argument*. Cambridge University Press, 1958.

Valadés, Diego. *Rhetorica Christiana*. Perugia, 1579.

Vieira, António, S. I. "Sermão da Sexagésima (1655)." *Sermões do Padre António Vieira*. Ed. by Margarida Vieira Mendes. Lisboa: Editorial Comunicação, 1987.

Whately, Richard. *Elements of Rhetoric*. Ed. by Douglas Ehninger. Southern Illinois University Press, 1963.

Wilson, Richard. "A Priest Smiles Back on 25 Years." *Catholic Digest*. St Paul, MN: University of St Thomas, September 1991.

Secondary Sources on Baltasar Gracián

Abbott, Don Paul, "Baltasar Gracián's *Agudeza*: The Integration of Inventio and Elocutio." *The Western Journal of Speech Communication* 50 (Spring 1986): 133–143.

Aguirre, J. M. "Agudeza o arte de ingenio y el Barroco." *Gracián y su época*. Zaragoza: Institución Fernándo el Católico, 1985.

Alonso, Santos. *Tensión semántica (lenguaje y estilo) de Gracián*. Zaragoza: Institución "Fernando el Católico", 1981.

Arco, Ricardo del. *Las ideas literarias de Baltasar Gracián y los escritores aragoneses*. Zaragoza: Institución "Fernando el Católico", 1950.

————. "Baltasar Gracián y los escritores conceptistas del siglo XVII." *Historia General de las Literaturas Hispánicas*. Ed. by D. Guillermo Días-Plaja. Barcelona: Ed Vergara, 1953.

Arellano Ayuso, Ignacio. "El ingenioso estilo de don Francisco de Quevedo. Otros aspectos." *Poesía Satírico Burlesca de Quevedo*. Pamplona: Ediciones Universidad de Navarra, S. A., 1984.

Ayala, Jorge M. *Gracián: vida, estilo y reflexión*. Madrid: Ed. Cincel, 1987.

Batllori, P. Miguel, S. I. *Gracián y el barroco*. Roma: Edizione di Storia e Letteratura, 1958.

Batllori, Miguel, S. I., and Ceferino Peralta, S. I. *Baltasar Gracián en su vida y en sus obras*. Zaragoza: Institución "Fernando el Católico", 1969.

Bethell, S. L. "Gracián, Tesauro, and the Nature of Metaphysical Wit." *Northern Miscellany of Literary Criticism* i (1953).

Chambers, Leland Hugh. "Baltasar Gracián's 'The Mind's Wit and Art.'" Diss., U of Michigan, 1962.

Correa Calderón, E. "Sobre Gracián y su *Agudeza y Arte de ingenio*." *Revista de Ideas Estéticas*. (1944): 73–87.

————. *Baltasar Gracián. Su vida y su obra*. Madrid: Editorial Gredos, 1961.

Coster, Adolphe. *Baltasar Gracián*. Trans. by Ricardo del Arco. Zaragoza: Institución Fernando el Católico, 1947.

Croce, Benedetto. "Los tratadistas italianos del conceptismo y Baltasar Gracián." *La Lectura. Revista de Ciencias y Letras*. 2nd ser. 12 (1912).

García Mercadal, José. *Baltasar Gracián*. Madrid: Compañía Bibliográfica Española, S. A., 1967.

Giménez, Gaudioso. "'El Comulgatorio' y la Oratoria Sagrada." *Gracián y su época*. Zaragoza: Institución Fernándo el Católico, 1985. 365–374.

Grady, Hugh H., "Rhetoric, Wit, and Art in Gracián's Agudeza." *MLQ* 41:21–37.

Guardiola Alcover, Conrado. *Baltasar Gracián. Recuento de una vida*. Zaragoza: Librería General, 1980.

Hafter, Monroe Z. *Gracián and Perfection, Spanish Moralists of the Seventeeth Century*. Cambridge: Harvard University Press, 1966.

Heger, Klaus. *Baltasar Gracián. Estilo lingüístico y doctrina de valores. Estudio sobre la actitud literaria del conceptismo*. Zaragoza: Institución "Fernando el Católico", 1960.

Hidalgo Serna, Emilio. "The Philosophy of *Ingenium*: Concept and Ingenious Method in Baltasar Gracián." *Philosophy and Rhetoric* 13.4 Fall: 1980.

Homenaje a Gracián. Zaragoza: Institución "Fernando el Católico", 1958.

Krauss, Werner. *La doctrina de la vida según Baltasar Gracián*. Madrid: Ed. Rialp, S. A., 1962.

May, T. E. "An Interpretation of Gracián's *Agudeza y Arte de Ingenio*." *Hispanic Review* XVI (1948): 257–300.

————. "Gracián's Idea of the concepto," *Hispanic Review* XVIII (1950): 15–41.

Menéndez Pelayo, Marcelino. "Poética conceptista: Baltasar Gracián." *Historia de las Ideas Estéticas en España*. Madrid: 1950.

————. *Historia de las Ideas Estéticas en España*. México: Ed. Porrúa, S. A., 1985.

Montesinos, José F. "Gracián o la picaresca pura." *Cruz y Raya*. 4 (Madrid: 1933).

Morreale, Margarita. "Castiglione y 'El Héroe': Gracián y 'Despejo.'" *Homenaje a Gracián*. Institución "Fernando el Católico," 1958.

Oltra Tomás, José Miguel. "Conformación de un texto de Gracián: El político Don Fernando." *Gracián y su época*. Zaragoza: Institución Fernando El Católico, 1986.

Peralta, Ceferino, S. I. "La ocultación de Cervantes en Baltasar Gracián." *Gracián y su Época*. Zaragoza: Institución Fernando el Católico. (1986) 137–156.

Ramos Foster, Virginia. *Baltasar Gracián*. Boston: Twayne Publishers, 1975.

Romera-Navarro, M. *Estudios sobre Gracián*. Austin: The University of Texas Press, 1950.

Rouveyre, Andrés. *El español Baltasar Gracián y Federico Nietzsche*. Trans. by Ángel Pumarega. Madrid: Ediciones Biblos, before 1936.

Rouveyre, Andrés, and Victor Bouillier. *Baltasar Gracián y Federico Nietzsche*. Madrid: Ediciones Biblos.

Sarmiento, Edward. "Gracián's *Agudeza y Arte de Ingenio.*" *The Modern Language Review* XXVII (Cambridge: 1932): 280–292, 420–429.

————. "On Two Criticism of Gracián's *Agudeza.*" *Hispanic Review.* III (1935): 23–35.

Woods, M. J. "Gracián, Peregrini, and the Theory of Topics." *Modern Language Review* 63 (1968).

General List of Secondary Sources

Alborg, Juan Luis. *Historia de la Literatura Española.* Madrid: Editorial Gredos, 1987. 4 vols.

Appollonio, Mario. *Storia della Letteratura Italiana.* Brescia: "La Scuola", Editrice, 1954.

Arendt, Hannah. *The Origins of Totalitarianism.* New York: Harcourt, Brace & World, Inc., 1966; first edited in 1951.

Atkinson, William C. *A History of Spain and Portugal.* Penguin Books, 1960.

Aullón de Havo, Pedro, et al. *Breve historia de la literatura española en su contexto.* Madrid: Ed. Playor, 1981.

Balthasar, Hans Urs von. *Thérèse of Lisieux. The Story of a Mission.* Trans. by Donald Nicholl. New York: Sheed and Ward, 1954.

Bataillon, Marcel. *Erasmo y España.* 2nd ed. México: F. C. E., 1966.

Beardsley, Monroe C. *Thinking Straight.* 4th ed. Englewood Cliffs, New Jersey: Prentice-Hall, Inc., 1975.

Bennet, W. Lance. *News. The Politics of Illusion.* 2nd. ed. New York and London: Longman, 1988.

Benzo Mestre, Miguel. *Teología para universitarios.* 6ª ed. Madrid: Ediciones Cristiandad, 1977.

Black, Edwin. "The Second Person." *The Quarterly Journal of Speech*. (April 1970): 109–119.

Blecua, José Manuel. *Historia y textos de la Literatura Española*. Zaragoza: Librería General, 1963.

Booth, Wayne C. *Modern Dogma and The Rhetoric of Assent*. The University of Chicago Press, 1974.

Braure, Maurice. *The Seventeenth and Eighteenth Centuries*. London: Burns & Oats, 1963.

Bunge, Mario. *Scientific Research*. Berlin, Heidelberg, New York: Springer-Verlag, 1967.

Burke, Peter. *Vico*. Oxford University Press, 1985.

"Casuística." *Enciclopedia Vniversal Ilvstrada Evropeo-Americana*. Barcelona: Hijos de Espasa, Editores. 12:415–418.

"Casuistry." *The Catholic Encyclopedia*. New York: Robert Appleton Company. 3:415–417.

Cerio, Gregory. "The Black Legend: Were the Spaniards That Cruel?" *Newsweek*. Special Issue. Fall/Winter, 1991.

Chávez, Ezequiel A. *Apuntes sobre la Colonia II, La Reeducación de Indios y Españoles*. México: Editorial Jus, 1958.

Cognet, Louis. *Post-Reformation Spirituality*. Trans. by P. Hepburne Scott. New York: Hawthorn Books·Publishers, 1959.

Conley, Thomas M. *Rhetoric in the European Tradition*. New York: Longman, 1990.

Copleston, Frederick, S. J. *A History of Philosophy Volume III Ockham to Suárez*. Westminster, Maryland: The Newman Press, 1959.

Cory, Herbert Ellsworth. *The Significance of Beauty in Nature and Art*. Milwaukee: The Bruce Publishing Company, 1947.

Curtius, E. R. *European Literature in the Latin Middle Ages.* New York: 1953.

Diez-Echarri, Emiliano, and José María Roca Franquesa, *Historia de la Literatura Española e Hispanoamericana.* Madrid: Editorial Aguilar, 1979.

Domínguez Ortiz, Antonio. *The Golden Age of Spain 1516-1659.* Trans. James Casey. London: Weidenfeld and Nicolson, 1971.

Dulumeau, Jean. *Catholicism between Luther and Voltaire: a new view of the Counter-Reformation.* London: Burns & Oates, 1977.

Eco, Umberto. *The Aesthetics of Thomas Aquinas.* Trans. Hugh Bredin. Harvard University Press, 1988.

Enciclopedia Vniversal Ilvstrada Evropeo-Americana. Barcelona: Ed. ESPASA, 1924: Tesauro's, Pallavicino's, and Pellegrini's entries.

Estrella Gutiérrez, Fermín. *Historia de la Literatura Española.* Buenos Aires: Editorial Kapelusz, 1945.

Fagothey, Austin. *Ética, teoría y aplicación.* México: Nueva Editorial Interamericana, 1973.

Fernández, Pelayo H. *Estilística.* Madrid: José Porrúa Turanzas, S. A., 1972.

Fumaroli, Marc. *La Age de L'Eloquence. Rhétorique et «res literaria» de la Renaissance au seuil de l'époque classique.* Genève: Librairie Droz, 1980.

Gambra Ciudad, Rafael. *Historia Sencilla de la Filosofía.* Madrid: Ediciones Rialp, S. A., 1981.

Gans, Herbert J. *Deciding What's News. A Study of* CBS Evening News, NBC Nightly News, Newsweek, *and* Time. New York: Vintage Books, 1979.

"Gaya Ciencia," *Enciclopedia Universal Ilustrada Europeo-Americana.* Barcelona: Ed. ESPASA, 1924. 4:1116.

Getto, Giovanni, et al. *Storia della letteratura italiana.* Milano: Rizzoli Editore, 1971.

Gilson, Etienne. *The Christian Philosophy of St. Thomas Aquinas.* New York: Random House, 1956.

Grassi, Ernesto. *Rhetoric as Philosophy. The Humanist Tradition.* The Pennsylvania State University Press, 1980.

――――. *Vico and Humanism. Essays on Vico, Heidegger, and Rhetoric.* New York: Peter Lang, 1990.

Gutiérrez Saenz, Raúl. *Introducción a la Lógica.* México: Editorial Esfinge, 1977.

Hage, Jerald. *Techniques and Problems of Theory Construction in Sociology.* New York: J. Wiley, 1972.

Helitzer, Melvin. *Comedy, Techniques for writers and performers. The HEARTS theory of humor writing.* Athens, Ohio: Lawhead Press, 1984.

Herrero García, Miguel. "La literatura religiosa." *Historia General de las Literaturas Hispánicas.* Ed. by D. Guillermo Díaz-Plaja. Barcelona: Ed. Vergara, 1953.

――――. *Ideas de los Españoles del Siglo XVII.* Madrid: Editorial Gredos, S. A., 1966.

Hooker, Edward N. "Introduction." *Essays on Wit* 1st. ser. 2 University of California: The Augustan Reprint Society, 1946.

Johnston, George Sim. *The Galileo Affair.* Scepter Publishers, 1994.

Kahn, Victoria. *Rhetoric, Prudence, and Skepticism in the Renaissance.* Cornell University Press, 1985.

Kuhn, Thomas S. *Structure of Scientific Revolutions.* 2nd. enlarged ed. University of Chicago, 1979.

López Piñero, José Mª. *La ciencia en la historia hispánica.* Barcelona: Salvat Editores, S. A., 1982.

Marañon, G. "La literatura científica en los siglos XVI y XVII," *Historia General de las Literaturas Hispánicas*. Barcelona: Editorial Vergara, 1953.

Martí, Antonio. *La preceptiva retórica española en el siglo de oro*. Madrid: Ed. Gredos, S. A., 1972.

Mazzeo, Joseph Anthony. "A Seventeenth-Century Theory of Metaphysical Poetry." *RR* 42 (1951).

————. "A critique of Some Modern Theories of Metaphysical Poetry." *MP* 50 (1952).

————. "Metaphysical Poetry and the Poetics of Correspondence" *JHI* 14 (1953).

McSorley. *An outline of History of the Church by Centuries. (From St Peter to Pius XII.)* B. Herder Book Co., 1947.

Meozzi, Antero. *Il secentismo europeo. Marinismo-Gongorismo-Preziosismo-Lilismo-Swhwulst*. Pisa: Nistri-Lischi Editori.

Milburn, D. Judson. *The Age of Wit 1650–1750*. New York: The MacMillan Company, 1966.

Millán Puelles, Antonio. *Fundamentos de Filosofía*. Madrid: Ediciones Rialp, S. A., 1978.

Monnot, Michel. *Selling America: Puns, Language, and Advertising*. Washington, D. C: University Press of America, 1981.

Montes de Oca, Francisco. *Lógica*. México: Editorial Porrúa, 1974.

Mooney, Michael. *Vico in the Tradition of Rhetoric*. New Jersey: Princeton University Press, 1985.

Moore, John A. *Fray Luis de Granada*, Boston: Twayne Publishers, 1977.

Mulkay, Michael. *On Humor. Its Nature and Its Place in Modern Society*. Basil Blackwell, Inc., 1988.

Murphy, James J. *Rhetoric in the Middle Ages. A History of Rhetorical Theory from St. Augustine to the Renaissance.* University of California Press, 1974.

O'Malley, John W. *Praise and Blame in Renaissance Rome.* Durham, North Carolina: Duke University Press, 1979.

Ong, Walter J. "Wit and Mystery: a revaluation in medieval Latin hymnody." *Speculum* 12 (1947).

————. *Method and the Decay of Dialogue. From the Art of Discourse to the Art of Reason.* Harvard University Press, 1983.

Orozco, Emilio. *Manierismo y Barroco.* Madrid: Ediciones Cátedra, 1981.

Ortuñez de Calahorra, Diego. *Espejo de Príncipes y Caballeros.* Edición, introducción y notas de Daniel Eisenberg. Madrid: Ed. Espasa-Calpe, S. A., 1975.

Osorio Romero, Ignacio. "La retórica en Nueva España." *Aproximaciones al mundo clásico.* Textos de Humanidades: 11. Universidad Nacional Autónoma de México: 1979.

Owen, Joseph. *An Elementary Christian Metaphysics.* Center for Thomistic Studies, 1985.

Owst, G. R. *Preaching in Medieval England, an introduction to sermon manuscripts of the period.* London: Cambridge University Press, 1926.

Paletz, David L., and Robert M. Entman. *Media. Power. Politics.* New York: The Free Press, 1981.

Parenti, Michael. *Inventing Reality. The Politics of the Mass Media.* New York: St. Martin's Press, 1986.

Parker, Alexander A. "'Concept' and 'Conceit': An Aspect of Comparative Literary History." *MLR* 77(4) (1982 Oct.): xxi–xxxv.

Paz, Octavio. *Sor Juana Inés de la Cruz, o las Trampas de la fe.* 1st. ed. Barcelona: Seix Barral, 1982.

Pius XII. Encyclical Letter *Divino afflante Spiritu.* (1943).

Poesía de Cancionero. Ed. by Alvaro Alonso. Madrid: Ed. Cátedra, S. A., 1986.

Porqueras Mayo, A. *La teoría poética en el Renacimiento y Manierismo españoles.* Barcelona: Ediciones Puvill.

————. *La teoría poética en el Manierismo y Barroco españoles.* Barcelona: Ediciones Puvill.

Purcell, William M. *"Transsumptio:* A Rhetorical Doctrine of the Thirteenth Century." *Rhetorica* Autumn 1987.

Raimondi, Ezio. *Letteratura Barocca. Studi sul Seicento Italiano.* Firenze: Leo S. Olschki-Editore, 1961.

Rico Verdú, José. *La retórica española de los siglos XVI y XVII.* Madrid: Consejo Superior de Investigaciones Científicas, 1973.

Río, Ángel del. *Historia de la Literatura Española.* New York: Holt, Rinehart and Winston, 1966.

Smith, Hilary Dansey. *Preaching in the Spanish Golden Age.* Oxford University Press, 1978.

Solana, Rafael. "Tratemos de conservar lo único que no se ha perdido: el humor." *Siempre!* (Agosto 8 de 1990).

Tedesco, John L. "Theology in the medieval tractates on preaching: a comparative study." *The Southern Speech Communication Journal* 41 Winter, 1976: 177–188.

"Theology." *The Catholic Encyclopedia.* New York: Robert Appleton Company. 14:600–611.

Trabalza, Ciro. *Storia dei Generi Letterari Italiani. La Critica Letteraria (Dai primordi dell'Umanesimo all'Età nostra) Vol. II (Secoli XV–XVI–XVII).* Milano: Casa Editrice Dottor Francesco Vallardi, 1915.

Ubieto, Antonio, et al. *Introducción a la Historia de España*. Barcelona: Editorial Teide, S. A., 1965.

Valbuena Briones, Ángel. *Literatura Hispanoamericana*. Barcelona: Editorial Gustavo Gili, S. A., 1962.

Valbuena Prat, Ángel. *Historia de la Literatura Española*. Barcelona: Editorial Gustavo Gili, S A, 1964.

Van Hook, John Williams. "'Concuspiscence of Wit': Baroque Poetics and the English Metaphysical Style." Diss., U of Washington, 1983.

Vargas Llosa, Mario. "¿Dios o la espada?" *El Norte*. Monterrey, México: 16 de febrero de 1992.

Vilanova, Antonio. "Preceptistas Españoles de los Siglos XVI y XVII." *Historia General de las Literaturas Hispánicas*. Ed. by D. Guillermo Díaz-Plaja. Barcelona: Ed. Vergara, 1953. 3: 567–692

Wallace, Robert, Jack L. King, and Gerald P. Sanders. *Biology the Science of Life*. Scott, Foresman and Company, 1986.

Weinberg, Bernard. *A History of Literary Criticism in the Italian Renaissance*. The University of Chicago Press, 1961. Vols. 1 and 2.

Whinnom, Keith. *La poesía amatoria de la época de los Reyes Católicos*. Durham: University of Durham, 1981.

Woods, M. J. "Sixteenth-Century Topical Theory: Some Spanish and Italian Views." *MLR* 63 (1968): 66–73.

Bibliographies

Gracián y Morales, Baltasar. *Obras Completas*. Ed., and "Introducción, recopilación y notas" by E. Correa Calderón. Madrid: M. Aguilar, 1944.

————. *Obras Completas.* Ed., and "Estudio preliminar, edición, bibliografía y notas" by Arturo del Hoyo. Madrid: Ed. Aguilar, 1960.

————. *Agudeza y Arte de Ingenio.* Ed. by E. Correa Calderón. Madrid: Editorial Castalia, 1969. 2 vols.

Porqueras Mayo, and A. Joseph L. Laurenti. *Estudios Bibliográficos sobre la Edad de Oro (Fondos raros y colecciones de la Universidad de Illinois).* Barcelona: Puvill Libros, S. A., 1984.

Index

RENAISSANCE AND BAROQUE
STUDIES AND TEXTS

This series deals with various aspects of the European Renaissance and Baroque. Studies on the history, literature, philosophy, and the visual arts of these periods are welcome. The series also will consider translations of important works, especially from Latin into English. These translations should, however, include a substantial introduction and notes. Books in the series will include original monographs as well as revised or reconceived dissertations. The series editor is:

Eckhard Bernstein
Department of Modern Languages
    and Literatures
College of the Holy Cross
Worcester, MA 01610